This fresh and important study contains more than the title suggests: it also revisits important topics like slavery and women in Paul, the provenance of Paul's letters, the meaning of *diakonos*, Pauline chronology, and more. Yet the title remains perfectly apt, for the book is the most comprehensive study of personages – every one of them – appearing in the (thirteen-letter) Pauline corpus of which I am aware. Abreast of recent scholarship yet discerning in its appropriation, Manuell models lexical, historical, and hermeneutical care and good judgment. Both scholars and students will want to draw from this compendium of information and insight.

ROBERT W. YARBROUGH
Professor of New Testament
Covenant Theological Seminary, St. Louis, Missouri, USA

This book is useful to a student of Paul's letters. It includes an entry with a fair amount of detail, surprisingly so, for every single person named in these letters! I also appreciate that Manuell is up front about his conservative historical assumptions. For example, he believes that Paul wrote all thirteen letters attributed to him. No, I do not agree with all of his specific historical conclusions or the details of every person described; but even in these cases, he usefully includes dissenting views.

ROBERT J. CARA
Provost, Reformed Theological Seminary,
Charlotte, North Carolina

THE PEOPLE IN PAUL'S LETTERS

A Compendium of Characters

GUY MANUELL

MENTOR

Hardback ISBN 978-1-5271-1198-1

E-book ISBN 978-1-5271-1285-8

10 9 8 7 6 5 4 3 2 1

Published in 2025 in the Mentor imprint
by
Christian Focus Publications Ltd,
Geanies House, Fearn, Ross-shire,
IV20 1TW, Great Britain.

www.christianfocus.com

Cover design by Daniel van Straaten

Printed and bound by Bell & Bain

Contents

Dedicated to the memory of those few thousand saints in the first century, many unknown but to God, who contended for the faith once for all time delivered to them (Jude 3) – even to death.

With gratitude to
John Cromarty and Allan Harman,
my brothers, friends, and mentors in Christ.

Foreword

When a book appears covering new ground, one wonders why the subject has not been tackled before. That is so with this book by Guy Manuell. He has brought together all the people mentioned in Paul's letters in the New Testament, and provided commentary on the Greek text that relates to them. This means that appropriate knowledge concerning these people is listed in the one source, and that makes this book such a convenient reference tool. The author, Guy Manuell, is already known for his competence in New Testament studies, which can be seen from his other writings, including his commentary on the Epistle of Jude. In the introduction he tackles some important issues, of which Paul's chronology is probably the most important. Footnotes and the bibliography show the width of his reading in the subject area, and they can quickly guide readers to much relevant material. I am sure that many New Testament scholars are going to be particularly thankful for the hard work that Guy Manuell has put into this resource, and I commend it heartily.

Allan M. Harman
Research Professor of Old Testament
Presbyterian Theological College
Melbourne, Australia

Author's Rationale and Acknowledgements

Much has been, and still is, written about the apostle Paul's teaching and theology via his thirteen letters in the New Testament (NT) to early Christian communities and individuals. It was Paul who unpacked the gospel of Jesus Christ and helped us to understand Christ's centrality to our salvation through His death on the cross and resurrection, making possible our justification by faith in God and the certain hope of an eternal relationship with the Triune God: Father, Son, and Holy Spirit.

Less has been written about the people in Paul's letters and the issues those relationships brought forth, which can relate so closely to day-to-day matters in our own lives – even though we are separated by twenty centuries. People are people no matter in what age they live. The problems, joys, and questions faced by the people in Paul's letters are still with Christians today. There is potentially much to be learnt from their interaction not only with Paul but also with one another and the world around them. Paul's reactions to them individually, and as members of Christian communities who were in communication with one another, provide relevant illustrations for our own time about a wide range of Christian issues.

My interest in the people in Paul's letters was sparked more than forty years ago by the need to choose a 'special subject' for my appearance on the TV programme *Mastermind*. The choice of 'People in Paul's Letters' seemed to fit the need for an unusual subject, one reference source and a limited amount of information that could be memorised for a few minutes of questions. Therefore, I learnt about these people and many of them had interesting (albeit sometimes brief) stories to tell. This book is the culmination of that experience and lessons learned in the meantime.

> A passage like this [Phil. 2:25-30] ought to serve as a constant reminder to all of us (scholar, pastor, student of the Bible) that the NT was written in the context of real people in a very real world. Biblical texts are too often the scholar's playground and the believer's rule book, without adequate appreciation for the truly human nature of these texts – texts written by one whose speech was ever informed by his theology, but who expressed that theology at a very personal and practical level.[1]

The papers on this subject rested peacefully in my filing cabinet for many years. I have dusted off the files, reviewed them in the light of current scholarship, and now share what is known about their lives with their successors in the faith nearly two thousand years later. It is necessary to appreciate the many nuances that can only be obtained from the original Greek text, reference to which is included for completeness, and these will be relevant to those familiar with that language. However, the subject matter can be readily understood by those without a knowledge of Greek.

The individuals who should be acknowledged in such a project are too numerous to name. The extent of the bibliography reflects my gratitude to many scholars, without whose contributions this book could not have been written. It is also clear that scholarship over the past forty years has improved our understanding of Paul's letters dramatically, causing me to write a more informed analysis than would have occurred when my interest in these people began. Sincere thanks to all those scholars and teachers who have made this possible – they are too numerous to name. Also, my gratitude to the staff of the Leon Morris Library at Ridley College, Melbourne, whose assistance was always available and valuable.

This book discusses people from the perspective that their names are in Paul's letters. Clearly, Paul's view will be prominent. John Piper has well described my attitude in dealing with this subject:

---

1. G. D. Fee, *Paul's Letter to the Philippians*, NICNT (Grand Rapids: Eerdmans 1995), p. 284.

> My controlling thought was, and is: What do the words and phrases and clauses and sentences and flow of thought *mean* in this text? Or to be more precise, my controlling thought was: What reality did this inspired writer *intend* to communicate to his readers, through the words and phrases and clauses and sentences and flow of thought in this text? What reality did this inspired author intend for me to see, through his use of words? And how did he intend for me to think about that reality, and feel about it, and apply it to my life and the lives of my people and the world? My first and controlling thought is not: How can I preach the gospel from this text? Rather, I am driven by the question: How can I see what this author sees? What glimpses of divine and human reality might he have for me, if I linger and look and look and look at what he actually said, with earnest prayer for God's help, and with heartfelt renunciation of all my sin that would distort my sight?[2]

That is my aim in writing this book.

I am a hoarder, and my wife is a clearer; so I thank Bernice sincerely not only for ongoing encouragement to put fingers to the keyboard but also for leaving these papers intact!

GUY MANUELL
Curlewis,
Australia

2. John Piper, *Exposition or Imposition? How Gospel-Centred Preaching Can Go Wrong* (June 28, 2020 [original emphasis]). See *https://www.desiringgod.org/messages/exposition-or-imposition*.

Abbreviations

AJT	*The American Journal of Theology*
BECNT	Baker Exegetical Commentary on the New Testament
BHGNT	Baylor Handbook on the Greek New Testament
BS	*Bibliotheca Sacra*
BTB	*Biblical Theology Bulletin*
ESV	English Standard Version
HCSB	Holman Christian Standard Bible
HSIBD	*The Hodder and Stoughton Illustrated Bible Dictionary*
HTR	*Harvard Theological Review*
ICC	International Critical Commentary
JBL	*Journal of Biblical Literature*
JETS	*Journal of the Evangelical Theological Society*
JSNT	*Journal for the Study of the New Testament*
KJV	King James Version
LXX	Septuagint (Old Testament in Greek)
MNTC	Moffatt New Testament Commentary
NASB	New American Standard Bible, 1995
NASBEC	*The Strongest NASB Exhaustive Concordance*
NCCA	New Covenant Commentary
NEB	New English Bible
NICNT	New International Commentary on the New Testament
NICOT	New International Commentary on the Old Testament
NIGTC	New International Greek Text Commentary
NIV	New International Version

NKJV	New King James Version
NRSV	New Revised Standard Version
NT	New Testament
NT	*Novum Testamentum*
NTC	New Testament Commentary
NTS	*New Testament Studies*
OT	Old Testament
PNTC	Pillar New Testament Commentary
RTR	*The Reformed Theological Review*
Strong	Strong, J. 'Greek Dictionary of the New Testament' in *The Exhaustive Concordance of the Bible*. Reprint 1970. London: Hodder and Stoughton, 1890
TBST	The Bible Speaks Today
TDNT	Theological Dictionary of the New Testament
TNTC	Tyndale New Testament Commentary
TynBul	*Tyndale Bulletin*
WBC	Word Biblical Commentary
WTJ	*The Westminster Theological Journal*
WUNT	*Wissenschaftliche Untersuchungen zum Neuen Testament*
ZETNC	Zondervan Exegetical Commentary Series on the New Testament
ZNW	*Zeitschrift für die Neutestamentliche Wissenschaft*

Introduction

Background to the Contents

This is a book about the people named in the apostle Paul's letters. Obviously, much of Paul's life cannot be omitted from the picture but there are several excellent books that focus specifically on him and his life.[1] My focus is on the people with whom he had to deal. Some are also mentioned in the Acts of the Apostles and 1 Peter; however, people only mentioned in those books are not included here. Without the Book of Acts we would know so much less about Paul and the people in his letters. However, just because someone (e.g. Luke) is mentioned in Paul's correspondence, I am not providing an overview of that person's entire life but comment only insofar as their relationship with Paul and the people or circumstances in his letters are concerned.

At the outset, I must declare that I assume (and believe) that the letters in the NT attributed to Paul were written by him. There will be little discussion of the endless academic debate about the authenticity of any letter.

Christianity involves relationships between God and humans and between humans themselves. The NT contains nine letters from Paul to early Christian communities, and four personal letters: two to Timothy and one each to Titus and Philemon. The most fulsome description of Paul's missionary journeys and preaching activity is contained in Acts, which provides invaluable additional facts about the circumstances in which Paul's letters were written. E. F. Scott noted that 'no section of Acts is more lacking in first-hand knowledge than that which deals with the

1. Excellent overviews of Paul's life are J. Pollock, *The Apostle*, third edition (London: Hodder and Stoughton 1987), and N. T. Wright, *Paul: A Biography* (San Francisco: HarperOne 2018).

events in Ephesus.'[2] Altogether, Paul's letters mention eighty-eight contemporary people, including fellow Christians, opponents, and some prominent people in secular society.

Paul dealt with people just like we would in various circumstances: wisely, sternly, humorously, lovingly, patiently, encouragingly, and even angrily. That is why considering his personal interactions with people is as much a part of understanding the gospel *in practice* as are his general directions about Christian thought (doctrine) and behaviour.

All these people had some influence on Paul personally, on his evangelical and pastoral ministries, and on the subjects discussed in his letters. One point that will become evident is that people travelled from place to place quite frequently due to the influence of *Pax Romana* throughout the region surrounding the eastern Mediterranean Sea. It was relatively easy and safe for personal travel and communication by land and sea during this time, which greatly assisted the expansion of the gospel of Jesus to many regions.

The *lingua franca* of the Roman Empire was Greek, hence all of Paul's letters were written in that language and some people's names and circumstances can only be properly understood by reference to the original Greek text. It is not easy to deduce a person's ethnic (or religious) origin in the first century by simply examining their name. A wide variety of people are discussed, many of whom called themselves Christians. Some were Jews with Jewish names; others were Jews with Gentile (Hellenistic or Roman) names: e.g. the apostle Saul (Jewish) who was widely known as Paul (Roman). Some were Gentiles who had become 'God-fearers', the Jewish name for non-Jews who embraced Judaism. Others were Gentiles who converted to Christianity from pagan religions. It must also be remembered that many new Christians were slaves or freed men and women with Hellenistic or Roman names, who could have moved across the Roman Empire from places as diverse as Britain, Germany, Syria, or Africa. Their

2. E. F. Scott, *The Epistles of Paul to the Colossians, to Philemon and to the Ephesians.* MNTC (London: Hodder and Stoughton reprinted 1942), p. 91.

slave names would bear no relationship to their place of origin. But this fact in itself may help to explain how the gospel spread so quickly across the known (Roman) world in the first two centuries after Christ, when freed slaves returned to their places of birth.

Understandably, the information in this book has been sourced from numerous commentaries and articles by scholars more expert in their subjects than me: hence the size of the bibliography. That is to the reader's benefit. I have undertaken the unenviable task of gauging various opinions (some quite contradictory) and concluding which is most likely to represent accurately the person or situation described based on the available facts. My preference is to take a conservative approach to the available data, rather than accept unlikely speculations. It is inevitable that this book is partly a travel guide for the lands around the eastern Mediterranean Sea, given the location of the people in Paul's letters and his own travels. It will become apparent that people in the first century A.D. travelled more frequently and over greater distances than we might initially assume.

One of the most surprising facts about Paul's letters is the significant differences in the number of people mentioned in individual letters. They range from only one in Ephesians, a city where Paul resided for over two years, to thirty-six people in Romans, even though he had not yet visited that city when he wrote to them. Similarly, twelve people are named in Colossians, where, again, Paul did not visit Colosse. The numerous people in 1 Corinthians contrast starkly with the mention of only three of his colleagues at the close of his personally difficult second letter to the Corinthians. There is also the foreboding of his future where Paul names nineteen people in the short letter of 2 Timothy, probably his last. The differences in Paul's letters reflect his humanity, his generosity of spirit towards many brothers and sisters, and his persistence in preaching one true gospel as in 1 Corinthians 1:23. It is an interesting aspect of Paul's ministry that he names sixty-two brothers and seventeen sisters in Christ, and nine other people in his letters. How many fellow believers known to us could we list? Our personal walk with Christ demands that we involve others in it.

Biblical Interpretation

It may seem that analysis of a list of names does not require much effort regarding the interpreting of Scripture but that is incorrect. My attitude towards Scripture is a vital component of what I have (and have not) written: not only in understanding the meaning of Paul's (Greek) text but also regarding an understanding of the reference books consulted in preparing this book.

Westminster Theological Seminary in Philadelphia was founded by scholars who rejected increasing liberalism in Christian theology and belief. I quote from part of the opening address of J. Gresham Machen, its first president, on 25 September 1929:

> If, then, the students of our seminary can read the Bible not merely in translations, but as it was given by the Holy Spirit to the church, then they are prepared to deal intelligently with the question what the Bible means. There we have the great subject of biblical exegesis or biblical interpretation. I hesitate to use that word 'interpretation', for it is a word that has been the custodian of more nonsense, perhaps, than any other word in the English language today. Every generation, it is said, must interpret the Bible and the creeds of the church in its own way. So it is said in effect by many modern leaders of the church: 'We accept the Apostles' Creed, but we must interpret the Apostles' Creed in a way that will suit the modern mind. So we repeat the assertion of the Creed, "The third day He rose again from the dead," but we interpret that to mean, "The third day He did not rise again from the dead."'
>
> *In the presence of this modern business of interpreting perfectly plain assertions to mean their exact opposite, do you know what I verily believe? I verily believe that the new Reformation, for which we long, will be like the Reformation of the sixteenth century in that it will mean a return to plain common honesty and common sense.* At the end of the middle ages the Bible had become a book with seven seals; it had been covered with the rubbish of the fourfold sense of Scripture and all that. The Reformation brushed that rubbish away. So again today the Bible has been covered with an elaborate business of 'interpretation' that is worse in some respects than anything that the middle ages could produce. The new Reformation will brush all that away. There will be a rediscovery of the great Reformation doctrine of the perspicuity of Scripture;

> *men will make the astonishing discovery that the Bible is a plain book addressed to plain men, and that it means exactly what it says.*
>
> In our work in exegesis at Westminster Seminary, at any rate, we shall seek to cultivate common sense. But common sense is not so common as is sometimes supposed, and for the cultivation of it true learning is not out of place. What a world of vagaries, what a sad waste of time, could be avoided if men would come into contact with the truly fine exegetical tradition of the Christian church! Such contact with the devout and learned minds of the past would not discourage freshness or originality. Far from it; it would help to shake us out of a rut and lead us into fields of fruitful thinking.
>
> ***In true biblical exegesis, the Bible must be taken as God has been pleased to give it to the church.***[3]

This is the methodology underpinning my examination of Paul's letters.

Slavery in the First Century A.D. and Earliest Christianity[4]

Many of the people mentioned in Paul's letters were slaves or freed slaves. It is important to understand the various roles and status of slaves in the first century A.D. A slave was the lowest position that a person could occupy in first-century society. There can be no doubt that most slaves in the Roman Empire were regarded as, and treated little better than, animals. Like animals, slaves were subject to the complete power of their masters. Nevertheless, there were slaves who occupied positions of responsibility and authority within wealthy Roman households. This is particularly relevant to a consideration of the names of slaves or freed men and women mentioned in Romans 16.[5]

---

3. J. G. Machen, 'Westminster Theological Seminary: Its Purpose and Plan' in *J Gresham Machen: Selected Shorter Writings*. Ed. D. G. Hart (Phillipsburg, NJ: P & R Publishing, 2004).

4. The comments on slavery reflect the text of G. Manuell, *The Letter of Jude: A Wake-Up Call to Christians in the Twenty-First Century* (Sydney: Tulip Publishing, 2022), pp. 70-5. See C. S. Keener, *Acts: An Exegetical Commentary* (Grand Rapids: Baker Academic, 2012-15), vol. 2, pp. 1906-42, for a comprehensive analysis of slavery in the first century A.D.

5. See W. L. Westermann, 'The Slave Systems of Greek and Roman Antiquity,' *Memoirs of the American Philosophical Society*, vol. 40 (New York:

As with Cephas,[6] James,[7] and Jude,[8] Paul calls himself 'a slave (δοῦλος – *doulos*) of Christ'.[9] This is one of the commonest early NT church descriptions of believers after the resurrection. It was also used of major figures in the LXX: 'Those called to special service in the OT were identified as the "slave" (δοῦλος) of the LORD: Abraham, Moses, Joshua, David, and the prophets: see Joshua 14:7; 24:29; 2 Kings 17:23; Psalm 89:4, 20.'[10] However, many English translations of δοῦλος in Scripture (especially those printed in the United States) cannot bring themselves to use 'slave'.[11] This may reflect widespread modern revulsion (and, to many, embarrassment) at the practice of slavery in the United States and England for centuries.

The NASB is regarded as one of the most literal translations of the Greek text, but it shows an inherent prejudice when translating δοῦλος. It never uses 'slave' whenever δοῦλος refers to someone (male or female) who is one of God's people, unless the notion of 'slave' is relevant to the particular text. Instead,

---

Noble Offset Printers, 1955). The most intensive consideration of the names listed in Romans 16 has been undertaken by R. Jewett, *Romans: A Commentary*. Hermeneia (Minneapolis: Fortress Press, 2007).

6. 1 Pet. 1:1.

7. James 1:1.

8. Jude 1.

9. Rom. 1:1; Gal. 1:10; Phil. 1:1; Titus 1:1.

10. T. R. Schreiner, *1, 2 Peter, Jude,* The New American Commentary (Nashville: Broadman and Holman, 2003), pp. 427-28. See also K. H. Rengstorf, '*doulos*', *TDNT*, vol. 2, ed. G. Kittel (Grand Rapids: Eerdmans, 1964), pp. 268, 276-77.

11. NIV, ESV, Good News, NEB, NRSV, RSV, and KJV use 'servant'; NASB and NKJV use 'bond-servant'. But The Message Bible, NetBible, and Recovery Version use 'slave'. P. H. Davids, *The Letters of 2 Peter and Jude,* PNTC (Grand Rapids: Eerdmans, 2006), pp. 33-4, uses the translation 'servant', but agrees that it means 'slave'; however, P. H. Davids, *2 Peter and Jude: A Handbook on the Greek Text,* BHGNT (Waco, TX: Baylor University Press, 2011), p. 1, and P. H. Davids, *A Theology of James, Peter and Jude,* Biblical Theology of the New Testament (Grand Rapids: Zondervan, 2014), pp. 265-6, use 'slave'. J. R. Bauckham, *Jude, 2 Peter,* WBC (Waco, TX: Word Books, 1983), pp. 19, 23, uses 'servant', while acknowledging that δοῦλος means 'slave'. Note Davids' change of emphasis in the importance of the 'slave' description between his two commentaries.

it uses euphemisms like 'bond-servant' or 'bond-slave'. But the NASB always uses 'slave' whenever the word is used in a general context. The Book of Revelation (NASB) is a clear example of this differentiation. The NIV deviates even further to comply with political correctness in its overwhelming use of 'servant' for δοῦλος rather than 'slave'. It must be emphasised that these are merely euphemisms.

K. H. Rengstorf says in reference to δοῦλος:

> All the words in this group serve either to describe the status of a slave or an *attitude corresponding to that of a slave*. ... The meaning is so unequivocal and self-contained that it is superfluous to give examples of the individual terms or to trace the history of the group. ... Hence we have a service which is not a matter of choice for the one who renders it, which he has to perform whether he likes it or not, because *he is subject* as a slave to an alien will, *to the will of his owner*.[12]

It has been argued that 'servant' is an appropriate term because Jesus regarded Himself as a servant in Matthew 20:28. However, the Greek in that verse uses the verb (διακονῆσαι – *diakonēsai*) for 'serving' (i.e. being a servant), not for being a slave. In any event, it is not the role of Jesus that is under scrutiny but the relationship of the believer to the Lord. Similarly, 'bond-servant' is favoured by those who argue that it often indicates one who sells himself into slavery to another. This view gives far too much credit to the one who becomes the 'slave' and fails to recognise Paul's reminder to the Corinthians, '*you have been bought* with a price' (1 Cor. 6:20, emphasis added). It is God's grace and sacrifice, not human effort, that enables us to become Christ's slaves *by the price He paid* as per Matthew 20:28. This view also has adverse implications for the doctrines of justification by faith and predestination.

Salvation by Christ is His work alone. Any suggestion that the redeemed person has contributed anything to their salvation (as per the analogy of selling oneself into slavery) cannot be sustained

---

12. Rengstorf, '*doulos*,' p. 261 (emphases added), but pp. 261-78 has the full explanation. See also G. L. Green, *Jude and 2 Peter*, BECNT (Grand Rapids: Baker Academic, 2008), pp. 45-6.

by Scripture (cf. Romans 4). Similarly, if the redeemed are chosen (elected) by God before the creation of the earth, there is no opportunity for a person to claim that they had anything to do with their salvation in their lifetime (cf. Eph. 1:4).

There is no excuse for mistranslating the original text just because the English meaning of the Greek word does not suit modern predispositions and sensibilities. This does no justice to the writer and thwarts the meaning he intended for his words. Nor does this reluctance to use 'slave' properly understand the role of a slave in the first century A.D. Although our modern impression of slavery is that it is wholly repugnant (and appropriately so from the perspectives of creation in Genesis 1:27 and human rights), this is of little help in understanding the concept in the first century. Westermann's comprehensive analysis of the institution of slavery in Greco-Roman times devoted a section to slavery in the context of the early Christians, which provides enlightenment on the use of δοῦλος by Paul and other NT writers. Some extracts follow to place our thoughts back in the first century:

> It would be self-deception if one failed to see that Jesus of Nazareth, the apostles and the Church, both in its formative period and in its later development, accepted the going system of labour of its time, including the slave structure, without hesitation or any expressed reluctance. It was there, and they took it.[13]
>
> To the apostle Paul, slavery and freedom were facts of everyday life which were to be accepted and which could be expressed in simple terms and grasped readily by simple people.[14] ... What Paul had done for slavery as it applied to Christian believers was to accept it as a physical fact, but to spiritualise that acceptance so that it became almost, if not fully, meaningless for those who were imbued with his own fervent conviction that Jesus of Nazareth was the ordained Saviour of mankind.[15]

---

13. Westermann, 'The Slave Systems of Greek and Roman Antiquity', p. 150. See also P. R. Coleman-Norton, *Studies in Roman Economic and Social History* (Princeton, NJ: Princeton University Press, 1951).

14. Westermann, 'The Slave Systems of Greek and Roman Antiquity', p. 149, who uses this view to consider Galatians 3:27–5:1.

15. ibid., p. 150.

> [t]he accepted social distinction of legal status ceased to exist in their [Christian] communities along with the differences of racial origin and former religious belief. This may be ascribed, in part, to the conviction which they held that the Day of judgment, and with it the end of the existing world, was not far distant.[16]

Since a slave was the lowest position that a person could occupy in first-century society, it can be argued that having come from the glory of the Father to life as a Nazarene carpenter, Jesus displayed the elements of utter debasement, only He went further. This would be demonstrated in the extreme (especially for Jews) by His dying on a cross (cf. Deut. 22:22-3). Nevertheless, there were many slaves who occupied positions of responsibility and authority within wealthy Roman households.[17] This latter understanding of the role of a slave would certainly have been within the knowledge of Paul, even if not within his experience. In any event, the particular role or physical circumstances of a slave is not the point at issue for Paul in his self-description. Paul uses δοῦλος simply to reflect the position of the most subservient people in his society. That is his understanding of his relationship to Jesus the Christ.[18]

> We need to remind ourselves of the abhorrence of the status of slavery in the Roman world, the paradoxical embrace of this term for one's relationship to King Jesus by the apostle Paul in its denotations of submission, obedience, and devotion to Christ, and therefore the revolutionary subordination at work when the early Christians began to see themselves now as slaves of Christ (e.g., Gal. 1:10; 1 Cor. 7:21-3; Rom. 1:1; 6:16-20; Eph. 6:6; Phil. 1:1).[19]

The reason for Paul's self-description as a slave rests on two premises: the first being the secular status of a slave. Slaves

---

16. ibid., pp. 150-1.

17. See P. Garnsey and R. Saller, *The Roman Empire: Economy, Society and Culture* (Berkeley: California University Press, 1987), pp. 119, 132.

18. See M. J. Harris, *Slave of Christ: A New Testament Metaphor for Total Devotion to Christ*, New Studies in Biblical Theology, vol. 8 (Downers Grove, IL: InterVarsity Press, 1999).

19. S. McKnight, *The Letter to the Colossians*, NICNT (Grand Rapids: Eerdmans, 2018), p. 103.

suffered from institutional limitations on their freedom of action and initiative. They had no freedom at all, nor did they have any entitlements.[20] A slave was his master's possession, with the same legal status as the master's other property, such as his house or horse. The slave's entire existence was determined by the master's will – for good or ill. As a slave of Christ, Paul is also subject to the will of His master, who will determine his role in life and control (own) his whole being.[21] In Paul's case, the master will control what happens to the slave in life *and death*. Unlike earthly equivalents, this slavery is not forced on Paul. It is a (low) status placed on him by God, to which he voluntarily and willingly submits because he wants to be wholly owned and directed by the One who died for him. It should be noted that, in the OT, the slave/master relationship is the 'commonest expression for the service of God in the sense of total allegiance and not just isolated acts of worship'.[22] This makes it less surprising that Paul uses this motif to describe his relationship to Jesus. The same, of course, could be said of the other apostles and members of the early NT church.[23]

---

20. Human rights as we know them today were non-existent in the first century; however, the concept of entitlements was recognised. The outcome of the ancient Greek philosophical belief that ideals can be worth even more than worthless (valueless) human beings meant that Plato considered that every man had the right to a fair trial – even a slave! A slave only received a fair trial because the importance of the argument for a fair trial had to be upheld – even if it needed to be applied to a slave or criminal! None of these concepts provide much comfort, in that ancient philosophers placed greater value on ideals than human beings and that the entitlement to claim 'rights' was on a high pedestal. See J. M. Rist, *Human Value: A Study in Ancient Philosophical Ethics* (Leiden: E. J. Brill, 1982), pp. 125-6. See Paul's analysis of his entitlements in 1 Corinthians 9:1-18 and his view of them.

21. cf. Paul's determination to fulfil Christ's will in his path to Jerusalem when faced with godly advice to the contrary in Acts 21:10-14.

22. C. E. B. Cranfield, *The Epistle to the Romans*, ICC (Edinburgh: T. & T. Clark, 1975), vol. 1: pp. 51-2, 320-30. See also D. B. Martin, *Slavery as Salvation: The Metaphor of Slavery in Pauline Christianity* (New Haven, NJ: Yale University Press, 1990).

23. See 2 Peter 1:1; Jude 1. This is emphasised in McKnight, *Colossians*, pp. 102-03. See also the entry for Epaphras.

Paul's second premise for describing himself as a slave is the status of the master of the slave.[24] Slaves in a prestigious Roman household enjoyed the status of their master. Better to be a slave in Caesar's palace than one in rural Tuscany. But Paul is a slave *of Jesus Christ!* There could be no higher honour than to be a member of Christ's household (the King of kings), no matter how menial the duties.[25] Given the nature of Christ (2 Cor. 10:1), it is absurd to regard the slave nomenclature as a reflection of base existence and ill treatment in a Christian context. On the contrary, slaves of Christ will eventually reign with Him (Rev. 20:6). This is a future for which no earthly slave could ever hope, let alone attain.

Again, the correct translation of δοῦλος is 'slave', not euphemisms like 'servant' or 'bond-servant', which entirely misrepresent both the relationship described *and the intention of the author.* Note the frequent use of 'servant' (διάκονος – *diakonos*) in the NT to differentiate a servant from the lowlier designation of slave (cf. Matt. 25:14-30). Mistranslations of δοῦλος attempt to minimise the servitude of Paul, whereas *he* wished to glory in his lowly position.[26]

Paul and Women

There are areas of exegesis where doctrinal positions matter. At the present time, one of the most controversial is the role(s) undertaken by women in the various Christian communities to which Paul travelled or wrote. The controversy regarding this issue in our present Christian society is a heated one.

The pre-fall bliss man and woman enjoyed in the Garden has given way to much confusion regarding man's and woman's place in God's

---

24. See Harris, *Slave of Christ,* p. 135. Davids, *The Letters of 2 Peter and Jude,* pp. 34-5, usefully notes that when Jesus is referred to as 'servant of the Lord' in Acts 3:13; 4:27, 30, παῖς (*pais*), not δοῦλος (*doulos*) is used for 'servant'.

25. cf. Psalm 84:10.

26. Harris, *Slave of Christ,* makes the same point, at greater length, in Appendix 3. See B. Witherington III, *The Letters to Philemon, the Colossians, and the Ephesians: A Social-Rhetorical Commentary on the Captivity Epistles* (Grand Rapids: Eerdmans 2007), pp. 26-30, 84-90, for a discussion of the issue of slavery regarding Onesimus and Philemon.

> world, in Christ's church, and in relation to one another. North American culture, with its emphasis on equality and the advances of feminism in this century, has pressed hard upon the church to conform its teachings to new societal standards. As is customary in American public life, special interest groups have been formed representing different sides of the 'gender issue' in an effort to influence the various segments within American evangelicalism toward their respective viewpoints.
>
> The last few decades have witnessed an increasing awareness of the importance of hermeneutical procedure in interpreting the gender passages in the NT. ...
>
> The present essay therefore seeks to readdress some of the issues taken up in earlier treatments, taking into account developments since these studies appeared. It also attempts to sharpen further the discernment of improper methodology. It is hoped that the critique of fallacious methodologies will contribute to better hermeneutical procedures. This, in turn, might lead to a greater convergence of exegetical conclusions.[27]

It is critical that women's roles fit consistently within the whole biblical framework of the OT and NT: especially Paul's instructions to Christians in his own day.

> Paul has been called everything from misogynist to misunderstood with regard to his stance on women in the ministry of the church, and a thorough re-examination of the role women played in the apostle's mission is needed to clear up some confusion. This is especially important since we are not dealing merely with the

---

27. A. J. Köstenberger, 'Gender Passages in the NT: Hermeneutical Fallacies Critiqued,' *WTJ* 56, no. 2 (1994): pp. 259-60. An example of this present confusion is illustrated in M. Mowczko, 'Wealthy Women in the First-Century Roman World and in the Church,' *Priscilla Papers* 32, no. 3 (2018), pp. 6-7. Footnote 7 says: 'The early church was attractive to women, including women of high status, "because within the Christian subculture women enjoyed far higher status than did women in the Greco-Roman world at large." Rodney Stark, *The Rise of Christianity* (New York: HarperOne 1996), p. 95.' This is a clear misunderstanding of the fact that 'status' (other than commitment to Christ) was irrelevant in Paul's Christian communities; cf. Galatians 3:28 as well as the entry for Phoebe.

> mission of one important individual, Paul. Ultimately, Paul's mission is *missio Dei*, the mission of God, and the mission of the Holy Spirit *through Paul.* Called and converted by the risen Christ, led by the Spirit, Paul's mission arguably transcends the man and his historical-cultural context. If this is true, it also and especially applies to the role women played in the Pauline mission, and it is here that we can ill afford not to listen and learn from the apostle; for today's churches are in dire need of an authoritative, definitive word on how women (and men) ought to function in the church.[28]

Acceptance of this framework is reflected in *Gender Wars in Christianity*,[29] which upholds a Reformed understanding of the authority of Scripture and God's designs for both the status and roles of men and women under God from a complementarian perspective. This controversy has transcended nearly two thousand years of scholarly acceptance but is now a major issue of debate.[30] Even later editions of the NASB include 'politically correct' additions to Scripture for the sake of including women. A glaring example is 2 Timothy 4:21, where the addition of 'and sisters' is completely unnecessary.

Put simply, the reality is that, regardless of the work, wealth, social status, or Christian status of the women described, none of them exercised leadership roles over men in accordance with both OT and NT principles for both genders (especially Paul's detailed requirements, which were followed in all the churches, as in 1 Corinthians 11:16 and Ephesians 5). Some commentators (often distinguished and, many of them, women) have tried to ascribe leadership roles for women, when no overt evidence exists for that assertion, often by distorting the meaning of Greek words. This book rejects that interpretation

---

28. A. J. Kostenberger, 'Women in the Pauline Mission', in *The Gospel to the Nations*, eds. P. Bolt and M. Thompson (Downers Grove, IL: Intervarsity Press, 2000), p. 221 (original emphasis).

29. G. Manuell, *Gender Wars in Christianity* (Brisbane: Connor Court, 2018).

30. This book reflects a complementarian view of men's and women's roles in life as described in J. Piper and W. Grudem, eds, *Recovering Biblical Manhood and Womanhood: A Response to Evangelical Feminism*, reprinted 2006 (Wheaton IL: Crossway Books, 1991).

of their work. It is inappropriate for commentators two millennia away to impose current social, political or gender standards on the behaviour of people in a different time and culture (*including the culture of earliest Christianity*), let alone to the immutability of God's Word as confirmed by Hebrews 13:8. Indeed, many of the 'politically correct' criticisms of some modern commentators on Paul's teachings only demonstrate their failure to appreciate (and accept) the *Christian culture* that Paul was trying to establish amongst these people. People today should be trying to replicate that early Christian culture if they are serious about being true followers of Jesus.

This is not to diminish the role of women in the early church. Indeed, a plain reading of the NT (especially Acts) indicates that much of what was achieved in the conversion of both Jews and Gentiles in the first century could not have been possible without the enormous contribution of *many* women (named and unnamed). Romans 16 is the outstanding example of this reality. But it was these women's profound new life in Christ that spurred their efforts; not attempts to become like men, let alone lead them.

Paul's Use of ἐν χριστῷ *(en Christō – in Christ)*

Paul often refers to the people named in his letters as being 'in Christ' or some similar expression, such as 'in the Lord'. J. S. Stewart commented on the significance of this phrase:

> We turn now to the brief but most important phrase in which Paul's intimacy with the risen Lord finds expression, the phrase 'in Christ'. So frequent and even commonplace has this phrase become in latter-day Christian usage that it is quite possible to miss its significance and fail to realise just how striking it is. It is worth reminding ourselves that no such words have ever been used, or indeed could ever be used, of any of the sons of men: we do not speak of being in St Francis or in John Wesley. The fact is that when we speak of being 'in Christ' we are consciously or unconsciously making a confession of faith; we are framing a Christology; if we are saying something about ourselves, we are saying something far more tremendous about Jesus. We are declaring that Jesus is no mere fact in history, no towering personality of the past, but a living, present Spirit, whose nature is the very nature of God. So far-reaching is this favourite apostolic phrase.

> It was a dictum of Luther's that all religion lies in the pronouns; and that there is a real truth in this, everyone who can speak with Paul of 'the Son of God, who loved me, and gave Himself for me' (Gal. 2:20) must realise. But Deissmann, going a step further than Luther, has virtually declared that religion resides in the prepositions, and in one of them in particular. The publication in 1892 of *Die neutestamentliche Formel 'in Christo Jesu'* heralded the dawn of a new era in Pauline study. Starting from the fact that 'in Christ' (or some cognate expression, such as 'in the Lord', 'in Him', etc.) occurs 164 times in Paul, but never in the Synoptics, Deissmann carried out a thorough examination of the use of ἐν with a personal dative in Greek literature in general and the Septuagint in particular, and came to the conclusion that Paul 'was the originator of the formula, not indeed as being the first to employ ἐν with a personal singular, but in the sense that he used an already existing idiom to create a new technical term' [reference = *Die neutestamentliche Formel*, 70] of religion. It is an instance of the way in which the creative power of the Christian experience makes itself felt even in the domain of language. New wine requires new bottles; and traditional thought-forms are often poor vehicles of expression for a man who has had his Damascus day. Where the Synoptics speak of the disciples' fellowship with Jesus, the preposition they use is μετά [*meta*], never ἐν [*en*]. Paul, on the other hand, uses ἐν constantly, μετά never. Take the long, typically Pauline sentence at the opening of the epistle to the Ephesians: within that single sentence 'in Christ' (or some derivative) occurs a dozen times. It is indeed the most characteristic phrase in the apostle's terminology.[31]

For Paul to designate someone as being 'in Christ' is a shorthand form of confirming the genuineness of that person's faith and devotion to the Lord. 'This common union with Christ is the fountain from which their mutual honour, respect, and love flows.'[32] Are we 'in Christ'?

Paul's Use of *σύν (sun)*

σύν is a small Greek word, used 128 times on its own in the NT. Its primary meaning is 'with'. However, Paul often combines

---

31. J. S. Stewart, *A Man in Christ* (London: Hodder and Stoughton 1935), pp. 154-5.

32. F. Thielman, *Romans*, ZECNT (Grand Rapids: Zondervan 2018), p. 729.

σύν with other words to form a sense of companionship and togetherness of people.[33] The most obvious reflection of this sense of community is found in the commonly used word (in Greek), συναγωγή (*sunagōgē* – synagogue), the meeting place of Jewish worship. Paulinisms using σύν at the start of nouns and verbs provide a sense of Paul's writing something like the English expression: 'we're all in this together.' The σύν words used by Paul are listed below. Not all words beginning with σύν have a 'with' context.

Greek	**Transliteration**	**English Meaning**	**Pauline Letters**
Συμπαραλαμβάνω	*symparalambanō*	taking with	Gal. 2:1
Συναγωνίζομαί	*sunagōizomai*to	struggle together	Rom. 15:30
Συναθλέω	*sunathleō*to	contend as one	Phil. 1:27; 4:3
Συναιχμάλωτος	*sunaichmalōtos*	fellow prisoner	Rom. 16:7; Col. 4:10; Philem. 23
Συναναμείγνυμι	*sunanameignumi*	associate with	1 Cor. 5:9, 11; 2 Thess. 3:14
Συναναπαύομαί	*sunanapauomai*	refreshed together	Rom. 15:32
Συναντιλαμβάνομαί	*sunantilambanomai*	help (by Holy Spirit)	Rom. 8:26
Συναπάγω	*sunapagō*	willing to associate	Rom. 12:16; Gal. 2:13
Συναποθνήσκω	*sunapothnēskō*	die with	2 Cor. 7:3; 2 Tim. 2:11
Συναποστέλλω	*sunapostellō*	sent with	2 Cor. 12:18

33. Over fifty years ago, Rev. L. J. Atkinson (Glengowrie Methodist Church, S.A.) encouraged me to look for σύν in Paul's letters. His advice is vindicated in this book.

GREEK	TRANSLITERATION	ENGLISH MEANING	PAULINE LETTERS
Συναρμολογέω	*sunarmologeō*	to join together	Eph. 2:21; 4:16
σύνδεσμος	*sundesmos*	to bind together	Eph. 4:3; Col. 2:19; 3:14
σύνδοξάζω	*sundoxazō*	share in glory	Rom. 8:17
σύνδουλος	*sundoulos*	fellow slave	Col. 1:7; 4:7
συνεγείρω	*sunegeirō*	raise up with	Eph. 2:6; Col. 2:12; 3:1
συνείδησις	*suneidēsis*	conscience	Rom. 2:15; 9:1; 13:5; 1 Cor. 8:7, 10, 12; 10:25, 27, 28, 29; 2 Cor. 1:12; 4:2; 5:11; 1 Tim. 1:5, 19; 3:9; 4:2; 2 Tim. 1:3; Titus 1:15
Συνεκδήμος	*sunekdēmos*	travelling companion	2 Cor. 8:19 (also Acts 19:29)
συνεργέω	*sunergeō*	to work together	Rom. 8:28; 1 Cor. 16:16; 2 Cor. 6:1
συνεργός	*sunergos*	fellow worker	Rom. 16:3, 9, 21; 1 Cor. 3:9; 2 Cor. 1:24; 8:23; Phil. 2:25; 4:3; Col. 4:11; 1 Thess. 3:2; Philem. 1, 24
συνέρχομαι	*sunerchomai*	come together	1 Cor. 11:17, 18, 20, 33, 34; 14:23, 26
Συνεσθίω	*sunesthiō*	eat with	1 Cor. 5:11; Gal. 2:12
σύνεσις	*sunesis*	under-standing	Eph. 3:4; Col. 1:9; 2:2; 2 Tim. 2:7
Συνετός	*sunetos*	intelligent	1 Cor. 1:19

GREEK	TRANSLITERATION	ENGLISH MEANING	PAULINE LETTERS
συνευδοκέω	*suneudokeō*	approve of	Rom. 1:32; 1 Cor. 7:12, 13
συνέχω	*sunechō*	compel	2 Cor. 5:14; Phil. 1:23
συνήδομαι	*sunēdomai*	delight	Rom. 7:22
συνήθεια	*sunētheia*	accustomed	1 Cor. 8:7; 11:16
συνηλικιώτης	*sunēlikiōtēs*	of own age	Gal. 1:14
συνθάπτω	*sunthaptō*	to bury with [Christ]	Rom. 6:4; Col. 2:12
συνίημι	*suniēmi*	understand	Rom. 3:11; 15:21; 2 Cor. 10:12; Eph. 5:17
Συνίστημι	*sunistēmi*	commend	Rom. 3:5; 5:8; 16:1; 2 Cor. 3:1; 4:2;
		hold together	5:12; 6:4; 7:11; 10:12, 18; 12:11; Gal. 2:18; Col. 1:17
σύνοιδα	*sunoida*	conscience is clear	1 Cor. 4:4
συνοικοδομέω	*sunoikodomeō*	built together	Eph. 2:22
συνοχή	*sunochē*	anguish	2 Cor. 2:4
συντελέω	*sunteleō*	finality	Rom. 9:28
συντέμνω	*suntemnō*	speed	Rom. 9:28
συντρίβω	*suntribō*	crush	Rom. 16:20
συντρίμμα	*suntrimma*	ruin	Rom. 3:16
συνυποκρίνομ	*αιsunupokrinomai*	joined in hypocrisy	Gal. 2:13
συνυπουργέω	*sunupourgeō*	help	2 Cor. 1:11
συστρατιώτος*su[n]*	*stratiōtos*	fellow soldier	Phil. 2:25

This use of σύν throughout his letters reflects Paul's humility in recognising the work of others as being part of God's whole plan for salvation.[34] His most common usage is συνεργός (*sunergos* – fellow worker) and it is used both with regard to individuals (e.g. Urbanus in Romans 16:9) and groups of named and unnamed people (e.g. Clement and the rest of my fellow workers in Philippians 4:3). Paul was but one part (important though he was) of Christ's body on earth, as noted in Ephesians 4:16.

The Role of διάκονος *(diakonos)*

διάκονος is a very broad term that Paul frequently employs to describe the ministry in which he and his colleagues are engaged.[35] In Paul's letters a number of men and women are designated by Paul as διάκονος. It is from this Greek work that the English term 'deacon' is derived. This word and its cognate, διακονια – *diakonia*, has raised considerable debate in recent decades over the roles and duties performed in a Christian community by a person (male or female) so designated. Given the debate between egalitarians and complementarians over women's roles in the church, an analysis of the translation and meaning of διάκονος cannot be avoided. It is one of the most contentious words in the debate about the *roles of men and women in the church*. An analysis of Paul's attitude to the relationships between men and women (especially Christians) *in the totality* of his letters compels us to examine the matter through *first-century eyes and facts* rather than the considerably different perspectives of the twenty-first century.

There are three relevant words in Greek to describe this function: a verb διακονέω (*diakoneō*) and two nouns, διακονία

34. See McKnight, *Colossians,* p. 103.

35. See Keener, *Acts,* vol. 3, p. 2789, n. 4931: 'A very broad term (διάκονος) that Paul frequently employs elsewhere for ministry of himself or his colleagues; cf. Streeter and Picton-Turbervill, *Woman,* p. 63; Keener, *Perspective,* pp. 216-17; *idem, Paul,* pp. 238-9; somewhat differently, see Belleville, *Leaders,* pp. 61-2 (translating 'deacon'). In a later period, see Blue, *House Church,* p. 183 (following Lightfoot, *Philippians,* pp. 95ff.)'

(*diakonia*) and διάκονος (*diakonos*).[36] The three words occur thirty-seven, thirty-four, and twenty-nine times, respectively, in the NT. Of the total one hundred occurrences, thirty-nine occur in the four gospels. They provide a good sense of what this group of words meant to the gospel writers in the first century. Without exception, they refer to a person engaged in serving others, never from a superior position. Luke 22:26-27 provides a typical example. These verses tell us how Jesus used this word:

> [26]But it is not this way with you, but the one who is the greatest among you must become like the youngest, and the leader like the servant (ὁ διακονῶν).
>
> [27]For who is greater, the one who reclines at the table or the one who serves (ὁ διακονῶν)? Is it not the one who reclines at the table? But I am among you as the one who serves (ὁ διακονῶν).

It is clear from the gospels, Paul's letters, and the remainder of the NT that διάκονος has nothing to do with leadership. That is discounted by Jesus' use of the word in comparing this role to 'greatness' or 'leadership'. This role has everything to do with serving or helping others. It is not a grandiose role and Paul never uses these words with that meaning. Attempts to foist significance on those who were described as having these positions in the early churches fail when the words are understood in the *culture of earliest Christianity.* This was quite different to the culture of the surrounding societies in which Christianity emerged. Yet many commentators incorrectly assume that the new Christian culture can only be understood by reference to 'worldly' culture.[37] Given Paul's instructions about male and female relationships, *which applied in all the churches*, a bias is evident in feminist commentary on the NT, where any mention of a woman by name gives rise to a claim that they occupied a leadership role – but see 'Mary' (Miriam) in the quotation below for legitimate attribution.

---

36. See NASBEC, p. 1519, ref. *1247, 1248, 1249*.

37. See S. E. Hylen, 'Women διάκονοι and Gendered Norms of Leadership', *JBL* 138, no. 3 (2019), pp. 687-702: as an example of this conflation of 'worldly' and Christian cultural values.

Note the comments in *Slavery in the First Century* A.D. *and Earliest Christianity* (in the introduction) about the slave-like *attitude* of the earliest believers. John the Baptist understood this principle of humility when he said, 'He must become greater; I must become less' (John 3:30, NIV). Even in Philippians 1:1, the English translation 'deacons' places them under the authority of 'overseers' (ἐπισκόποις – *episkopois*). There can be no doubt that these terms referred to some type of recognised positions for men and women in the earliest Christian groups, but their precise nature is impossible to determine. However, it seems clear that this nomenclature of διάκονος for men *and women* in the early churches involved serving others but without any implication of leadership. To insist on some administrative hierarchy in earliest Christianity is to overstate the organisational structure of this diverse group of small communities.

> In these cases it [διάκονος] still does not denote specific tasks or tasks formally given, but rather tasks voluntarily undertaken at their own initiative – that is, denoting a sensitivity to needs within a new congregation and willingness to expend energy and time in meeting them (cf. the Roman inscription *CIG* 9592, cited by Deissmann, *Light*, p. 313). *Thus it does not denote a leadership function as such (cf. 1 Thess. 5:17* [sic]*); Paul's point elsewhere is rather that those who do so devote themselves to working for the good of the church ought to be given recognition* (1 Cor. 16:16; 1 Thess. 5:12; for προϊσταμένους there, see on [Rom.] 12:8). Nevertheless, it is noticeable here that Mary is picked first for such commendation, confirming that women played a not insignificant part in the emerging roles of leadership within the infant Christian communities – the weightier the significance of κοπιάω (Harnack), the more significant their role.[38]

38. J. D. G. Dunn, *Romans 9-16*, WBC (Dallas, TX: Word Books 1988), p. 894 (emphasis added). For a contrary view, see S. Mathew, *Women in the Greetings of Romans 16.1-16: A Study of Mutuality and Women's Ministry in the Letter to the Romans*, Library of New Testament Studies 471 (London: T. and T. Clark 2014), pp. 109-10. Dunn's reference to 1 Thessalonians 5:17 appears to be an error and the verses may be (more appropriately) verses 12, 13. The Greek προϊστάμενος (*proistamenos*) in Romans 12:8 refers to 'leadership' – see NASBEC, p. 1560, ref. *4291b*.

To the extent that the role of διάκονος involved any attribution of leadership, it was a lowly position and subject to the leader of the Christian community. (The entry for Phoebe in this book is particularly relevant to this discussion.) Cranfield's understanding is that Phoebe held a 'definite office ... with reference to the practical service of the needy'.[39] Note that Philippians 1:1 refers to 'overseers *and deacons*', suggesting that deacons do not have leadership responsibilities. Haldane comments that '[a]s deacons were appointed to attend to the poor, so deaconesses were specially set apart in the churches in order to attend to the wants of their own sex.'[40]

This understanding of διάκονος should be applied to every person with that description in Paul's letters.

Letters from Prison: Ephesians, Philippians, Colossians and Philemon

Paul's letters to the Ephesians, Philippians, Colossians and Philemon are generally known as the Letters from Prison, as cited in Ephesians 6:20; Philippians 1:17; Colossians 4:10; and Philemon 23. For centuries it has been agreed that these four letters were written during Paul's two-year incarceration in Rome described in Acts 28:30-31; but there is a growing number of eminent commentators (for more than a century) who argue for an origin of some of these letters during a time (or times) when Paul was imprisoned in Ephesus. Although the provenance of these letters does not necessarily have much effect on their broad theological content, it does have critical importance to our understanding of what the people mentioned in them did, where they were, and the relationships between them and Paul, and themselves.

---

39. C. E. B. Cranfield, *The Epistle to the Romans*, ICC (Edinburgh: T. & T. Clark 1979), vol. 2: p. 781.

40. R. Haldane, *An Exposition of Romans* (Grand Rapids: Evangelical Press, reprinted 1958), p. 633. See J. Murray, *The Epistle to the Romans,* NICNT (Grand Rapids: Eerdmans, reprinted 1973), p. 226; C. Hodge, *Romans,* Geneva Series of Commentaries (Edinburgh: Banner of Truth, reprinted 1975), p. 447.

The first to suggest an Ephesus imprisonment was A. Deissmann in 1897;[41] then the matter was considered by B. W. Robinson in 1910. He noted, 'The transfer of the authorship of the imprisonment epistles from Rome to Ephesus is an opinion that will progress but slowly even if a very great preponderance of evidence in its favour should be accumulated.'[42] He makes the following relevant observation:

> He [Paul] was not so very far from Rome when he wrote Romans, not so very far from Corinth when he wrote Corinthians, probably not so very far from Galatia when he wrote Galatians, not so very far from Thessalonica when he wrote Thessalonians. It would at least introduce the element of consistency in the matter of writing his letters from places reasonably near to their destination if we were willing to say that Philemon, Colossians, Ephesians, and perhaps, Philippians were written from Ephesus.[43]

This book is not the place for a long dissertation on the origin of the Letters from Prison; nevertheless, their provenance must be considered, and conclusions formed because of their critical impact on the biographical information of so many people discussed in this book. Disagreement amongst distinguished scholars is difficult to unravel and mere status is no answer to a complex question. That eminent scholars like Scott, Moffatt, and Lightfoot (and many more recent ones) offer differing analyses speaks of the uncertainty surrounding this issue. Scott considered that 'There seems to be no sufficient reason for abandoning the generally accepted view that the epistles date from the period of the Roman captivity,'[44] yet he recognised that 'the case in favour of this view [the Ephesian imprisonment] has been ably presented in the Commentary on *Philippians* in this series.'[45]

---

41. A. Deissmann, *Paul: A Study in Social and Religious History,* 2nd ed, trans. W. E. Wilson (New York: Harper, 1927), p. 17, n. 1.

42. B. W. Robinson, 'An Ephesian Imprisonment of Paul,' *JBL* 29, no. 2 (1910): p. 188.

43. Robinson, 'An Ephesian Imprisonment of Paul,' p. 181, n. 1, p. 189. See also J. A. Doole, 'Was Timothy in Prison with Paul?' *NTS* 65, no. 1 (2019), pp. 59-77.

44. Scott, *Colossians,* p. 5.

45. Scott, *Colossians,* p. 4.

Letter to the Philippians

Although the text of Philippians seems to shout 'Rome!' as its place of origin, it is a matter of judging probabilities. There are arguments for an Ephesian provenance,[46] but they are, in my view, strongly outweighed by the evidence for Rome; the arguments in the commentaries of Witherington and Fee should be accepted.[47] The strongest arguments for Paul being in custody in Rome are:

1. The two 'Rome' references of ἐν ὅλῳ τῷ πραιτωρίῳ (*en holō tō praitōriō* – in the whole praetorium) in Philippians 1:13 and οἱ ἐκ τῆς καίσαρος οἰκίας (*hoi ek tēs kaisaros oikias* – those from Caesar's household) in Philippians 4:22 cannot be ignored or downplayed. It is reasonably presumed that the first reference is to the emperor's Praetorian Guard. Even if it referred to a 'governor's palace', there was not a *praetorium* in Ephesus because it was situated in a senatorial, not imperial, province.[48] Similarly, 'Caesar's household' seems to be self-explanatory of a location in Rome.[49]

2. Paul describes himself as 'being in chains' (Phil. 1:7, 13, 14, 17). This does not necessarily denote being in a prison but, as described in Acts 28:16, suggests that Paul was chained to a Roman soldier in his own rented quarters.[50]

3. The letter to the Philippians has a 'feel' about it that a considerable time has elapsed between the initial establishment of the church and the writing of this letter (Phil. 4:14-16). In this letter Paul expects to be released and to return to Philippi: see Philippians 1:26; 2:24. If a Rome

46. For an Ephesian imprisonment for Philippians, see M. F. Bird and N. K. Gupta, *Philippians*, New Cambridge Bible Commentary (Cambridge: Cambridge University Press, 2020), pp. 20-3.

47. G. D. Fee, *Paul's Letter to the Philippians,* NICNT (Grand Rapids: Eerdmans, 1995); B. Witherington III, *Paul's Letter to the Philippians: A Social-rhetorical Commentary* (Grand Rapids: Eerdmans, 2011).

48. Fee, *Philippians,* pp. 34-5, esp. n. 87; Witherington, *Philippians,* p. 10.

49. See entries for Aristobulus and Narcissus.

50. Witherington, *Philippians,* pp. 9-10.

> provenance is accepted, this suggests a period towards the end of the two years of his being in custody. Fee proposes that 'the internal evidence of Philippians would put the writing of this letter toward the latter end of the imprisonment, rather than early on, thus closer to 62 than to 60'.[51]

Therefore, Philippians is regarded as one of Paul's later letters, written from Rome during his first imprisonment there as described in Acts 28:30-31.

Letters to the Colossians and Philemon

It must be noted that, in Acts, Luke provides little information about Paul's ministry in Ephesus. There is considerable reliance on 1 Corinthians 15:32 and 2 Corinthians 11:23-9 for some of Paul's experiences in Ephesus and in other places well before his incarceration in either Caesarea or Rome. See the entry for Aristarchus, which provides further facts supporting Ephesian imprisonment(s) of Paul. To avoid writing a book within a book, I am quoting the discussion of the matter by McKnight (in 2018):

> What, then, is the best defence for the traditional imprisonment location in Rome? First, a subscript to manuscripts K and L says 'written from Rome by Tychicus and Onesimus'. Second, Eusebius informs his readers that Paul was taken to Rome, and 'Aristarchus was with him; whom also somewhere in his epistles he suitably calls a "fellow prisoner" (*Ecclesiastical History 2.22.1*)'. This comment connects to Col. 4:10 but also to Rome, since the Macedonian Aristarchus accompanied Paul to Rome (Acts 27:2). In addition, what we know from Acts 28 about Paul's Roman imprisonment can be squared with what we find in Colossians, namely, a measure of freedom to visit friends, which would entail the freedom to communicate with others. However, this impression hardly establishes a Roman imprisonment, since the same kind of imprisonment conditions would obtain empire-wide. *What most harms the*

51. Fee, *Philippians,* p. 37.

> *Roman imprisonment theory is distance from Colossae, some 1,200 miles – it requires all these Lycus Valley believers to be present in Rome, have the financial wherewithal to return, and then again go back to Rome.*

We can tighten the arguments by looking at the names of people that appear in the letters that impinge on the location of the imprisonment. There is slightly more connection in the names to an imprisonment in Rome than in Ephesus, but the argument is not foolproof. In one dense footnote Michael Bird put this argument into exquisite shape, so I quote his summary:

> (1) Timothy can be placed in Ephesus (Acts 19:22; 1 Cor. 16:10; 1 Tim. 1:3) but not to Rome (unless Phil. 1:1 was written from Rome). (2) Tychicus is linked to Rome and Ephesus (2 Tim. 4:12) but towards the end of Paul's imprisonment. (3) Aristarchus was apparently in Ephesus during the riot there (Acts 19:29) and he probably sailed on to Rome with Paul (Acts 27:2). (4) Demas is only linked with Paul in his final imprisonment and noted for his desertion (2 Tim. 4:10). (5) If Luke was Paul's travelling companion after Troas (Acts 16:11) he may have been with Paul in Ephesus and probably accompanied him to Rome, hence 'we came to Rome' (Acts 28:14, 16; cf. 2 Tim. 4:11). (6) John Mark had broken off from Paul (Acts 15:37-41) during an earlier missionary journey so the reference to him with Paul in Col. 4:10 and Philem. 24 is all the more peculiar. It means that reconciliation has probably occurred. He is placed in Rome by 1 Pet. 5:13 and in Ephesus by 2 Tim. 4:11.[52]

The names, then, do not resolve the issue.

As indicated above, there is a problem for the Roman imprisonment theory: that is, at the same time, an opportunity for the Ephesian theory: namely trips are mentioned in these letters that make Rome far less likely than Ephesus. That is, one needs to consider indications of travel in Colossians 1:7-8,

---

52. McKnight's quotation is from M. F. Bird. *Colossians and Philemon*, A New Covenant Commentary (Eugene, OR: Cascade Books 2009), p. 11, n. 37. Bird is in error regarding Demas, who is (importantly for our purposes) mentioned in Colossians 4:14 and later in 2 Timothy 4:10.

Philemon 8-12, Colossians 4:7-8, and Ephesians 6:22, as well as Philemon 12, 22. Four trips, all to the same region of Asia Minor, sometimes involving less prominent people (Onesimus being chief – back and forth, as it turns out; see Philemon 15). How such people could all be in Rome is harder to explain than an Ephesian imprisonment. *In fact, I am inclined to think that, for the slave Onesimus, travelling 1,200 miles to Rome, being sent back home 1,200 miles to Colossae, and then, at Paul's request, returning 1,200 miles to Rome yet again beggars the imagination at the level of historical realities.* How long did Paul imagine he'd be imprisoned in Rome? With this hesitation about Rome in mind now, there is, one might suggest, a sense of proximity to Colossae in the comments found at Colossians 4:9-12: Mark 'if he comes to you'; Epaphras, 'who is one of you'. And on a Roman origination, 'They will tell you everything that is happening here' runs the risk of being seriously outdated by the time the travellers would be arriving. These considerations tip the balance in favour of Ephesus, and like others, I have myself resiled from the traditional Roman imprisonment theory.

Along this line and leading in the same direction, Bird makes the point that the 'circumstances of Philippians and Timothy are crucial for the provenance and date of Colossians/Philemon'. Here is how he puts it:

> [Timothy] is named as co-sender of Colossians and Philemon (Col. 1:1; Philem. 1). To that we can add the observations that Timothy is also named as co-sender of Philippians (Phil. 1:1), Philippians is also written from captivity (Phil. 1:13-14), and Philippians is similar to Philemon in at least two other respects: both look forward to Paul's eventual release from prison (Philem. 22; Phil. 1:19-26; 2:24), and there are several stylistic similarities between them, as noted by Francis Watson.[53] The final and perhaps strongest pieces of evidence are: (1) that Aristarchus is in prison with Paul (Col. 4:10), and he was arrested in Ephesus according to Acts 19:29. In addition, (2) Paul tells Philemon to

53. The reference is to F. Watson, *Paul, Judaism, and the Gentiles: Beyond the New Perspective*, 2nd ed. (Grand Rapids: Eerdmans, 2007), pp. 141-2.

> prepare a room for him as he is coming there (Philem. 22), but the book of Romans has already indicated that Paul was on his way west to Spain after being in Rome, not back to Asia Minor (Rom. 15:14-33). Philemon 22, thus, suggests Ephesus as the origin.
>
> If we take an Ephesian origin for this letter, one is tempted to hear Ephesian [sic] echoed in the letter. Thus, Paul argued with Jews in the synagogues (Acts 18:19; 19:8-9), and one might wonder, then, whether the very Jewish-sounding problems at Colossae could be Paul's transference to Colossae of issues arising with Jews in Ephesus (e.g. Col. 2:16-7, 21-2). The 'savage wolves'[54] of Paul's speech to the Ephesian elders (Acts 20:29-30) is another possible instance of transferring to the Letter to the Colossians the sorts of problems he's finding in Ephesus, which will no doubt also be the case in the Lycus Valley. The presence of exorcists and powers at Ephesus (Acts 19:13-20, 23-41) might help explain their presence and theology of defeat in Colossians 2 as well. *If Colossians was written from Ephesus, we would need to date the letter in the mid-50s, or perhaps even 57, one date for the riot of Demetrios (Acts 19:23-41).*[55]

The descriptions of Epaphras and Aristarchus in Ephesus are different in Colossians and Philemon, which have important implications for those who support the idea that Paul suffered one or more imprisonments in Ephesus.[56] It has been assumed by some commentators that the letters to the Colossians and to Philemon were sent to the Colossian church at the same time, with Onesimus joining Tychicus to deliver them. However, this assumption is flawed for the following reasons.

---

54. This description should be compared with the hyperbole of 1 Corinthians 15:32.

55. McKnight, *Colossians*, pp. 37-9 (emphasis added). See C. H. Talbert, *Ephesians and Colossians* (Grand Rapids: Baker Academic 2007), p. 12.

56. This has been examined in detail by Talbert who suggests two different imprisonments of Paul in Ephesus. See Talbert, *Ephesians and Colossians*, 244-6. I do not agree with all of Talbert's conclusions.

Letter to Philemon

1. Onesimus was a slave who deserted his master, Philemon. He found Paul in Ephesus, was converted and, eventually returned to Colosse with Paul's letter to Philemon in an attempt to be received back by his master with something other than the severity that he deserved.
2. Philemon received him back, then freed him and sent him to be Paul's coworker. He did this job well and became known as 'the faithful and beloved brother' (τῷ πιστῷ καὶ ἀγαπητῷ ἀδελφῷ – *tō pistō kai agapētō adelphō*).
3. Epaphras is Paul's 'fellow prisoner' (ὁ συναιχμάλωτός μου – *ho sunaichmalōtos mou*) in the letter to Philemon (v 23), but not in Colossians.
4. In Philemon Paul expects to be set free and asks Philemon to prepare a room for him (v. 22).
5. Tychicus, who is identified as the bearer of the letters to the Ephesians and Colossians, is not mentioned in Philemon.

Letter to the Colossians

1. In Colossians, Aristarchus is 'Paul's fellow prisoner' (Col. 4:10). Although Paul is a prisoner in both letters, his fellow prisoners are different.
2. In Colossians, Onesimus (from Colosse) is described by Paul as 'the faithful and beloved brother' (Col. 4:9). Paul could only call him a 'faithful brother' if sufficient time had elapsed for him to earn this commendation.
3. Philemon is not mentioned at all in Colossians, although in the letter to Philemon his was the house in which the church met. Colossians mentions only his son, Archippus, who is now said to have a ministry. Has his father died?[57]

---

57. See A. Kirkland, 'The Beginnings of Christianity in the Lycus Valley: An Exercise in Historical Reconstruction', *Neotestamentica*, 29, no. 1 (1995), pp. 109-24.

4. In Colossians there is no expectation of a release from prison. If it is the same imprisonment, then has the apostle lost all hope of release? If it is a later imprisonment, does Paul now consider that he has less chance of release than he did when writing to Philemon?

The factual differences between the two letters suggests that Colossians was written later than Philemon. How much later depends on whether or not we are dealing with two different imprisonments. The list of the same coworkers in the two letters seems to argue for a relatively short lapse of time. The assumed chronology is best reconstructed thus: Paul was imprisoned in Ephesus and wrote to Philemon concerning Onesimus. Philemon sent Onesimus back to Paul to help him. At a later time, Paul was again imprisoned in Ephesus and, with Timothy, wrote Colossians and sent it by Tychicus and Onesimus, both of whom he commended. This analysis supports the conclusion that both letters were written during different imprisonments in Ephesus.

> The delivery of the letters as well usually involved persons from the circle of Paul's coworkers. Messengers were more than mere letter carriers. They probably read the letters to the churches and also explained the letter in an authoritative manner, adding unique personal information not contained in the text. At times coworkers from the receiving congregation were present in the authorial community during the production of the letter (cf. Col. 4:9, 'Onesimus, who is one of you').[58]

There is, however, an issue which none of the commentators in favour of an Ephesian imprisonment have raised, but it seems to be a vital piece of the puzzle regarding the nature and length of imprisonment(s), if it (they) happened. Paul travelled to Ephesus after he had visited Philippi. In Philippi he was imprisoned in harsh conditions and resorted to *claiming his rights as a Roman citizen*, described in Acts 16:35-9. The embarrassment suffered by the officials of a major Roman city regarding the improper

58. Talbert, *Ephesians and Colossians*, pp. 247.

treatment of a Roman citizen was probably not lost on Paul. If he was imprisoned in Ephesus, the Philippian precedent of Roman citizenship could well have been used to mitigate the severity of the conditions of his confinement: e.g. meeting people and writing letters.[59] It may well have also shortened the period of his incarceration(s) because Paul was obviously released.

Letter to the Ephesians

An initial starting point is that there is a close linguistic relationship between the letters to Colosse and Ephesus.

> Without fear of contradiction it may be said that there are more numerous and more sustained similarities between Ephesians and Colossians than between any other two New Testament Epistles. It is said that, with varying degrees of similarity, 75 of the 125 verses of Ephesians are found in Colossians. There are different categories in which the parallels between the two Epistles should be considered.[60]

Debate continues as to whether Paul's letter described as 'to the Ephesians' was or was not initially addressed to that group of Christians but was more of an encyclical to various churches in the province of Asia. To the extent that the latter view is supported, a provenance of Ephesus seems more strongly confirmed and I agree with that conclusion. Scholars from different eras hold this view.

> 'In form', said Goodspeed, 'it is an encyclical.' This is a widely held view, to which some support is given by the textual evidence of the prescript, which throws doubt on the mention of Ephesus as the place to which the letter was to be sent. It might be called

---

59. The Hellenistic city wall, erected under King Lysimachus and at least nine kilometres long, was built in 30 B.C. Today more than three kilometres of it is extremely well preserved on the Bulbuldag. Strabon, one of the famous writers in antiquity, wrote that the city wall was 2.5–3 metres thick and fortified by watch towers. There is an important, well-preserved tower, which was called St Paul's prison, near the ancient harbour on the hill. See https://ephesus.us/ancient-ephesus/hellenistic-city-wall/. There is a section entitled 'Hellenistic City Wall'. See also Robinson, *An Ephesian Imprisonment of Paul*, p. 181.

60. F. Foulkes, *Ephesians*, TNTC (Leicester, InterVarsity Press, 1956), p. 20.

> a general letter to Gentile Christians, more particularly in the province of Asia – Gentile Christians who (like the readers of 1 Peter) needed to be shown what was involved in their recent commitment to the way of Christ. ... If, then, they live in the province of Asia, we shall not look for them in Ephesus or its neighbourhood, but in some region of the province which Paul himself had not visited.[61]

> Though there is no mention of Paul's coworkers here in the postscript, this material is so dependent on Col. 4:7-8 that in verse 22 he says 'how *we* are' (*ta peri hēmōn*). Two more pointers to the encyclical nature of this document are the absence of personal greetings here at the end of the document and the blessing in verse 24 'with *all* who love our Lord Jesus'...[62]

'You also' in verse 21 suggests that this document is sent along with another to a specific audience in Colossians. There are thirty-two consecutive words copied directly from Colossians, which means that the scribe had Colossians before him while composing Ephesians. This book accepts Ephesus as the place of origin of Colossians, Philemon, and Ephesians for the combination of reasons provided above. Philemon was written first, followed by the joint delivery of Colossians and 'Ephesians' by Tychicus, noted in Colossians 4:7 and Ephesians 6:21, respectively.

Time Between Two Roman Imprisonments

The Book of Acts 28:31 ends with Paul in custody in Rome for two years, yet 'preaching the kingdom of God and teaching concerning the Lord Jesus with all openness, unhindered'. Paul's activities before his second and final imprisonment in Rome (while awaiting execution as noted in 2 Timothy 4:6ff.) are unknown other than some clues from his letters, Titus and 1 Timothy. Importantly, for our purposes, the period of time between Paul's two Roman imprisonments could be a span of

61. Bruce, *Ephesians*, p. 230.

62. See Witherington, *Ephesians*, pp. 356-7. It is equally possible that the scribe copied the text of Ephesians to produce the ending of Colossians.

several years, during which he could have accomplished journeys both to the west (Spain, as per his desire in Romans 15:24) and to the east (the Mediterranean region).

It has been widely assumed by commentators, with which I agree, that, upon his release in Rome around A.D. 62, Paul continued his ministry in the east, during which time he composed Titus and 1 Timothy.[63] Paul's first release from Roman imprisonment is noted in 1 Clement 5:7.[64] With Titus (and possibly Timothy) Paul evangelised Crete, leaving Titus there to instruct believers and organise the new churches (Titus 1:5). He then went to Ephesus, where Timothy remained (1 Tim. 1:3-4). Having been so close to Colosse, he may well have fulfilled the invitation of Philemon to visit him there (Philem. 22). In due course Paul reached Macedonia (1 Tim. 1:3) where he would have visited the Philippian Christians (Phil. 2:4). From this region (and probably this city) Paul wrote first to Titus and, a little later, to Timothy.

In Titus 3:12 Paul mentions his intention to spend the winter in Nicopolis, a town on the east coast of the Adriatic Sea. There is no reason to think that Titus did not join him there in A.D. 63-64.

> If the apostle was ever able to fulfil his great ambition to evangelise Spain (Rom. 15:24, 28), it must have been in the following spring that he set sail. Clement of Rome in his famous letter to the Corinthians (chapter 5) said that Paul had 'come to the extreme limit of the west'. He may have been referring only to Italy, but an allusion to Gaul or Spain – and even Britain (as some have suggested) – seems more likely.[65]

---

63. B. Witherington III, *Letters and Homilies for Hellenised Christians: A Socio-Rhetorical Commentary on Titus, 1-2 Timothy and 1-3 John* (Downers Grove, IL: InterVarsity Press, 2006). See also T. C. Oden, *First and Second Timothy and Titus: Interpretation: A Bible Commentary for Teaching and Preaching* (Louisville: Westminster John Knox Press, reprinted 2012); J. R. W. Stott, *The Message of 2 Timothy*, TSBT (Leicester: InterVarsity Press, 1973), pp. 16-18.

64. Witherington, *Letters and Homilies for Hellenised Christians*, p. 65.

65. Stott, *The Message of 2 Timothy*, p. 17.

I think it unlikely that Paul ever travelled further west than Rome.

From his winter retreat Paul would have visited Timothy in Ephesus (1 Tim. 3:14, 15), then continued to Miletus where Trophimus became ill and was left there (2 Tim. 4:20), and from there to Troas. It was from Troas that Paul began his ministry in Europe and, ironically, the place from which he would make his final, long journey to Rome. The text of 2 Timothy 4:14-15 should be read in the light of the comments on Alexander of Troas because it is possible that his vociferous opposition to Paul led to his arrest. This would explain why he did not have time to collect his personal possessions from Carpus in Troas (2 Tim. 4:13).

Paul's second letter to Timothy was written during Paul's second (and final) imprisonment in Rome. In the fourth century A.D. Eusebius accepted this fact and there is no evidence to the contrary.[66] Ben Witherington III considers that 2 Timothy was written from Rome close to Paul's execution by Nero. In his commentary he suggests that the destination of 1 and 2 Timothy was Ephesus.[67] One factor that suggests that Timothy was in Ephesus is the mention of people associated with Ephesus, such as Prisca and Aquila, and Tychicus and Trophimus. A stronger inference is 1 Timothy 1:3: 'As I urged you upon my departure for Macedonia, *remain on at Ephesus* so that you may instruct certain men not to teach strange doctrines' (emphasis added).

Romans 16

The longest list of people greeted by Paul is in Romans 16. The question may be asked how Paul could greet so many people with such familiarity if he himself had never visited Rome. Several of these people were Jews or Hellenistic Jews. The most plausible explanation is that Romans was written from Corinth in A.D. 56, well after Claudius' edict in A.D. 49 that the Jews should leave Rome. Many went west to the Roman provinces in (modern) Greece and Turkey. It is known that the population of Corinth

---

66. *Eusebius*, 2.22.2, p. 96. Oden, *First and Second Timothy and Titus*, p. 26.
67. Witherington, *Letters and Homilies for Hellenised Christians*, pp. 66-8.

included many Jews. Things having quietened down in the imperial capital, it would not be surprising if many of these people returned to their homes (and families) in Rome before Paul wrote to the Christians in that city.

One of the most significant aspects of Romans 16 is the number of women greeted by Paul. It is particularly noteworthy that their consistent hard work for the gospel is emphasised. There has been a bias in some recent commentaries (many by feminists) to portray these (and other) women as leaders of the church(es).[68] However, this analysis needs to take account of Paul's specific instructions for male and female (and especially married) relationships, as well as the significantly different Christian culture that emerged.

Issues of Clarification

The standard practice in this book is to use the names of people as written in Paul's letters: e.g. Cephas is preferred to Peter; Silvanus to Silas, etc.

Analysis of the original Greek text is critical to a correct understanding of many subtleties not easily expressed in an English translation. The Greek text used is the *Greek New Testament*, Nestlé–Aland 27th edition, 1993. Some words used individually may have a different punctuation apparatus from the Nestlé-Aland edition, being words used in KJS.[69] Unless otherwise indicated, all Scripture quotations are from the New American Standard Bible, 1995. Almost all English translations of NT *names* in Greek use the English '**y**' for the Greek letter 'υ'. I have followed that practice for personal names but, other than in the case of quotations, the Greek letter 'υ' is transliterated by the English letter '**u**' for consistency.

The personal entries are listed in alphabetical order for ease of reference. Because the accounts in Scripture provide both

68. See S. Mathew. *Women in the Greetings of Romans 16.1-16*, Library of New Testament Studies 471 (London: T. and T. Clark, 2014).

69. J. R. Kohlenberger III, E. W. Goodrick and J. A. Swanson, eds., *The Greek English Concordance to the New Testament with the New International Version* (Grand Rapids: Zondervan, 1997).

expansive and few facts about different individuals, it is inevitable that the length of the entries for different people will vary greatly. Comments relating to more than one person are sometimes repeated under each relevant entry to avoid the need for constant reference back to other people.

Chronology of Paul's Life

Historical Methodology

In historical research there are two sources of chronological information: internal and external. The letters of Paul provide 'internal' evidence as to the progression of his life, while the 'external' sources are Luke's Book of Acts and records of historical events in the Roman Empire of the first century A.D., which are independently verifiable. Internal data is always regarded as superior to external data.

> These data from the letters have intrinsic superiority over anything contained in Acts. In the first place they are the earliest information available to us, antedating the material in Acts by a number of years, if not decades. Secondly, these details are not motivated by chronological considerations or any assumption regarding the periodisation of the church's history. Thirdly, material from letters such as these must be classed as primary historical data and thus have an intrinsic priority over secondary materials such as a history of the type Luke works out. This evaluation does not depend upon theological or personal criteria; whether one is theologically inclined toward Paul or Luke, the fact remains that methodological considerations force one to give unequivocal priority to chronological details in the [Pauline] letters.
>
> The result is that the general outline of Paul's life must be worked out on the basis of the evidence from the letters and these alone. ... To compromise between Luke's general outline and that reflected in the Pauline letters is to open the door to a subjective chaos that can never be tamed by the whim of the scholar. A general rule therefore is that material from Acts is usable in the chronological experiment only when it does not conflict with evidence in the letters.[1]

1. R. Jewett, *Dating Paul's Life* (London: SCM Press, 1979), pp. 23-4.

Chronological Issues

Paul's early life was dominated by Judaism. Born the son of a Pharisee in Tarsus (Acts 22:3), he was sent to Jerusalem to be instructed in the faith of his fathers by Gamaliel (Acts 22:3), one of Judaism's acknowledged great teachers. As a Pharisee Paul was a strict adherent to the law of Moses. As a young man he was present at the stoning to death of Stephen (Acts 7:57), the first Christian martyr. His dedication to the Jewish Law saw him become one of the chief persecutors of the early Christian church, in Jerusalem and beyond, earning him a fearful reputation.

His enthusiasm led him to request the High Priest in Jerusalem for authority to arrest Christians as far away as Damascus, approximately 135 miles (225 km) north of Jerusalem (Acts 9:2). He was on this journey of persecution when he met the risen Christ, who asked, 'Paul, why are you persecuting *me*?' (Acts 9:5).

The Book of Acts describes people in the life of Paul after that devastating encounter; however, several gaps remain in that chronology, especially Paul's time in Ephesus, coinciding with Luke's absence from that city. It needs to be noted that, at the beginning of Acts, Luke does not claim to present a complete history (let alone a precise chronology) of everything that occurred to the early Christians up to the time of Paul's Roman imprisonment in Acts 28. Even the end of his account ceases before the death of Paul. He was clearly present during the 'we' parts of Acts but was clearly absent from other scenarios which he described from second-hand information.

It was necessary to consult many chronologies of Paul's life by respected scholars in the subject to determine a more precise dating of certain events.[2] While general trends exist between

---

2. Primary references used for the chronology are L. C. A. Alexander, 'Chronology of Paul' in *Dictionary of Paul and His Letters*, eds. G. F. Hawthorne, R. P. Martin and D. G. Reid (Downers Grove, IL: InterVarsity Press, 1993); F. F. Bruce, *Paul: Apostle of the Free Spirit* (Exeter: Paternoster Press, revised edition, 1980); D. A. Campbell, 'An Anchor for Pauline Chronology: Paul's

them for particular events, there are also some clear differences of opinion. One of the helpful markers is Roman history, where precision can be made in dating a few facts. Jewett makes the critical observation that most Pauline chronologists show a 'tendency to downplay evidence in Paul's letters to accommodate contradictions with the book of Acts'.[3] This preference has resulted in some impossible dating conclusions.[4] I have ended up creating my own chronology of Paul's life. It will be up to readers to form their own assessment of its usefulness; however, Donfried's warning must be kept in mind.

> [i]t must be acknowledged that no matter from what perspective one views the data, *there can be no absolutely definite chronology of this period*; all attempts must be tentative and subject to correction and revision.[5]

Flight from the "Ethnarch of King Aretas,"' *JBL* 121, no. 2 (2002): pp. 279-302; D. B. Capes, R. Reeves and E. R. Richards, *Rediscovering Paul: An Introduction to His World, Letters and Theology* (Downers Grove, IL: InterVarsity Press Academic, 2017); D. E. Graves, *Biblical Archaeology Volume 1: An Introduction with Recent Discoveries that Support the Reliability of the Bible* (Moncton, NB, Canada: Electronic Christian Media, 2015); Jewett, *Dating Paul's Life*; F. Josephus, *Jewish Antiquities, Books 18-19,* translated by L. H. Feldman (Loeb Classical Library, 1965); G. Ogg, *The Chronology of the Life of Paul* (London: Epworth, 1968); S. E. Porter, *The Apostle Paul: His Life, Thought, and Letters* (Grand Rapids: Eerdmans, 2016); R. Riesner, *Paul's Early Period: Chronology, Mission Strategy, Theology* (Grand Rapids: Eerdmans, 1998); B. Witherington III, 'The Case of the Imprisonment that did not Happen: Paul at Ephesus,' *JETS* 60, no. 3 (2017): pp. 525-32; N. T. Wright, *Paul: a biography* (San Francisco: HarperOne, 2018).

3. Jewett, *Dating Paul's Life*, p. 69.

4. See Jewett, *Dating Paul's Life*, pp. 1-2 for examples of the widely varying dates claimed for Pauline chronologies. His 'deductive-experimental method' is explained in pp. 2-6. He quotes: 'Scientific hypotheses and theories are not *derived* from observed facts, but *invented* in order to account for them' from C. G. Hempel, *Philosophy of Natural Science* (Englewood Cliffs, NJ: Routledge and Keegan Paul, 1961), p. 15 (original emphasis).

5. K. P. Donfried, 'Chronology: New Testament' in *Anchor Bible Dictionary*, eds. D. N. Freedman, G. A. Herion, D. F. Graf and J. D. Pleins (New York: Doubleday, 1996), vol. 1: p. 1017.

Paul's Visits to Jerusalem

The issue most discussed in academic debate on Pauline chronology is the number of times that Paul visited Jerusalem; the critical issue being a reconciliation of the facts described in Acts 11:27-30; 15:1-30 with Galatians 2:1-10. My conclusion is that the Acts passages refer to four separate visits by Paul to Jerusalem (the first, three years, and the third, fourteen years, after his conversion) and that the correct chronology is recorded in Galatians 2. The second journey (the famine visit) to Jerusalem is considered below. His final journey to Jerusalem ended with his arrest by the Roman authorities.

In Galatians 1:21 Paul notes that he went to the regions of Syria and Cilicia after his first visit to Jerusalem,[6] three years after his conversion. Acts 11:29-30 records the so-called 'famine visit' by Paul and Barnabas in verse 46, which is not mentioned in Galatians. This was Paul's second visit to Jerusalem.

The events of Acts 15 demonstrate the ongoing resistance of some (now Christian) Jews in Jerusalem to abandon the need of circumcision for Gentiles. Acts 15:1 demonstrates this determination of the Judaisers by their going from Jerusalem to Antioch, where they caused serious trouble amongst the believers. Having previously (they may have thought) put the matter to rest during Paul's first visit to Jerusalem (meeting with Cephas), Paul and Barnabas understandably 'had great dissension and debate with them' (Acts 15:2). This wrangling had to cease. Paul went to Jerusalem because of a revelation, noted in Galatians 2:2, accompanied by Barnabas, Titus, and other brothers. The Jerusalem Conference was held, and the matter was settled by the decision of James in Acts 15:13-29. Acts 15:1-30 records the meeting of the Jerusalem Council in A.D. 48, which is summarised in Galatians 2:1-9, where the matter of circumcision was (perhaps) finalised in Paul's mind. But the issue kept on re-occurring. It is evident from Paul's disclosure

6. At this time, the province of Galatia bordered the northern part of the province of Cilicia. See L. C. A. Alexander, 'Chronology of Paul' in *Dictionary of Paul and His Letters*, eds. G. F. Hawthorne, R. P. Martin and D. G. Reid (Downers Grove, IL: InterVarsity Press, 1993), pp. 117, 121-3. See Map 1.

in Galatians 2:11-21 of the subsequent Cephas (Peter) incident in Antioch – obviously after the Jerusalem Council decision – that Paul was infuriated with this persistent issue of partiality between Jew and Gentile (mainly because of circumcision). Having finally dealt with that matter, Paul and Barnabas then set out on their second missionary journey (Acts 16:36).[7]

The chronological puzzle rests on the assertion by some commentators, using Galatians 1:18; 2:1, that Paul wrote that he only visited Jerusalem on two occasions, a view supported by Marshall.[8] However, in my opinion, Cole clarifies this apparent inconsistency by his interpretation of πάλιν (*palin* – again) in Galatians 2:1.

> But does the *palin*, *again*, necessarily mean a second visit? Or could it refer to a third, or any subsequent visit? ... But in that case [if it refers to a third visit] what has happened to the account of the second visit? No man could suspect Paul of deliberately falsifying, the more so as he is virtually 'on oath' by his own choice. On a matter like this it is inconceivable that his memory could be at fault. He was not travelling so constantly to and from Jerusalem that he could accidentally miss out the account of one visit. And it is unthinkable that he should suppress the account of one visit in such a context. The only possibility, if this verse [Gal. 2:1] does refer to the Council visit and not the famine visit, is that Paul regarded the latter as completely irrelevant, since it had nothing to do with theological matters, and thus deliberately omitted it without any intention of deceiving.[9]

The conclusion is that Paul made four visits to Jerusalem (as per Acts) and experienced the incident with Cephas in Antioch after the Jerusalem Council but before writing Galatians; however, only two of the visits (those of theological importance) are recorded in Galatians 2.[10]

---

7. See Map 2.

8. See I. H. Marshall, *A Fresh Look at the Acts of the Apostles* (Sheffield, UK: JSOT Press, 1992), p. 95.

9. R. A. Cole, *The Epistle of Paul to the Galatians.* TNTC (Leicester: InterVarsity Press, reprinted 1983), pp. 60-1.

10. P. Barnett, 'Galatians and Earliest Christianity', *RTR* 59, no. 3 (2000): pp. 112-29. In pp. 114-15 he comments: 'My own reading of the letter urges

Near the End of Paul's Life

The end of Paul's life after his first release from imprisonment in Rome can only be deduced from the letters to Titus and 1 Timothy. The following summary by Oden describes the situation.

> It is likely that Paul was arrested either immediately before or shortly after the intended winter in Nicopolis. At some point in this sequence (the particular time is unclear) he went to Miletus, where he left Trophimus (2 Tim. 4:20), and then to Troas with Carpus (2 Tim. 4:13) and then to Corinth (2 Tim. 4:20). Somewhere in this area he was arrested and taken to Rome, where Titus was with him temporarily. By the time of the writing of Second Timothy, Paul was still in prison at Rome, where he appears to have been incarcerated for some time (2 Tim. 1:17). Titus had gone on to Dalmatia (2 Tim. 4:10), and Timothy presumably was still at Ephesus. In Rome, Paul had a preliminary hearing before a Roman tribunal (2 Tim. 4:16-18) and was required to remain in prison for subsequent trial. During his imprisonment Onesiphorus of Ephesus came to Rome, sought him out (perhaps under difficult circumstances), and brought him up-to-date on the (probably deteriorating) events at Ephesus (2 Tim. 1:15-18). Paul was already feeling abandoned by some he had trusted (e.g. Demas, 2 Tim. 4:9). Crescens had gone to Galatia; Titus to Dalmatia. Paul decided under these difficult circumstances to recall Timothy to Rome and send Tychicus to Ephesus (2 Tim. 4:12). It is likely to surmise that Tychicus delivered the second letter to Timothy, asking him to come immediately to Rome (2 Tim. 4:21). 'Luke alone is with me. Get Mark and bring him with you' (2 Tim. 4:11). These complex movements cannot be fitted into the chronology of Acts.[11]

---

the earlier date as the more likely. Paul's reference to the Galatians' faith having been overturned "so quickly" (1:6) makes more sense in relation to a recent missionary tour of Paul than to the advent of later troubles among the Galatians ... An early date for Galatians (late forties) carries the powerful implication that this letter is the earliest surviving document of early Christianity, as Stephen Mitchell has observed! Thus Paul's Letter to the Galatians lies closer to the historical figure of Jesus and the origins of Christianity than any other document of the New Testament.' Of course, Paul later made a fourth visit to Jerusalem (Acts 21:15).

11. Oden, *First and Second Timothy and Titus*, p. 22.

Roman History

Some dates are more easily identified from known historical occurrences recorded by contemporary historians, such as the reign of Aretas IV, noted in 2 Corinthians 11:32; the proconsulship of Gallio[12] noted in Acts 18:12; and the roles of Felix (Acts 23:24), Porcius Festus (Acts 24:27), and King Agrippa (Acts 25:13) in Judea. These provide an historical framework for other facts. A chronology of Paul's life is provided below.

CHRONOLOGY OF PAUL'S LIFE

DATE	REFERENCE	COMMENT
c 6[13]	Acts 22:3 Rom. 11:2 Phil. 3:5	Born a Roman citizen to Jewish parents (father a Pharisee) in Tarsus (in modern south-eastern Turkey). An Israelite of the tribe of Benjamin. Circumcised on the eighth day, 'a Hebrew of Hebrews'.
c 20–33	Acts 22:3 Phil. 3:5	Studies the Torah in Jerusalem with Gamaliel; becomes a Pharisee and committed to Judaism.
32		Crucifixion of Jesus.[14] (Friday, 7 April 30).
33	Acts 7:58 Gal. 1:13-4 Phil. 3:6 Acts 8:1-3	Stoning of Stephen. Saul was 'a young man' (Acts: νεανίας – *neanias*) when Stephen was killed, and the Galatians reference implies that he was a young adult. Persecution of early church in Jerusalem.
34	Acts 9:1-2 Acts 9:3-22 Gal. 1:17	Persecution of early church and desire to go to Damascus. Conversion near Damascus. To Arabia.

12. For the term of the appointment of Gallio as proconsul of Achaia (Acts 18:12), see the entry on Sosthenes.

13. All dates are A.D.

14. For a detailed confirmation of the date, see N. Geldenhuys, *Commentary on the Gospel of Luke* (London: Marshall, Morgan & Scott, 1950), pp. 649-70. Both Bruce, *Paul: Apostle of the Free Spirit*, p. 475; and Capes, *Rediscovering Paul*, p. 78 agree with this date.

DATE	REFERENCE	COMMENT
35	Gal. 1:17	Arabia/Damascus.
36	Acts 9:23-5 2 Cor. 11:32-3 Gal. 1:18-20 Acts 9:26-9 Acts 9:29-30	In Damascus, but plot by Jews to kill Paul. Escape (from ethnarch Aretas IV). ***First visit to Jerusalem three years after conversion***, aided by Barnabas. Meets with Cephas and James (the Lord's brother) for fifteen days. Plot to kill Paul. Goes from Jerusalem to Tarsus via Caesarea.
37	Roman history	Aretas IV controlled Damascus up to A.D. 37.
36–45	Gal. 1:21	Paul in Tarsus. Evangelistic activity in Syria and Cilicia.
39	Roman history	Death of Aretas IV.
44	Roman history Acts 12:19-23	Death of Herod Agrippa ***(Josephus cites March)***.
45	Acts 11:25-9	Visit to Tarsus by Barnabas to bring Paul to Antioch. Paul in Antioch. Famine prophesied by Agabus in Antioch.
46	Acts 11:26 Acts 11:29-30 Acts 12:25	Paul in Antioch. For a whole year Barnabas and Paul met with the church. Paul and Barnabas take the famine gift to Jerusalem ***(second visit)***. John Mark accompanies them back to Antioch.
47–48	Acts 13:4 Acts 13:5-12 Roman history Acts 13:13 Acts 13:14-51 Acts 13:51–14:5	Paul's ***first missionary journey*** from Antioch with Barnabas and John Mark. From Seleucia to Cyprus. Met proconsul of Cyprus, Sergius Paulus.[15] Sailing from Paphos (Cyprus) to Perga (Pamphylia). John Mark goes back to Jerusalem. To Pisidian Antioch and eventually persecution (v. 50). To Iconium. Eventually, persecution (14:5). To Lycaonia, Lystra, Derbe ***(home of Timothy)*** and surrounding region.

15. Bryan Windle, 'Sergius Paulus: An Archaeological Biography,' Bible Archaeology Report, November 15th 2019. See *https://biblearchaeologyreport.com/2019/11/15/sergius-paulus-an-archaeological-biography/* for archaeological evidence on Cyprus for this man.

DATE	REFERENCE	COMMENT
47–48 (cont.)	Acts 14:19-20	Eventually, persecution in Lystra. Jews from Pisidian Antioch and Iconium came to Lystra and stoned Paul, leaving him for dead outside the city.
	Acts 14:20	To Derbe.
	Acts 14:21-3	Returned via these cities to Pisidian Antioch.
	Acts 14:24-5	Through regions of Pisidia and Pamphilia to Perga and preached the gospel.
	Acts 14:26	To Attalia, then to Antioch. ***End of first missionary journey.***
48	Gal. 2:1-10	Antioch.
	Acts 15:1-29	Men came from Jerusalem demanding circumcision of the Gentiles. Paul went to Jerusalem with Barnabas, Titus and other brothers because of a 'revelation'.
		This visit was *14 years after Paul's conversion* (Gal. 2:1).
		The Jerusalem Council – Paul's ***third*** visit to Jerusalem before writing ***Galatians***.
	Gal. 2:11-14	Circumcision of Gentiles was a main issue for discussion and Titus was not circumcised. The issue of circumcision was finally dealt with by James' declaration.
	Gal. 1:6	Cephas' and Barnabas' hypocrisy in Antioch. Paul vindicated by the Jerusalem Council. Paul writes ***Galatians*** in Antioch after first missionary journey.
49	Roman history	Claudius' edict for Jews to leave Rome.
	Acts 18:2	Paul in Antioch.
	Acts 15:36, 40	***Second missionary journey*** from Antioch.
	Acts 15:37-9	Disagreement between Paul and Barnabas over John Mark.
49–50		***Second missionary journey.***
	Acts 15:40-1	Paul and Silvanus (Silas) travel to Syria, Cilicia.
	Acts 16:1	Then to Derbe.
	Acts 16:2-5	To Lystra, Iconium and other towns where there were Christians.
	Acts 16:6-7	Through the regions of Phrygia and Galatia; but not permitted to go to the regions of Asia or Bithynia by the Holy Spirit.

DATE	REFERENCE	COMMENT
49–50 (cont.)	Acts 16:8-10	Bypassed the region of Mysia and arrived in Troas. Paul's vision of the man in Macedonia.
	Acts 16:11-2	Troas to Samothrace to Neapolis to Philippi (Macedonia).
	Acts 16:13-40	In Philippi, conversion of Lydia. Paul and Silvanus beaten and put in prison overnight. They were released when Paul claimed Roman citizenship.
	Acts 17:1-9	Passed through Amphipolis and Apollonia. Arrival in Thessalonica and subsequent persecution.
	Acts 17:10-14	Journey to Berea, where further persecution occurs.
	Acts 17:15-34 1 Thess. 3:1-2	Paul taken to Athens and stays there. Silvanus and Timothy sent back to Thessalonica.
50		***Second missionary journey.***
	Acts 18:1	Paul arrives in Corinth in late 50.
	Acts 18:2-3	Paul meets Prisca and Aquila in Corinth where he stays 18 months.
		Writes ***1 and 2 Thessalonians*** in Corinth.
51		***Second missionary journey.***
	Roman history	Proconsulship of Gallio in Corinth (1 July 51–30 June 52).
	Acts 18:12-7	Proceedings before Gallio in Corinth. It is likely that the Jews would have taken their case to the proconsul early in his tenure before he had an opportunity to become more familiar with the political and religious climate in the city. Gallio held his position for less than one year.
52		***Second missionary journey.***
	Acts 18:18	Paul remains in Corinth.
	Acts 18:19-21	Paul leaves Corinth with Prisca and Aquila and they sail to Ephesus. Paul in Ephesus for a short time.
	Acts 18:22	Paul leaves Ephesus and goes to Caesarea, Jerusalem ('the church') and back to Antioch.
		End of second missionary journey.
	Roman history	Felix, procurator of Judea (52/53-60) arrives in Palestine.

DATE	REFERENCE	COMMENT
53	Acts 18:23	'Some time' in Antioch. From Antioch – ***Third missionary journey.*** Paul travels through the regions of (south) Galatia and Phyrgia 'strengthening all the disciples'.
	Acts 19:1	Through Pisidia ('the upper country') and arrives in Ephesus for two and a half years. Paul in Ephesus and probably stays at the home of Prisca and Aquila.
	1 Cor. 16:19	***1 Corinthians*** written from Ephesus.[16] Paul writes: '*there are many adversaries*'.
	1 Cor. 16:9	Likely imprisonment in Ephesus *(see analysis in introduction).*
		Philemon written in Ephesus.
54		***Third missionary journey***
	2 Cor. 1:8; 6:3-10; 11:23-7	Severe hardships in Asia (Ephesus). Likely imprisonment in Ephesus *(see analysis in introduction).*
		Ephesians, Colossians written in Ephesus.
55		***Third missionary journey.***
	1 Cor. 16:8	***Intention*** to stay in Ephesus until Pentecost (25 May) – ***but not realised.***
	1 Cor. 16:5	Intention to go to Macedonia and spend winter in Corinth, then back to Macedonia on the way to Judea.
	2 Cor. 1:16	Riot at Ephesus. Paul leaves Ephesus and goes to Macedonia.
	1 Cor. 16:8 Acts 19:23-41 Acts 20:1-2 Rom. 15:19	Departure for Macedonia, going as far north as Illyricum.
56		***Third missionary journey.***
	2 Cor. 7:5; 8:1; 9:2 Acts 20:2	***2 Corinthians*** written from Macedonia (Philippi), spending some months going through that district.
	2 Cor. 1:16 Acts 20:2-3	Stayed in Greece (Corinth) for three months. Writes ***Romans***. Paul's third visit to Corinth. Plot by Jews to kill Paul, so he returns to Macedonia (Philippi).

16. See D. Graham, 'The Placement of Paul's Composition of 1 Corinthians in Troas: A Fresh Approach', *Themelios* 46, no. 3 (2021): pp. 592-607. This conclusion is rejected because of chronological inconsistences with Acts 16:9-10.

DATE	REFERENCE	COMMENT
57		*Third missionary journey.*
	Acts 20:5-6	Sailed from Philippi 'after the Days of Unleavened Bread' to Troas.
	Acts 20:13-36	From Troas to Assos to Mitylene to Chios to Samos to Miletus. Paul called for elders from Ephesus and farewelled them.
	Acts 21:1-9	From Miletus to Cos, Rhodes, Patara, Tyre, Caesarea, and eventually back to Antioch.
		End of third missionary journey.
	Acts 21:10-14	Prophecy of Agabus concerning Paul's fate.
	Acts 21:15-7	Paul's *fourth* (final) journey to Jerusalem.
	Acts 21:27–23:35	Arrested in Jerusalem and held in Roman custody at Caesarea. Felix was procurator of Judea.
58	Acts 24:27	Roman custody at Caesarea for more than two years under Felix and Porcius Festus.
59		Roman custody at Caesarea.
	(Roman history Acts 24:27)	Transfer of governorship of Judea from Felix to Porcius Festus.
	Acts 25:6-12	Paul examined before Porcius Festus and appeals to Caesar.
	Acts 25:13–26:32	Account of Paul's testimonies to Festus, King Agrippa and Bernice.
	Acts 27:1-13	(Late 59) Paul's journey to Rome sails from Adramyttium with centurion Julius, going to Myra in Licia. Then to Fair Havens in southern Crete. Paul's prediction of danger is ignored.
	Acts 27:13-44	Paul sets sail from Fair Havens. Predicted storm occurs and the ship eventually founders on Malta.
	Acts 28:1-10	Three months on Malta.
60	Acts 28:11-16	(Early 60) Paul sails from Malta via Syracuse, Rhegium, and Puteoli, Italy. Travels to Rome.
61–62	Acts 28:17-31 Phil. 1:13-14.	Paul in custody in Rome for two years but lives on his own in relative freedom with a soldier guarding him. Writes ***Philippians***.
62–64		Released from custody but Paul's activities are unknown.

DATE	REFERENCE	COMMENT
62–64 (cont.)	Rom. 15:24, 28	It is possible that Paul travelled to Spain (no evidence exists) but Paul resumed travel in the eastern Mediterranean area.
	Titus 3:5	On Crete with Titus. Writes ***Titus*** from Macedonia (Philippi) and encourages him to go to Nicopolis for the winter.
	1 Tim. 1:3	Writes ***1 Timothy*** from Macedonia.
	2 Tim. 4:14-5	Arrested (probably Troas?) and sent to Rome.
64	2 Tim. 1:8; 4:6	Imprisoned and writes ***2 Timothy***. Nero criticised for large fire in Rome.
64/65 or later	Christian historian Eusebius	Executed under Nero.

Chronology of Paul's Letters

Chronology and Origin

Estimating the date and origin of Paul's letters is not the primary purpose of this book. However, without these data it is a much more speculative task to write about the people in them, where they were, and what they were doing. This chronology is deliberately as brief as is necessary to comment accurately on the provenance of Paul's letters.

The chronology and origin of Paul's letters is probably of lesser importance to their theological value (other than as a guide to the development of Paul's theological ideas) but they are critical to an evaluation of the people mentioned in them. For example, 'though the question [regarding the destination of the letter] has important historical, exegetical, and interpretative ramifications, the deriving of either doctrinal insight or spiritual benefit from Paul's letter to the Galatians is not dependent on a final solution as to provenance.'[1] Ordering the letters chronologically assists in examining the relationship of verses in one letter to verses in the others from a time perspective; importantly, to Luke's recordings of events in Acts; and, particularly, to the relationship of one person to another and to Paul.

Calculating a chronology of Paul's letters is a speculative task to say the least! I have undertaken the unenviable task of assessing multiple chronological opinions and presenting my own summary of those opinions – without the expectation of strong endorsement! This necessitates relying on many respected biblical scholars (see Bibliography) to guide my conclusions. Of course, the final dating is my determination and none of them should be thought responsible for these conclusions. We have already seen Donfried's warning above. It is inevitably difficult to ascribe some letters precisely to an individual year. To assist the accuracy of

1. R. N. Longenecker, *Galatians*, WBC (Dallas: Word Books 1990), p. lxviii.

this process, scholars have taken specific events and people in Roman history to aid their linkage of these events with Paul's activities at the same time.

There are widespread opinions about the order in which Paul wrote his letters as well as the years and locations in which they were composed. It is clear from Scripture that Romans, 1 and 2 Corinthians, Galatians, and 1 and 2 Thessalonians were not composed in prison. Of the others, there is consensus that 1 Timothy and Titus were composed while Paul was in Macedonia prior to his second Roman imprisonment. Second Timothy was probably written later, closer to Paul's death in Rome. The most controversial chronological issue concerning Paul's letters revolves around the so-called Letters from Prison (Ephesians, Philippians, Colossians, and Philemon). Were they composed during Paul's imprisonment in Rome or Ephesus?

After considering many arguments in many commentaries, I conclude that Ephesians, Colossians, and Philemon were composed during one or more imprisonments of Paul in Ephesus. Evidence for this is provided particularly in the introduction (*Letters From Prison: Ephesians, Philippians, Colossians, and Philemon*) and in the entries for Aristarchus and Epaphras. Philippians was written in Rome during the imprisonment of Acts 28.

It has long been argued that Paul's Letter to the Ephesians was actually a circular letter to several churches and the Ephesians received a copy of it: 'To whom was the epistle addressed? Many answers have been given to this question, but nothing is certain except that the letter was not written to the Ephesians.'[2] For this reason, it is quite reasonable to suppose that the letter was actually composed in Ephesus.

Chronology of Paul's Letters

Assuming that three of the Letters from Prison were written in Ephesus, the table which follows provides an estimate of the

2. Scott, *Colossians*, pp. 121-2. See also Foulkes, *Ephesians*, pp. 17-20.

chronology of Paul's correspondence, which in some cases may have been written during the preceding or following year of that nominated.

Letter	Place of Origin	Year of Composition
Galatians	Antioch	48
1 Thessalonians	Corinth	50
2 Thessalonians	Corinth	50
1 Corinthians	Ephesus	53
Philemon	Ephesus	53
Colossians	Ephesus	54
Ephesians	Ephesus	54
2 Corinthians	Macedonia	56
Romans	Corinth	56
Philippians	Rome	61
Titus	Macedonia	63
1 Timothy	Macedonia	63
2 Timothy	Rome	64

The People in Paul's Letters
Individual Entries

Achaicus

1 Corinthians 16:15-18

[15] *Now I urge you, brethren (you know the household of Stephanas, that they were the first fruits of Achaia, and that they have devoted themselves for ministry to the saints), ...*

[16] *... that you also be in subjection to such men and to everyone who helps in the work and labours.*

[17] *I rejoice over the coming of Stephanas and Fortunatus and Achaicus, because they have supplied what was lacking on your part.*

[18] *For they have refreshed my spirit and yours. Therefore acknowledge such men.*

The name Achaicus means 'belonging to Achaia',[1] which, in Paul's time, was a Roman province of Greece whose capital was Corinth.[2] Achaicus is a Latin name, probably that of a slave or freed man, but would not have originated in Greece. According to Meeks, Achaicus (or his father) 'must have lived for a time in Italy, received the name there, and then returned to Corinth, probably as one of the freed men colonists'.[3] Moffatt assumed that he and Fortunatus belonged to the household of Stephanas (either as slaves or freed men) and this seems likely.[4] They were

1. HSIBD, p. 13.

2. See J. A. Fitzmyer, *First Corinthians: A New Translation with Introduction and Commentary*, The Anchor Yale Bible (New Haven, CT: Yale University Press, 2008), p. 625.

3. W. A. Meeks, *The First Urban Christians: The Social World of the Apostle Paul* (New Haven, CT: Yale University Press, 2003), p. 56.

4. See J. Moffatt, *The First Epistle of Paul to the Corinthians*, MNTC (London: Hodder and Stoughton, reprinted 1947), p. 279; R. E. Ciampa and B. S. Rosner, *The First Letter to the Corinthians*, PNTC (Grand Rapids: Eerdmans, 2010), p. 859.

members of the Corinthian church. The mention of the 'household of Stephanas' implies that he was a person of some means who could employ slaves or freed men.

Corinth is nearly 900 miles (1,450 km) from Ephesus by land. These three may have walked the journey, but it is much more likely that they crossed the Aegean Sea in about two weeks during Paul's extended stay in Ephesus (A.D. 53 to 55). First Corinthians 7:1 suggests that they brought with them a letter with questions for the apostle to answer. Paul urges the Corinthian church 'to submit to such people and to everyone who joins in the work and labours at it':

> Thus we may have here people, including two of relatively low social standing, who are to be honoured for their 'serving' of the people, characterised in part by their refreshing of both Paul's spirit and that of others. The anomaly of 'servant' figures being 'respected' for their labouring is made all the more stark by Paul's insistence in 1 Corinthians 16:16 that these figures be submitted to precisely because of their labour. This verb implies the attribution of authority – an unexpected command in the wider Graeco-Roman context given the social status of the individuals concerned.[5]

The NASB translates τοῖς ἁγίοις (*tois hagiois*) 'of the Lord's people' but the Greek text refers to 'the saints' (of Corinth and Achaia): 'The military echoes in the imperatives of v. 13 have probably inspired Paul's use of τάσσω – *tassō* [ἔταξαν – *etaxan*] and ὑποτάσσω – *hupotassō* here (vv. 15, 16), both of which also have military connotations.'[6] The use of συν- in συνεργοῦντι – *sunergounti* in this context indicates that 'certain ones are worthy of more exceptional regard than others'.[7]

---

5. A. D. Clarke, '"Refresh the Hearts of the Saints": A Unique Pauline Context,' *TynBul* 47, no. 2 (1996): p. 288. See G. D. Fee, *The First Epistle to the Corinthians*, NICNT (Grand Rapids: Eerdmans, 2014), pp. 918-20 for a detailed analysis of the relationship between Stephanas, Achaicus, and Fortunatus, reflecting Paul's new Christian society in practice.

6. T. A. Brookins and B. W. Longenecker, *1 Corinthians 10-16: A Handbook on the Greek Text*, BHGNT (Waco, TX: Baylor University Press, 2016), p. 202.

7. ibid., pp. 202-3.

The three men visited Paul in Ephesus while he was writing his letter to the Corinthians. It is possible that they took a letter back to Corinth on their return journey. Paul writes to the Corinthians that he rejoiced over their visit because 'they have supplied what was lacking on your part'. There is no implied criticism that these men did something that the Corinthian church could not (or would not) do. The sense of the words is that, by coming to Paul personally, they have brought a little bit of Corinth with them (v. 17).[8]

Paul tells the Corinthian church that their visit 'refreshed my spirit and yours'. The word for 'refreshed' (ἀναπαύω – *anapauō*) is the same as that used by Jesus in Matthew 11:28 when He talks about giving 'rest' to those who labour and are heavy-laden.[9] Perhaps their presence lifted a burden of concern from Paul's shoulders about the state of the Corinthian church. Morris also comments about the end of verse 18 that '*And yours* is an interesting addition. Not only was it good for Paul to receive news from Corinth; it was good for the Corinthians to send the messages to Paul that they had done through these three men. The believers should acknowledge people like this; i.e. know them for what they are, and ascribe to them their true worth.'[10]

In verse 18 Paul concludes that Achaicus and his companions should be highly esteemed by the Corinthian Christians, only reinforcing his commendation in verse 15. The use of ἐπιγινώσκω (*epiginōskō*) should be understood as meaning 'appreciate (or recognise) these men for what they are'.[11]

ALEXANDER

There are a number of Alexanders in the NT and two are mentioned in Paul's letters to Timothy. The name means

---

8. Moffatt, *1 Corinthians*, p. 280. See Brookins and Longenecker, *1 Corinthians 10-16*, p. 203.

9. Compare this with the use of ἀναψύχω (*anapuchō*) regarding Onesiphorus (2 Tim. 1:16).

10. L. L. Morris, *The First Epistle of Paul to the Corinthians*, TNTC (Leicester: InterVarsity Press, 1983), p. 245 (original emphasis).

11. M. Zerwick and M. Grosvenor, *A Grammatical Analysis of the Greek New Testament* (Rome: Biblical Institute Press, 1979), vol. 2: p. 533.

'defender of men'.[12] Another Alexander is mentioned in Acts 19:33ff. Alexander was a common name in the Hellenistic world and, although there are arguments to identify the two men named in 1 and 2 Timothy as one and the same person, they are dealt with separately below. I regard them as two distinct people. This name was used by both Jews and Gentiles.[13]

Alexander

1 Timothy 1:18-20

[18] *This command I entrust to you, Timothy, my son, in accordance with the prophecies previously made concerning you, that by them you fight the good fight, ...*

[19]*... keeping faith and a good conscience, which some have rejected and suffered shipwreck in regard to their faith.*

[20] *Among these are Hymenaeus and Alexander, whom I have handed over to Satan, so that they will be taught not to blaspheme.*

This Alexander lived in Ephesus, where Timothy was then residing. Paul wrote to Timothy from Macedonia after being released from his first imprisonment in Rome, described in Acts 28:30-31.[14] Paul warns Timothy that some people 'have turned their backs' (ἀπωθέω – *apōtheō*) on the faith.[15]

> 'Rejected' translates a word (*apōtheō*) used six times in the NT, three of those in Acts, where it refers to a literal pushing aside of Moses (Acts 7:27) in a physical scuffle and then a rejection of his spiritual leadership by the wayward children of Israel in the exodus (Acts 7:39). Paul and Barnabas dramatically charge their synagogue audience with rejecting God's word (Acts 13:46), resulting in a historic shift in their mission so that they will henceforth target the Gentiles. Paul used the same word twice in Romans 11, once in the historical question 'Did God reject His people?' (v. 1) and again with

12. HSIBD, p. 34.

13. Jewish uses of Alexander in the NT are the son of Simon of Cyrene (Mark 15:21) and a person in the High Priest's family (Acts 4:6).

14. See Stott, *The Message of 2 Timothy,* pp. 16-18 for a summary of Paul's possible travels between his first and second imprisonments in Rome. This description is also applicable to Hymenaeus and is used there.

15. Zerwick and Grosvenor, *Grammatical Analysis,* vol. 2, p. 629.

> the insistence 'God did not reject His people' (v. 2), adapting words from the LXX. Usage in Josephus and Philo indicates that the word often connotes a rash and violent dispersal of something or putting someone to flight. Paul may be understood as describing, not a less-than-perfect faith or a spiritual outlook not completely congruent with his own, but a determined or even vehement blockage. His implied critique in this verse is by no means petty.[16]

They rejected it so completely that Paul describes their fate as a 'shipwreck' (ἐναυάγησαν – *enauagēsan*). By this time, Paul was well aware of the outcome of being in a shipwreck, his experiences being described in 2 Corinthians 11:25 and Acts 27:9-44.

> These misunderstandings are in fact culpable and wilful distortions that wreak havoc on what believers affirm and confess to their salvation – indicating that to follow their mistaken lead would be fatal betrayal of the means of grace embodied in the truth of the gospel (see Col. 1:5). Paul refers to people like someone who receives the keys to an impressive new car and then promptly takes it out and wrecks it. The reckless driver may live to drive again, but the car is totalled. Timothy is up against persons at Ephesus whose religious bent – whose bogus belief and unredeemed conscience – would result in total wreckage of the apostolic conviction Paul and Timothy champion, were that possible.[17]

Hymenaeus and Alexander were among the casualties. Perkins notes that 'the expression ναυαγεῖν περί [*nauagein peri*] + accusative [v. 19] in the majority of cases refers to geographical locations'.[18]

> Although these examples are not plentiful, they suggest that in 1 Tim. 1:19 'the faith' may be the element against which the shipwreck occurs. The writer may be saying that these believers have been wrecked on the rock of the faith. If this is a correct reading of the metaphor, then 'the faith' – i.e., the gospel teaching – in this setting becomes the shoal on which these people's lives are foundering

---

16. R. W. Yarbrough, *The Letters to Timothy and Titus*, PNTC (Grand Rapids: Eerdmans, 2018), p. 133.
17. ibid., p. 134.
18. L. J. Perkins, *The Pastoral Letters: Handbook on the Greek Text*, BHGNT (Waco, TX: Baylor University Press, 2017), p. 27.

> because they are pursuing a false gospel and placing themselves in danger of God's judgment.[19]

With his authority as an apostle, Paul 'handed [them] over' (παραδίδωμι – *paradidōmi*) to Satan.[20] Paul uses exactly the same verb to describe their fate as he uses to describe the judgment of God in Romans 1:23, where he writes that people 'exchanged the glory of the incorruptible God for an image in the form of corruptible man and of birds and four-footed animals and crawling creatures'. As a consequence, Romans 1:24 says that 'God gave them over' (παραδίδωμι – *paradidōmi*). Both verbs are in the aorist tense, reflecting the finality of the matter.[21] Paul's purpose was so that they might 'be taught' (παιδεύω – *paideuō*) not to blaspheme (about what we do not know). This word is more forceful than 'taught' (NASB); it relates more to discipline.[22]

> The verb translated 'be taught' (from *paideuō*) is used elsewhere by Paul to refer to restorative instruction rather than blind punishment or vengeance. (See 1 Cor. 11:32; 2 Tim. 2:25; Titus 2:12.) Paul's action is intended to bring or restore them to saving faith rather than allowing them to continue to misrepresent that faith, slander it, or otherwise speak evil of it, the sorts of meanings that attach to NT occurrences of 'blaspheme'.[23]

---

19. ibid., p. 28. See A. J. Köstenberger, *Commentary on 1–2 Timothy and Titus*, Biblical Theology for Christian Proclamation (Nashville, TN: Holman, 2017), p. 89, n. 103. Note also the analogy of shipwreck in Jude 12.

20. This is a passage subject to various interpretations but the general conclusion revolves around excommunication. See P. H. Towner, *1-2 Timothy and Titus*, IVP New Testament Commentary Series (Downers Grove, IL: IVP Academic, 1994), pp. 59-60. Perkins, *Pastoral Letters*, p. 29 provides lengthy comments about παιδευθῶσιν (*paideuthōsin*) and βλασφημεῖν (*blasphēmein*).

21. See the use of the same verb in Ephesians 5:2, 25 where Christ 'gave Himself up' for the church. There is a finality about this.

22. See NASBEC, p. 1553, ref. *3811*. Perkins, *Pastoral Letters*, p. 29 suggests that the sense is 'so they might discipline/train themselves not to defame [the faith] profanely'. He notes that '[T]he verb as well as the cognate noun and adjective occur frequently within the PE [Pastoral Epistles] (seven times) to describe actions and roles that profane the faith.'

23. Yarbrough, *Letters to Timothy and Titus*, p. 135.

Paul uses this same expression in 1 Corinthians 5:5; see also Job 2:6 (LXX) for a similar action. No one seems to be sure of its meaning and implications for the offender. Nevertheless, it is an extreme form of discipline in the Christian community.

> It apparently signifies excommunication (see 1 Cor. 5:2, 7, 13). The idea underlying this is that outside the Church is the sphere of Satan (Eph. 2:12; Col. 1:13; 1 John 5:19). To be expelled from the Church of Christ is to be delivered into that region where Satan holds sway. It is a very forcible expression for the loss of all Christian privileges.[24]

It appears that Hymenaeus continued to sin because of his mention in 2 Timothy 2:17-18.

ALEXANDER

2 TIMOTHY 4:14-15

[14] Alexander the coppersmith did me much harm; the Lord will repay him according to his deeds.

[15] Be on guard against him yourself, for he vigorously opposed our teaching.

In spiritual terms, this is a dangerous man. This is one of Paul's strongest condemnations of an individual. In writing 2 Timothy 1:8 from his prison cell in Rome, Paul warns Timothy (still in Ephesus) in the strongest terms that a 'coppersmith' (χαλκεὺς – *chalkeus*, a worker of hollowing out copper or brass) named Alexander 'did me much harm'. The use of πολλά – (*polla*) reflects a great deal of harm.[25] 'But because this man rose against God with malice and sacrilegious hardihood, and openly attacked known truth, such impiety had no claim to compassion.'[26]

---

24. Morris, *1 Corinthians*, p. 88. See D. Guthrie, *The Pastoral Epistles*, TNTC (Leicester: InterVarsity Press, reprinted 1983), pp. 68-9; Köstenberger, *1–2 Timothy and Titus*, p. 90. D. Prior, *The Message of 1 Corinthians*, TBST (Leicester: InterVarsity Press, 1985), pp. 72-9 provides a fuller discussion of church discipline regarding this matter.

25. See Miriam and Persis for the other end of the scale concerning this word.

26. J. Calvin, 'Commentaries on the Second Epistle to Timothy', *Calvin's Commentaries*, trans. W. Pringle (Grand Rapids: Baker Book House, 1979), vol. 21: p. 268.

Then comes a grave omen. Paul reminds Timothy that the Lord will repay (ἀποδιδωμι – *apodidōmi*; cf. the opposite (reward) in 2 Timothy 4:8) this man according to his deeds. Given Paul's commitment to the gospel, 'We may be quite sure that it was Paul's concern for the truth of the message, and not personal pique or vindictiveness, which led him to express his belief (it is a statement according to the best MSS, not a wish or a prayer): the Lord will requite him for his deeds.'[27] Various commentators regard this Alexander as the same person described in 1 Timothy 1:20; others consider him to be a different person. I accept the latter view.

> An Ἀλέξανδρος appeared in 1 Tim. 1:20, an opponent of Paul linked with Hymenaeus, who with him had been 'handed over to Satan'. He is presumably the same person. Opinions differ whether he was located in Ephesus (one of the opponents in 1 Cor. 16:8; cf. Brox, 274), Rome or elsewhere. If he lived in Troas, this would explain the association of ideas (Easton, 73). He is described as a χαλκεὺς (*chalkeus*), 'coppersmith', hence generally 'blacksmith, metalworker' [see Gen. 4:22; 2 Chron. 24:12]. The suggestion that the description is given to distinguish him from the other Alexander of 1 Tim. 1:20 falls down on the fact that this is a different literary context. There was a guild of coppersmiths at Troas, and the suggestion has been made that Alexander was a member of it; this would tie in with the sudden reference to him after the mention of Troas in the previous verse.
>
> Against the identification of him with the Alexander of 1 Tim. 1:20 it has been objected that, although he was excommunicated there, he is here carrying on his activities unhindered. Such an objection is anachronistic. We do not know enough about how far 'handing over a person to Satan' was effective in discouraging their activities in the church.[28]

Given the specific reference to Alexander's occupation, it has been suggested that he is not the same man referred to in 1 Timothy 1:20.[29] The mention of Troas in 1 Timothy 4:13 may indicate that this

27. Stott, *2 Timothy*, p. 122. See Yarbrough, *Letters to Timothy and Titus*, p. 452.

28. I. H. Marshall, *A Critical and Exegetical Commentary on the Pastoral Epistles*, ICC (Edinburgh: T. and T. Clark, 1999), p. 821.

29. Guthrie, *Pastoral Epistles*, p. 174.

Alexander is in Troas, where there was a guild of coppersmiths.[30] If so, Timothy is being warned ahead of time should he visit Troas. The other location for Alexander would be Ephesus. Marshall not only regards the two Alexanders as one and the same person but also suggests that 'Alexander thus emerges as the leader of an anti-Pauline faction, hardly as a non-Christian attacker of the church'.[31]

This person spoke 'strongly' (λίαν – *lian*) against Paul's preaching. This word emphasises a particularly vociferous and forceful opposition.[32] The word chosen does not suggest physical harm but a serious impediment to Paul's preaching activity. Timothy is warned to have nothing to do (φυλάσσω – *phulassō*) with this person: 'to keep clear of him' (cf. Titus 3:10).[33] It appears that Alexander strongly opposed the spread of the gospel for some years. The severity of Paul's use of the verb ἀνθίστημι (*anthistēmi* – 'opposed') is reflected in its use in 1 Timothy 3:8 concerning the opposition of Jannes and Jambres to Moses.[34] Some commentators have suggested that, through his adverse comments concerning Paul, he may have been responsible for Paul's arrest in Troas and return to imprisonment in Rome.[35]

> The mention of having had to leave his coat and books in Troas reminds Paul of the cause of his arrest, Alexander the metalworker, whom he now cautions Timothy also to be on his guard against when he goes through there. In any case, Paul has full confidence in God's

30. Marshall, *Pastoral Epistles,* p. 821, n. 25.

31. Marshall, *Pastoral Epistles,* pp. 821-2. Perkins, *Pastoral Letters*, p. 233, agrees with this conclusion but it should be rejected if two different men are called Alexander.

32. See Perkins, *Pastoral Letters*, p. 235: 'This is the only occurrence of this adverb in the PE [Pastoral Epistles]. It means "to a high degree" (BDAG, 594) and indicates a very strong opposition.'

33. Zerwick and Grosvenor, *Grammatical Analysis*, vol. 2, p. 645. The opposite 'strength' of φυλάσσω is found in Jude 24, where it refers to Christ's power to prevent Christians from stumbling. See Manuell, *The Letter of Jude*, p. 192.

34. See Yarbrough, *Letters to Timothy and Titus*, pp. 45-52, 414, who notes its use in Romans 9:19; 13:2; Galatians 2:11 and Ephesians 6:13.

35. See Marshall, *Pastoral Epistles,* p. 822; Köstenberger, *1–2 Timothy*, p. 283; G. D. Fee, *1 & 2 Timothy, Titus* (Peabody, MA: Hendrickson, 1998), p. 296.

> justice and therefore expects Alexander to come under eschatological judgment: The Lord will repay him (the same verb as in v. 8) for what he has done (words reminiscent of Psalm 28:4 and 62:12).[36]

This explanation of how Paul may have been arrested in Troas and returned to Rome is strengthened by Perkins' analysis of the Greek text.

> **πολλά ... κακὰ.** Accusative direct object of ἐνεδείξατο. Its position prior to the verb gives it focal prominence. The adjective κακὰ functions substantively ('evils'). The meaning of the expression πολλά κακὰ depends upon the interpretation of the main verb. If ἐνεδείξατο means that Alexander 'showed, displayed' certain behaviours, πολλά κακὰ refer to evil deeds in general. If, however, the verb is used in its legal sense 'to inform against', then πολλά κακὰ refer to specific accusations Alexander made in some court proceedings.
>
> **ἐνεδείξατο.** Aor. mid. ind. 3rd sg ἐνδείκνυμι. For other uses of this verb in the PE [Pastoral Epistles], see 1 Tim. 1:16; and Titus 2:10; 3:2. Quinn and Wacker (812-3) propose that the writer uses this verb in its legal sense, i.e., 'bring charges against'. On this view, Alexander would be one who has brought particularly evil charges against him, contributing to the writer's arrest. Marshall (822) and Johnson (2001, 411) opt for a more general meaning (i.e., 'he did me much evil)' because the circumstances surrounding this person are unclear.[37]

AMPLIATUS (also known as **AMPLIAS**)

ROMANS 16:8

> [8] *Greet Ampliatus, my beloved in the Lord.*

This was a common Latin slave name meaning 'large' or 'enlarged',[38] especially in Rome, where it was found in inscriptions of the imperial household. It was also known in Ephesus.[39] Some documents refer to him as Amplias, but the best ancient sources use his full name.

---

36. Fee, *1 & 2 Timothy, Titus*, p. 219.
37. Perkins, *Pastoral Letters*, p. 233-4.
38. HSIBD, 45. See Jewett, *Romans*, p. 964.
39. J. D. G. Dunn, *Romans 9-16*, WBC (Dallas, TX: Word Books, 1988), p. 895.

Throughout Paul's letters (and especially Romans) we have the command 'greet' (ἀσπάσασθε – *aspasasthe*). This is its first occurrence in this book: 'In this context, to greet is to honour and welcome one another, probably with the hug, kiss, handshaking, or bowing that gave expression to greeting in the ancient world; the original meaning of the Greek term ἀσπάζομαι [*aspazomai*] ("greet") [was] to embrace by wrapping one's arms around another.'[40]

Paul greets him as '*my* beloved in the Lord' (emphasis added). Clearly, Ampliatus is a person for whom Paul had particular affection, reflected by his use of 'my'. All Christians are 'in Christ',[41] but the direct connection of this phrase with the name of Ampliatus indicates that he had a special devotedness to Christ and a special place in Paul's heart. This indicates that Paul knew him personally and that he had moved (back?) to Rome by the time this letter was written. Matthew Henry noted that 'Where the law of love is in the heart the law of kindness will be in the tongue. Endearing language should pass among Christians to express love, and to engage love.'[42]

There is common reference by commentators linking Ampliatus to the Catacomb of Domitilla in Rome.

> There is a burial chamber in the Catacomb of Domitilla containing two inscriptions which may perhaps bear on the present verse. In one not earlier than the second century A.D. (and apparently Christian) an Aurelius Ampliatus is named. It is natural to suppose that he was a descendant of the person commemorated by the other, which consists of the single word AMPLAT[I]. The tomb which bears this single name, inscribed in bold, well-formed lettering, belongs – to judge from its decoration – to the first or early second century A.D. Its character suggests that it is the tomb of someone who was especially esteemed. There seems to be a real possibility – we cannot put it more strongly – that this Ampliatus is the person greeted by Paul, and that it may have been through him – a slave – that the gospel first

---

40. Jewett, *Romans*, p. 952.
41. See introduction – Paul's Use of *ἐν χριστῶ (en Christō - in Christ).*
42. M. Henry, *Commentary on the Whole Bible: Genesis to Revelation*. ed. L. F. Church (Grand Rapids, MI: Zondervan, 1961), p. 1799.

> penetrated into the noble household to which Flavia Domitilla, the emperor Domitian's niece and wife of Flavius Clemens belonged.[43]
>
> Flavia Domitilla was a Christian lady of the imperial household who was banished to the island of Pandateria, off the Campanian coast, by her uncle Domitian in A.D. 95, but was released after his death in the following year, and whose name is perpetuated in the 'Cemetery of Domitilla'.[44]

Barclay suggests that the style of the tomb reflected the lack of social discrimination in the early church. 'The distinction of rank and place were so completely wiped out that it was possible for a man at one and the same time to be a slave and a prince of the church.'[45] Dodd comments that 'we have early evidence of a Roman Christian family bearing this name'.[46]

Dunn notes that 'Ampliatus is a common slave name, attested in Rome but also elsewhere (Pompeii, Spain, Athens, Ephesus). … Its frequency weakens the case for linking Ampliatus to the imperial household (as suggested by Lightfoot).'[47] Thielman's conclusion is that the comments above about Domitilla are pure speculation.[48]

ANDRONICUS see also **JUNIAS**

ROMANS 16:7

[7]Greet Andronicus and Junias, my kinsmen and my fellow prisoners, who are outstanding among the apostles, who also were in Christ before me.

Andronicus is a Greek name meaning 'conquer',[49] and is associated with slaves in the imperial household.[50] There has been much discussion on whether the other person's name is Junia (f.) or

---

43. Cranfield, *Romans*, vol. 2, p. 790. See Jewett, *Romans*, p. 964.

44. F. F. Bruce, *The Epistle of Paul to the Romans*, TDNC (Leicester: InterVarsity Press, 1963), p. 273.

45. W. Barclay, *The Letter to the Romans*, The Daily Study Bible (Edinburgh: St Andrew Press, 1957), p. 232.

46. C. H. Dodd, *The Epistle of Paul to the Romans* (London: Hodder and Stoughton 1932), p. xxiii.

47. Dunn, *Romans 9–16*, p. 895.

48. Thielman, *Romans*, pp. 720-1.

49. HSIBD, p. 47.

50. Cranfield, *Romans*, vol. 2, p. 788.

Junias (m.). Either name is possible and arguments for both are provided in the entry for Junia(s).

'The article-noun-και-noun construction τοὺς συγγενεῖς μου καὶ συναιχμαλώτους (*tous suggeneis mou kai sunaichmalōtous*) ['*my kinsmen and my fellow prisoners*'] applies both descriptors to Andronicus and Junia(s) and is an example of the Granville Sharp Rule'.[51] Commentators have varied in their interpretation of Andronicus and Junia(s) as 'my kinsmen' (ὅι συγγενοι μου – *hoi suggenoi mou*). Some suggest that they were relatives of Paul;[52] others that, as in Romans 9:3, Paul is referring to fellow Jews.[53]

---

51. J. D. Harvey, *Exegetical Guide to the Greek New Testament* (Nashville, TN: B&H Academic, 2017), p. 379. There are many examples of the rule in the NT. For example, in Jude 4, the terms 'Master' and 'Lord' both refer to the same person. The construction in Greek is known as the Granville Sharp Rule, named after the English philanthropist-linguist who first clearly articulated the rule in 1798. Sharp pointed out that in the construction 'article-noun-καί-noun' (where καί [*kai*] = 'and'), when two nouns are singular, personal, and common (i.e., not proper names), they *always* had the same referent. Illustrations such as 'the friend and brother', 'the God and Father', etc. abound in the NT as examples of the rule; e.g. Titus 2:13; 2 Pet. 1:1.

Granville Sharp (1735–1813) was an English political reformer, slavery abolitionist, and Greek language scholar known for his contributions regarding the translation of NT Greek as it relates to the divinity of Christ. Sharp believed strongly in the deity of Christ and studied the NT in its original language to more ably prove Christ's deity. The Granville Sharp Rule was first noted in 1798 in his book, *Remarks on the Uses of the Definitive Article in the Greek Text of the New Testament: Containing Many New Proofs of the Divinity of Christ, from Passages Which Are Wrongly Translated in the Common English Version.*

The Granville Sharp Rule states, 'When the copulative *kai* connects two nouns of the same case, [viz. nouns (either substantive or adjective, or participles) of personal description, respecting office, dignity, affinity, or connexion, and attributes, properties, or qualities, good or ill], if the article *ho*, or any of its cases, precedes the first of the said nouns or participles, and is not repeated before the second noun or participle, the latter always relates to the same person that is expressed or described by the first noun or participle.' (*Remarks on the Uses of the Definitive Article*, 3). See *https://www.gotquestions.org/Granville-Sharp-Rule.html.*

52. See Hodge, *Romans*, p. 449; Haldane, *Romans*, p. 637.

53. See Murray, *Romans*, p. 229; Bruce, *Romans*, p. 272; Cranfield, *Romans*, vol. 2, p. 788.

The NIV always translates συγγενής as referring to a familial relative, with the exception of Romans 9:3 where the alternative of 'my race' is clear. This word is used by Paul only in Romans 16:7, 11, 21: he refers to six people with this word. It seems highly unlikely to imagine that so many members of Paul's personal family would be in Rome. Importantly, Strong regards the singular (συγγενίς – *suggenis*) as referring to a personal relative but the plural (συγγενής – *suggenēs*) as referring by extension to a fellow-countryman (i.e. for Paul, a Jew).[54] It seems clear that Paul uses this word not to refer to part of his personal family but to fellow members of the family of Abraham through faith in Christ. The Pauline use of this word is to refer to fellow Jews. The necessity of this description may reflect the fact that, even though they were Jews, Andronicus and Junia(s) had what looked like Hellenistic and Roman names, respectively.

> Having this kind of special theological interest in emphasising the Jewish kinship of Christians in Romans – and only in Romans – Paul probably applies the term 'kins(wo)men' rather consistently to all Jewish Christians he can identify in the group of Romans 16.[55] The list, then, shows that only a small minority of Jewish Christians existed among the twenty-six persons of this Roman group (15 per cent).
>
> Several times in Romans Paul presumes that the vast majority in the Roman church is Gentile. These clear and direct statements seem to contradict the impression that much of the contents of Romans could be understood only by people who were trained in Jewish culture. The solution of the paradox is at hand if we assume that most people in the Roman church were of Gentile origin but had lived as sympathisers on the margins of the synagogues before they became Christian.[56]

---

54. Strong, *Greek Dictionary of the New Testament*, p. 67, ref. *4772, 4773*.

55. The only exception seems to be Aquila, a Jewish Christian according to Acts 18:2. Paul reports so many other things about him and his wife that the ethnic attribute is understandably left unremarked.

56. P. Lampe, 'The Roman Christians in Romans 16' in *The Romans Debate*, ed. K. Donfried, rev. and expanded ed. (Peabody, MA: Hendrickson, 1977), pp. 224-5.

They were also, at some stage, Paul's 'fellow prisoners', (συναιχμαλώτους μου – *sunaichmalōtos mou*) reflecting their preparedness to suffer for Christ. This word is also used in relation to Aristarchus in Colossians 4:6, and Epaphras in Philemon 23. Although there is no mention of their imprisonment in the NT, two possibilities arise. First, it is possible that Andronicus and Junia were imprisoned with Paul in some unreported incident. This is likely to be an imprisonment in Ephesus.[57] The inclusion of μου *(mou* – 'my') may indicate this. Second, it is less likely that they were imprisoned on their own for their gospel work. In either case, Paul's comment must be taken as an authentic statement that, at some time, they were in custody: in my judgment, imprisonment with Paul in Ephesus seems more likely.[58]

Then comes the controversial statement that this couple were 'outstanding among the apostles' (ἐπίσημοι ἐν τοῖς ἀποστόλοις – *episēmoi en tois apostolois*).[59] No one else in the NT is accorded such high praise regarding their relationship with the apostles. There are two alternatives: they were themselves to be accorded the distinctive title 'apostle', or they were highly regarded by that group known as '*the* apostles'.

> Some would claim that, while ἐπίσημοι may mean 'well-known, acknowledged,' had Paul wished to say that Andronicus and Junia were well-known to the apostles, he would have used the Greek preposition ὑπο followed by the genitive τῶν ἀποστόλων, and not ἐν followed by the dative τοῖς ἀποστόλοις. Moreover, the phrase ἐπίσημοι ἐν τοῖς ἀποστόλοις has consistently been interpreted by Church Fathers in an inclusive sense. Thus there is no valid reason not to translate the phrase as 'prominent among the apostles.' Some of these scholars go on to claim that the attempt to interpret the phrase as 'well known to, and acknowledged by, the apostles' stems from a theological bias in order to deny or downplay the fact

57. See *Letters From Prison: Ephesians, Philippians, Colossians, and Philemon* in the introduction.

58. See Jewett, *Romans*, pp. 962-3.

59. The only other use of ἐπίσημος in the NT is the description of Barabbas (Matt. 27:16).

that women once served as apostles.[(1)] However, in two subsequent scholarly articles published in 2009 and 2015 by David Huttar and M. H. Burer respectively,[(2)] the authors cited further extrabiblical texts that used similar words and similar grammatical constructions and made a strong case that it is plausible to render ἐπίσημοι ἐν τοῖς ἀποστόλοις in Rom. 16:7 as 'well known to the apostles.' The paper by Burer also demonstrated that Paul would have said ἐπίσημοι τῶν ἀποστόλων had he wanted to say that Andronicus and Junia were themselves prominent among the apostles. Here I will make no attempt to adjudicate between the two views. My objective is merely to point out that the common rendering of 'prominent among the apostles' is not unassailable truth.[(3)] [60]

(1) Thus Belleville concludes by saying, 'The sole basis is a theological and functional predisposition against the naming of a woman among the first-century cadre of apostles.' See her 'Re-examination,' 248. It is nonetheless noteworthy that neither Bauckham, nor Belleville, nor Epp could deny that there were indeed instances cited by Burer and Wallace that can support the non-inclusive view. Belleville merely discounted the evidence as too early (!) to be relevant (247).

(2) David Huttar, 'Did Paul'; M. H. Burer, ''ΕΠΙΣΗΜΟΙ 'ΕΝ ΤΟΙΣ 'ΑΠΟΣΤΟΛΟΙΣ in Rom. 16:7 as "Well Known to the Apostles": Further Defense and New Evidence,' JETS 58.4 (2015): 731–55. In his article, Burer broadened his search of similar Greek constructions in extrabiblical texts, answered the rebuttals of his critics, and laid an even stronger foundation for the 'non-inclusive' view. He also cited other scholars who agreed with his position.

(3) In my opinion, the following extrabiblical texts cited by Huttar and Burer strongly support the non-inclusive view: Euripides, Hipp. 103 (Huttar, 'Did Paul,' 750); inscription Asia Minor FdXanth VII 76.6 (Burer, 'Further Defense,' 741); Lucian, Harm. 1.17 (Burer, 'Further Defense,' 742–43); Ephraem Syrus Theol. Ad imitationem proverbiorum, p. 187, line 6 (Burer, 'Further Defense,' 749); Prolegomena de Comoedia, De comoedia, line 22 (Burer, 'Further Defense,' 750).

Paul then acknowledges that 'they were in Christ before me'.

Paul's description of Andronicus and Junia as before him in Christ is not an afterthought, tacked on merely as further praise. Paul adds

---

60. E. Y. L. Ng, 'Phoebe as Prostatis,' *Trinity Journal* 25, no. 1 (2004): pp. 517-33, 526.

> this clause because he has named other apostles, and in doing so he never fails to return to his own role as the last and the 'least'. In fact, the only other time Paul uses προ ἐμοϋ is in Gal. 1:17, in reference to other apostles: 'nor did I go up to Jerusalem to those who were already apostles before me, but I went away at once into Arabia, and afterwards I returned to Damascus'.[61]

This places them amongst the earliest Christians and raises the possibility that they may have been among the 500 to whom Christ appeared before His ascension, referred to in 1 Corinthians 15:6.[62] They were probably two of those Hellenistic Jews who believed after Pentecost: see Acts 6:1. Given the early date of their conversion, we cannot exclude the possibility (even likelihood) that, like Paul's self-reference in 1 Corinthians 9:1, Andronicus and Junia(s) were regarded by Paul as apostles.

> As Andronicus and Junia were Christians before Paul, who was converted (on a reasonable chronology) not more than two or three years after the Crucifixion, we must connect them with the primitive church at Jerusalem. As they were Jews bearing Greek or Graeco-Latin names, they would naturally belong to the Hellenistic group whose leaders were Stephen, Philip and their associates. Like others of this group (Acts 8:4-5; 11:21), they became missionaries, or 'apostles' in the wider sense. In the stricter sense 'the Apostles' were the Twelve appointed by Christ Himself; or the Eleven of them who remained faithful, together with Matthias who was appointed in place of Judas. But the Acts of the Apostles gives the title also to Paul and Barnabas (14:14). Paul (1 Cor. 15:5-7) seems to distinguish 'the twelve' from 'all the apostles' as a wider body. He gives the title also to delegates of churches (2 Cor. 8:23). … It seems clear, therefore, that the title was widely given to persons properly commissioned by the Church to preach the Gospel.[63]

'In situations like this, it seems prudent to turn to the oldest Greek commentators on Romans, who spoke as their native tongue the language in which Paul was writing. All who

---

61. Y-J. Lin, 'Junia: An Apostle before Paul', *JBL* 139, no. 1 (2020): p. 208.

62. Bruce, *Romans*, p. 272; Cranfield, *Romans*, vol. 2, p. 789; Thielman, *Romans*, pp. 719-20.

63. Dodd, *Romans*, pp. 237-8.

comment on the passage assume without debate that Andronicus and Junia were apostles.'[64]

> All we can say with certainty is that this couple had functioned as Christian apostles for more than two decades before Paul wrote this letter to Rome requesting that they be greeted by other believers in Rome who evidently were not inclined to acknowledge their accomplishments and status.[65]

My conclusion is that Andronicus was one of the earliest Christians and that it is likely he was an apostle. Alternatively, he was highly regarded by 'the apostles'. He was obviously well known to, and highly regarded by, Paul.

Apelles

Romans 16:10

[10] Greet Apelles, the approved in Christ.

This is a fairly common Greek name (meaning 'separation')[66] and was also used by Hellenistic Jews. It is also associated with the imperial household.[67] Paul describes Apelles as 'the approved in Christ' (τὸν δόκιμον ἐν Χριστῷ – *ton dokimon en Christō*). Lampe suggests that 'Paul's appraisal of Apelles as "approved in Christ" (16:10) could hardly be said without a personal acquaintance'; however, he is incorrect when stating that '*dokimos* is defined as "serving Christ" in the everyday love and care of interhuman relations (Rom. 14:15-21)'.[68] This view quite understates the 'testing' that is implied by *dokimos* and its cognates.[69] The significance of δόκιμος is that it is elsewhere used by Paul to describe someone who is tested and proven, as in Romans 14:8; 1 Corinthians 11:19; 2 Corinthians 13:7; 2 Timothy 2:15; also James 1:12.[70] It is clear

64. Thielman, *Romans*, p. 719.

65. Jewett, *Romans*, p. 964.

66. See *'Apelles', She Knows, https://www.sheknows.com/baby-names/name/apelles/*

67. Cranfield, *Romans*, vol. 2, 791; Bruce, *Romans*, p. 273.

68. Lampe, *The Roman Christians*, p. 220.

69. See NASBEC, p. 1522, ref. *1381a-1384*.

70. See W. J. Dumbrell, *Romans*, A New Covenant Commentary (Eugene, OR: Wipf and Stock, 2005), p. 142.

that Apelles had undergone some serious testing of his faith and withstood the opposition.[71]

Paul's description that he was '*the* approved *in Christ*' reflects a personal commendation applied to few individuals by the apostle.[72] Paul was clearly aware of Apelles' faithfulness in Christian work and this greeting reflects a very personal respect and love for this brother who had (by now) moved (back?) from the eastern mission fields to Rome. The desire to afford honour to brothers and sisters in Christ does not come readily to many Christians. Paul's inclusion of τὸν (*ton* – 'the') must be noted for its uniqueness in his letters. Haldane puts Apelles' commendation in the following context:

> Apelles is here distinguished as a tried disciple. It is mentioned to his honour that he was tried and *approved in Christ*. The Lord's people have various and diversified characteristics as Christians. The Apostle selects that peculiar trait in the characters of those of whom he writes for which they are severally distinguished. Some of them are tried with particular afflictions, and their obedience to their Lord is put to the severest test. When they stand this fiery trial, it is the most distinguished honour, and their trials in the service of Christ ought to be held up to notice. This is due to them from their brethren, and it is a great encouragement to others who are similarly tried. All the Lord's people are not exposed to trials equally severe; and when the Lord calls any of them to glorify His name by suffering peculiarly for His sake, we are here taught to treat them with peculiar honour. How very unfounded, then, and unscriptural, are the views of those who would fear the encouragement of a proud legal spirit, were they to utter a word of praise with respect to the characters of any of the Lord's servants. From perceiving an extreme on the one hand, they plunge into the opposite. But they confound things entirely distinct. That praise which a worldly spirit is accustomed to seek or give, is quite different from that which the Apostle confers. The latter excites to

71. See Dunn, *Romans 9-16*, p. 896; Schreiner, *Romans*, p. 764; Jewett, *Romans*, p. 966.

72. See *Paul's Use of ἐν χριστῷ (en Christō – in Christ)* in the introduction.

greater devotedness; but the former puffs up, and is quite opposite to the spirit of the Gospel. 'How can ye believe', says Christ, 'who receive honour one of another?' Such persons love the praise of men more than the praise of God. But the honour which is given by the Lord's servants, after the example of Paul, is to the honour of the Lord, and for the interest of His cause.[73]

Concerning Apelles, who is here said to be approved in Christ (v. 10), a high character! He was one of known integrity and sincerity in his religion, one that had been tried; his friends and enemies had tried him, and he was as gold. He was of approved knowledge and judgment, approved courage and constancy; a man that one might trust and repose a confidence in.[74]

Apollos

Acts 18:24-28

[24] Now a Jew named Apollos, an Alexandrian by birth, an eloquent man, came to Ephesus; and he was mighty in the Scriptures.

[25] This man had been instructed in the way of the Lord; and being fervent in spirit, he was speaking and teaching accurately the things concerning Jesus, being acquainted only with the baptism of John; ...

[26]... and he began to speak out boldly in the synagogue. But when Priscilla and Aquila heard him, they took him aside and explained to him the way of God more accurately.

[27] And when he wanted to go across to Achaia, the brethren encouraged him and wrote to the disciples to welcome him; and when he had arrived, he greatly helped those who had believed through grace, ...

[28]... for he powerfully refuted the Jews in public, demonstrating by the Scriptures that Jesus was the Christ.

Acts 19:1

[1] It happened that while Apollos was at Corinth, Paul passed through the upper country and came to Ephesus, and found some disciples ...

1 Corinthians 1:12

*[12] Now I mean this, that each one of you is saying, '**I** am of Paul,'[and] '**I** of Apollos,' [and] '**I** of Cephas,' [and] '**I** of Christ.'* (Emphasis added.)

---

73. Haldane, *Romans*, p. 638.

74. M. Henry, *Commentary on the Whole Bible*, p. 1799. See Mathew, *Women in the Greetings of Romans 16.1-16*, p. 38.

1 CORINTHIANS 3:4-6

4 For when one says, 'I am of Paul,' and another, 'I am of Apollos,' are you not mere men?

5 What then is Apollos? And what is Paul? Servants through whom you believed, even as the Lord gave opportunity to each one.

6 I planted, Apollos watered, but God was causing the growth.

1 CORINTHIANS 3:22

22 Whether Paul or Apollos or Cephas or the world or life or death or things present or things to come; all things belong to you,

1 CORINTHIANS 4:6

6 Now these things, brethren, I have figuratively applied to myself and Apollos for your sakes, so that in us you may learn not to exceed what is written, so that no one of you will become arrogant in behalf of one against the other.

1 CORINTHIANS 16:12

12 But concerning Apollos our brother, I encouraged him greatly to come to you with the brethren; and it was not at all his desire to come now, but he will come when he has opportunity.

TITUS 3:13

13 Diligently help Zenas the lawyer and Apollos on their way so that nothing is lacking for them.

1. Alexandria and Background[75]

The name Apollos, a shortened form of Apollonius or its cognates, means 'destroyer';[76] however, the destruction wrought by Apollos was to pull down the kingdom of Satan by his preaching. 'It is however of unusual interest as it [the name Apollos] seems to be almost unexampled outside Egypt, but is conspicuously common there.'[77] 'The evidence at least suggests that "Apollos" was a peculiarly Egyptian abbreviation of "Apollonius", whereas other forms prevail elsewhere.'[78] Notwithstanding his Gentile name, 'a

75. A lengthy commentary on Alexandria and Apollos is provided in Keener, *Acts,* vol. 3, pp. 2797-814.

76. HSIBD, p. 77.

77. C. J. Hemer, *The Book of Acts in the Setting of Hellenistic History, WUNT* 49 (Tübingen: J. C. B. Mohr, 1989), p. 233.

78. ibid., p. 234, n. 37.

Jew named Apollos, an Alexandrian by birth, an eloquent man, came to Ephesus; and he was proficient in the Scriptures' as noted in Acts 18:24 NASB. Some further explanation is required. Most English translations (from KJV onwards) describe Apollos as 'an eloquent man' (ἀνὴρ λόγιος – *anēr logios*); however, as Bruce points out, 'the adjective means "learned" in both classical and Modern Greek; the meaning "eloquent" is secondary'.[79] Only the NIV uses 'learned man'. The word for 'proficient' (δυνατὸς – *dunatos*) is often associated with motive power (e.g. dynamo), but here δυνατὸς refers to a 'thorough knowledge' of the Scriptures.[80] Both descriptions emphasise his superior intellectual ability. It was Martin Luther who first proposed that Apollos was the author of the Letter to the Hebrews.[81]

> Egyptian Alexandria, home of the greatest Jewish intellectual of the period [first century A.D.] (added), Philo, was the second city of the Roman Empire and renowned throughout the ancient world for, among other things, its *Mouseion*, which included its famous royal library. Alexandria could boast of a variety of philosophical schools and a rich intellectual life. Its reputation as a centre of learning would last for centuries.[82]

Apollos arrived in Ephesus in the period between Paul's departure from that city (to travel to Syria and Judea) and his return to Ephesus. It is not necessarily the case that Apollos learned about Jesus in Alexandria, although that seems likely. Acts 19:25 presents us with a strange situation in which the description of Apollos' knowledge about Jesus is perplexing. It claims that he 'had been instructed in the way of the Lord' and spoke 'accurately the things concerning Jesus', yet he only knew about (and presumably had

79. F. F. Bruce, *The Book of the Acts*, NICNT (Grand Rapids: Eerdmans, 1988), p. 358, n. 64.

80. As in NIV. See M. Zerwick and M. Grosvenor, *Grammatical Analysis of the Greek New Testament* (Rome: Biblical Institute Press, 1974), vol. 1: p. 414.

81. F. F. Bruce, *The Pauline Circle* (Grand Rapids: Eerdmans, 1985), p. 57.

82. M. den Dulk, 'Aquila and Apollos: Acts 18 in Light of Ancient Ethnic Stereotypes,' *JBL* 139, no. 1 (2020): pp. 177-8.

received) the baptism of John the Baptist. He had been 'instructed orally' (κατηχημένος – *katēchēmenos*),[83] and perhaps his teachers only passed on whatever information they themselves knew about the Way of the Lord. This does suggest an oral tradition from earliest Christianity. Various commentators have worked their way through this dilemma. Käsemann basically claimed that Luke had concocted a fictious version of Apollos' Johannine baptism.[84] A better analysis of the facts is provided below.

> We do not know where Apollos became a Christian. Although there is every reason to suppose that the faith would have come at an early date to Alexandria, we know nothing about its beginnings there, and the first Christianity of which we do hear was characterised by Gnostic tendencies. It would not be surprising if Apollos had picked up some garbled understanding of Christianity there. Certainly the description of his Christian status is odd. He had received Christian instruction *in the way of the Lord*, and he was able to teach accurately about Jesus. He was enthusiastic *in spirit* (Rom. 12:11), but he understood only the baptism of John. This description raises difficult questions: Does Luke mean that Apollos possessed the Spirit although he had not received Christian baptism with water? And if Apollos had not received Christian baptism, why was he not baptised like the twelve men at Ephesus (Acts 19:5)? The problem is treated by Käsemann who argues that in the face of the heretics of his day Luke could not countenance the existence of freelance missionaries like Apollos who worked independently of the mainstream church. He therefore showed how Apollos had to be properly instructed by Priscilla and Aquila in order to be an effective missionary. He did not dare to report the rebaptism of one who was known to be possessed by the Spirit and gifted for missionary service, but he fabricated the detail that Apollos had merely received Johannine baptism, and by linking the story with that of the twelve men at Ephesus he attempted to make Apollos at least 'guilty by association'. As Haenchen (p. 551) puts it, Luke did not dare to say more than that Apollos did not 'understand' Christian baptism.

---

83. Zerwick and Grosvenor, *Grammatical Analysis*, vol. 1, p. 414.

84. E. Käsemann, *Essays on New Testament Themes* (London: SCM Press, 1964), pp. 136-48.

This view of the passage faces strong objections. First, in view of the heretical character of much of early Christianity in Alexandria, it would not be surprising if Apollos had picked up defective ideas of the faith. Secondly, the existence of the twelve men at Ephesus shows that it was possible for people to think of themselves as disciples while merely having received John's baptism (unless with Käsemann we deny that they thought of themselves as Christians). Thirdly, Luke knew that it was possible in exceptional cases for people to receive the Spirit apart from Christian baptism with water (cf. Acts 10:44-8); Apollos differed from the twelve men in that they had clearly *not* received the Spirit, while he probably had received the Spirit. Fourthly, it is possible that there were groups of former disciples of John who had moved on to faith in the coming One without having been baptised in the name of Jesus. Did Luke shrink from the historical fact that so mighty a preacher as Apollos nevertheless needed to be baptised in the name of Jesus? This would lead us to exactly the opposite view of the passage from Käsemann, but on the whole it is more probable that, since Apollos had received the Spirit, he did not need to be rebaptised with water.[85]

2. Paul Meeting Prisca and Aquila

Being a Jew, but without knowing Paul's habits (see Acts 17:1-2, 10), Apollos adopted Paul's strategy and began to speak boldly (παρρησιάζεσθαι – *parrēsiazesthai*) to Jews first (Acts 18:25-26) in synagogues in Ephesus. The reference to Jews before Gentiles may be part of Paul's 'Jews first' principle as noted in Romans 2:9-10.[86] However, although he spoke about Jesus, Apollos' knowledge of Christian doctrine was limited to the baptism of John the Baptist.

It is interesting that, although Christians, Prisca and Aquila continued to attend the synagogue in Ephesus (see Acts 18:26), presumably for evangelism. When Apollos began his preaching ministry at the synagogue in Ephesus, Prisca and Aquila heard him. They were concerned that his message had some shortcomings, particularly because he only knew about the baptism of John the

85. I. H. Marshall, *The Acts of the Apostles*, TNTC (Leicester: InterVarsity Press, 1980), pp. 303-4.

86. See McKnight, *Colossians*, p. 387.

Baptist. Baptism in the name of Jesus, as practised in Acts 2:38, was apparently unknown to him.

Prisca and Aquila 'took him aside and explained to him the way of God "more accurately" (ἀκριβῶς – *akrib*'). The verb for 'took aside' (προσλαμβάνω – *proslambanō*) indicates that the faithful couple gently spoke to Apollos without causing him embarrassment. The context in which this verb is used suggests that it may not be going too far to propose that they invited Apollos home for a meal and a discreet chat about the essence of the gospel, as described in the NIV translation of Acts 18:26. Alternatively, they may have invited Apollos to join their fellowship group to learn more about Christian doctrine. Bruce's translation and commentary explicitly come to this conclusion but the Greek text does not permit that reading conclusively.[87] Nevertheless, here is a lesson for those who see the need to correct public statements by Christians. Bruce reminds us 'how much better it is to give such private help to a teacher whose understanding of his subject is deficient than to correct or denounce him publicly'.[88] Both Prisca and Aquila had sufficient knowledge and authority not only to 'explain' (ἐξέθεντο – *exethento*) 'carefully' (ἀκριβέστερον – *akribesteron*) to the already knowledgeable Apollos about the Way of the Lord but also to gain his respect and acknowledgement of the correctness of their message. Undoubtedly, Paul's tutoring of Prisca and Aquila in the gospel of Jesus would have strongly influenced their instruction of Apollos, both in content and manner of instruction. In due course, Apollos would carry this Pauline-influenced understanding of the gospel to his ministry in Corinth (Acts 18:27-8); however, the Scriptures never mention Paul teaching anything to Apollos.

The contrast would have been apparent to Luke's readers between the learned Apollos from Alexandria and his teacher(s) from Pontus, which was regarded as a backward and primitive region.[89]

---

87. Bruce, *Acts*, pp. 358, 360.

88. ibid., p. 360.

89. See den Dulk, *Aquila and Apollos*, pp. 177-89.

Acts 18:25-6 uses a very early Christian self-description of their movement: 'the Way' (Acts 9:2; 19:9), which may have been Apollos' means of initially identifying himself with the Christians in Ephesus.[90]

3. Apollos and Corinth

It is clear that Apollos had become a leader in the Corinthian church by the time that Paul wrote 1 Corinthians. Early in that letter he addressed divisions in the congregation, where some people had placed their allegiance behind certain leaders. In 1 Corinthians 1:12, he names the groups who follow Paul, Apollos, Cephas, and Christ. The language used by Paul in this verse is important. 'Thus, no item here receives more or less prominence than any other; all items are on equal footing (see also 15:39).'[91] Paul uses the style μέν ... δὲ ... δὲ ... δὲ. This is best translated into English by emphasising the pronoun: ***I*** am for Paul; ***I*** am for Apollos, etc.[92] It reflects the personal preferences of different people in the Corinthian congregation rather than an assertion by Paul as to anyone's superiority. 'The masculine gender of ἕκαστος should not be taken as narrowing the identity of the culprits for as a rule, "the masculine is used for person in general" Smyth §1015).'[93]

Paul uses this literary style again in 1 Corinthians 3:4. First Corinthians ascribes no blame at all to either Apollos or Cephas for these quarrels and divisions in the church. I quote from Ciampa and Rosner, who assess this issue in considerable detail.[94] It is clear that the key verse to the origin of the problems is 1 Corinthians 1:26.

---

90. See Isaiah 30:20-21. '"Way" conveys the idea of manner of life, and this instruction ties in with the warning of Deuteronomy 28:14. In the Acts of the Apostles "way" is probably a Hebraism used in reference to the early church (see Acts 9:2; 19:9, 23; 24:14, 22)' in A. M. Harman, *Isaiah: A Covenant to be Kept for the Sake of the Church* (Fearn: Christian Focus, 2005), p. 206.

91. Brookins, T. A. and B. W. Longenecker, *1 Corinthians 1-9: A Handbook on the Greek Text*, BHGNT (Waco, TX: Baylor University Press, 2016), pp. 16-17.

92. See Zerwick and Grosvenor, *Grammatical Analysis*, vol. 2, p. 499.

93. Brookins and Longenecker, *1 Corinthians 1–9*, p. 16.

94. Ciampa and Rosner, *1 Corinthians*, pp. 77-82.

Paul explains more of the nature of the reported 'divisions' and 'quarrels'. The Corinthians were divided, rallying around particular figures whom they held to be superior to the others. Such a personality-focused approach to leadership, with its emphasis on the high rank of the leader and the status conferred on the follower, betrays the influence of Corinthian society. The Corinthians made too much of specific leaders and specific styles of leadership.[95]

> Two things about Paul's behaviour there [in Corinth] may have led some to oppose him or at least prefer Apollos or Peter to him. Paul's unimpressive style of speaking apparently had some looking down on him. Additionally, his refusal to accept financial support from the Corinthians, preferring instead to ply his trade (see 9:1-27), would probably have offended some of the wealthier and more influential members of the congregation.[96]
>
> The appearance of Apollos's name six times in 1:10-4:17 suggests that in Paul's view the Apollos party lay at the heart of the divisions in Corinth. However, as Barrett observes, 'Paul never suggests any difference between Apollos and himself, but rather goes out of his way to represent Apollos as his colleague (3:6-9)'. Any difference between Paul and Apollos was a matter of style rather than substance.[97]

This is hardly surprising given the instruction that Apollos received from Prisca and Aquila. The 'Christ party' is the most mysterious and may well have been sardonic humour on Paul's part.[98] This subject is raised again in 1 Corinthians 3:4-6, where the rivalry is narrowed down to people choosing between Paul and Apollos; however, Paul gives credit where it is due: 'I planted, Apollos watered'. Paul insists that he and Apollos are only servants. Paul's emphasis of the lowly status of Apollos and him before God is emphasised in that 'διάκονοι stands in stark contrast to ὁ κύριος.'[99]

---

95. Ciampa and Rosner, *1 Corinthians*, pp. 77-8. See similar divisions, criticised by Jude, probably in Antioch, in Manuell, *The Letter of Jude*, 39-42, 137-9.

96. Ciampa and Rosner, *1 Corinthians*, p. 78.

97. ibid., p. 79. See Bruce, *Pauline Circle*, p. 56.

98. See Ciampa and Rosner, *1 Corinthians*, p. 80.

99. Brookins and Longenecker, *1 Corinthians 1-9*, p. 69.

> Aside from quotations from the OT, κύριος in Paul's letters usually refers to Christ; in view of the following verse, however, it seems in this case to refer to God the Father (so Fitzmyer, p. 194). The variable inclusion and exclusion of the article reflects Paul's varying usage of the word, now as a name, now as a title; it is perhaps a title here; but compare 3:20; 4:4.[100]

In 1 Corinthians 3:22 Paul returns to naming the three men.

> Paul here recalls the party slogans of 1:12, but now juxtaposes them with a Stoic maxim: 'all things belong to you'. Paul, however, cleverly alters the Stoic sense of the slogan: it is not the philosopher's virtues that 'belong' to the Corinthians, but all the blessings of salvation in Christ. Repetition of the connective εἴτε gives us polysyndeton. Among NT writers, use of the correlatives εἴτε ... εἴτε is virtually unique to Paul, who has a special fondness for the construction (a total of fifteen times in the Corinthian letters alone).[101]

It is not necessary here to explore the theological implications of 1 Corinthians 1–4 other than to say that Paul was particularly anxious to avoid factionalism in the Corinthian congregation.[102] Apollos and Cephas were the supposed 'leaders' of different factions in the congregation. Perhaps Apollos' knowledge of the (Hebrew) Scriptures and eloquence attracted some, while Cephas' close association with the Lord Jesus may have compelled others to join the 'Cephas faction'. It is noteworthy that Paul does not criticise the supposed leaders themselves but the sin of forming factions in the first place.[103] The use of Apollos in 1 Corinthians serves two purposes. Firstly, it identifies him as one of the so-called leaders of a faction within the church. Secondly, it suggests that the 'Apollos' faction may have been composed not only primarily of Gentiles (the Jews possibly being more committed to the 'Cephas' faction) but also of those Gentiles (see 1 Corinthians 1:26) more

---

100. ibid., p. 70.

101. ibid., p. 90.

102. See M. M. Mitchell, *Paul and the Rhetoric of Reconciliation: An Exegetical Investigation of the Language and Composition of 1 Corinthians* (Louisville: Westminster John Knox Press, 1992).

103. See Fitzmyer, *First Corinthians*, p. 193.

attuned to Apollos' eloquence and sophistication than to Paul's gospel of grace alone.

Note that Paul regards Apollos' efforts as equal to his own. There is no rivalry or dispute about seniority or leadership here. The comment (below) by Moffatt may be old but it has new vitality in an age where preachers (especially on television and in the media) compete for public attention (and their dollars!), ranking fame and fortune higher than the integrity of the 'gospel' they preach. It is clear that neither Paul nor Apollos were of that mind.

> In deprecating partisanship and factiousness (1 Cor. 3:4f., 18), he [Paul] has tactfully chosen himself **and Apollos**, without mentioning any others, in order to disarm criticism. 'Let no one suppose that we consider ourselves exempt from the risks of party-felling in leaders and followers, on which I have been reading you a lesson. Only, I have shown you in our case how absurd it is to play off one against another, as if we were rival apostles with programs of our own, or anything but **servants** and **stewards** alike. That is what **I** have been trying **to teach you**. We two, at any rate, are an illustration of the baselessness of exalting **one teacher** over **another**'. This is the obvious meaning of the sentence.[104]

There has been much discussion over the meaning of the verb μετεσχημάτισα (*meteschēmastisa*) in 1 Corinthians 4:6, which basically means 'to change the form of'. Fitzmyer discusses a wide range of opinions for this word and then moves on to discuss a variety of opinions on the following five words: τὸ μὴ ὑπὲρ ἃ γέγραπται (*to mē huper ha gegraptai* – 'beyond that which is written').[105] Its most compacted meaning is a reference to 1 Corinthians 1:31: 'so that, just as it is written, "Let him who boasts, boast in the Lord."'[106] Wagner adds, 'Far from being an irrelevant reminder, Paul's reference to the scriptural command, "Let the one who boasts, boast in the Lord", undergirds and advances his censure of the Corinthians' behaviour and his call to

104. Moffatt, *1 Corinthians*, p. 46 (original emphasis).

105. See Fitzmyer, *First Corinthians*, pp. 214-15.

106. See J. R. Wagner, '"Not Beyond the Things that are Written": A Call to Boast Only in the Lord (1 Cor. 4-6)'. *NTS* 44, no. 2 (1998): pp. 279-87.

imitate the example of the apostles in 1 Cor. 4:6-13.'[107] A broader, and widely accepted, interpretation is that 'what is written' is a reference by Paul to the OT Scriptures.[108] The NT Scriptures would also be relevant today. Clearly, Apollos would have approved of this instruction: he and Paul are at one on this matter. It is a reflection of the relative immaturity of the Corinthian church that Paul highlights the need for cessation of factions based on human wisdom and needs to highlight the matter so forcefully in 1 Corinthians 4:6: 'Now, brothers and sisters, I have applied these things to myself and Apollos for your benefit, so that you may learn from us the meaning of the saying, "Do not go beyond what is written." Then you will not be puffed up in being a follower of one of us over against the other.'[109]

> Two purpose clauses in verse 6 explain what Paul has been aiming at up to this point in the letter. He wants the Corinthians, first, 'to learn to live according to Scripture' (RSV) and, secondly, to refrain from arrogant rivalries. As it turns out, the two are virtually synonymous. The second purpose clause confirms our interpretation of the first (see above). What does the command mean, *Do not go beyond what is written?* It means *not [to] be puffed up in being a follower of one of us against the other.* Arrogant claims to wisdom or rhetorical skill are at the heart of Corinthian factionalism, and they contravene Scripture's judgment on human wisdom fulfilled in the cross. 'to be puffed up', a prominent term in 1 and 2 Corinthians (1 Cor. 4:6, 18,

---

107. ibid., p. 287.

108. See M. D. Hooker, '"Beyond the Things Which Are Written": An Examination of 1 Cor. 4.6.' *NTS* 44, no. 2 (1963-64): pp. 129-32, which is a correct understanding of the verse as per its translation in the following text.

109. I have used the translation of Ciampa and Rosner, *1 Corinthians*, p. 174, which best reflects the point Paul is making about the needless factional rivalry in Corinth. This verse was used by John Calvin to formulate the 'Regulative Principle', which is described in Chapter 21.1 of the *Westminster Confession of Faith*, 1646: 'But the acceptable way of worshipping the true God is instituted by Himself, and so limited by His own revealed will, that He may not be worshipped according to the imaginations and devices of men, or the suggestions of Satan, under any visible representation or any other way not prescribed in the holy Scripture.' Some Reformed churches still adhere to this.

19; 5:2; 8:1; 13:4; 2 Cor. 12:20), is one of Paul's central accusations against the Corinthians. As Marshall notes, such pride 'results from a failure of self-knowledge'. This is seen in Paul's rebuke in 8:1-3, where the crucial thing is not to know God but to be known by Him, and in the three rhetorical questions in 4:7.[110]

4. The Call from Corinth[111]

Acts 18:24-8 records that, in due course, Apollos wished to cross the Aegean Sea to minister to the Christians in Achaia, of which Corinth was the capital city. He was encouraged to do so by the Ephesian Christians, who wrote a letter of commendation to the Corinthian Christians, no doubt similar to Romans 16:1-2 regarding Phoebe. After his instruction from Prisca and Aquila, the arrival of Apollos in Ephesus 'greatly helped (συνεβάλετο πολὺ – *sunebaleto polu*; from συμβάλλω – *sumballō*) those who had believed through grace' (Acts 18:27).[112] Acts 18:28 records that Apollos 'vigorously' (εὐτόνως – *eutonōs*) 'refuted' (διακατελέγχομαι – *diakatelegchomai*) the Jews '*in public*' (δημοσίᾳ – *dēmosia*)! Clearly, Apollos was no shrinking violet and debated with the Jews publicly as well as in their synagogue(s). While Apollos was in Corinth, Paul was in Ephesus.

By the time 1 Corinthians was written, Apollos had returned to Ephesus because Paul discusses another visit by Apollos to Corinth in 1 Corinthians 16:12. In the event, Apollos did not go to Corinth with 'the brethren' but remained in Ephesus. There needs to be a major clarification as to why he did not go at that time. My judgment is that *virtually all translations of his reason are quite wrong*, effectively defaming Apollos. Some translations make him look petulant. Virtually every English Bible (e.g. ESV, KJV,

110. Ciampa and Rosner, *1 Corinthians*, pp. 176-7.

111. This is a shortened version of G. Manuell, 'Apollos in 1 Corinthians: Praised by Paul but Defamed by Translators', *Evangelical Action* 4 (2021), pp. 26-31.

112. Zerwick and Grosvenor, *Grammatical Analysis*, vol. 2, pp. 414-15 note two possible translations of Acts 18:27: '**διὰ τῆς χάριτος** *those who by (God's) grace were believers* (cf. RSV, NEB) or, taken with συνεβάλετο, *by (God's) grace he made a great contribution to the faithful* (cf. JB)'. The first alternative is preferred.

NASB, NIV, NKJV, RSV) makes it clear in its translation that *Apollos* definitely did not want to go. Most commentators are content with the current translation, trying to find reasons why Apollos would not go.[113] Fitzmyer comments, 'there being no indication in the Greek as to whose will is meant; but it must be Apollos' will since *there is no reason to think* that God's will is implied, although some commentators have understood it that way (J Weiss, *1 Cor.*, p. 385; Kümmel in Lietzmann, *1 Cor.*, p. 196; *TDNT*, 3:59; Barrett, *1 Cor.*, p. 391; Bruce, *1 Cor.*, p. 160; Héring, *1 Cor.*, p. 153).'[114] Even Calvin criticises Apollos for remaining in Ephesus![115]

The Greek text is πάντως οὐκ ἦν θέλημα ἵνα νῦν ἔλθῃ (*pantōs ouk ēn thelēma hina nun elthē*) and the critical words are πάντως οὐκ **ἦν** θέλημα ('not at all **the** will'). The question is: whose will is Paul talking about? The Greek text says '***the*** will', not '***his*** will'. In addition to those noted above, I consider that the following translations correctly understand Paul's message: 'it was definitely not God's will for him to do so then' (J. B. Phillips Bible); 'it is not the will of God that he should visit you' (Moffatt).[116] The ESV translation is 'it was not at all his [Apollos'] will' but has a marginal note, 'Or *God's will for him?*' I have no doubt that this is the correct understanding of Paul's comment. Other than by direct linkage with a human person,[117] Paul always uses θέλημα in his letters with reference to the will of God. Apollos did not go to Corinth at that time because *God* did not want him to go. It is

---

113. See Ciampa and Rosner, *1 Corinthians*, pp. 853-4; B. W. Powers, *First Corinthians: An Exegetical and Explanatory Commentary* (Eugene, OR: Wipf and Stock, 2008), pp. 467-8.

114. J. A. Fitzmyer, *First Corinthians: A New Translation with Introduction and Commentary*, The Anchor Yale Bible (New Haven, CT: Yale University Press, 2008), pp. 622-3 (emphasis added).

115. J. Calvin, 'The Argument on the First Epistle to the Corinthians,' *Calvin's Commentaries* 22 vol., trans. J. Pringle (Grand Rapids: Baker Book House, 1979), pp. 72, 74-5.

116. For a fuller explanation of his position, with which I agree, see Moffatt, *1 Corinthians*, pp. 274-5.

117. 1 Cor. 7:37 (the man who marries); Eph. 2:3 (the sinful nature); 2 Tim. 2:36 (the devil).

surprising that so many commentators ignore the action of the Spirit in directing Apollos' life in this instance.[118]

This incident concerning Apollos reminds us that two wills vie against one another for supremacy in our lives: our will and the will of God. If Apollos obeyed his own will in this instance, the text shows him to be petulant and self-absorbed. If Apollos in fact obeyed the will of God, no criticism can be levelled at him at all.

5. Concluding Note

The only other reference to Apollos in the NT is Titus 3:13 where Paul asks Titus to assist Zenas the lawyer and Apollos on their journey. The logical conclusion is that Zenas and Apollos were visiting Titus on Crete before travelling elsewhere. Unless they were with Titus personally, he could not have been able to fulfil their needs as thoroughly as Paul requested.

> Paul's decision to spend the winter in Nicopolis favours that the commanded diligence includes Titus's coming before winter's onset. For sailing during winter, as Titus would have to do when leaving the island of Crete, was dangerous and usually avoided (see Acts 27 for Paul's recognition of the danger, involving Crete). So the commanded diligence in a sending of Zenas the lawyer and Apollos is also likely to include action taken before winter's onset (compare 2 Tim. 4:9, 21). …
>
> He [Apollos] seems to have ministered cooperatively but independently from Paul. Since Paul addresses Titus alone, at the time of writing Zenas and Apollos have yet to arrive in Crete. They're probably carrying Paul's letter to Titus. But Paul wants them to rejoin him. Titus's sending forward Zenas and Apollos while he himself waits for the arrival of Artemas or Tychicus before going himself to Paul – this sending forward includes supplying Zenas and Apollos with whatever they need for their journey to Paul: food, money, and such like. And for a supply that will leave nothing lacking, Cretan Christians (whom Paul calls 'our [people]') are 'to be engaging in good deeds', which in this case means supplying Zenas's and Apollos's 'essential needs'. These Cretans will be learning by the actual doing (compare 1 Timothy 5:4, 13). 'Also to be learning'

118. See Bruce, *Paul: Apostle of the Free Spirit*, p. 257, esp. n. 32 for support of my view.

> seems to mean learning by doing as well as learning by listening to Titus's exhortations.[119]

As to their destination, 'Since he [Apollos] was from Alexandria, it is suggested that he and Zenas may have been heading in a southerly direction from Paul, to Crete, and then finally on to Alexandria. This is only a possibility, however.'[120] Regarding Apollos' presence on Crete, Wieland comments:

> It was not only Alexandrians who might be predisposed to 'stupid controversies, genealogies, dissensions, and quarrels about the law' (Titus 3.9), but if the sort of Hellenistic Judaism that flourished in Alexandria furnished part of the environment envisaged by the author, who better to help than Apollos (Titus 3:13), the learned Alexandrian Jew encountered in Acts 18.24-28; 1 Cor. 3.4-6, and so on?[121]

We do not know the fate of Apollos.

Apphia

PHILEMON 1-2

> *[1] Paul, a prisoner of Christ Jesus, and Timothy our brother,*
> *To Philemon our beloved brother and fellow worker,*
>
> *[2] and to Apphia our sister, and to Archippus our fellow soldier, and to the church in your house:*

This woman has a Phrygian name meaning 'endearment'.[122]

> Her name is a rare example of a Phrygian name in the New Testament, Apphia of Colossae, in Phrygia (Philem. 2). This raises the question of the boundaries of places nominated by Luke in Acts. [In Acts 14:6] [T]he implication is that the crossing from Iconium to Lystra involved a passage across a linguistic and administrative boundary from Phrygia to Lycaonia, a fact reflected in onamastics of the district. This name ... is common in inscriptions of Phrygia and rare elsewhere. ... The varied testimonies of the literary texts must be understood in this context of a

---

119. R. H. Gundry, *Commentary on First and Second Timothy, Titus* (Grand Rapids: Baker Academic, 2010), pp. 72-3.

120. Yarbrough, *Letters to Timothy and Titus*, p. 557.

121. G. M. Wieland, 'Roman Crete and the Letter to Titus', *NTS* 53, no. 3 (2009): p. 353.

122. HSIBD, 79. See Witherington, *The Letters to Philemon, the Colossians, and the Ephesians: A Social-Rhetorical Commentary on the Captivity Epistles*, p. 54, n. 6.

> well-defined ethnic identity which occupied a territory including both [Pisidian] Antioch and Iconium over many centuries. ... It must be noted that Roman administrative boundaries were imposed for historic or strategic reasons which took no account of older national identities.[123]

Apphia is mentioned in the context of a letter from Paul to Philemon. The reference to 'our sister' (lit. 'the sister') confirms that Apphia was a Christian.[124] She lived in Colosse, in the Roman province of Asia (south-western Turkey).

There is general agreement amongst commentators that Apphia and Archippus were the wife and son, respectively, of Philemon.[125] There was a house church in Philemon's home. Apphia would have had responsibility for overseeing the slaves and routines of the household.[126] See the entries for Archippus and Philemon for more background information about Colosse.

AQUILA (see PRISCA AND AQUILA)

ARCHIPPUS

COLOSSIANS 4:17

[17] Say to Archippus, 'Take heed to the ministry which you have received in the Lord, so that you may fulfil it.'

PHILEMON 1-2

[1] Paul, a prisoner of Christ Jesus, and Timothy our brother,
To Philemon our beloved brother and fellow worker,

[2] and to Apphia our sister, and to Archippus our fellow soldier, and to the church in your house:

Archippus means 'chief groom'.[127] Most commentators agree that he was the son[128] of Philemon and Apphia in Colosse, in the

---

123. Hemer, *The Book of Acts*, pp. 228-30.

124. See the entry for Phoebe concerning the use of 'sister' by Paul.

125. R. C. Lucas, *The Message of Colossians and Philemon*, TBST (Leicester: InterVarsity Press, 1980), pp. 184-5; W. Hendriksen, *Philippians, Colossians and Philemon*, NTC (Edinburgh: Banner of Truth, reprinted 1981), p. 210; Bird, *Colossians and Philemon*, p. 134.

126. Bird, *Colossians and Philemon*, p. 134.

127. HSIBD, p. 90.

128. F. F. Bruce, *The Epistles to the Colossians, to Philemon, and to the Ephesians*, NICNT (Grand Rapids: Eerdmans, 1984), pp. 184-6, 206; McKnight, *Colossians*, p. 396.

Roman province of Asia (south-western Turkey), whose capital city was Ephesus. He was one of the people greeted by Paul in his letter to Philemon. He is described as 'our fellow-soldier' (τῷ συστρατιώτῃ ἡμῶν – *tō sustratiōtē hēmōn*) in Paul's letter to the Colossian church. Paul uses this description only twice in his correspondence, the other referring to Epaphroditus in Philippians 2:25. 'In other words, Archippus battled alongside in what Paul elsewhere describes as a war against spiritual opposition (2 Cor. 7:5; 10:3).'[129] It is clear that Paul's use of 'our' (ἡμῶν – hēmōn) in Philemon 2 signifies some (unknown) personal association of Paul with Archippus' ministry.[130]

To better understand Paul's letters to Philemon and to the Colossians, it is necessary to be aware of the location of this town. About 100 miles (160 km) east of Ephesus there were the towns of Hieropolis, Laodicea, and Colosse (Col. 4:13), located in the Lycus Valley in the Roman province of Asia. Through this valley flows the Lycus River, an offshoot to the right of the larger Maeander (now Menderes) River. Hieropolis was located on the northern side of the Lycus River, Laodicea was on the southern side about ten kilometres south, and Colosse was a small town that lay on both sides of the river about twenty kilometres to the south-east of Laodicea. They were cities known for dyeing cloth. The general area was very fertile. [131]

The letter to Philemon precedes the letter to the Colossians because Colossians 4:9 helps to explain why Paul knew of Archippus' ministry in the Lycus Valley (see also entries for Epaphras and Philemon) and the need to spur him on via the whole Colossian church: 'Take heed to the ministry which you have received in the

---

129. Dunn, *The Epistles to the Colossians and Philippians*, p. 288.

130. Bruce, *Colossians*, p. 206.

131. For a comprehensive description of this region, see Bruce, *Colossians*, pp. 3-13; Hendriksen, *Philippians, Colossians and Philemon*, pp. 6-14. For an accurate (and moving) description of first-century Colosse and its history, see H. C. G. Moule, *Colossian and Philemon Studies: Lessons in Faith and Holiness* (London: Pickering & Inglis, 1902), pp. 18-20: 'But by the Christian era Colossae was small and obscure; a place which hovered between town and village, a townlet, a *polisma* (p. 18).' See also the entry for Apphia.

Lord, that you may fulfil it' (Col. 4:17). The verbs εἴπατε (*eipate*– 'say') and βλέπε (*blepe* – 'see to … that …') are imperatives. They are specific commands to the members of the church.

> This remark is not addressed to him personally, instead it is given to the Colossians in general: Say to Archippus, 'See to it that you fulfil the ministry to which you have received in the Lord'. Notably, the word for 'Say' is in the plural and the believers are corporately to encourage Archippus to fulfil his ministry as something exercised in the sphere of the Lord's authority. What that ministry exactly was, is not stated. It could be to preach, teach, or relate to the collection for the Jerusalem church.[132]

The Greek verb for 'fulfil' is πληρόω (*plēroō*), which has the sense of 'continually fulfil' (NASB) or 'complete' (NIV).[133] As a young man he had a destiny to fulfil for God. Undoubtedly, his ministry would have been exercised in Hieropolis, Laodicea and Colosse. Archippus' ministry is described by the words τὴν διακονίαν (*tēn diakonian*), related to the English term 'deacon'.[134]

> The Colossians knew Archippus, and what his ministry was. We don't. Had Paul heard that Archippus was discouraged, under some pressure, growing weary? We don't know. We simply hear Paul giving this word of encouragement to one member of the Colossian fellowship to complete his God-given ministry.[135]

It was proposed by John Knox in his 1935 doctoral thesis that Archippus was actually the owner of the slave, Onesimus.[136] Bruce correctly rejected that argument and suggested that 'It was quite

---

132. Bird, *Colossians and Philemon*, p. 126. See C. R. Campbell, *Colossians and Philemon: A Handbook on the Greek Text*. BHGNT (Waco, TX: Baylor University Press, 2013), p. 77.

133. See NASBEC. p. 1558, ref. *4137*.

134. See *The Role of διάκονος (diakonos)* in the introduction for a fuller understanding of this term and role.

135. J. Woodhouse, *Colossians and Philemon: So Walk in Him*, Focus on the Bible Commentary Series (Fearn: Christian Focus, 2011), p. 268. This possibility is discussed in Bird, *Colossians and Philemon*, p. 126; Dunn, *Colossians*, p. 288.

136. J. Knox, *Philemon among the Letters of Paul* (Nashville, TN: Abingdon Press, 1959), pp. 49-51.

probable that the ministry which Archippus was to fulfil had something to do with Laodicea, since it is mentioned immediately after the reference to "the letter to Laodicea."'[137]

Aretas IV

Acts 9:23-5

[23] *When many days had elapsed, the Jews plotted together to do away with him,*

[24] *but their plot became known to Saul. They were also watching the gates day and night so that they might put him to death;*

[25] *but his disciples took him by night and let him down through an opening in the wall, lowering him in a large basket.*

2 Corinthians 11:32

[32] *In Damascus the ethnarch under Aretas the king was guarding the city of the Damascenes in order to seize me,*

Galatians 1:17

[17] *nor did I go up to Jerusalem to those who were apostles before me; but I went away to Arabia, and returned once more to Damascus.*

The Dead Sea Scrolls scholar, Geza Vermes, has written about historical characters living around the time of Jesus, including Aretas IV.[138] Extracts from Vermes concerning Aretas IV are provided to illustrate the person referred to by Paul. For background, (Herod) Antipas was the second son of Herod the Great.

> The career of Antipas was profoundly affected by his marital affairs. His first wife was a daughter of Aretas IV, King of the Nabateans (9 B.C–A.D. 40). The union was politically useful as it protected Peraea, the Transjordan territory of Antipas, from marauding Arab nomads. However, things went sour later when Antipas decided to divorce his wife after falling in love in Rome with the wife of his half-brother Herod, son of Mariamme II, the high priest's daughter. …

---

137. Bruce, *Colossians*, p. 199.

138. G. Vermes, *Who's Who in the Age of Jesus* (London: Penguin, 2005), pp. 47, 111, 253. See also P. Barnett, *The Second Epistle to the Corinthians*, NICNT (Grand Rapids: Eerdmans, 1997), pp. 553-5; M. J. Harris, *The Second Epistle to the Corinthians: A Commentary on the Greek Text* (Grand Rapids: Eerdmans, 2005), pp. 820-3 for detailed analysis of Acts 9:23-25.

> The rumour about Antipas' marital plans reached his wife: gossip-mongering flourished in the Herodian royal courts. The shrewd Nabatean princess obtained permission from her naïve husband to leave Galilee and travel to the fortress of Machaerus in southern Transjordan from where she could easily cross the border to Petra, the capital of the Nabateans. With the rejected and humiliated wife safe with her father, Aretas was free to wage a war of revenge against Antipas.[139] [The war was lost by Antipas.]
>
> Vitellius[140] was ordered by Tiberius to capture the Nabatean king Aretas IV and punish him for the defeat he had inflicted on Herod Antipas, tetrarch of Galilee. Vitellius, who disliked Antipas, half-heartedly obeyed the imperial command, but on hearing the news of the death of Tiberius in March A.D. 37, while on his way with his army to the Nabatean capital, Petra, he stopped the enterprise and returned to Syria.[141]

Acts 9:23-25 describes Paul's escape from Damascus over the city wall in a basket or net. Kruse correctly notes Paul's description of this event in 2 Cor. 11:32 as an example of his rejection of boasting.

> This was probably Paul's first taste of the ignominy of persecution, and it must have left an indelible imprint upon him. It was a humiliating experience, and its inclusion here seems to constitute a parody of the whole purpose of boasting.[142]

The reason for Paul's escape from Damascus varies in these accounts. In Acts, Luke ascribes his escape to a plot by the Jews to assassinate him, whereas Paul attributes his peril to the ethnarch of the city in 2 Corinthians 11:32-3. It is not unlikely that the plotting Jews had involved the authorities in their search for Paul. Far more important, though, from a chronological perspective is the

---

139. Vermes, *Who's Who in the Age of Jesus*, p. 47.

140. 'Lucius Vitellius, consul in A.D. 34 and father of the future emperor Vitellius (A.D. 69), was appointed legate to Syria by Tiberius in A.D. 35, and recalled by Caligula in A.D. 39. An excellent administrator, he was repeatedly involved in Jewish matters.' Vermes, *Who's Who in the Age of Jesus*, p. 253.

141. Vermes, *Who's Who in the Age of Jesus*, p. 253.

142. C. G. Kruse, *2 Corinthians: An Introduction and Commentary*, TNCT (Downers Grove, IL.: InterVarsity Press, 2015), p. 259.

technical detail about Aretas IV which was the Graecised name of many kings of Arabia, similar to the title 'Pharaoh' used in Egypt. The 'ethnarch' was a governor under his rule.[143] A significant extract from an article by D. A. Campbell is included because of its importance in assessing Paul's chronology from historical facts. I accept his conclusions in my chronological calculations.

> At one point in his letters Paul briefly recounts his flight – by means of a basket lowered out of an opening in the walls of Damascus – from an ethnarch responsible to King Aretas (see 2 Cor. 11:32-33 and Gal. 1:15-24, esp. verse 18; an incident echoed by Acts 9:23-25). The king referred to by Paul here must be Aretas IV, king of Nabataea from 8 B.C.E. *Although it was clearly not Paul's intention, his concise account of this dramatic episode creates the prospect of an absolute chronological marker for his life – a datum, if it proves determinable, of near incomparable importance since it would be our only such reference from his letters.* This would then also link up with his sequence of Jerusalem visits, one of our most important sets of chronological data, since Paul went directly on this flight to Jerusalem for his first visit to the holy city since his call some three years earlier (so Gal. 1:18, 21; 2:1). *Thus, it could constitute the chronological anchor that Pauline biographers so desperately need; one to which an entire biographical framework for his life could eventually be connected.*
>
> The simple schema below should serve as the starting point for Pauline chronology, and any subsequent biography – it arises for the most part directly out of the apostles' letters. So:

1. Paul's call	A.D. 33 (mid to late)
2. 'after three years' (Gal. 1:18): first visit to Jerusalem (from the Aretas datum)	+ 3 years A.D. 36 (late)
3. [stays in Tarsus and Syrian Antioch]	
4. mission on Cyprus (from Acts 13:4-12)	A.D. 37 (mid)

143. See R. V. G. Tasker, *The Second Epistle of Paul to the Corinthians*, TNTC (Leicester: InterVarsity Press, 1963), pp. 167-8; Bruce, *The Book of the Acts*, p. 191.

5. 'after fourteen years' (Gal. 2:1):	+14 years (from point 2 above):
Second visit to Jerusalem	A.D. 51 (early to mid)

Robert Jewett stated correctly some time ago that 'this [i.e. Paul's escape from King Aretas] is a datum whose historical solidity is capable of anchoring a chronology'.[144]

Aristarchus

Acts 19:29

[29] *The city was filled with the confusion, and they rushed with one accord into the theatre, dragging along Gaius and Aristarchus, Paul's travelling companions from Macedonia.*

Acts 20:3-4

[3] *And there he spent three months, and when a plot was formed against him by the Jews as he was about to set sail for Syria, he decided to return through Macedonia.*

[4] *And he was accompanied by Sopater of Berea, the son of Pyrrhus, and by Aristarchus and Secundus of the Thessalonians, and Gaius of Derbe, and Timothy, and Tychicus and Trophimus of Asia.*

Acts 27:2

[2] *And embarking in an Adramyttian ship, which was about to sail to the regions along the coast of Asia, we put out to sea accompanied by Aristarchus, a Macedonian of Thessalonica.*

Colossians 4:10-11

[10] *Aristarchus, my fellow prisoner, sends you his greetings; and also Barnabas's cousin Mark (about whom you received instructions; if he comes to you, welcome him);*

[11] *and also Jesus who is called Justus; these are the only fellow workers for the kingdom of God who are from the circumcision, and they have proved to be an encouragement to me.*

Philemon 23-4

[23] *Epaphras, my fellow prisoner in Christ Jesus, greets you,*

[24] *as do Mark, Aristarchus, Demas, Luke, my fellow workers.*

---

144. D. A. Campbell, 'An Anchor for Pauline Chronology: Paul's Flight from the "Ethnarch of King Aretas."' *JBL* 121, no. 2 (2002): p. 301. The reference is to Jewett, *Dating Paul's Life*, pp. 30-3. See also Barnett, *2 Corinthians*, p. 555.

Aristarchus (meaning 'best ruler')[145] was a close associate of Paul for many years. However, he is virtually unknown to modern Christians. Notwithstanding his name, Aristarchus was a Macedonian Jew from Thessalonica (Acts 20:4; Col. 4:11).

> While the name itself is unremarkable, it is interestingly attested from Thessalonica, notably in a text where an Aristarchus son of Aristarchus heads a list of politarchs (Dimitsas, 368, ascribed to the first or second century of Roman rule).[146]

He was obviously converted by Paul on his visit to that city, but we are suddenly introduced to him via a riot in Ephesus (Acts 19:23ff.) concerning the possible devaluing of silver shrines made for the Greek goddess, Artemis, caused by Paul's preaching. A crowd dragged Paul's two travelling companions from Macedonia, Gaius[147] and Aristarchus, to the theatre (Acts 19:29). Although described as 'travelling companions', the word συνεκδήμος (*sunekdēmos*) literally means 'be away from one's own people'; they had gone some distance with Paul. In Ephesus there was an open-air theatre, which has been excavated and is estimated to have been capable of holding an audience of about 25,000 people.[148] However, Paul's 'friends' (including some prominent citizens) urged him not to go to the theatre for fear of his life. 'It has been conjectured that the vividness of Luke's description of what went on in the theatre owes something to the account given by one or the other of these two men.'[149] In due course the crowd was subdued and Paul, after encouraging the local Christians, departed for Macedonia. Gaius and Aristarchus apparently departed the riot without harm.

Paul had made it clear that his aim was to travel from Ephesus to Jerusalem (Acts 19:21). However, due to various circumstances, including an assassination plot, Paul began

---

145. HSIBD, p. 97.

146. Hemer, *The Book of Acts*, p. 236.

147. This Gaius from Macedonia is a different person to Gaius from Derbe (Asia) (Acts 20:4) and Gaius Titius Justus (Acts 18:7).

148. Marshall, *Acts*, p. 318.

149. Bruce, *Acts*, p. 376.

by going in the opposite direction (north) via Greece and Macedonia. We are informed of the circuitous route over which he travelled by foot. That could have taken a couple of years to accomplish (Acts 20-1).

Luke informs us that Paul was accompanied by Sopater of Berea (son of Pyrrhus). Parsons and Culy suggest that Acts 20:4 should be understood as 'Sopater accompanied him [Paul]. Aristarchus and Secundus of the Thessalonians, Gaius of Derbe, Timothy, and Tychicus and Trophimus – Asians – these went on ahead.'[150] Some of these men are never mentioned in Paul's letters and, therefore, omitted from this book.

The mention of Aristarchus in Colossians 4:10-11 and Philemon 23-24 raises the critical issue of the place(s) from which these letters were written. For completeness, it is necessary to consider Aristarchus' circumstances as being imprisoned with Paul in *either* Ephesus *or* Rome. See *Letters from Prison: Ephesians, Philippians, Colossians and Philemon* in the introduction. The Ephesus possibility is discussed below, followed by the Rome possibility.

The Ephesus Possibility

The following view reflects the possibility that Colossians and Philemon were written in Ephesus during Paul's supposed imprisonment there.

> Paul's letters to the church at Colosse and to Philemon include greetings from Aristarchus, who is a 'fellow prisoner' (συναιχμάλωτός – *sunaikmalōtos*) with Paul in Ephesus (Col. 4:10). Technically, συναιχμάλωτός means 'prisoner-of-war', reflecting the spiritual warfare in which Paul and his fellow workers were engaged. The only other people of whom Paul used this description are Andronicus and Junia (Rom. 16:7) and Epaphras (Philem. 23). In Col. 4:11, Aristarchus, Mark and Jesus Justus are given a unique description in the NT: 'fellow-workers for the kingdom of God' (οὗτοι μόνοι συνεργοὶ εἰς τὴν βασιλείαν τοῦ θεοῦ – *outoi monoi sunergoi eis tēn*

150. M. C. Parsons and M. M. Culy, *Acts: A Handbook on the Greek Text*, BHGNT (Waco, TX: Baylor University Press, 2003), p. 384.

> *basileian Theou*). They were also the only Jews supporting Paul in Ephesus when he wrote to the Colossians and Philemon. Given the uproar against Jews in general at the theatre (Acts 19:33-5), it is hardly unsurprising that few of his fellow countrymen would wish to support Paul in that riotous and volatile situation. The others (Gentiles) mentioned here (Col. 3:10-14) are Epaphras, Luke and Demas. Again, the reference to Jews before Gentiles may be part of Paul's 'Jews first' principle (cf. Rom. 2:9-10).[151]

The reference to only three Jews (ἐκ περιτομῆς – *ek peritomēs*, 'from the circumcision') assisting Paul in his Ephesian imprisonment again raises the constant reminder that even Judaisers amongst the Christians presented a constant threat and harassment to Paul's gospel work among the Gentiles (e.g. Acts 15:1).

Paul's letter to Philemon ends with greetings from some eminent Christians, who must have known him personally. Philemon 24 names Mark, Aristarchus, Demas, and Luke, 'my fellow workers' (οἱ συνεργοί μου – *hoi sunergoi mou*). All of them must have assisted Paul in his imprisonment(s?) in Ephesus.

The next appearance of Aristarchus in Acts (27:2) is where he accompanies Paul and Luke by ship from Jerusalem on the voyage to Rome. It must be the case that Aristarchus was with Paul for most of his (Aristarchus') converted life, for he would not have journeyed from Ephesus (let alone Thessalonica) to Jerusalem just to accompany Paul on this long journey.

If Aristarchus is present during Paul's imprisonment in Ephesus, the events in Acts 27:2 would mean that Aristarchus may have left Paul at Myra and returned home to Thessalonica (see below). The Ephesus possibility also has implications for our understanding of the actions and movements of Demas, Epaphras, Jesus Justus, Luke, Mark, Onesimus, Timothy, and Tychicus. Each of these people will be examined under their own entries.

The Rome Possibility

The following view reflects the possibility that Colossians and Philemon were written in Rome during Paul's first imprisonment.

151. See McKnight, *Colossians*, p. 387.

Bruce, referring to W. M. Ramsay's conclusions,[152] comments on Acts 27:2:

> It is not said explicitly that he [Aristarchus] went all the way to Rome with Paul, and some have thought that he accompanied him only as far as Myra, where they trans-shipped (Acts 27:5-6), and then went home to Thessalonika. But we are more probably intended to understand that he accompanied him to Rome – that he remained one of the company designated by the pronoun 'we' as far as Acts 28:16 ('and when we came into Rome …'). At any rate he was with Paul and Timothy when this letter was on the point of being dispatched, and is described by Paul as his 'fellow-prisoner' – literally his fellow-prisoner-of-war. Ramsay suggested that Aristarchus shared Paul's captivity voluntarily, perhaps passing as his servant. One who looked on himself as a soldier of Jesus Christ, as Paul did, would not unnaturally think of himself during his captivity as a prisoner-of-war.[153]

However, Bruce's argument does nothing to add to the plausibility of a Rome provenance for Colossians or Philemon unless Aristarchus can be placed in Rome.

> Aristarchus is not expressly named later in this narrative; it is possible, therefore, that he was travelling home to Thessalonica and did not join the second ship which took the party in the direction of Italy. On the other hand, if Colossians and Philemon are to be dated in the course of Paul's Roman captivity, he was in Paul's company when those letters were written (Col. 4:10; Philem. 24), so he may have gone all the way with Paul on this occasion; in that case he is no doubt included in Luke's 'we' throughout the narrative. It is impossible to be sure. Ramsay argued that Luke and Aristarchus 'must have gone' as Paul's slaves, not merely performing the duties of slaves … but actually passing as slaves. In this way not merely had Paul faithful friends always beside him; his importance in the eyes of the centurion was much enhanced, and that was of great importance. The narrative clearly implies that

---

152. W. M. Ramsay, *St Paul the Traveller and Roman Citizen* (London: Hodder and Stoughton, 1942).

153. Bruce, *Colossians*, p. 178. This view was supported by J. B. Lightfoot, *St Paul's Epistle to the Philippians* (London: MacMillan, reprinted 1908), pp. 11, 35.

> Paul enjoyed much respect during this voyage, such as a penniless traveller without a servant to attend on him would never receive either in the first century or the nineteenth. While Ramsay's argument merits the respect due to his great knowledge of social history in the Roman Empire of the first century A.D., it is not the prima facie inference which one would draw from the narrative, and is really improbable. Aristarchus may have gone as a fare-paying passenger; Luke (if a reader's imagination may be indulged) perhaps signed on as a ship's doctor.[154]

In Colossians 4:10-11 Paul writes that Aristarchus, Mark, and Jesus Justus are the only Jews with him at that time if Colossians was written in Rome. The reference to only three Jews (ἐκ περιτομῆς – *ek peritomēs*, 'from the circumcision') being with Paul in his (first) Roman imprisonment again raises the constant issue that Judaisers amongst the Christians (throughout the Empire) presented a constant threat and harassment to Paul's gospel work among Jews (and Gentiles). However, it is apparent from Romans 16 that some Jews in Rome strongly supported Paul's gospel of grace. It seems to me unlikely that not one of them would have supported Paul in his first imprisonment given the greetings to several Jews in Romans 16 and the circumstances described in Acts 28:30-1.

This supports the view that Colossians and Philemon were not composed in Rome. However, it is evident from Acts 27:2 that Aristarchus did accompany Paul at least part of the way (if not the whole journey) from Caesarea to Rome.

In terms of long-term involvement with the apostle's work, Aristarchus must rank as one of Paul's most devoted fellow workers.

Aristobulus

Romans 16:10b

10b Greet those who are of the household of Aristobulus.

This is a Greek name, meaning 'best adviser'.[155] It seems clear that Aristobulus was not a Christian, otherwise he would have

154. Bruce, *Acts*, pp. 477-8. Stott, *Acts*, p. 387, regards this conclusion as 'plausible'. See also Marshall, *Acts*, p. 404.

155. HSIBD, p. 97.

received the personal greeting which was directed to 'those of the household of Aristobulus' (τοὺς ἐκ τῶν ἀριστοβούλου – *tous ek tōn aristoboulou*), presumably referring to *some* of the slaves in his employ.[156] In any event, Aristobulus was a wealthy Roman citizen.[157] Because they only receive this brief acknowledgement by Paul without comment, it seems likely that he knew of these believers by reputation rather than personal association.

> The name Aristobulus is rare in Roman records and inscriptions and is likely to belong to someone who was born elsewhere. It was much used in the Hasmonean dynasty and in the family of Herod the Great. Cranfield (*Romans*, 2:791-792), Dunn, (*Romans 9-16*, 896) and Jewett (*Romans*, 964-966) consider the possibility that this Aristobulus was the grandson of Herod the Great, who came to Rome as a hostage with his brother Herod Agrippa I and was educated with the future emperor Claudius. He died between A.D. 45 and 48.[158]

It is agreed that Aristobulus was a man of some importance in Rome. Lightfoot maintains that he was a grandson of Herod the Great and a brother of the elder Agrippa and of Herod (king of Chalcis).[159] He lived in Rome as a private citizen and was believed to have been on intimate terms with the Emperor Claudius. Although disputed, there has never been concrete proof to dismantle Lightfoot's claim.

> We know of an Aristobulus who came to Rome as a hostage along with his brother, Herod Agrippa, that they were educated with the future emperor Claudius and that Aristobulus later appeared before the procurator Petronius to protest Caligula's placement of his statue in the Jerusalem temple (Josephus *Ant.* 18.273-76).

---

156. See Lampe, *The Roman Christians*, p. 222.

157. See Cranfield, *Romans*, vol. 2, p. 791; Murray, *Romans*, p. 230.

158. D. G. Peterson, *Commentary on Romans*, Biblical Theology for Christian Proclamation (Nashville, TN: B&H Publishing, 2017), p. 541.

159. J. B. Lightfoot, 'Caesar's Household', in J. B. Lightfoot, *Saint Paul's Epistle to the Philippians,* pp. 174-5. Support for Lightfoot is found in L. L. Morris, *The Epistle to the Romans,* PNTC (Grand Rapids: Eerdmans, 1988), p. 534; Dumbrell, *Romans*, p. 142.

> It is plausible, therefore, that this particular Aristobulus was the grandson of Herod the Great, who died sometime after A.D. 45, having apparently willed his household to his friend the emperor Claudius, who thereupon incorporated the administrative slaves into his imperial bureaucracy. If so, the strategic setting of this congregation within the bureaucracy indicates not only how far Christianity had penetrated into government circles but also how they could have been helpful in clearing the way for the Spanish mission. ... Since Paul makes no personal reference to them, it is clear that his knowledge is second-hand. He had probably heard of this remarkable group from other Roman believers whom he had met during their exile between A.D. 49 and 54. If the link to the Herodian family is valid, their association with their now deceased Jewish patron, Aristobulus, who had forcefully interceded on behalf of his compatriots in the Caligula incident, undoubtedly meant that they were sympathetic to the viewpoint of the Jewish Christians within Rome. It is significant that Paul honours them here as worthy of the same acceptance as the members of the church of Prisca and Aquila, who would have been more sympathetic to Paul's mission to the Gentiles.[160]

The fact that the next person in Paul's list in Romans 16 is Herodion (a Christian and probably a slave) may be more than a coincidence if the link with Herod's family is correct.[161]

Artemas

Titus 3:12

[12] When I send Artemas or Tychicus to you, make every effort to come to me at Nicopolis, for I have decided to spend the winter there.

His name is related to the Greek god, Artemis (Acts 19:24), being a shortened form of Ἀρτεμίδορος (*Artemidoros*), meaning 'gift of Artemis'.[162]

---

160. Jewett, *Romans*, pp. 966-7.

161. See Jewett, *Romans*, p. 967, and the entry for Herodion.

162. Marshall with Towner, *Pastoral Epistles*, p. 341; Perkins, *Pastoral Letters*, p. 284. However, Yarbrough, *Letters to Timothy and Titus*, p. 556, comments that Artemas 'was a common name, not to be confused with the female goddess Artemis'.

Titus (Gal. 2:3), one of Paul's fellow workers from before his first missionary journey, was ministering to the Christians on Crete (Titus 1:5). At the conclusion of his letter Paul asks Titus to join him in Nicopolis. 'Although several cities have this name, the most probable location is in Epirus, a region located on the western coast of Greece and the site of the Actian games.'[163] Paul planned to spend the winter there. Clearly, Paul was not in prison at this time.[164] Paul plans to send Artemas or Tychicus (who is mentioned in several letters) to replace Titus. 'Assuming the plan held good, apparently it was Artemas who replaced Titus – not Tychicus, who is placed in Ephesus in 2 Timothy 4:12. With the arrival of his replacement, Titus was able to make his way to Nicopolis, where Paul planned to spend the winter.'[165] The tense of the Greek verb κέκρικα (*kekrika* – 'decided') indicates that Paul had already decided on this course of action.[166]

We know nothing more about Artemas;[167] but the fact that he could minister to the Cretan Christians in the absence of Titus speaks volumes for his faith, capacity, and Paul's confidence in him.

Asyncritus

Romans 16:14

[14] Greet Asyncritus, Phlegon, Hermes, Patrobas, Hermas, and the brethren with them.

Asyncritus is a Greek name meaning 'incomparable'.[168] He is greeted with Phlegon, Hermes, Patrobas, and Hermas. All of these are masculine names of Gentile slaves or freed men. Given the common greeting afforded to them, it is most likely that they worked in the same household or were members of a particular house church in

---

163. Perkins, *Pastoral Letters*, p. 284.

164. See the entry for Titus.

165. Towner, *1–2 Timothy and Titus*, p. 263.

166. Perkins, *Pastoral Letters*, p. 285. Page 221 refers to the use of this verb in 2 Timothy 4:1 and comments that 'These are the only occurrences of this verb in the PE [Pastoral Epistles]'.

167. See W. Barclay, *The Letters to Timothy, Titus and Philemon*, The Daily Study Bible, revised edition (Edinburgh: St Andrew Press, 1975), p. 265; Gundry, *Commentary on First and Second Timothy, Titus*, p. 72.

168. HSIBD, p. 116.

Rome. This possibility is supported by Paul's addition of 'and the brethren with them'.[169] It was clearly a larger group whom Paul knew to be associated with one another and were committed Christians but probably not known to him personally.[170] However, they had not worked with Paul, only being described as 'brothers'. Jewett notes that 'the fact that this Asynkritos belongs with a group of other persons whose servile status is indisputable leads me to concur with Lampe that he is probably a slave or freed man'.[171]

> Here a number of brethren are selected without distinction. This mark of brotherly attention would gratify those whom the Apostle here names, beside the brethren who were with them. The Lord's people are not equally distinguished, but they are all brethren equally related to Him who is the Elder Brother of His people. Some of them are eminent, and others are without peculiar distinction. They are all, however, worthy of love. A Church is not to consist of the most eminent believers, but of believers, though some be of the lowest attainments. A church of Christ is a school in which their education is to be perfected. And all the saints which are with them – that is the believers in their families and neighbourhood. These might not be personally known to the Apostle, but as believers they were worthy of his notice.[172]

BARNABAS

ACTS 4:36-37

[36] *Now Joseph, a Levite of Cyprian birth, who was also called Barnabas by the apostles (which translated means Son of Encouragement),*

[37] *owned a tract of land. So he sold it, and brought the money and laid it at the apostles' feet.*

ACTS 9:27

[27] *But Barnabas took hold of him and brought him to the apostles and described to them how he had seen the Lord on the road, and that He had talked to him, and how he had spoken out boldly in the name of Jesus at Damascus.*

---

169. See Cranfield, *Romans*, vol. 2, p. 795.
170. See Peterson, *Romans*, p. 543.
171. Jewett, *Romans*, p. 970.
172. Haldane, *Romans*, p. 640.

Acts 11:19-30

[19] So then those who were scattered because of the persecution that occurred in connection with Stephen made their way to Phoenicia, Cyprus, and Antioch, speaking the word to no one except to Jews alone.

[20] But there were some of them, men of Cyprus and Cyrene, who came to Antioch and began speaking to the Greeks as well, preaching the good news of the Lord Jesus.

[21] And the hand of the Lord was with them, and a large number who believed turned to the Lord.

[22] The news about them reached the ears of the church in Jerusalem, and they sent Barnabas off to Antioch.

[23] Then when he arrived and witnessed the grace of God, he rejoiced and began to encourage them all with resolute heart to remain true to the Lord; ...

[24] ... for he was a good man, and full of the Holy Spirit and faith. And considerable numbers were added to the Lord.

[25] And he left for Tarsus to look for Saul;

[26]... and when he had found him, he brought him to Antioch. And for an entire year they met with the church and taught considerable numbers of people; and the disciples were first called Christians in Antioch.

[27] Now at this time some prophets came down from Jerusalem to Antioch.

[28] One of them, named Agabus, stood up and indicated by the Spirit that there would definitely be a severe famine all over the world. And this took place in the reign of Claudius.

[29] And to the extent that any of the disciples had means, each of them determined to send a contribution for the relief of the brethren living in Judea.

[30] And they did this, sending it with Barnabas and Saul to the elders.

Acts 12:25

[25] And Barnabas and Saul returned from Jerusalem when they had fulfilled their mission, taking along with them John, who was also called Mark.

Acts 13:1-2

[1] Now there were at Antioch, in the church that was there, prophets and teachers: Barnabas, and Simeon who was called Niger, and Lucius of Cyrene, and Manaen who had been brought up with Herod the tetrarch, and Saul.

[2] While they were ministering to the Lord and fasting, the Holy Spirit said, 'Set apart for Me Barnabas and Saul for the work to which I have called them.'

ACTS 13:7

[7]... who was with the proconsul, Sergius Paulus, a man of intelligence. This man summoned Barnabas and Saul and sought to hear the word of God.

ACTS 13:43, 46, 50

[43]Now when the meeting of the synagogue had broken up, many of the Jews and the God-fearing proselytes followed Paul and Barnabas, who were speaking to them and urging them to continue in the grace of God.

[46]Paul and Barnabas spoke out boldly and said, 'It was necessary that the word of God be spoken to you first. Since you repudiate it and consider yourselves unworthy of eternal life, behold, we are turning to the Gentiles'.

[50]But the Jews incited the devout women of prominence and the leading men of the city, and instigated a persecution against Paul and Barnabas, and drove them out of their region.

ACTS 14:12-14

[12]And they began calling Barnabas, Zeus, and Paul, Hermes, since he was the chief speaker.

[13]Moreover, the priest of Zeus, whose temple was just outside the city, brought oxen and garlands to the gates, and wanted to offer sacrifice with the crowds.

[14]But when the apostles Barnabas and Paul heard about it, they tore their robes and rushed out into the crowd, crying out

ACTS 14:20

[20]But while the disciples stood around him [Paul], he got up and entered the city. The next day he left with Barnabas for Derbe.

ACTS 15:1-2

[1]Some men came down from Judea and began teaching the brethren, 'Unless you are circumcised according to the custom of Moses, you cannot be saved.'

[2]And after Paul and Barnabas had a heated argument and debate with them, the brothers determined that Paul and Barnabas and some others of them should go up to Jerusalem to the apostles and elders concerning this issue.

ACTS 15:12

[12]All the people kept silent, and they were listening to Barnabas and Paul as they were relating what signs and wonders God had done through them among the Gentiles.

ACTS 15:22, 25, 26

[22] *Then it seemed good to the apostles and the elders, with the whole church, to choose men from among them to send to Antioch with Paul and Barnabas: Judas who was called Barsabbas, and Silas, leading men among the brothers,*

[25] *... it seemed good to us, having become of one mind, to select men to send to you with our beloved Barnabas and Paul,*

[26] *... men who have risked their lives for the name of our Lord Jesus Christ.*

ACTS 15:35-9

[35] *But Paul and Barnabas stayed in Antioch, teaching and preaching with many others also, the word of the Lord.*

[36] *After some days Paul said to Barnabas, 'Let's return and visit the brethren in every city in which we proclaimed the word of the Lord, and see how they are.'*

[37] *Barnabas wanted to take John, called Mark, along with them also.*

[38] *But Paul was of the opinion that they should not take along with them this man who had deserted them in Pamphylia and had not gone with them to the work.*

[39] *Now it turned into such a sharp disagreement that they separated from one another, and Barnabas took Mark with him and sailed away to Cyprus.*

1 CORINTHIANS 9:6

[6] *Or do only Barnabas and I have no right to refrain from working?*

GALATIANS 2:1

[1] *Then after an interval of fourteen years I went up again to Jerusalem with Barnabas, taking Titus along also.*

GALATIANS 2:9-13

[9] *... and recognizing the grace that had been given to me, James and Cephas and John, who were reputed to be pillars, gave to me and Barnabas the right hand of fellowship, so that we might go to the Gentiles, and they to the circumcised.*

[10] *They only asked us to remember the poor – the very thing I also was eager to do.*

[11] *But when Cephas came to Antioch, I opposed him to his face, because he stood condemned.*

[12] *For prior to the coming of some men from James, he used to eat with the Gentiles; but when they came, he began to withdraw and separate himself, fearing those from the circumcision.*

[13] *The rest of the Jews joined him in hypocrisy, with the result that even Barnabas was carried away by their hypocrisy.*

COLOSSIANS 4:10

[10] *Aristarchus, my fellow prisoner, sends you his greetings; and also Barnabas' cousin Mark (about whom you received instructions; if he comes to you, welcome him);*

1. Background

Barnabas was one of the most important and influential people in earliest Christianity. Most of our information about Barnabas comes from Acts but he is also mentioned in three of Paul's letters. He was a cousin of (John) Mark (Col. 4:10) and had relatives in Jerusalem (Acts 12:12). Having the real name of Joseph, Barnabas was a Jew of the priestly tribe of Levi, born in Cyprus, and resident in Jerusalem. His Jewish lineage would have made him eligible to serve in the Temple in Jerusalem in a minor capacity. The name Barnabas was a nickname, meaning *Son of Encouragement*, which stuck with him forever.[173] He was a man of good conscience and good character.

In Acts 11:24 Barnabas is described as ἀνὴρ ἀγαθὸς (*anēr agathos*), 'a good man' (cf. Matt. 25:21 where the same adjective is used) and numbered among the 'prophets and teachers' in Antioch. His commitment to Christ was clearly evident to all: 'a good man, and full of the Holy Spirit and of faith' (ἦν ἀνὴρ ἀγαθὸς καὶ πλήρης πνεύματος ἁγίου καὶ πίστεως. – *ēn anēr agathos kai plērēs pneumatos hagiou kai pisteōs*). There is one other person in Acts who is described as 'doing good': Dorcas, Acts 9:36. This is a rare tribute to two great Christians. Paul uses ἀγαθὸς in his letters but never as a description of a specific individual. Perhaps he had in mind the saying of Jesus in Luke 18:19: 'Why do you call me good? No one is good except God alone.'

---

173. Zerwick and Grosvenor, *Grammatical Analysis,* vol. 1, p. 363 note that this name is 'not possibly a translation of Barnabas'. See also Marshall, *Acts,* p. 109.

Barnabas' sale of land[174] and gift of the whole proceeds to the apostles [clearly a reference to the Twelve] was noteworthy. It was in stark contrast to the immediately following story of Ananias and Sapphira (Acts 5:1-11). The two stories reflect the pattern of life practised among the early disciples, of which deeds like that of Barnabas were clearly more common. Coming to faith in Christ may have prompted Joseph Barnabas to reflect on the Mosaic law, where the ownership of land by Levites is prohibited (Num. 18:20; Deut. 10:9; but see Jer. 32:7). Although no longer necessary under the new Christian dispensation, this Mosaic law may have been a stimulus to his decision. Regardless, it was an act of considerable generosity and clearly a proof and encouragement to everyone as to the sincerity of his faith.

2. Meeting with Saul

After Saul's dramatic vision on the road to Damascus and conversion, he eventually sought to meet the *disciples* in Jerusalem, but he still must have had such a fearsome reputation for persecution that they were afraid of him. (At this stage Paul is still called Saul in Acts.) But Barnabas had sufficient courage to take him to meet the *apostles* (Acts 9:27) but, by Paul's own account (Gal. 1:18-20), he only met Cephas and James (the Lord's brother). Barnabas spoke on Saul's behalf and repeated what he had done and said in Damascus. Saul was now a member of the Christian community, a brother in Christ. It becomes apparent (cf. Acts 11:22) that, after Paul's departure, Barnabas remained in Jerusalem.

> True conversion always issues in church membership. It is not only that converts must join the Christian community, but that the Christian community must welcome converts, especially those from a different religious, ethnic or social background. There is an urgent need for modern Ananiases and Barnabases who overcome their scruples and hesitations, and take the initiative to befriend newcomers.[175]

---

174. This is the only occasion where ἀγρός (*agros*) is used for 'land' in the NT. See Bruce, *Acts*, p. 101, n. 59.

175. Stott, *Acts*, p. 178.

When it became evident to the apostles in Jerusalem that Gentiles had heard and believed the gospel, they sent Barnabas to Antioch (Acts 11:22). He was an obvious choice given his Cyprian birth and the Cyprian nationality of some of the new converts. When he saw that the grace of God was mightily at work among Jews and Gentiles, he naturally used his gift of encouragement.

Barnabas left Antioch for Tarsus to find Saul and, having done so, they returned to Antioch. Staying there for a year, they enjoyed a fruitful ministry in that city, which was the first place where the believers were called 'Christians' (Acts 11:26). The text συναχθῆναι ἐν τῇ ἐκκλησίᾳ (*sunachthēnai en tē ekklēsia*) (Acts 11:26) indicates that Paul and Barnabas met with the church 'as part of the communal worship experience'.[176] In response to a word from God ('through the Spirit') the Jerusalem prophet, Agabus, announced in Antioch that there would be a famine in the inhabited world, which did indeed occur (Acts 11:28). In response, Barnabas and Saul were chosen by the Antioch church to take a gift for the relief of the Christians in Judea. Zerwick and Grosvenor translate verse 29 as a contribution 'of the disciples each one of them in the measure that (καθὼς – *kathōs*) he could afford (εὐπορεῖτό – *euporeito*) assigned (pl.) [a sum] to send as relief to the brethren who were living in Jerusalem'.[177] Note that, as a leader of the church of Antioch, Barnabas is given precedence over Saul in this and following accounts until Cyprus (see below); however, by this stage, Saul's recognition as a Christian was increasing.

3. From Antioch to Cyprus: From Saul to Paul

When Barnabas and Saul returned to Antioch from their mission to Jerusalem, they were accompanied by Barnabas' cousin John, who was also called Mark, the future writer of one of the gospels (Acts 12:25).

While at Antioch, Barnabas and Saul were recognised as being among the teachers and prophets in that place. The Holy

176. Parsons and Culy, *Acts*, p. 228.

177. Zerwick and Grosvenor, *Grammatical Analysis*, vol. 1, p. 388.

Spirit then set them aside for work which the Lord had chosen for them (Acts 13:1-2).

> The preposition [κατὰ-Acts 13:1] is probably used distributively to indicate something that was characteristic of the church at Antioch: there were prophets and teachers throughout the various house churches in Antioch, or there were many prophets and teachers in the Antioch church.[178]

Concerning οὖσαν (*house* – 'that was there' [in Antioch], Acts 13:1), Parsons and Culy provide an important understanding of the circumstances of earliest Christianity which may have faded from the church by the time that Luke wrote Acts, possibly some forty years after the event: 'It is possible that Luke was *looking back on a world that had since changed* and that the participle connotes "*existing at that time*".'[179] This may reflect the lack of 'prophetic' utterances in the church even by A.D. 65.

Barnabas and Saul travelled from Seleucia (Piera), which was located five miles from the mouth of the Orontes River and served as the port of Antioch, to Cyprus, Barnabas' birthplace. They also had John Mark as their assistant (ὑπηρέτης – *hupēretōs*) (Acts 13:5). They travelled most of the length of Cyprus from Salamis in the east to Paphos at the western end of the island. Being Jews, Barnabas and Saul spoke the gospel message in Jewish synagogues.[180] However, we should note the increased prominence of Saul over Barnabas in Luke's account of their missionary work in Cyprus.

In Paphos (Acts 13:6-12), Barnabas and Saul were summoned by Sergius Paulus, the Roman proconsul[181] (ἀνθύπατος – *anthupatos*, the Greek equivalent of proconsul as per Acts 18:12; 19:38) of Cyprus,

---

178. Parsons and Culy, *Acts*, p. 243.

179. ibid., p. 243. (The first emphasis is mine.)

180. In regard to Luke's reference to 'Jewish synagogues', see the entry for Sosipater.

181. A proconsul, as the name implies, acted on behalf of the two consuls elected in Rome and was a senior official in the Roman Empire. In this case, he was the civil governor of Cyprus but without military authority. It is possible that his one-year tenure places this event around A.D. 45–46. See APXIOC Institute of Biblical Archaeology, *https://apxaioc.com/?p=20*.

'an intelligent man' (ἀνδρὶ συνετῷ – *andri sunetō*),[182] who wanted to hear the Word of God. However, in his palace, was a magician and 'Jewish false prophet' (ψευδοπροφήτης ἰουδαῖος – *pseudoprophētēs ioudaios*), called Bar-Jesus in Hebrew and Elymas in Greek.[183] He was trying to persuade the proconsul to reject the gospel. At this time some important changes occur in Luke's account.

First, Acts 13:2, 7 refer to 'Barnabas and Saul'. Secondly, in Acts 13:9, Luke reveals that Saul is also known as Paul, the first occurrence of this fact in the NT. Thirdly, and much more importantly, Paul was 'filled with the Holy Spirit' and placed a curse on Elymas that was immediately fulfilled. Consequently, Sergius Paulus became a Christian: at that stage he was the highest ranked Roman to do so. But this event marks a major turning point concerning Paul and Barnabas. It appears that Barnabas did not speak during this event. Fourthly, after Cyprus, Luke then refers to 'Paul and his company'. In Luke's mind, the leadership has changed. Acts then concentrates on Paul and what he preaches.

4. Paul's First Missionary Journey

After leaving Cyprus they travelled to Pamphylia, where John Mark left Barnabas and Paul, returning to Jerusalem. They then went on to Pisidian Antioch, near the middle of modern Turkey.

> Pisidia was a wild mountainous country infested with bandits. When Paul wrote that he had been 'in perils of robbers' (2 Cor. 11:26), he may have been referring to his dangerous journey through the mountains of Pisidia. While in Perga Paul intended to travel north through this rugged and dangerous mountain terrain to Antioch of Pisidia.[184]

Acts 13 quotes a lengthy sermon from Paul to the Jews in their synagogue in Pisidian Antioch. It was during this event that Paul made the critical decision to turn from the Jews to the Gentiles (Acts 13:44-46). The Greek text οὐκ ἀξίους κρίνετε (*ouk axious krinete*

---

182. Although both are learned men, Luke uses ἀνὴρ λόγιος for Apollos (Acts 18:24) but ἀνδρὶ συνετός for Sergius Paulus (Acts 13:7).

183. Zerwick and Grosvenor, *Grammatical Analysis*, vol. 1, p. 392, note that 'the connection between Elymas and Bar-Jesus (v. 6) is not clear'.

184. HSIBD, p. 844.

– 'consider yourselves unworthy') (v. 46) contains emotive language. 'The fronting … of the adjectival complement … along with the use of the verb κρίνω in a negative statement makes this clause drip with sarcasm.'[185] In Acts 13:47 Paul and Barnabas quote the latter part of Isa. 49:6: '"I will also make you a light of the nations so that My salvation may reach to the end of the earth" as justification for their Gentile ministry.'[186] There is an interesting occurrence when the Jews protested against Paul in his second week of preaching there. Acts records many instances where women were attracted to the gospel and were converted; however, in this case 'the Jews incited the *devout women of prominence* and the leading men of the city' (Acts 13:50) to oppose Paul and Barnabas. The reaction to Paul came in a severe response from three groups: Jews, 'devout women of prominence' (NASB) (τὰς σεβομένας γυναῖκας τὰς εὐσχήμονας – *tas sebomenas gunaikas tas euschēmonas*), and prominent men.[187] Their persecution was so severe that they drove Paul and Barnabas not only from the city but also from their 'region' (όπιων – *opiōn*).

Acts 14 reflects the determination of Paul and Barnabas to preach the gospel despite the ongoing persecution that followed them. Jews from Pisidian Antioch followed them to Iconium and stirred up both Jews and Gentiles to the extent that they might be stoned (Acts 14:4). Their next destination was Lystra, the hometown of Timothy. They faced the confusion of pagan religion when, after performing a miracle in Lystra, Barnabas and Paul were mistaken for Zeus and Hermes, his messenger, respectively. This mistaken identification highlights that it was now Paul who was the main speaker in these towns. However, the pursuing Jews from Pisidian Antioch were joined by their fellow antagonists in Iconium and, together, they stirred up the

---

185. Parsons and Culy, *Acts*, p. 268.

186. Harman, *Isaiah*, p. 342.

187. The NIV presumes that the women were Jewish, using the term 'God-fearing'. This cannot be confirmed because σεβομένας (*sebomenas*) means 'devout' without ascribing a religion to the person. It is difficult to tell from the text whether the (devout) prominent women were Jewish or pagan worshippers. That they and the prominent men were Gentiles seems more likely.

crowds sufficiently for Paul to be stoned and left for dead outside Lystra (Acts 14:19). It appears that Barnabas was spared this severe treatment. However, the pair continued their preaching journey on to Derbe and had the courage to return to both Iconium and Pisidian Antioch to strengthen those who had become Christians in those towns. Barnabas showed as much courage as Paul on this lengthy journey. They could return home to Antioch to tell the church 'all the things that God had done with them *and how he had opened a door of faith to the Gentiles*' (Acts 14:27). This news would have world-wide implications for Christianity.

After Acts 15 (see below), Barnabas is no longer mentioned for the remainder of Acts. After the Cyprus events, Luke alternates between 'Paul and Barnabas' (Acts 13:43, 46, 50) and 'Barnabas and Paul' (Acts 14:12, 14).[188] In this latter case the reversal of order seems to be only because of the ascription of the names of Greek gods to the two apostles: Zeus (Barnabas) ranked higher in Greek deities than Hermes (Paul).

5. The Issue of the Gentiles

The chronology of the facts provided by Luke in Acts 15 and Paul in Galatians 2 has been the subject of huge academic research, with quite varying conclusions reached by distinguished scholars.

Throughout Acts 15 we have both orders of the two men's names again, but verse 2 emphasises *their unanimity in rejecting the need for the Gentiles to be circumcised.* In due course, Jews came to Antioch from Judea (Jerusalem). Paul and Barnabas had to face 'great dissension and debate' (στάσεως καὶ ζητήσεως οὐκ ὀλίγη - *staseōs kai zētēseōs ouk oligē*) from them. This English translation understates the seriousness of the disputation. The Greek word στάσις is only otherwise used in the NT to describe an insurrection or violent riot (e.g. Luke 23:19; Acts 23:10), although no violence was used here. But harsh words would have been spoken.[189] Nevertheless, some residual support for

188. See comments on this change of order in Stott, *Acts*, pp. 221, 246; Marshall, *Acts*, p. 220; Bruce, *Acts*, pp. 251, 276.

189. cf. Galatians 1:7; 5:10.

the circumcision party remained with some Jews in Antioch, as seen in Gal. 2:11–4 (see below). This event is described in Acts 15:1-2.

Eventually, Paul, Barnabas (note the name order twice in Acts 15:2)[190] and others (including Titus – Gal. 2:2-3) were sent by the church at Antioch to meet with the apostles for the famous Council of Jerusalem, where Cephas and James were the prominent speakers after listening to 'Barnabas and Paul' (Acts 15:12). James' critical speech, which settled the matter, mentions 'Paul and Barnabas' (v. 22) and 'Barnabas and Paul' (v. 25), indicating the high respect accorded both men, each of whom were given 'the right hand of fellowship' by James, Cephas, and John (note the order in Gal. 2:9) in recognition of their mission to the Gentiles. In his speech, James observes that 'we [the Jerusalem church] have heard that some of our number *to whom we gave no instruction* have disturbed you with their words, unsettling your souls' (Acts 15:24, emphasis added). A wise description of the type of people represented by these Jewish zealots is provided (in a different context but applying the same principle) by Moffatt in his commentary on 1 Corinthians.

> In a final article on the Oxford Movement, written in 1839, just before he went over to the Roman Church, Newman remarked that in any such movement 'there will ever be a number of persons professing the opinions of the party ... too young to be wise, too generous to be cautious, too warm to be sober, or too intellectual to be humble. Such persons will be very apt to attach themselves to particular persons, to use particular names, to say things merely because others do, and to act in a party-spirited way'.[191]

Acts 15:26 is translated 'men who have risked their lives' (NASB, NIV); however, this seems to be an exaggeration when seen in comparison with the deeds of Prisca and Aquila (Rom. 16:4). A more appropriate translation of παραδεδωκόσι (*paradedōkosi*)

---

190. Bruce, *Acts*, p. 291 raises the issue in the context of Acts 15:12.

191. Moffatt, *1 Corinthians*, p. 9. This was, of course, especially applicable to 1 Corinthians 1:11. See the entry for Chloe.

– from παραδίδωμι (*paradidōmi*), a word with many meanings[192] – is the literal meaning: men 'who have handed over their souls'.[193]

6. The Incident at Antioch

This incident is one of the most critical points in the development of Christian theology concerning justification by faith alone. It is dealt with more fully in the entry for Cephas.

At some time, Cephas himself stayed in Antioch (Gal. 4:11), the timing of which is an important piece of the Pauline chronological puzzle. Cephas was there for sufficient time for him to be seen enjoying table fellowship with Gentile Christians. However, in Galatians 2:11–4, Paul wrote that he 'opposed him to his face' because, after the arrival of pro-circumcision Jews 'from James',[194] Cephas 'feared the party of the circumcision' and began to revert to Jewish dietary customs (Gal. 2:12). This background is necessary because it involved Barnabas, who had been such a faithful companion of Paul: from his introduction of Paul to the Jerusalem church to his emphatic support of Paul over the critical issue that Gentile Christians did not need to be circumcised. Together, they achieved one of the most important early defences of justification by faith alone.

> *The other Jews* will mean other converted Jews in Antioch. We have no way of knowing how many of them there were, but clearly there were enough to create a problem for people like Paul. That they *dissembled* means that they were acting hypocritically. Paul doubtless expected strong support from Barnabas, who had been with him on the notable first missionary journey when so many Gentiles had been brought into the church without any suggestion that they ought to be circumcised. But *even Barnabas* was caught up in the movement that urged that Jews be Jews even if they were Christians. He does not think of Barnabas as doing this out of conviction and willingly, but as one *carried away with their hypocrisy.* Until now Barnabas had gone along with Paul, but evidently felt that he could not oppose Peter. Paul and Barnabas had been through a lot

---

192. See NASBEC, p. 1554, ref. *3860*.

193. Parsons and Culy, *Acts*, p. 299.

194. This may be the event described by James in Acts 15:24, where these men may have been of the 'James party' in Jerusalem. See the entry for Cephas regarding these men.

> together. Barnabas had brought Paul into the fellowship of believers in Jerusalem when those believers were all afraid of him, doubting the reality of his conversion (Acts 9:26-28). And it was Barnabas who brought Paul into the church at Antioch (Acts 11:25-26), Barnabas who accompanied Paul to Jerusalem with gifts to the poor saints there (Acts 11:30), and Barnabas who worked with Paul on that first missionary journey (Acts 13:2f.). So it is not surprising that Paul evidently took this man's defection very hard. He of all men would have been expected to stand with Paul. Paul does not speak of his colleague as taking the initiative, he was *carried away*.[195]

Unfortunately, Cephas' backsliding to accommodate the visiting Jews was undoubtedly the first falling out between Paul and Barnabas because Paul writes that 'The rest of the Jews joined him [Cephas] in hypocrisy, with the result that even Barnabas was carried away by their hypocrisy' (Gal. 2:13). The Greek word for 'carried away' (συναπήχθη – *sunapēchthē*) can mean 'seduce', which seems appropriate here.[196] Commentators seem to ignore the fact that Barnabas was a Levite (of the priestly tribe) and that this may have been an unconscious bias in his siding with the circumcision group. Paul must have felt let down that his close associate was enticed to compromise such a critical issue of Christian doctrine that they had defended at great personal risk to Barnabas' reputation in the Jerusalem church. Notwithstanding his difficult circumstances, 'Like Jesus, Paul remained unmoved. His steadfastness of character was upset neither by flattery nor by opposition.'[197]

> If Paul had not taken his stand against Peter that day, either the whole Christian church would have drifted into a Jewish backwater and stagnated, or there would have been a permanent rift between Jewish and Gentile Christendom, 'one Lord, but two Lord's tables'

---

195. L. L. Morris, *Galatians: Paul's Charter of Christian Freedom* (Leicester: InterVarsity Press, 1996), pp. 79-80. D. J. Moo, *Galatians*, BECNT (Grand Rapids: Baker Academic, 2013), pp. 141-52, provides an excellent and lengthy comment on this incident but virtually ignores Barnabas' involvement. The same can be said of the excellent commentary in T. R. Schreiner, *Galatians*, ZETNC (Grand Rapids: Zondervan, 2010), pp. 135-49.

196. Strong, *Greek Dictionary of the New Testament*, p. 69, ref. *4879*.

197. Stott, *Acts*, 233; see also Bruce, *Acts*, p. 302.

(Lightfoot). Paul's outstanding courage on that occasion in resisting Peter preserved both the truth of the gospel and the international brotherhood of the church.[198]

7. The Dispute over Mark

Regrettably, things eventually fell apart between Paul and Barnabas, as described in Acts 15:35-39. Regarding τόν … βαρναβᾶν in Acts 15:39, Parsons and Culy note that,

> Levinsohn (1987, 103) argues that the use of the article with the proper name here indicates that that the reader's attention is being directed away from Barnabas as he leaves the scene. Indeed, Luke does not mention Barnabas again at all.[199]

Their 'sharp disagreement' (παροξυσμὸς – *paroxusmos*) as to whether John Mark should accompany them (on a return journey to see how believers were faring) could only be resolved by their separation. This Greek word for disagreement is associated with great distress (Acts 17:16) and, probably, anger (cf. 1 Cor. 13:5) between two men who had been so close to one another.[200] Perhaps Barnabas was trying to protect the reputation of his close relative, Mark (a relationship never mentioned by Luke). This and the incident with Cephas in Antioch would reflect Barnabas' personality as 'son of encouragement', where his nature was to smooth over differences rather than resort to the 'hard' tactics of Paul.[201] In the event, Barnabas left Antioch and sailed to Cyprus with Mark.

> It is a pity that the dispute was allowed to generate such bitterness; it might not have done so but for the memory of the incident at Antioch when 'even Barnabas', as Paul says, followed Peter's example in withdrawing from the society of Gentile Christians (Gal. 2:13). After that, it is doubtful that Paul and Barnabas could ever be so happy in their association as they had once been. The old mutual

---

198. J. R. W. Stott, *The Message of Galatians* (Leicester: InterVarsity Press, 1968), p. 52.

199. Parsons and Culy, *Acts*, p. 304.

200. With regard to this dispute, see the advice of Motyer in settling such differences in the entry for Euodia and Syntyche.

201. See Marshall, *Acts*, p. 258. For a lengthy comment on this issue, see R. A. Cole, *The Epistle of Paul to the Galatians*, p. 76.

confidence had been damaged and could not be restored: 'never glad confident morning again'. It is not Luke's policy to record such disagreements on points of principle, but the disagreement on a personal matter which he does record here can be read with greater understanding in the light of Paul's account in his letter to the Galatians. Even so, the present disagreement was overruled for good: instead of one missionary journey and pastoral expedition there were two, Barnabas took Mark and went back to Cyprus to continue the evangelisation of his native island; Paul visited the young churches of Anatolia.[202]

8. Concluding Comments

One can see divine intervention in the separation of Paul and Barnabas for missionary work (Eph. 1:11). Had Barnabas journeyed with Paul to Philippi, for example, as a Jew he would not have been protected as Paul was by Roman citizenship (notwithstanding the treatment received by him and Silvanus), which in those circumstances, could have proved to be fatal for Barnabas (see Acts 16:22-4; 22:25).

We do not know the fate of Barnabas, but he was known to the church at Corinth because of 1 Corinthians 9:6, otherwise Paul could not mention the same issue regarding them both. It is clear that Barnabas and Paul were not in Corinth at the same time; however, the same issue of not working (while preaching) was a matter of dispute among the Corinthians. It is relevant to note that 1 Corinthians 9 discusses the entitlements of an apostle.[203] By Barnabas' inclusion in this issue, Paul not only recognises Barnabas as apostle but also as one who was devoted to preaching the gospel in preference to working for a living as per Paul (see Acts 18:5). No commentator argues that Barnabas may have actually been *in Corinth* at some stage, but it is probable given this direct reference to him.

---

202. Bruce, *Acts*, p. 302.

203. While 'human rights' must be excluded, it is clear from the Greek philosophers that 'entitlements' were due to many different people in the ancient world: see Rist, *Human Value*. Paul takes up this point to counter those who considered themselves 'wise' in human terms.

> *Barnabas* is mentioned for the first and only time in this letter [1 Corinthians]. Presumably, he was known to the Corinthians; otherwise Paul would not be mentioning him .... This reference to Barnabas was written from Ephesus toward the end of Paul's third missionary journey, and the way Paul refers to him implies that they are still good friends.[204]

The final mention of Barnabas is in Colossians 4:10, in which Paul sends greetings from 'Mark, the cousin of Barnabas'. Mark was the reason for Paul's separation from Barnabas but reconciliation with Paul has now occurred and it is fitting for Paul to note his relationship with the friend who first befriended him in Jerusalem. The mention of his name in Col. 4:10 suggests that Barnabas had also travelled to the province of Asia, presumably Ephesus. He may also have ventured further westward so that he was known (by reputation, at least) in the towns around Colosse since his name would otherwise mean nothing in Col. 4:10. Given his exclusion from the latter part of Acts, we do not know precisely where he travelled.

Barnabas must be recorded as one of the most outstanding members of earliest Christianity.

Carpus

2 Timothy 4:13

[13] When you come, bring the cloak which I left at Troas with Carpus, and the books, especially the parchments.

Carpus (a Latin name meaning 'fruit'),[205] was a Christian living in Troas, which was the seaport of the Roman province Mysia in what is now north-western Turkey (near the Dardanelles). Troas derived its name from the nearby ancient ruins of Troy. 'Paul visited Troas in earlier times and ministered there (Acts 16:8, 11; 20:6-12; cf. 2 Cor. 2:12).'[206] Paul informs Timothy that he had left his cloak with Carpus and requests that Timothy brings it to him before winter. Fellows suggests that Carpus 'may have been

204. Fitzmyer, *First Corinthians*, p. 360.

205. HSIBD, p. 210.

206. Yarbrough, *Letters to Timothy and Titus*, p. 450.

Paul's host in Troas'.[207] This may be the same winter that Paul was planning to spend in Nicopolis (Titus 3:12).

This sentence provides much interest when the Greek text is considered because it contains a number of unique or rare inclusions in the NT. The following quotations are from Perkins' analysis of the text:

> **τὸν φαιλόνην**. A NT *hapax legomonon*. BDAG (p. 1046) indicates that this may be a transliteration of a Latin word, *paenula*. This term refers to a 'woollen outer garment covering the whole body, a kind of cloak or mantle worn on journeys and also in the city in rainy weather' (Lewis and Short, p. 1289). Placing the object first in the clause gives it some prominence and marks it as the topic of the discourse.
>
> **ἀπέλιπον**. The verb can describe things or people left behind in certain locations (2 Tim. 4:20; Titus 1:5). These are the only uses in the Pauline Epistles.
>
> **παρὰ κάρπῳ**. This is the only use of παρὰ + dative in the Pauline Epistles. The personal name κάρπος may be Latin in origin and is known from the papyri, but it is a *hapax legomenon* in the NT.
>
> **Φέρε**. This verb only occurs here in the Pauline Epistles.[208]

A description of Paul's cloak follows: 'In Greek, it was called a φαιλόνης (*phailonēs*), a circular outer garment made of heavy cloth with a hole in the middle for the head to go through.'[209] 'It was made by sewing two pieces of cloth together with slits, rather than sleeves, for the arms and it fell below the knees. It was particularly needed as a winter garment because it was used to cover its owner while sleeping.'[210] This was especially the case for the poor, of whom Paul was a member (cf. Exod. 22:27). It is of note, given Calvin's comments below, that Strong's Concordance refers to φελόνη (without ς), whereas the UBS Greek text uses φαιλόνης, which may have another meaning as claimed by Calvin.[211]

---

207. R. G. Fellows, 'Name Giving by Paul and the Destination of Acts', *TynBul* 67, no. 2 (2016): p. 261.

208. Perkins, *Pastoral Letters*, pp. 232-33.

209. Guthrie, *Pastoral Epistles*, p. 173.

210. HSIBD, p. 312.

211. Strong, *Greek Dictionary of the New Testament*, p. 75, ref. 5341.

The text does not make it clear whether 'the books, especially the parchments' were also held by Carpus, but it is probable that they were. Two different items are mentioned here. Paul is particularly concerned that Timothy brings to him 'the books' (τὰ βιβλία – *ta biblia*) (translated 'scrolls' in the NIV) and, 'especially' (μάλιστα – *malista*, a word of special emphasis, used infrequently in the NT), the parchments (τὰς μεμβράνας – *tas membranas*). The books (scrolls) were probably writings on papyrus, but the more valuable parchments would have been writings on animal skins. One can only speculate as to their contents: there may have been some letters from churches, passages of Scripture or, perhaps, documents like Paul's proof of Roman citizenship.

However, Calvin's commentary on 2 Timothy 4:13 introduces a completely different interpretation of the verse:

> *Bring the cloak which I left at Troas.* As to the meaning of the word φελόνη, commentators are not agreed; for some think that it is a chest or box for containing books, and others that it is a garment used by travellers, and fitted for defending against cold and rain. Whether the one interpretation or the other be adopted, how comes it that Paul should give orders to have either a garment or a chest brought to him from a place so distant, as if there were not workmen, or as if there were not abundance both of cloth and timber? If it be said, that it was a chest filled with books, or manuscripts, or epistles, the difficulty will be solved; for such materials could not have been procured at any price. But, because many will not admit the conjecture, I willingly translate it by the word *cloak*. Nor is there any absurdity in saying that Paul desired to have it brought from so great a distance, because that garment, through long use, would be more comfortable for him, and he wished to avoid expense.
>
> Yet (to own the truth) I give the preference to the former interpretation; more especially because Paul immediately afterwards mentions *books and parchments*. It is evident from this, that the Apostle had not given over reading, though he was already preparing for death. Where are those who think that they have made so great progress that they do not need any more exercise? Which of them will dare to compare himself with Paul? Still more does this expression refute the madness of those men who – despising

> books, and condemning all reading – boast of nothing but their own ἐνθουσιασμοὺς divine inspirations. But let us know that this passage gives to all believers a recommendation of constant reading, that they may profit by it.
>
> Here someone will ask, 'What does Paul mean by asking for a robe or cloak, if he perceived that his death was at hand?' This difficulty also induces me to interpret the word as denoting a chest, though there might have been some use of the 'cloak' which is unknown in the present day; and therefore I give myself little trouble about these matters.[212]

Notwithstanding this comment, the word φαιλόνης is generally accepted as meaning 'cloak'. Marshall with Towner comment that Calvin's view is 'The older view, no longer accepted'.[213] However, they offer lengthy comments about the documents left with Carpus.[214] There is lengthy debate about the nature of the documents and the materials on which they were written (papyrus and parchment). At one point, they state that 'It should be remembered, however, that copies of books of the OT would be quite bulky!'[215] In these circumstances, the interpretation by Calvin may well be valid. Given the numerous Christians in Rome who knew Paul's situation by the time this letter was written (cf. Romans 16), it seems more than likely that a cloak could have been made available to Paul far more quickly than waiting for it to be delivered from distant Troas.

CEPHAS (also known as SIMON PETER)

1 CORINTHIANS 1:12

[12] *Now I mean this, that each one of you is saying, '**I am** with Paul', or '**I am** with Apollos', or '**I am** with Cephas', or '**I am** with Christ'.* (Emphasis added.)

---

212. Calvin, 'Commentaries on the Second Epistle to Timothy', *Calvin's Commentaries*, vol. 21, pp. 265-6. Although this request is discussed in Yarbrough, *Letters to Timothy and Titus*, p. 450, the name of Carpus is not mentioned.

213. Marshall, *Pastoral Epistles*, p. 818, n. 14. I suspect that Calvin may be closer to the truth than many imagine.

214. Marshall, *Pastoral Epistles*, p. 819-21.

215. ibid., p. 820.

1 Corinthians 3:22

[22] whether Paul or Apollos or Cephas, or the world or life or death, or things present or things to come; all things belong to you,

1 Corinthians 9:5

[5] Do we not have a right to take along a believing wife, even as the rest of the apostles and the brothers of the Lord, and Cephas?

1 Corinthians 15:5

[5] and that he appeared to Cephas, then to the twelve.

Galatians 1:18

[18] Then three years later I went up to Jerusalem to become acquainted with Cephas, and stayed with him for fifteen days.

Galatians 2:7-14

[7] But on the contrary, seeing that I had been entrusted with the gospel to the uncircumcised, just as Peter had been to the circumcised

[8] (for he who was at work for Peter in his apostleship to the circumcised was at work for me also to the Gentiles), ...

[9] ... and recognising the grace that had been given to me, James and Cephas and John, who were reputed to be pillars, gave to me and Barnabas the right hand of fellowship, so that we might go to the Gentiles, and they to the circumcised.

[10] They only asked us to remember the poor – the very thing I also was eager to do.

[11] But when Cephas came to Antioch, I opposed him to his face, because he stood condemned.

[12] For prior to the coming of some men from James, he used to eat with the Gentiles; but when they came, he began to withdraw and separate himself, fearing those from the circumcision.

[13] The rest of the Jews joined him in hypocrisy, with the result that even Barnabas was carried away by their hypocrisy.

[14] But when I saw that they were not straightforward about the truth of the gospel, I said to Cephas in the presence of all, 'If you, being a Jew, live like the Gentiles and not like the Jews, how is it that you compel the Gentiles to live like Jews?'

1. Background

Cephas is better known to Christians as Simon Peter, one of the first disciples called by Jesus (Matt. 4:18-20; Mark 1:16-8;

Luke 5:1-11). Paul's letters only refer to 'Cephas', not 'Peter'; therefore, only that name is used in this book despite the NASB use of 'Peter'.[216] A book could be written about Cephas alone; however, this entry deals primarily with the relationship between Paul and Cephas. According to John's Gospel, Cephas was the second disciple of Jesus, having been introduced to the Lord by his brother Andrew (John 1:40). Andrew was a follower of John the Baptist. This verse tells us that, when introduced to the Lord, 'Jesus looked at him, and said, "You are Simon the son of John; you shall be called Cephas" (which is translated Peter)'. The Greek is σὺ κληθήσῃ κηφᾶς ὃ ἑρμηνεύεται πέτρος – *su klēthēsē Cēphas ho ermēneuetai Petros. Cephas* is Aramaic for 'rock' and *Petros* is the same word in Greek. In his letters, Paul used the name assigned to this man by the Lord, reflecting Paul's respect both for Jesus' nomenclature and for Peter's role as leader of the Twelve.

Cephas and his brother, Andrew, were fishermen on Lake Galilee. They lived in Bethsaida (John 1:44), near the entrance of the River Jordan into the north of Lake Galilee; both Capernaum and Bethsaida were located on its western shore. Cephas was married and Jesus healed his mother-in-law (Matt. 8:14-5).

While there is great reliance on the Book of Acts for historical information on earliest Christianity, Luke makes no mention of the interaction of Paul and Cephas, who last appears in Acts 15:7.[217] Therefore, we only have Paul's letters as evidence for his interactions with Cephas.

2. Jerusalem

Acts 9:27 notes that Barnabas took Paul to meet 'the apostles' three years after his conversion.[218] From Galatians 1:18 we know that Paul met with Cephas, staying with him for fifteen days. During that time, he did not meet 'any other of the apostles, except James, the Lord's brother'.

---

216. The one exception, where Paul uses 'Peter', is Galatians 2:8, 9.

217. Similarly, Barnabas disappears from Luke's account in Acts after chapter 15.

218. Moo, *Galatians*, p. 108.

In Acts 15, Luke describes at length the mission of Paul, Barnabas, Titus, and other believers to Jerusalem fourteen years later to meet the leaders of the church there (the Jerusalem Conference).[219] A major topic of discussion was whether circumcision was necessary for Gentile believers. Having described their experiences, the Jerusalem leaders were convinced that the Holy Spirit rested on the visitors (both Jew and Gentile) and that grace had been given to them (Gal. 2:9; cf. Acts 10:47; 15:8, 9).

In Galatians 2:9 Paul writes: 'And having recognised [γνόντες – *gnontes*] the grace having been given to me, James and Cephas and John, "the ones having the reputation of being pillars" [οἱ δοκοῦντες στῦλοι εἶναι – *hoi dokountes stuloi einai*], gave the right hand of fellowship [κοινωνίας – *koinōnias*] to me and Barnabas, that we should go to the Gentiles [τὰ ἔθνη – *ta ethnē*] and they to the circumcised [τὴν περιτομήν – *tēn peritomēn*].' This verse needs careful examination.

Paul acknowledged that James and Cephas and John recognised him as a fellow believer (note the use of κοινωνία – *koinōnia*). In the NT the verb for 'reputed' (δοκέω – *dokeō*) is often used with an air of scepticism about the authenticity of a person's claim (cf. Luke 22:24; Phil. 3:4; James 1:26). Although the Jerusalem leaders had accepted Paul's understanding of the gospel, it may be the case that, within his own spirit, Paul was yet to be fully convinced of the Jerusalem leaders' complete repudiation of the Mosaic Law and acceptance of the *gospel of grace alone*. A more conciliatory analysis regarding James is provided by Cole.[220] The subsequent episode at Antioch recorded in Galatians 2 may provide some justification for Paul's reservations at that time.

> Acts 15 shows a puzzled but loyal James accepting the palpable differences of approach and method in a kind of 'interim agreement'; but his real embarrassment is manifest in Acts 21:17-26. The irony of the situation is seen in the fact that it was this attempted compromise

219. Like F. F. Bruce, *Peter, Stephen, James & John: Studies in Non-Pauline Christianity* (Grand Rapids: Eerdmans, 1979), p. 28, n. 31, and many other commentators, I consider the 'fourteen years' to date from Paul's conversion.

220. See Cole, *Galatians*, pp. 64-70.

> that, humanly speaking, caused Paul's arrest, imprisonment, and ultimate death, although to Paul this had a deeper explanation and meaning in the purposes of God.[221]

This issue of Paul's comments about the 'pillars' is considered at length by R. N. Longenecker, whose conclusion follows.

> The ironic or dismissive tone in Paul's usage need not, however, be viewed as stemming from either (1) a feeling that to call the Jerusalem apostles 'pillars' devalued his own apostleship (so Wilckens) or (2) a theology of merit being so bound up with the pillars of Israel that to call the Church's leaders by a title associated with them would only tend to confuse the gospel (so Aus). Rather, the Jewish Christians of Jerusalem had legitimately, from their perspective, applied the term 'pillars' to their three leaders, the Judaisers, it seems, were using that attribution for their own purposes. So we may believe that Paul had no objection to the title in its original Christian context (cf. *1 Clem.* 5, where the title is applied to both Peter and Paul), connoting, as it did, a theology and ecclesiology with which he agreed. What he seems to be opposed to is the Judaisers' inflated adulation of the Jerusalem leaders and their use of the title, setting both them and it against Paul.[222]

3. 'Peter' Named in Galatians 2:7-8

The Greek text of Galatians 2:7-8 is unusual because of the change in name chosen by Paul to describe the first apostle. Paul uses Πέτρος (*Petros*) here but elsewhere in Galatians 2 (and all his other letters) he uses Κηφᾶς (*Cephas*). Some commentators have overlooked this point. Comments by Bruce and Morris help to clarify the issue.[223] R. N. Longenecker is quoted below.

> There are, however, two features of language in this statement that appear somewhat non-Pauline: (1) the references to 'a gospel to the

---

221. Cole, *Galatians*, p. 69. But see G. S. Duncan, *The Epistle of Paul to the Galatians*, MNTC (London: Hodder and Stoughton, 1934), p. 57, concerning the attitude of James regarding the incident at Antioch, described below.

222. R. N. Longenecker, *Galatians*, pp. 57-8, but see pp. 43-59 for his full discussion of Galatians 2:1-10.

223. Bruce, *Peter, Stephen, James & John*, pp. 30-2; Morris, *Galatians*, pp. 72-3, esp. n. 28.

uncircumcised' and another gospel 'to the circumcised', which seem at variance with the insistence on only one gospel in 1:6-9; 2:11-16, passim, and (2) the use of 'Peter' rather than 'Cephas', which occurs in Paul's letters only here (contra P46 A D G etc.; for Paul's use of 'Cephas', see Gal. 1:18; 2:9, 11, 14; 1 Cor. 1:12; 3:22; 9:5; 15:5). Furthermore, the material between the participles ἰδόντες, 'when they saw', of verse 7a and γνόντες, 'knowing', of verse 9a – which appears to be introduced by a ὅτι *recitativum* (i.e., a 'that' which introduces a cited portion) – can be abstracted from its context without destroying the sentence.

Now it is possible, of course, to lay too much weight on the difference between two kinds of gospels here and Paul's insistence elsewhere that there is only one gospel, for the point here is not with regard to content but audience and type of outreach. And it may, indeed, be that Paul used 'Cephas' and 'Peter' rather indifferently, with their easy interchangeability evident only here in his writings. Yet such linguistic and structural features as cited above suggest the possibility that Paul here is using expressions and words of others for his own purposes, as he frequently does elsewhere in his letters.

Oscar Cullman proposed that Paul 'here cites an official document, in the Greek translation in which the form Πέτρος was used' (*Peter*, 20; idem, *TDNT* 6:100). And Eric Dinkler, in support of Cullman, has attempted to reconstruct that official document, assuming that at the Jerusalem Council an official decree was in both Aramaic and Greek and that Paul is here quoting verbatim the Greek version to buttress his argument (*VF*1-3 [1953-55] pp. 182-3). Such a reconstruction of events and documents, however, is somewhat hypothetical, particularly on a 'South Galatian' view of provenance. Betz's evaluation of the matter, whether with reference to the Jerusalem Council or some earlier meeting, is much to be preferred: (1) that 'the non-Pauline notions of the 'gospel of circumcision' and 'of uncircumcision' as well as the name 'Peter' may very well come from an underlying official statement', but (2) that 'rather than "quoting" from the written protocol, Paul reminds the readers of the agreements by using terms upon which the parties had agreed' (*Galatians*, p. 97).[224]

224. R. N. Longenecker, *Galatians*, pp. 55-6. Dumbrell, *Galatians*, p. 27, suggests that 'the reference may be solemn or official'. See also Duncan, *Galatians*, pp. 48-54.

4. Corinth

From the various mentions of Cephas in 1 Corinthians, it seems apparent that Cephas had at some stage visited the Christians in Corinth, probably after Paul's departure from that city.

In 1 Corinthians 1–3 Paul challenges the Corinthian church about various factions that have arisen, including the separation of believers into various groups that claimed to be following a particular leader. In his lengthy exposition about the need for unity, Paul notes that one of the leaders being followed was Cephas (1 Cor. 1:12; 3:22), another being Apollos and, of course, Paul. Paul is most critical of the Corinthians' behaviour, but he does not deny the leadership qualities attributed to each person. He wants unity in Christ. The use of Cephas in 1 Corinthians 1–3 serves two purposes. First, it identifies him as the nominal head of a faction within the church. Secondly, it suggests that the 'Cephas' faction may have been composed primarily of Jews or, possibly, Jews more committed to Jewish customs than to Paul's gospel of grace alone.

In asserting the entitlements of apostles in his first letter to the Corinthians, Paul defends Cephas for taking his wife with him on missionary work. Paul states that this was a right of 'the rest of the apostles, and the brothers of the Lord' (1 Cor. 9:5). Luke never mentions this in Acts. Paul is well aware of Cephas' history (e.g. 1 Cor. 15:5). As an apostle, he had certain entitlements, which were strongly defended by Paul. Barnabas was also included as one who shared the same rights (1 Cor. 9:1-12).

> Although Cephas would be part of the 'apostles' mentioned earlier in the verse, he is singled out and mentioned last simply because of his importance in the early church and because his influence was already invoked in Corinth (1:12 [see NOTE there]; 3:22). Here Paul is saying that Cephas was accompanied on his ministry by his wife, whose name is unknown (see Klauck, *Hausgemeinde*, pp. 30, 59). To see Cephas as the head of the opposition to Paul in Corinth goes beyond the evidence provided in this letter [1 Corinthians].[225]

225. Fitzmyer, *First Corinthians*, p. 360.

Similarly, in 1 Corinthians 15:5, Cephas is mentioned in relation to Christ's resurrection not only because of the readers' familiarity with him but also because he was the leader of the Twelve.

> The fourth element of the kerygmatic fragment [see earlier comments, p. 548] mentions Christ's appearance to Cephas, thus preserving an ancient recollection, which Luke also records independently in his Gospel (24:34, *ontōs ēgerthē ho kyrios kai ōphthē Simōni*, 'the Lord has truly been raised and has appeared to Simon'). This independent attestation makes it almost certain that *ōphthē kēphā* was the real ending of the primitive kerygma, which has sometimes been questioned. The mention of Cephas takes for granted that he is well known. Apart from Gal. 2:7-8, it is the name Paul normally uses for Simon Peter (see Note on 1:12; cf. 3:22; 9:5). Cf. the later (independent?) narrative of the risen Christ's appearance to Peter in John 21:7. Cephas is mentioned first because of the prominence that he already enjoyed among the followers of Jesus; cf. John 21:15-18. As used here, it is a pre-Pauline Peter formula. *Pace* Conzelmann ('On the Analysis', p. 22), this appearance to Cephas did not make 'him the foundation' of the church and leader of the Twelve; it was the other way round: He appeared to Cephas because he was already the leader.[226]

The question as to whether and when Cephas was in Corinth is impossible to answer from Scripture alone, but Eusebius did suggest that, at one stage, Cephas was in Corinth.[227]

As for *Cephas*, Peter's name in Aramaic, although we cannot be certain, it is likely that he had also visited Corinth after Paul's departure. Barrett argues for this on the basis of the four references in 1 Corinthians in which Paul mentions Peter. Taken together, these make more sense if Peter had visited the city. In 1 Corinthians 1:12, Barrett contends that the genitive case of the names signifies agencies of conversion, with verses 13-17 referring to the baptism of converts by those persons named in verse 12 (obviously excluding Christ): 'converts tended to align themselves with the evangelist under whom they had been won to the faith.' Secondly, Paul, Apollos, and Cephas may be listed in 3:22 as teachers from whom

226. ibid., p. 549.

227. See ibid., pp. 143-5.

the community had directly benefited. Thirdly, 9:5 may hint that Peter had visited Corinth with his wife, both of whom enjoyed their hospitality. And in 15:5 Paul may single out Cephas as someone with whom the Corinthians were personally familiar. If Peter had been to Corinth, and some Corinthians had used his name as a rallying point, Paul's silence in regard to him in his response to Corinthian factionalism, except in 3:22, indicates that the Peter group was not as much a problem as the Apollos party. If Peter himself had somehow been at fault in the Corinthian situation facing Paul, we would have expected a direct and robust response from Paul, as in his disagreement with Peter reported in Galatians 2.[228]

5. The Incident in Antioch

The majority view holds that Galatians 2:1-10 relates to Acts 15 and that, therefore, the Antioch crisis occurred after the Jerusalem council. Moreover, despite the liberal ruling on circumcision in favour of Paul's position in Acts 15:19, the Jerusalem decree by James also favored Jewish conservatism, because to abstain 'from what is strangled and from blood' in Acts 15:20 probably referred to the kosher laws, effectively regulating table fellowship between Jewish and Gentile Christians on Jewish terms. Contra the majority view, I seek to support Richard Bauckham's proposal that the Antioch crisis was the lead-up to the Jerusalem council and that the Jerusalem church remained central by providing authoritative direction for the entire Christian mission.[229]

Cephas is mentioned in Galatians concerning two meetings with Paul, one in Jerusalem and a later one in Antioch. Galatians 2:11–6 records one of the most critical events in Christian doctrine and belief. 'This is without doubt one of the most tense and dramatic

228. Ciampa and Rosner, *1 Corinthians*, p. 79.

229. C. Bennema, 'The Ethnic Conflict in Early Christianity: An Appraisal of Bauckham's Proposal on the Antioch Crisis and the Jerusalem Council', *JETS* 56, no. 4 (2013): pp. 753-4. See R. J. Bauckham, 'James and the Jerusalem Church' in *The Book of Acts in its First Century Setting, vol. 4: The Book of Acts in its Palestinian Setting*, ed. B. W. Winter (Grand Rapids: Eerdmans, 1995), pp. 415-80.

episodes in the New Testament. Here are two leading apostles of Jesus Christ face to face in complete and open conflict.'[230] Hundreds of pages must have been written by commentators on the theological implications of this confrontation; however, this book is interested primarily in examining those mentioned in Paul's letters as *people* – human beings with actions, roles, thoughts, and emotions.

I accept the view that, after the Jerusalem Council (see above),[231] Cephas visited Antioch. Following the revelation to Cephas described in Acts 11:1-18, he was pleased to eat and have fellowship with Jews and Gentiles in that city which was about 240 miles (400 km) north of Jerusalem. But when 'certain men from James' (ἐλθεῖν τινας ἀπὸ ἰακώβου – *elthein tinas apo Iakōbou*) arrived in Antioch, Cephas changed his behaviour completely and would not eat (i.e. have fellowship) with Gentiles.

This behaviour contrasts so starkly with the account in Acts 11 where Cephas goes to considerable trouble to justify to the circumcision party his eating with Gentiles. Acts 11:18 notes that, earlier in Jerusalem when Cephas' detractors heard his explanation, they 'became silent' (ἡσύχασαν – *hēsuchasan*). Given that experience, he should have been ready to defend himself against such accusations by the same group.

> Then one day a group arrived in Antioch from Jerusalem. They were all professing Christian believers, but they were Jewish in origin, indeed strict Pharisees (Acts 15:5). They came 'from James' (Gal. 2:12), the leader of the Jerusalem church. This does not mean that they had his authority, for he later denied this

230. Stott, *Galatians*, p. 49. In pp. 49-58 he provides an excellent analysis of the personal issues for Cephas, Paul, *and us* in these verses. He could be quoted at length.

231. The chronology of these two meetings is disputed by many scholars. For example, Duncan, *Galatians*, p. 55, and Cole, *Galatians*, p. 69, suggest that the text in Galatians seems to indicate that the Antioch visit occurred after the Jerusalem Council. Stott, *Galatians*, p. 55, is of the opposite view, but I regard Duncan and Cole as correct. *Regardless of the chronology, the Antioch incident is a critical turning point for the gospel of grace and justification by faith alone.*

> (Acts 15:24), but rather that they *claimed* to have it. They posed as apostolic delegates.[232]

Regardless of the authority of the men from James, Paul would have none of their criticism.

> James was the head of the church in Jerusalem, already mentioned in [Gal.] 1:19; 2:9; and we may take it that these men had come with his authority and approval, probably bearing letters of commendation from him (cf. 2 Cor. 3:1) – had they merely made use of his name to add weight to their pretensions, Paul would have made that plain.[233]

Stott and Duncan appear to discount Acts 15:24, where James says, 'we have heard that some of our number *to whom we gave no instruction* have disturbed you with their words' (emphasis added).

In any event, Paul confronted (ἀντέστην – *antestēn*) Cephas personally: 'to his face' (κατὰ πρόσωπον – *kata prosopon*). This is strong language. The strength of the verb ἀνθίστημι is reflected by Paul's use of it in Ephesians 6:13 ('stand your ground,' NIV) and Acts 6:10 ('stand up against,' NIV). The accusation was made before everyone (Gal. 2:14); this was not a private dispute. Paul acted so forcefully because Cephas stood condemned (κατεγνωσμένος – *kategnōsmenos*). The NASB provides a marginal note: 'or self-condemned.' He was guilty of one of Jesus' most condemned behaviours: hypocrisy.

> Paul's charge is serious, but plain. It is that Peter and the others acted in insincerity, and not from personal conviction. Their withdrawal from table-fellowship with Gentile believers was not prompted by any theological principle, but by craven fear of a small pressure group. In fact, Peter did in Antioch precisely what Paul had refused to do in Jerusalem, namely yield to pressure. The same Peter who had denied his Lord for fear of a maidservant now denied Him again for fear of the circumcision party. He still believed the gospel, but failed to practice it. His conduct 'did not square' with it (NEB). He

232. Stott, *Galatians*, p. 50.

233. Duncan, *Galatians*, p. 57. In pp. 55-63 he provides an important analysis of the theological and cultural issues at stake for Paul and Peter. See Barnett, *Galatians and Earliest Christianity*, p. 118.

> virtually contradicted it by his action, because he lacked the courage of his convictions.[234]

Given what he writes in Galatians 2:11-16 concerning Cephas' behaviour in Antioch, my impression is that Paul was not fully convinced (*as he wrote Galatians 2:9*) of the supposedly high standing attributed to James (the Lord's brother) and Cephas by the Jerusalem church. John (the apostle) does not appear to be criticised.[235] There may have been some reciprocal concern on the part of Cephas. 'Cephas is treated summarily in [Gal.] 2:11; and 2 Pet. 3:15-16 shows what may be regarded as a very cautious attitude to "our beloved brother Paul" that was doubtless characteristic of Cephas in later days at least. Once bitten, twice shy.'[236] I have some sympathy with Cole's view.

6. Summary

Cephas was a complex character, variously convinced of Christ's Messiahship (Mark 8:29), full of bravado (Mark 14:29) and then cowardice (Mark 14:72). He did not react well to unexpected pressure (e.g. Matt. 17:1-4; Gal. 2). Yet he was loyal to his Saviour until the end. It must be said in Cephas' defence that he was only human. Just because he was a disciple with Jesus Himself and a leader of the Jerusalem church, this did not place him beyond fault. Many of us may react as Cephas did when faced with circumstances of pressure or disagreement within our churches when highly contentious issues of doctrine or practice are under examination and the *koinonia* of the fellowship is under threat. But we have the forgiveness offered by Christ.

When the truth of the gospel is at stake, the better choice (cf. Luke 10:41-42) is to unhesitatingly oppose those who wish to change it in any way, as Paul did in Antioch and Jerusalem. The two letters of Peter in the Scriptures confirm his complete acceptance of, and agreement with, the gospel of justification by

---

234. Stott, *Galatians*, p. 52.

235. See entries for James and John for further analysis of this issue regarding each of them.

236. Cole, *Galatians*, p. 69.

faith in Christ alone. Despite his human frailty, Cephas was one of the most outstanding men in earliest Christianity.

Chloe

1 Corinthians 1:11

[11] For I have been informed concerning you, my brethren, by Chloe's people, that there are quarrels among you.

Chloe means 'tender sprout', whose springtime colour was of a greenish-yellowish appearance.[237] In this verse, which has been translated with a variety of meanings, we begin with Paul's precise description of the source of his information about rival parties in the Corinthian church. Paul writes that his informants are 'from the *ones* of Chloe' (ὑπὸ τῶν χλόης – *hupo tōn Chloēs*). This is the same construction used by Paul (ἐκ τῶν ἀριστοβούλου – *ek tōn Aristoboulou*) in Romans 16:10 when he refers to the household of Aristobulus. Therefore, he is not referring to Chloe's family but to some of the slaves in her household.

> He [Paul] mentions explicitly the source of his information so that the Corinthians cannot contest its correctness. We have no other information concerning *Chloe* or *her household*. Chloe, 'the fair or the blonde', is a surname of the goddess Demeter and Chloe may have been a liberated slave. *The household* is to be understood as the *familia*, that is the slaves. Chloe may have been the head of a business, as Lydia was at Philippi (cf. Acts 16:14). Paul did not receive his information from Chloe herself. Her slaves must have come to Ephesus, called on Paul and informed him of the conditions at Corinth. The words *it has been signified unto me concerning you* suppose that Paul at first did not believe conditions were so bad at Corinth, but that, upon questioning the slaves of Chloe, he could only conclude that there were contentions in the church.[238]

These people obviously travelled between Paul's location in Ephesus and Corinth. The greatest difficulty is determining

237. HSIBD, p. 219.

238. F. W. Grosheide, *Commentary on the First Epistle to the Corinthians*, NICNT, reprint 1984 (Grand Rapids: Eerdmans, 1953), p. 35. See Ciampa and Rosner, *1 Corinthians*, p. 55.

where she lived: Ephesus or Corinth? Both locations have their adherents, and some commentators express no opinion. While Grosheide suggests Corinth, Morris suggests that she lived in Ephesus because Paul has named her and that seems plausible.[239] It is more likely that informants would be named if they were not present in the disturbance so as to avoid conflict with the accused.

Calvin insists that Paul is not acting on rumours. These people made it clear ('informed', ἐδηλώθη – *edēlōthē*) to Paul that factions existed in Corinth. The same verb (δηλόω – *dēλόω*) is used in 1 Corinthians 3:13.[240] Paul knows that the Corinthians would know Chloe herself and who 'Chloe's people' were (as surely as we do not know who they were) because Paul names her.

> And that he [Paul] may not be charged with believing too readily what was said, as though he lightly lent his ear to false accusations, he speaks with commendation of his informants, who must have been in the highest esteem, as he did not hesitate to adduce them as competent witnesses against an entire Church.[241]
>
> The reference is probably to her slaves, employees or partners travelling between Ephesus and Corinth on her behalf. Chloe may have been a widow since, as Theissen notes, members of a family were normally identified through the name of the father rather than the mother. That Paul uses her name suggests that she and her relatives or associates belong to the church in Ephesus and have regular links with Corinth. Both cities were vibrant centres for trade.[242]

'Chloe's people' were not circulating gossip; but they were conveyors of critical information to Paul to assist his management of the Corinthian church.

---

239. Morris, *1 Corinthians*, p. 39. Powers, *First Corinthians*, p. 26 (citing Sir William Ramsay) suggests Ephesus, but Fitzmyer, *First Corinthians*, p. 141, suggests that Chloe lived in Corinth. Ephesus is to be preferred.

240. In 1 Corinthians 3:13, Zerwick and Grosvenor, *Grammatical Analysis*, vol. 2, p. 502, translate δηλώσει as 'make clear, show'. See Ciampa and Rosner, *1 Corinthians*, p. 77.

241. Calvin, 'The Argument on the First Epistle to the Corinthians', *Calvin's Commentaries*, p. 64.

242. Ciampa and Rosner, *1 Corinthians*, p. 77. See Fee, 1 *Corinthians*, p. 55.

Because Paul mentions her, that does not mean that she was one of 'the outstanding woman leaders' of the Corinthian church, *pace* Schüssler Fiorenza (*In Memory*, p. 219). Nothing in the text suggests that she was the overseer of a house church or that she sent them to Paul with a message or report; they seem to have been in Ephesus for some other reason and simply told Paul of the situation. In any case, there is no evidence that these people belonged to any of the groups mentioned. Hitchcock ('Who Are') claims that Paul would not have mentioned a Corinthian lady by name in connection with a report that reflected discredit on Corinthian Christians.[243]

The seriousness of the matter and the earnestness of Paul's entreaty to the church is reflected in his use of ἀδελφοί **μου** (*adelphoi* ***mou*** – '***my*** brothers'). This expression is also used in 1 Corinthains 11:33; 15:8.[244]

CLAUDIA

2 TIMOTHY 4:21

[21] Make every effort to come before winter. Eubulus greets you, also Pudens, Linus, Claudia, and all the brethren.

Claudia was a common female Latin name in the first century, meaning 'lame'.[245] This woman was a faithful Christian who remained as a helper to Paul when he was imprisoned for the second time in Rome near the end of his life (2 Tim. 4:6, 17).[246] She was obviously known to Timothy, sending him greetings. She is not mentioned elsewhere in the NT but, again, we see another brave woman willing to assist the gospel.

Since Paul passes on their greetings to Timothy, one wonders why they did not support Paul at his trial (v. 16). Perhaps they lacked social standing to make any difference in such a situation, or perhaps it would have exposed them to inordinate danger to appear to stand at Paul's side. Paul

243. Fitzmyer, *First Corinthians*, p. 141. Hitchcock's comment strengthens the argument for Chloe's residence in Ephesus.

244. Brookins and Longenecker, *1 Corinthians 1-9*, p. 15.

245. HSIBD, p. 239.

246. Stott, *2 Timothy*, p. 118.

> does not feel it necessary to account for these details to Timothy ... The Greek verb is singular because in a series, the verb usually takes its number from the nearest subject nominative ... Claudia was a common name with possible royal associations,[397] but the significance of this possibility for the person named here is uncertain.[398] [247]

Clement

PHILIPPIANS 4:3

[3] *Indeed, true companion, I ask you also, help these women who have shared my struggle in the cause of the gospel, together with Clement as well as the rest of my fellow workers, whose names are in the book of life.*

Clement, a common name of the time (meaning 'merciful'),[248] was a Christian in Philippi, whom Paul regarded as a fellow worker (συνεργός – see *Paul's Use of σύν (sun)* in the introduction) along with a number of others. We do not know why Clement was singled out other than that he was personally known to Paul. He is named after Euodia and Syntyche (Phil. 4:2).

> In their contending for the cause of the gospel they were exposed to the suffering and opposition that always attended Paul's own struggle. The notion of fellowship or participation is brought out in the repetition of the prefix συν- in the terms σύζυγος, συναθλέω, and συνεργός. They were highly valued coworkers who had energetically participated in Paul's apostolic mission, perhaps even when the congregation at Philippi was founded ...
>
> μετὰ καὶ κλήμεντος καὶ τῶν λοιπῶν συνεργῶν μου (*meta kai Klēmentos kai tōn loipōn sunergōn mou*). 'Together with Clement and the rest of my fellow worker.' This phrase should be joined

247. Yarbrough, *Letters to Timothy and Titus*, p. 459. References in this quotation are: [397]R. F. Collins, *1& 2 Timothy and Titus*, New Testament Library (Louisville: Westminster John Knox, 2002), p. 292; [398]For concise assessment of the ancient references and their value, see R. Van Neste, 'Claudia' in H.-J. Klauck et al., *Encyclopaedia of the Bible and its Reception* (Berlin: de Gruyter, 2009), vol. 5, pp. 398-9: 'In the end, there is far too little evidence to make any certain identification of the Claudia mentioned in 2 Tim. 4:21.' For additional reflection on the names in this verse, see H.-W. Neudorfer, *Der zweite Brief des Paulus an Timotheus*, Historisch-theologische Auslegung (Witten: Brockhaus, 2017), pp. 297-8.

248. HSIBD, p. 240.

to συνήθλησάν μοι (*sunēthlēsan moi* – 'contended with me'), not συλλαμβάνου αὐταῖς (*sullambanou autais* – 'help them'). 'Clement' is otherwise unknown to us. His name is Latin, and he may well have been a Philippian Christian who was well known within the church because Paul does not need to identify him.[249]

These three and other unknown fellow workers (συνεργοί) will have their names written in the 'book of life', as per Luke 10:20; Hebrews 12:23, and especially Revelation 3:5; 13:8; 17:8; and 20:15. An OT allusion to the book of life is Isaiah 4:3.

The suggestion that this man is the same person as Clement of Rome is untenable.[250] Interestingly, Clement is not mentioned in Motyer's commentary on Philippians.[251]

It may be the case that the supposedly unnamed person called 'true companion' (γνήσιε σύζυγε – *gnēsie suzuge*) was a person called Syzygus. See the entry under that name. However, most commentators nominate Epaphroditus.

Crescens

2 Timothy 4:10

[10]... for Demas, having loved this present world, has deserted me and gone to Thessalonica; Crescens has gone to Galatia, Titus to Dalmatia.

Crescens is a common Latin name that occurs infrequently in Greek,[252] meaning 'growing'.[253] Crescens was supporting Paul during his second imprisonment in Rome. Nearing his end, Paul writes to Timothy that Crescens 'has gone to Galatia'. There is actually no verb in the Greek text for 'the going' of either Crescens or Titus. There is no sense that Crescens has deserted Paul; nor faithful Titus. Perkins notes that ἐπορεύθη – *eporeuthē* (from the verb πορεύομαι (*poreuomai*), meaning 'to go') is 'implied' in its

249. P. T. O'Brien, *The Epistle to the Philippians: A Commentary on the Greek Text* (Carlisle, UK: Paternoster Press, 1991), pp. 481-2.

250. See Hendriksen, *Philippians*, p. 191, n. 174, and the lengthy note by Lightfoot, *Philippians*, pp. 168-70.

251. J. A. Motyer, *The Message of Philippians*, TBST (Leicester: InterVarsity Press, 1984), pp. 203-4.

252. Marshall with Towner, *Pastoral Epistles,* p. 816; see also Perkins, *Pastoral Letters*, p. 231.

253. HSIBD, p. 264.

reference to Crescens and Titus.[254] We do not know why Crescens left the apostle, but it was probably at Paul's direction that he departed for further missionary work in Galatia.

Crispus

Acts 18:8

[8] Crispus, the leader of the synagogue, believed in the Lord together with his entire household; and many of the Corinthians, as they listened to Paul, were believing and being baptised.

1 Corinthians 1:13-15

[13] Has Christ been divided? Paul was not crucified for you, was he? Or were you baptised in the name of Paul?

[14] I am thankful that I baptised none of you except Crispus and Gaius,

[15] … so that no one would say you were baptised in my name.

Given his Latin name (meaning 'curly'),[255] Crispus was a Hellenised Jew who was leader of the synagogue (ἀρχισυνάγωγος – *archisunagōgos*) in Corinth. Acts 18 describes Paul's attempts to speak to the 'Jews and Greeks' in the synagogue on several Sabbath days but they resisted his attempts to proclaim the gospel and he departed from them. However, Crispus and his household were converted to belief in Christ. As ἀρχισυνάγωγος, Crispus would have been a man of some wealth. It is quite possible that his larger home might, in time, have become a meeting place for a house church.

> Although Luke reports that many were converted, the conversion of a synagogue leader and his household invited special comment (18:8). On ἀρχισυνάγωγος, see comment on Acts 13:15; such a title appears to have been usually based on status, and his conversion may have both embarrassed the detractors and led to more conversions. (As noted at 13:15, some who bore this title could be Gentile benefactors; that the God-fearer Titius Justus did not receive this title in 18:7, however, could suggest that in Corinth it applied to Jewish leaders.)[256]

---

254. Perkins, *Pastoral Letters*, p. 231.

255. HSIBD, p. 265.

256. Keener, *Acts*, vol. 3, p. 2748. On page 2749, n. 4514, he adds 'More likely, Sosthenes was simply a fellow synagogue ruler with Crispus or his replacement; for further discussion, see comment on Acts 18:17.' See the entry on Sosthenes.

It is clear that Apollos had become a leader in the Corinthian church by the time that Paul wrote 1 Corinthians. Early in that letter he addressed divisions in the congregation, where some people had placed their allegiance behind certain 'leaders'. In 1 Corinthians 1:12, he names the groups who followed Paul, Apollos, Cephas, and Christ. The language used by Paul in this verse is important. 'Thus, no item here receives more or less prominence than any other; all items are on equal footing (see also 15:39).'[257] Paul uses the style μέν ... δὲ ... δὲ ... δὲ. This is best translated into English by emphasising the pronoun: ***I*** am for Paul; ***I*** am for Apollos, etc.[258] It reflects the personal preferences of different people in the Corinthian congregation rather than an assertion by Paul as to anyone's superiority. In 1 Corinthians 1:11, the masculine gender of ἕκαστος 'should not be taken as narrowing the identity of the culprits for as a rule, "the masculine is used for person in general" Smyth §1015.'[259]

Paul uses this literary style again in 1 Corinthians 3:4. First Corinthians ascribes no blame at all to either Apollos or Cephas for these quarrels and divisions in the church. From 1 Corinthians 1:13-17 it is clear that the issue of the baptiser's name had developed significance in furthering these divisions. It was not Paul's usual practice to baptise converts but, given the absence of any other Christians in Corinth during the city's initial evangelisation, Paul had no alternative.

Brookins and Longenecker make the following comments about the nature of this baptism:

> **εἰς τὸ ὄνομα.** Not 'in the name', but 'into the name'. Harris (p. 228-9) identifies 'three principal views' about the meaning of this phrase, arranged 'in descending order of probability': (1) It may denote 'the establishment of a relationship of belonging and possession, and so a transference of ownership'; (2) it may mean 'with respect to', denoting the 'fundamental reference or purpose of some thing, rite, or action', in such a way as to distinguish it from other rites or actions; or, (3) especially when the context pertains to baptism,

257. Brookins and Longenecker, *1 Corinthians 1-9*, pp. 16-17.
258. See Zerwick and Grosvenor, *Grammatical Analysis*, vol. 2, p. 499.
259. Brookins and Longenecker, *1 Corinthians 1-9*, p. 16.

> it may indicate that a person is endowed with the benefits of the salvation accomplished therein. The first option seems best, but this could be stated in a manner more resonant with Paul's notion of 'being in Christ'. To be 'baptised into the name of Christ' means to be united with or incorporated into the One to whom the baptised person gives his/her allegiance. Cf. εἰς τὸν μωϊσῆν ἐβαπτίσθησαν in 10:2; see also Rom. 6:3; Gal. 3:27.[260]

In 1 Corinthians 1:14 Paul declared that he had baptised Crispus and Gaius, but this was the exception, not the rule, for Paul.

> Paul repeats the idea expressed in the third question of verse 13 in a different way. The conj. *hina* expresses result (ZBG ʃ352; BDF ʃ391.5). Paul thus insists that no matter what relationship the Paul-group of Corinth might be claiming to him, it does not stem from him as their baptiser. Some interpreters have argued that this was the nature of the rival groups, that Corinthians who had been baptised by a certain preacher developed a bond of allegiance to him. Now Paul would be countering that claim.[261]

Since Crispus was a leading Jew, his baptism by the apostle himself would have confirmed the sincerity of his conversion. It is quite possible that, given his seniority in Judaism and his conversion to Christianity, he was the one who baptised those new converts mentioned in the latter part of Acts 18:8. Other baptisers may have been Stephanas, the first convert in Corinth, and Gaius Titius Justus.

In explaining his role as a preacher of the gospel and not as a baptiser of believers, Paul concedes in 1 Corinthians 1:16 that he did baptise the household of Stephanas in Corinth. Other examples of households being baptised are described in Acts 16:15, 32-33. Concerning 1 Corinthians 1:16:

> **δὲ**. Introduces an additional consideration, but which Paul takes to be of minimal consideration. Lightfoot (156) proposes that the verse is an 'afterthought'; but the effect could be deliberate, calculated to brush aside the fact that Paul did actually perform a few baptisms.

260. ibid., p. 19.

261. See Fitzmyer, *First Corinthians*, p. 147.

> Vis-à-vis verse 14, the addition has almost concessive force ('I baptised no one except Crispus and Gaius ... Now, admittedly, I did baptise the household of Stephanas.').[262]

From 1 Corinthians 1:15, it may appear that Paul was not particularly concerned who baptised whom.[263] He wrote that he had not come to baptise but to preach the gospel (1 Cor. 1:17). However, the phrase εἰς τὸ ἐμὸν ὄνομα (***eis to emon** omona* – '***into my*** name') is similar to εἰς τὸ ὄνομα (*eis to onoma*) in verse 13 above it. This fact might be quite important to Paul in the light of the divisions within the Corinthian church. The literal meaning '*into my* name' may be important in the light of 1 Corinthians 1–3 where one group of believers is 'the Paul group' and may be claiming some special status. All have been baptised not into any person but into Christ. Paul is emphasising that *his* baptism of people is not the significant issue.[264]

> **εἰ μὴ**. [v. 14] An idiom meaning 'but', 'except' (= πλήν). To say, 'I baptised no one except', rhetorically downplays Paul's involvement in baptisms more than if he said, 'I baptised only'.[265]
>
> Some in Corinth may have thought it to be personally advantageous to be associated with Paul, Apollos or Peter via the administration of baptism. This type of thinking was rife in Corinth, where personality-centred politics and status-seeking 'hangers-on' were the norm in secular society. If so, Paul's comments in these verses would have given such Corinthian Christians no encouragement. In what must be the greatest disappointment in Paul's otherwise impressive history of giving thanks, the apostle is grateful that he performed so few baptisms in Corinth! He wants no part in petty rivalries, even if indirectly, and is happy not to have unwittingly played into anyone's hands. In the context of his arguments in the unit, not having baptised many of the Corinthians contributes to Paul's depiction of the nature of Christian ministry as a 'shared partnership'.

---

262. Brookins and Longenecker, *1 Corinthians 1-9*, p. 21.
263. See Ciampa and Rosner, *1 Corinthians*, p. 84.
264. For a technical discussion of the alternative interpretations of εἰς τὸ ἐμὸν ὄνομα, see Brookins and Longenecker, *1 Corinthians 1-9*, pp. 19, 21.
265. Brookins and Longenecker, *1 Corinthians 1-9*, p. 20.

The only two that Paul does admit to baptising, at least initially (see v. 16), are *Crispus* and *Gaius*, presumably early converts in the city. *Crispus* is probably the synagogue ruler mentioned in Acts 18:8. Murphy O'Connor notes inscriptional evidence that this honorific title was bestowed on wealthy patrons who had donated something substantial to the synagogue, like part of a building, a mosaic floor, or other accoutrements.[266]

Demas

Colossians 4:14

[14] *Luke, the beloved physician, sends you his greetings, and Demas does also.*

2 Timothy 4:9-10

[9] *Make every effort to come to me soon;*

[10] *... for Demas, having loved this present world, has deserted me and gone to Thessalonica; Crescens has gone to Galatia, Titus to Dalmatia.*

Philemon 23-24

[23] *Epaphras, my fellow prisoner in Christ Jesus, greets you,*

[24] *... as do Mark, Aristarchus, Demas, and Luke, my fellow workers.*

Demas is 'an abbreviation of Δημήτριος (*Dēmētrios*) or Δημάρατος (*Dēmaratos*). It occurs in inscriptions or papyri'.[267] Demetrios means 'devotee of the goddess Demeter'. He provides greetings in Paul's letters to the church at Colosse and to Philemon, so he was known to them, although he was probably from Thessalonica (2 Tim. 4:10). His being mentioned in the letters to Colossians and Philemon supports the argument that these letters were penned in Ephesus. In Colossians, he is mentioned in the same breath with Doctor Luke. In Philemon, he is described as a fellow worker who was obviously known to Philemon and is included in such illustrious company as Mark, Aristarchus, and Luke. Demas was clearly a close associate of Paul who would have been known by the churches in Asia, including Ephesus. However, if Philemon was written before Colossians, there may be a subtle hint in the

---

266. Ciampa and Rosner, *1 Corinthians*, pp. 83-4.

267. Perkins, *Pastoral Letters*, p. 230. See also Marshall, *Pastoral Epistles*, p. 815, n. 3.

second letter in the fact that Demas is not given any description.[268] Perhaps Paul was already sensing some weakening in Demas' commitment to the strenuous nature of Paul's missionary work, although he ended up with imprisoned Paul in Rome.

But something went terribly wrong by the time Paul was imprisoned for a second time in Rome near his death. Paul wrote to Timothy that he should 'make every effort' (σπούδασον – *spoudason*; cf. Titus 3:12; Heb. 4:11; 2 Pet. 3:14) to come to Paul 'quickly' (ταχέως – *taxeōs*). There is an urgency in his request; the verb is in the aorist imperative, indicating that it is more of an order than request, followed by 'quickly'. The reason is provided in the next verse: Demas has 'deserted (ἐγκατέλιπεν – *egkatelipen*) me and gone to Thessalonica.' Throughout the NT this verb has a sense of finality about it. 'ἐγκαταλείπω implies not simply that Demas has departed and left Paul but that he has forsaken and deserted him.'[269]

It appears that Demas, 'having loved this present world' (ἀγαπήσας τὸν νῦν αἰῶνα – *agapēsas ton nun aiōna*), was unable to face the increasing rigours placed on Christians in Rome: especially, at the time of writing, the possibility of martyrdom. The verb ἀγαπήσας indicates that this state of mind is continuing.[270] 'This present world' is to be contrasted with 'the world to come' (Titus 2:12). This is a condemnatory description of Demas' lack of willingness to suffer any further than he had to for the gospel. A similar situation is found with some followers of Jesus in John 6:66. 'Perhaps Paul was already aware of Demas's spiritual slide because he was the only one of the six [in Colossians 4] about whom there was no comment in the greeting.'[271]

---

268. R. K. Hughes, *Colossians and Philemon*. Westchester, IL: Crossway, 1989, p. 151; Dunn, *Colossians*, p. 283.

269. Marshall with Towner, *Pastoral Epistles*, p. 15. See its use in 2 Timothy 4:21.

270. Perkins, *Pastoral Letters*, p. 219, suggests an ongoing affection by Demas in his translation: 'For Demas, because he is in love with this present age, has deserted me.' He suggests that the use of this verb [ἀγαπήσας] may be to highlight the distinction between Demas and its use in describing 'all who have loved His [Christ's] appearing' earlier in 2 Timothy 4:8.

271. Hughes, *Colossians*, p. 151.

> 'For' implies that Paul will now give one or more reasons why he feels acute need for Timothy's speedy arrival. The first matter he raises concerns Demas. Only a few years previous, he was a loyal coworker alongside Paul's valued lieutenant Luke (Col. 4:14; Philem. 24). He has 'deserted' Paul, who used the same word to describe the not uncommon lot in Christian life: 'persecuted, but not abandoned [= deserted]' (2 Cor. 4:9). He means that God does not abandon those whose faithfulness leads them into dire straits for Jesus's sake. But people, including fellow believers once deemed trustworthy, may prove fickle. Demas is a case in point.
>
> Demas tripped up on inordinate affection for 'this world'. Whether this was an act of apostasy is uncertain. Calvin's gracious analysis is attractive though not verifiable: 'We are not to suppose that he completely denied Christ and gave himself over again to ungodliness or the allurements of the world, but only that he cared more for his own convenience and safety rather than for the life of Paul.'[272] The 'world' Demas loved is not *gē* (planet earth, humanity) or *kosmos* (the created universe with or without its inhabitants). Paul does not disparage Demas for embodying a positive view of the created order. Paul refers rather to the current *aiōn* (age, era, as in 'The Age of Reason'). Every time and place has its tone and trends. Those who follow Christ seek to love his priorities and 'appearing' (see [2 Tim.] 4:8); they heed the command, 'Do not conform to the pattern of this world [*aiōn*]' (Rom. 12:2). The message of the lordship of Christ is 'not the wisdom of this age [*aiōn*] or of the rulers of this age [*aiōn*], who are coming to nothing' (1 Cor. 2:6). Paul uses this same word with this meaning in two Pastoral Epistle passages (1 Tim. 6:17; Titus 2:12). Whereas the Christian mandate is to love God and your neighbour as yourself, Demas has set his affection at least to some extent on this crumbling world order, not the kingdom of God. We do not know why he went to Thessalonica or what he may have sought there.[273]

Demas is generally condemned for his desertion from Rome to Thessalonica, but Marshall notes that 'it remains possible that he

---

272. Calvin, 'Commentaries on the Second Epistle to Timothy', *Calvin's Commentaries*, vol. 21, pp. 264-5. See Towner, *Letters to Timothy and Titus*, p. 623.

273. Yarbrough, *Letters to Timothy and Titus*, pp. 447-8.

continued actively as a Christian, even as a missionary'.[274] Calvin's commentary (above) reflected the same possibility. Demas' behaviour reflects that of Cephas in a similar position (Mark 14:50, 66-72) and it was only his future rehabilitation by Christ post-resurrection that has ennobled his name. Could the same have applied to Demas to a lesser extent? It would appear that Demas was one of Paul's helpers, like Crescens (cf. 2 Tim. 4:10).

> Demas ([2 Tim. 4:] 10) had served in a similar role until he apparently abandoned it under duress during Paul's final imprisonment. Demas had been with Paul during his first Roman imprisonment (Col. 4:14; Philem. 24), a house arrest which involved less risk than this final Roman imprisonment. Paul now poignantly described Demas as 'in love with this present world' (cf. 1 John 2:15). Demas lacked only one thing – the willingness to suffer on behalf of the truth, but that was the one thing necessary. He had left Paul in the lurch and gone to Thessalonica. This did not imply that he became apostate but that 'he merely preferred his private convenience, or his safety' (Calvin, p. 264). 'Having loved his own ease and security from danger, he has chosen rather to live luxuriously at home, than to suffer hardships' with Paul (Chrysostom, p. 513). No one could continue long in a leadership position in the early church without risk, troubles, loss, bodily injury, and finally death. One gets the sense of disappointment and grief in his abrupt reference that Paul had expected more of Demas. The fact that Demas had served well earlier did not ensure that he would remain steady under stress. Commitment to the gospel must be renewed daily. A whole series of new appointments to service had apparently been made and missioners dispatched to distant parts. The changing of the guard was occurring in the gentile missions.[275]

EPAENETAS

ROMANS 16:5

[5]*... also greet the church that is in their house. Greet Epaenetas, my beloved, who is the first convert to Christ from Asia.*

---

274. Marshall, *Pastoral Epistles,* p. 816. See Köstenberger, *Commentary on 1–2 Timothy and Titus,* pp. 280-1.

275. Oden, *First and Second Timothy and Titus,* p. 171.

Epaenetas was almost certainly a Gentile and his name means 'praiseworthy'.[276] It was not an uncommon name in Greek, and was probably associated with slaves or freed men, being found in places as diverse as Sicily, Corinth, and Ephesus.[277] He is greeted by Paul as '**my** beloved' (τὸν ἀγαπητόν **μου** – *ton agapēton* ***mou***). Paul regards him as 'beloved', as he does Ampliatus (Rom. 16:8), Stachys (Rom. 16:9), and Persis (Rom. 16:12). This title 'indicates a significant measure of personal attachment'[278] to him and gratitude for his support of Paul and his ministry.

> The description of Epaenetas as Paul's 'beloved' is not to be taken to imply that he was more beloved than those who are not so described. Paul seems to have tried to attach some expression of kindly commendation to all the individuals he mentions. He has managed to keep this up (apart from v. 10b) right to the end of v. 13; but with v. 14 he simply lists names.[279]

However, that comment understates Paul's greeting and the revelation of a startling fact.

> The fact that this person who had been converted in Ephesus is now in Rome along with Prisca and Aquila has been taken to indicate that he may have been either their slave or a freed man in their employ. But this is rendered unlikely by Paul's reference to him as ἀπαρχὴ τῆς ἀσίας εἰς χριστόν (*aparchē tēs Asias eis Christon*) ('first fruit of Asia for Christ'), which places Epainetos [sic] in the same status as the household of Stephanos [sic] in 1 Cor. 16:15, the earliest and thus most honoured convert in the province. ... These considerations confirm the inference that Epainetos was probably associated with Prisca and Aquila's house church on the basis of his conversion during the period of their Ephesian residence.[280]

The Greek translates more accurately as '***the*** first fruits in Asia': ἀπαρχὴ **τῆς** (*aparchē* ***tēs***).[281] It is a Jewish term for anything set

276. HSIBD, p. 342.
277. See Cranfield, *Romans*, vol. 2, p. 786.
278. Jewett, *Romans*, p. 960.
279. Cranfield, *Romans*, vol. 2, p. 786-7.
280. Jewett, *Romans*, p. 960.
281. For a similar description, see the entry for Stephanas.

apart to God before the remainder could be used (Exod. 23:16, 19; 34:24, 26; Num. 15:17-21; cf. 1 Cor. 15:20).[282] This conversion is offered to Christ with praise. Epaenetas represents the first fruits of Paul's missionary activity with Prisca and Aquila in the province of Asia, centred around Ephesus, its largest city.[283] Although he was the first Christian convert in Asia (the Roman province in the south-western part of modern Turkey), he is not mentioned anywhere else in the NT. Jewett regards Paul's description of first fruits as 'clearly honorific', but this must be rejected.

> Since Paul worked with Prisca and Aquila, who were missioning in Ephesus prior to his arrival in circa A.D. 53 (Acts 18:26), the early conversion of Epainetos [sic] provides grounds for associating him with their ministry. Since their slaves and family would undoubtedly become members of their house church, and would have accompanied them to Ephesus, no such person would be likely to be described as the 'first fruits of Asia'. Since he was a resident in 'Asia', presumably from Ephesus, there is no reason to associate him with slavery; he was probably a free man.[284]

That the gospel took him to Rome indicates that he was, certainly by that time, a free man.

> The fact that he is given such prominence and mentioned immediately after Prisca and Aquila is presumably explained by the following phrases, but it could be that he belonged to the house church of Prisca and Aquila, or had been converted by them, or, indeed, had joined the business of Aquila and Priscilla [sic] and had returned with them from Asia to Rome. ἀγαπητός, as also in verses 8, 9, 12, simply denotes a warm personal relationship.[285]

---

282. See Haldane, *Romans*, p. 636. See 1 Corinthians 16:15, where the household of Stephanas is regarded as a singular entity. This singular use of ἀπαρχὴ is justified in the case of Epaenetas.

283. Schreiner, *Romans*, pp. 764-5, regards Epaenetas as 'one of the first people converted in Asia'.

284. Jewett, *Romans*, p. 960.

285. Dunn, *Romans 9-16*, p. 893. See Lampe, *The Roman Christians*, pp. 220-1; 222, n. 28.

Notwithstanding our understanding that Paul saw everyone as equal in Christ, it would nevertheless be surprising if Paul did not have some special affection for one of the earlier Christians outside of Judaea and did not acknowledge this by listing him as one of the first people greeted in this letter. Epaenetas' standing among the Roman Christians would have been important in verifying the authenticity of the earlier contents of the letter. Paul's love for this man would also surely reflect the fact that, at the time of writing, Epaenetas had been a faithful witness for a long time within the relatively short history of Christianity among the Gentiles.

Since he would have known Prisca and Aquila in Ephesus, he may have been a member of the house church meeting in their home in Rome.

Epaphras

Colossians 1:7-8

[7] *... just as you learned it from Epaphras, our beloved fellow bond-servant, who is a faithful servant of Christ on our behalf,*

[8] *... and he also informed us of your love in the Spirit.*

Colossians 4:12-13

[12] *Epaphras, who is one of your own, a bond-servant of Christ Jesus, sends you his greetings, always striving earnestly for you in his prayers, that you may stand mature and fully assured in all the will of God.*

[13] *For I testify for him that he has a deep concern for you and for those who are in Laodicea and Hierapolis.*

Philemon 1:23

[23] *... Epaphras, my fellow prisoner in Christ Jesus, greets you, ...*

Epaphras is a shortened form of Epaphroditus, but he is a different person to another individual called Epaphroditus (see an entry for Epaphroditus below). Epaphras 'became a name in itself',[286] and is a Gentile name meaning 'charming'.[287] He

286. McKnight, *Colossians*, p. 101, n. 119.
287. HSIBD, p. 342.

was initially a resident of Colosse (Col. 4:12). He would have travelled to Ephesus where he was presumably converted by Paul during his stay there. Paul notes that Epaphras went 'on our behalf' (Col. 1:7) – i.e. Paul and Timothy – as Paul's messenger for Christ.[288] Epaphras' return journey with the gospel took him about 100 miles (160 km) east of Ephesus to the towns of Hieropolis, Laodicea and Colosse (Col. 4:13). The towns were located in the Lycus Valley in the Roman province of Asia (now south-western Turkey). Through this valley flows the Lycus River an offshoot to the right of the larger Maeander (now Menderes) River. Hierapolis was located on the northern side of the Lycus River, Laodicea was on the southern side of the river about 6 miles (10 km) south, and Colosse was a small town that lay on both sides of the river about 12 miles (20 km) to the south-east of Laodicea. They were cities known for dyeing cloth. The general area was very fertile.[289]

It was from Epaphras that the church at Colosse (and those in Hierapolis and Laodicea) 'learned' (ἐμάθετε – *emathete*) the gospel. 'The verb used for learning here (μανθάνω – *manthanō*) evokes a relationship of discipleship and theological content. It is reasonable to imagine their being discipled, or spiritually formed, at the feet of Epaphras, who himself extends Paul's ministry'.[290] Epaphras was 'a conscientious and thorough teacher

---

288. The Greek in the text means 'on your behalf'; however, there is much conjecture as to whether ὑμῶν should be ὑμῶν. Hendriksen, *Colossians*, p. 53, n. 34 comments: 'With ARV, RSV, Bruce, C. F. D. Moule, Ridderbos, Robertson, etc., I accept the reading ὑμῶν instead of ὑμῶν. It is true that either reading would make sense. Yet, the phrase "minister ... on our behalf" would seem to harmonise most exactly with the words "*our* fellow-servant".' For the alternative view, see McKnight, *Colossians*, p. 103, n. 127.

289. For a comprehensive description of this region, see Bruce, *Colossians*, pp. 3-13; Hendriksen, *Philippians, Colossians and Philemon*, pp. 6-14. For an accurate (and moving) description of first-century Colosse and its history, see H. C. G. Moule, *Colossian and Philemon Studies*, pp. 18-20: 'But by the Christian era Colossae was small and obscure; a place which hovered between town and village, a townlet, a *polisma* (p. 18).'

290. McKnight, *Colossians*, pp. 101-2.

of the gospel message. His mission had been no hit-and-run affair with minimal instruction. The truth had been fully explained and applied'.[291] McKnight provides a comprehensive overview of Epaphras' character and ministry.[292]

We conclude that Philemon was written before Colossians (see Colossians 4:8 and *Letters From Prison: Ephesians, Philippians, Colossians and Philemon* in the introduction) and both were written in Ephesus. Therefore, we have two occasions on which Paul was imprisoned there (cf. Philem. 10, 23; Col. 4:10). On the first occasion Epaphras was with him in prison (Philem. 23), and at the time that Colossians was written, Aristarchus was in the Ephesian prison with Paul (Col. 4:10).

One of Epaphras' converts in Colosse was Philemon, although he is not mentioned in Colossians. Given their brotherhood in Christ, Epaphras sends his greetings in Paul's letter to Philemon (v. 23). Note Paul's continuous use of συν regarding Epaphras (Col. 1:7) and, in this letter, he describes Epaphras as 'my fellow prisoner in Christ Jesus' (ὁ συναιχμάλωτός μου ἐν χριστῷ ἰησοῦ – *ho sunaichmalōtos mou en Christō Iēsou*). This term is also reserved for Andronicus and Junia (Rom. 16:7) and Aristarchus (Col. 4:10).[293] However, only Epaphras is accorded the additional 'in Christ Jesus'.

On his return from (one of several visits to) the Lycus Valley, Epaphras would have brought news to Paul about the spiritual state of the Christians in these towns. Some was good: the Colossians displayed Paul's highest gift, 'love in the Spirit' (Col. 1:8). However, some not so good: heretical teaching was creeping into their understanding of the gospel (Col. 2:8), causing Paul to write his letter to them (Col. 4:7-8).

The Colossians understood the grace of God in truth (Col. 1:6):

> Grace is not just mercy to the undeserving (incongruity as the whole of it) [sic] but the kind of mercy that achieves holistic redemption

291. Lucas, *Colossians and Philemon*, p. 33.

292. McKnight, *Colossians*, pp. 102-5; 391-3. See also Hughes, *Colossians*, pp. 150-1.

293. Technically, συναιχμάλωτός means 'prisoner-of-war': Bruce, *Colossians*, p. 224, n. 106.

> (effective and at times circular). In Colossians grace accumulates into the perfection of the circular (e.g. 1:10-12 and esp. 1:23).[294]

Epaphras is described by Paul as 'my beloved fellow bond-servant': τοῦ ἀγαπητοῦ συνδούλου – *tou agapētou sundoulou* (Col. 1:7). All widely used English Bibles translate συνδούλος as 'fellow servant'. A few lesser-known translations use the correct term, 'fellow slave'. See *Slavery in the First Century A.D. and Earliest Christianity* in the introduction regarding Paul's use of δοῦλος. This is Paul's only use of συνδούλος in his letters other than in Colossians 4:7 with respect to Tychicus.[295] Paul repeats δοῦλος in his description of Epaphras in Colossians 4:12 ('bond-servant', NASB), who sends his greetings in this letter. McKnight's reticence over the plain meaning of συνδούλος and δοῦλος is puzzling, although he does recognise the lowly state to which it refers.

> Second, Epaphras was a 'fellow-servant'. It is not entirely clear whether this term *syndoulos* means one who is in prison alongside Paul (as is the case with Epaphras at this time; see Philem. 23), or whether the *syn*-compound, of which Paul is so fond, refers to a status as a fellow slave of Christ. Because both Col. 1:17 and 4:12 connect slavery or servanthood to Christ, one is inclined to see here a metaphoric relationship of serving Christ. We need to remind ourselves of the abhorrence of the status of slavery in the Roman world, the paradoxical embrace of this term for one's relationship to King Jesus by the apostle Paul in its denotations of submission, obedience, and devotion to Christ, and therefore the revolutionary subordination at work when the early Christians began to see themselves now as slaves of Christ (e.g. Gal. 1:10; 1 Cor. 7:21-23; Rom. 1:1; 6:16-20; Eph. 6:6; Phil. 1:1).[296]

It is an outstanding endorsement of Epaphras' commitment to the gospel and the Lord since δοῦλος is the word Paul uses to describe his own relationship to Christ Jesus.[297]

---

294. McKnight, *Colossians*, p. 101.

295. The only other occurrences of συνδούλος in the NT are in Matthew (four times) and Revelation (three times).

296. McKnight, *Colossians*, pp. 102-3.

297. Romans 1:1; Galatians 1:10; Philippians 1:1; Titus 1:1.

> The words used by Paul in the three verses where he mentions Epaphras are sufficient to form an impression of the man's pastoral work: dear, fellow servant, faithful minister, servant, 'always wrestling in prayer for you', and fellow prisoner with Paul (1:7; 4:12; Philem. 23). ... The word 'dear' may not contain enough weight to suggest to English readers Paul's use of *agapētos*, a word evoking election in Israel's history (Isa. 41:8; 44:1; Jer. 31:20) that Paul uses twenty-seven times, most often for the new kind of love in Christian fellowship. Epaphras, if we use our understanding of love defined at [Col. 1:]4, is the object of Paul's covenant commitment of presence, advocacy and direction.[298]

This takes us back to *Paul's* meaning when he uses διάκονος (*diakonos*). This must be one of the most controversial words in the Pauline letters; but see the comments in *The Role of διάκονος (diakonos)* in the introduction. In Philippians 1:1 a διάκονος appears to be subordinate to an 'overseer' (ἐπίσκοποις – *episkopos*). We can conclude that, whatever the importance of their work for God, a person called διάκονος, like Epaphras, is another lowly servant of Christ, as was Paul, δοῦλος χριστοῦ ἰησοῦ (Rom. 1:1).

Colossians 4:12-13 demonstrates Epaphras' concern for the spiritual wellbeing of the Christians in his home region; we could describe them as his children in Christ, using Paul's analogy in Philemon 10.[299] Epaphras 'is always wrestling (ἀγωνιζόμενος – *agōnizomenos*) in prayer for you, that you may stand firm in the will of God, mature and fully assured. I vouch for him that he is working hard for you and for those at Laodicea and Hierapolis.' The word ἀγωνιζόμενος is quite important in understanding Epaphras' commitment to his prayers. It is the word Paul uses

298. McKnight, *Colossians*, p. 102.

299. Bruce, *Colossians*, p. 181, n. 53, is incorrect in ascribing the word παρηγορία – *parēgoria* (a NT *hapax legomenon*) to Epaphras ('a true bondman of Christ'), although it was no doubt true. The word is applied to the three Jewish Christians mentioned above in Colossians 4:10-11. Bruce's comment is: 'παρηγορία (not elsewhere in the NT). "The idea of consolation, comfort, is on the whole predominant in the word", because it and its derivates "were used especially as medical terms, in the sense of 'assuaging', 'alleviating'"' (Lightfoot, [*Philippians*], *ad loc.*).

in 1 Corinthians 9:25 to describe 'competing in the games'. It emphasises strenuous and committed effort, as required by athletes. It is one of a series of similar words used by Paul in his letters.[300] Having put in so much effort to teach the Colossian church (Col. 1:7), Epaphras' prayer is that the seed he planted will come to 'full flower' as it were (cf. 1 Cor. 3:6), standing 'mature and fully convinced' (τέλειοι καὶ πεπληροφορημένοι – *teleioi kai plērophorēmenoi*) of the will of God.[301] Indeed, in Colossians 4:13, Paul vouches that Epaphras is working hard for the three churches but we have no specific details. The NASB translates πολὺν πόνον (*polun ponon*) as 'has a deep concern' but this is too weak; the words should be 'working hard', 'a term that means labour and toil and describes physical exertion, if not also pain'.[302]

The descriptions of Epaphras (and Aristarchus) in Ephesus are different in Colossians and Philemon, which have important implications for those who support the idea that Paul suffered more than one imprisonment in Ephesus.[303] Bruce makes the plausible suggestion that 'It may well have been he [Epaphras] who brought Paul and Onesimus together.'[304]

> In Col. 1:7-8 he seems to be considered the founder of the Colossian church, and this is undoubtedly why he is mentioned first.
>
> ... he was most likely a Gentile Christian. He later became a bishop of Colossae and a martyr for the Christian faith (feast day in the Roman Martyrology: July 19).[305]

---

300. See V. C. Pfitzner, 'Paul and the *Agon* Motif', *NTest* Supplement 16. (Leiden: E. J. Brill, 1967); Manuell, *The Letter of Jude*, p. 91: Jude 3 uses an extreme form of the word.

301. τέλειος can be translated 'perfect' or 'complete' as earlier in Colossians 1:28 (NASB); however, it should be noted that these words could only be applied as a wish for the future rather than an actuality when written because 'perfection' in Christ cannot be attained in this life. 'Mature' seems to suit the text better: see Lucas, *Colossians*, p. 178. See the detailed description of Epaphras' impressive prayer life in Dunn, *Colossians*, pp. 280-1.

302. McKnight, *Colossians*, p. 393, n 74.

303. See *Letters to the Colossians and Philemon* in the introduction.

304. Bruce, *Colossians*, p. 224.

305. J. A. Fitzmyer, *The Letter to Philemon* (New York: Doubleday, 2000), p. 123.

It is evident that Epaphras is another of those unsung first-century heroes of the faith in the region of Ephesus, without whom the spread of the gospel would have been much more difficult. He was dearly loved by Paul.

Epaphroditus

Philippians 2:25-30

[25] *But I thought it necessary to send to you Epaphroditus, my brother and fellow worker and fellow soldier, who is also your messenger and minister to my need,*

[26] *because he was longing for you all and was distressed because you had heard that he was sick.*

[27] *For indeed he was sick to the point of death, but God had mercy on him, and not only on him but also on me, so that I would not have sorrow upon sorrow.*

[28] *Therefore I have sent him all the more eagerly, so that when you see him again you may rejoice and I may be less concerned about you.*

[29] *Receive him then in the Lord with all joy, and hold people like him in high regard,*

[30] *because he came close to death for the work of Christ, risking his life to compensate for your absence in your service to me.*

Philippians 4:18

[18] *But I have received everything in full and have an abundance; I am amply supplied, having received from Epaphroditus what you have sent, a fragrant aroma, an acceptable sacrifice, pleasing to God.*

Epaphroditus is the longer (formal) form of Epaphras[306] (see entry above), but they are two distinct people in the NT. Epaphroditus (a Gentile name meaning 'charming', like Epaphras) came from Philippi to visit Paul during his first imprisonment in Rome.[307] Philippi was an important Roman colony in eastern Greece, the first city in Europe evangelised by Paul. It was among the first Christians there that Epaphroditus was converted. He may have even heard Paul

306. This is the same relationship as the formal 'Prisca' is to the familiar 'Priscilla'.

307. See *Letters From Prison: Ephesians, Philippians, Colossians and Philemon* in the introduction.

preach the gospel (Acts 16:40). Of all the less well-known Christians mentioned in Paul's letters, commentaries on the person and role of Epaphroditus are some of the most voluminous. There are quite varied interpretations of his visit to Paul; therefore, a summary of the most reasonable interpretations is analysed here, with many references in footnotes. There are also many disputed issues concerning the Greek text, some of which are considered below.

Paul's letter to the Philippian church mentions Epaphroditus twice. Philippians 2:25-30 is the longest description of one of his fellow workers in the NT. Clearly, there was a close relationship between the two men.

Epaphroditus is described by five terms as τὸν ἀδελφὸν καὶ συνεργὸν καὶ συστρατιώτην μου, ὑμῶν δὲ ἀπόστολον καὶ λειτουργὸν τῆς χρείας μου (*ton adelphon kai sunergon kai sustratiōtēn mou, humōn de apostolon kai leitourgon mou* – 'my brother and fellow worker and fellow soldier, who is also your messenger and minister'). Philippians 2:25 is another example of the Granville Sharp Rule, although not mentioned by commentators. The first three descriptions refer to his relationship with Paul and the last two refer to his relationship with the church sending him on this mission. This description of Epaphroditus is like the introductions of people who delivered Paul's letters (e.g. Rom. 16:1-2; 1 Cor. 16:15-18; 2 Cor. 8:16-24; Eph. 6:21-22; Col. 4:7-9), even though he is well-known to the Philippians. This reflects Paul's sincere affection for '*my* brother' as well as a deep appreciation of his diligence and faithfulness. This lengthy description is not unprecedented: see the same order of words in Philemon 1:2, although applying to different people. Paul sometimes used two epithets to describe and commend fellow believers (e.g. Rom. 16:1; 1 Cor. 4:17; 1 Thess. 3:12).

> The very fact that Paul compounds these designations so often (see preceding n.) argues for the opposite, namely that their semantic range does *not* sufficiently overlap for only one of them to be used.[308]

---

308. Fee, *Philippians*, p. 275, n. 14 (original emphasis). E. E. Ellis, *Prophecy and Hermeneutic in Early Christianity* (Grand Rapids: Baker, 1993), pp. 13-15, had earlier argued that these were just alternatives for 'coworker'.

Epaphroditus is described as 'my fellow soldier' (τὸν συστρατιώτην μου – *ton sustratiōtēn mou*). Paul uses this description only twice in his correspondence, the other referring to Archippus in Philemon 2. It is apparent that Epaphroditus, like Archippus, had endured some severe hardships or persecution (perhaps even imprisonment) to warrant this military-style recognition. Paul's use of ἀπόστολος (*apostolos*) should be interpreted in its common meaning of 'messenger'; O'Brien uses 'envoy', which suits the role perfectly.[309] It replaces the oft-used διάκονος (*diakonos*).

> Epaphroditus is λειτουργός [vv. 25, 30] ('minister'): he had been sent by the Philippians to minister to Paul's need (τῆς χρείας μου)'. As already noted λειτουργέω ('serve') and its cognate λειτουργία ('service') had to do with all kinds of public service in the Greek world, while in the LXX the word group was used almost exclusively for the service of priests and Levites in the temple. In the NT, however, the word appears infrequently. Through Christ and His death upon the cross there is no need for a priestly caste to provide access to God. The new community has no priests, for it is a priestly kingdom in which all may enter God's presence directly. λειτουργία is employed noncultically of other kinds of service rendered to meet the needs of men and women.[310]

Epaphroditus travelled from Philippi to Rome with a gift of money for Paul to sustain him in difficult circumstances. Paul says that he had a need, not for his ministry, but for himself (τῆς χρείας **μου** – for *my* need'). It is clear from Philippians 4:11, 12, 16 that Paul was willing to accept financial assistance from the Philippians. Epaphroditus was again meeting that need. He was a little bit of the Philippian church with Paul (Phil. 4:30) in the same way that Stephanas and his colleagues were a little bit of Corinth when they went to Paul in Ephesus (1 Cor. 16:17). This gift is described in Philippians 4:18 as 'a fragrant aroma, an acceptable sacrifice, well-pleasing to God.'

> There are many references to 'a fragrant offering' in the Bible, but the first sets the scene for the rest. After the Flood, Noah offered a burnt offering to God, and we read, 'when the LORD smelled the pleasing

309. O'Brien, *Philippians*, p. 332.

310. O'Brien, *Philippians*, p. 332. See also Witherington, *Philippians*, p. 175: 'the service he undertook was taking Paul some needed funds.'

> odour, the LORD said in his heart, "I will never again curse the ground because of man ...'" (Gen. 8:21). The picture is homely, the teaching plain. The burnt offering expresses obedient consecration to God, and God delights in His people dedicated to himself. Paul teaches here that when Christians take note of Christian needs and generously sacrifice to meet them, it is, for God, the burnt offering all over again, and He delights to accept it.[311]

We now turn to the controversy concerning the actual purpose of Epaphroditus' visit to Paul. If Epaphroditus was carrying a large sum of money to Paul, he would have been accompanied by others from the church (cf. the groups travelling with collections, 1 Cor. 16:3; 2 Cor. 8:19; 11:9; Acts 20:4; 24:17). The remainder of the party presumably returned to Philippi (from Rome) to report on Epaphroditus' illness. The delivery of the monetary gift is clear, but was there a second aspect to the visit?

This revolves around the issue of Epaphroditus' illness, concerning which there are two tangents. Many commentators *assume* that his illness occurred on the journey from Philippi, but there is no indication at all where it occurred, and it is quite possible that Epaphroditus fell ill while with Paul.[312] The addition of καὶ γὰρ (*kai gar* – 'for indeed') at the beginning of 2:27 emphasises the seriousness of the illness. Epaphroditus became distressed (ἀδημονῶν – *adēmonōn*) when he heard that the Philippians were worried about him. This is the word used to describe Christ's deep distress in the Garden of Gethsemane (Mark 14:33). 'This was provoked in Epaphroditus by the simple fact that they were anxious about him! Far from feeling gratified that he was the centre of attention back home, it drove him to mental torment that he was being a worry.'[313] Paul tells us more about this illness in 2:30. Epaphroditus 'risked his life' (παραβολευσάμενος – *paraboleusamenos*)[314] for the work

311. Motyer, *Philippians*, pp. 216-17. cf. Ephesians 5:2; 2 Corinthians 2:14-16.

312. Being ill *on the journey to Paul* is advocated by Fee, *Philippians*, pp. 277, 278, n. 30, 283. For a contrary view, see O'Brien, *Philippians*, pp. 334-5.

313. Motyer, *Philippians*, p. 143.

314. This is a gambling term. See Lightfoot, *Philippians*, p. 124; Motyer, *Philippians*, p. 144.

of Christ. Indeed, he nearly died. 'So Paul might be saying that Epaphroditus rolled the dice, risking his very life to supply Paul's needs.'[315] The sovereignty of God is evident in Paul's description of the illness (cf. Rom. 8:28) and God's mercy in restoring his brother to health, which avoided the apostle from having 'sorrow upon sorrow' (Phil. 2:27).[316]

> Far fewer people in antiquity recovered from death's door. In saying 'God had mercy on him', therefore, Paul probably does not mean simply that in God's good mercy Epaphroditus simply got better, but that God had a direct hand in it. ... Paul's emphasis rests altogether on the mercy of God evidenced by Epaphroditus's recovery, which in turn does not so much stress generosity toward the underserving – although that is always true as well – but the *experience* of mercy itself.[317]

The phrase 'for the work of Christ' (τὸ ἔργον χριστοῦ – *to ergon Christō*) (Phil. 2:30) is its only occurrence in Paul's letters.

> The translation *not regarding his life* is based on a probably corrupt reading *parabouleusamenos.* Many MSS, omitting one Greek letter, have the participle *paraboleusamenos* with the meaning 'hazarding his life'. This is illustrated by Deissmann, who quotes an inscription found at Olba on the Black Sea, dated at the end of the second century, in honour of a certain Carzoazus who 'exposed himself to dangers (*paraboleusamenos*) as an advocate in (legal) strife (by taking his clients' cases even) up to (*mechri*) the emperors (Augustus and Tiberius)'.
>
> This reading gives a better meaning, as is accepted by modern editors generally. It is a gambling term. Epaphroditus staked his life for the service of Christ, in the interest of the apostle and on behalf of the Philippian community whose lack of help was unavoidable since they were many miles away. Such a word brings its own challenge and rebuke to an easy-going Christianity which makes no

---

315. Witherington, *Philippians*, p. 177.

316. In his *Sermon Preached at the Funeral of Mr Samuel Lawrence, Minister of Nantwich*, Matthew Henry uses the illness of Epaphroditus as an example in his sermon, using the phrase 'sorrow upon sorrow' (Phil. 2:27) thirty-one times. See M. Henry, *The Complete Works of Matthew Henry: Treatises, Sermons, and Tracts* (Grand Rapids: Baker Books, reprinted 1979), vol. 2: pp. 362-5.

317. Fee, *Philippians*, p. 279.

> stern demands, and calls for no limits of self-denying, self-effacing sacrifice. Here is a man who gave little thought to personal comfort and safety in order to discharge his responsibility; and we cannot accept Michael's rather uncharitable suggestion that he may have acted in a specially foolhardy way and brought harm upon himself.
>
> There is no touch of harshness or mention of complaint concerning the Philippians as the AV *to supply your lack of service to me* might suggest. The thought is simply 'to complete your service to me' (RSV), with a parallel in 1 Cor. 16:17, where the coming of Stephanus, Fortunatus and Achaicus make up for the absence of the Corinthians.[318]

In the above quotation, Martin expresses a critical issue with regard to translations from the Greek. This is an important case in point. He has provided AV and RSV translations above and explained why the Philippians (hundreds of miles away) cannot help Paul. The NASB translation of Philippians 2:30 sounds harsh and critical ('risking his life to *complete what was deficient in your service to me*'), while the NIV translation ('risking his life to make up for *the help you could not give me*') (my emphases) touches a gentler and more sympathetic tone reflecting what Paul meant in his letter. It is well and good to translate accurately but the emotion of the letter ought to be transmitted to the reader as well.[319]

The second tangent to this illness stems from an assumption by J. H. Michael that part of Epaphroditus' task was to remain with Paul as long as the apostle needed him.[320] Many commentators have wrongly adopted this argument which has no foundation in the

318. R. P. Martin, *2 Corinthians*, WBC (Grand Rapids: Zondervan, 2014), pp. 133-4.

319. In our modern world, with the frequent use of electronic communication via email, SMS, Facebook, Twitter, etc., how often do we find the 'written' (if some of it deserves the term 'writing'!) word causes unnecessary distress to the reader when the intonations of the spoken word would have eliminated much uncertainty about the underlying intention and meaning of the sender.

320. J. H. Michael, *The Epistle of Paul to the Philippians*, MNTC (New York: Harper and Brothers Publishers, 1928), pp. 118-19. His theory is primarily based on the position of ἀναγκαῖον ('necessary') at the beginning of verse 25: 'But I thought it necessary to send to you Epaphroditus …'

text.[321] 'That the church had sent Epaphroditus on a "double mission" is pure conjecture; what Paul actually says here and in 4:18 implies a single mission. In any case that is all Paul explicitly refers to.'[322]

> So intent are some [commentators] on finding ulterior motives that they are quite ready to overthrow what Paul does say in favour of reading between the lines – or else make Epaphroditus out to be emotionally unstable (see esp. Martin, 'nervous disorder'; Hawthorne, 'emotional instability'). All of this fails to take the letter genre ('friendship') seriously. It is as though because so much in Paul's letters is polemical, one must read even friendship through polemical bifocals.[323]

Given his successful mission, recovery from illness, and speedy return to Philippi, there was every reason for the church to greet Epaphroditus with gladness and rejoicing. With his ministry to all the saints foremost in his mind, Paul determines that Epaphroditus should return to Philippi not only for his personal reasons but also that Paul will know (from a future message) that all is well at that church (Phil. 2: 28).

Erastus

Acts 19:22

[22] And after he [Paul] sent into Macedonia two of those who assisted him, Timothy and Erastus, he himself stayed in Asia for a while.

2 Timothy 4:20

[20] Erastus remained at Corinth, but I left Trophimus sick at Miletus.

There are two men named Erastus in the NT. This relatively common Latin name means 'beloved'.[324] This is not the man identified in Romans 16:23.[325] Acts 19 describes Paul's activities in

---

321. Scholars who have adopted Michael's position include P. T. O'Brien, R. P. Martin, F. F. Bruce, W. H. Ollrog, and G. F. Hawthorne. See O'Brien, *Philippians*, pp. 332-3. The strongest opposition to this view comes from Fee, *Philippians*, p. 273. See also Witherington, *Philippians*, p. 174, n. 19.

322. Fee, *Philippians*, p. 275, n. 12. I accept Fee (fourteen pages) as the most accurate commentator on Epaphroditus.

323. Fee, *Philippians*, p. 273, n. 8.

324. HSIBD, p. 349.

325. Guthrie, *Pastoral Epistles*, p. 178; Dunn, *Romans 9-16*, p. 911. Yarbrough, *Letters to Timothy and Titus*, p. 458 is uncertain whether both are one and the

Ephesus and 19:21 notes his intention to travel to Jerusalem after he had passed through Macedonia and Achaia. Prior to doing so, he sent Timothy and Erastus ahead of him to Macedonia. In 1 Corinthians 16:10 Paul writes that Timothy will visit Corinth on his way to Macedonia, but no mention is made of Erastus, probably because he was unknown to the Corinthians. These latter two are described as 'two of those who ministered to him' (δύο τῶν διακονούντων αὐτῶ – *duo tōn diakonountōn autō*). The use of the verb related to the noun διακονος (*diakonos*) underscores the relative lowliness of this term. The underlying meaning of the term is that of service and help.[326]

This Erastus is described as but one of a number of helpers to Paul in Ephesus. It is worthy of note that he is placed after Timothy, one of Paul's more senior assistants.

He is most likely the same person who is described in 2 Timothy 4:20. Paul's second letter to Timothy was written near the end of the apostle's life when Timothy resided in Ephesus. At the end of this letter Paul informs Timothy that Erastus remained at Corinth. In view of their earlier work together (see above), Timothy would have been interested to know of this brother's current work.[327] Given his role as one of Paul's trusted assistants, who could travel ahead of him to prepare things, it is not surprising that he now has a ministry in Corinth.[328]

ERASTUS

ROMANS 16:23

[23] *Gaius, host to me and to the whole church, greets you. Erastus, the city treasurer, greets you, and Quartus, the brother.*

---

same man. T. Thompson, 'Erastus' in H.-J. Klauck et al., eds. *Encyclopaedia of the Bible and its Reception* (Berlin: de Gruyter, 2009), vol. 7: p. 1126 argues that they are two different people, whereas Marshall, *Pastoral Epistles*, pp. 828-9 asserts the opposite opinion. I think that they are different men.

326. See *The Role of διάκονος (diakonos)* in the introduction.

327. See Guthrie, *Pastoral Epistles*, p. 178.

328. Keener, *Acts*, vol. 3, pp. 2863-5 analyses the arguments for and against the two men being the same person.

This second Erastus is a senior official in the Roman administration of Corinth and is clearly not the Erastus described above.[329] Bruce provides a cogent explanation of the term ὁ οἰκονόμος τῆς πόλεως (*ho oikonomos tēs poleōs*). He was the city treasurer of Corinth.

> This Erastus has been identified with the civic official of that name mentioned in a Latin inscription on a marble paving-block discovered at Corinth in 1929 by members of the American School of Classical Studies at Athens: 'ERASTVS PRO: AED: S: SP: STRAVIT' ('Erastus, commissioner for public works, laid this pavement at his own expense'). The pavement belongs to the first century A.D., and may well have been laid by Paul's friend. The public offices, however, are not the same: in Greek the commissioner for public works, or 'aedile', is called *agoranamos*, whereas the city treasurer (as here) is *oikonomos tēs poleōs*. If we have to do with the same Erastus, he had presumably been promoted to the city treasurership from the lower office of 'aedile' by the time Paul wrote this Epistle. (If anyone prefers to suppose, on the contrary, that he had been demoted from the higher to the lower office on account of his Christian profession, there is no evidence against this supposition!) There is no good reason to identify this Erastus with the Erastus of Acts 19:22 or 2 Tim. 4:20; the name was common enough.[330]

However, exactly what position is referred to by the Greek text is subject to considerable debate. The most extensive research into the position occupied by Erastus (ὁ οἰκονόμος τῆς πόλεως) has been undertaken by Goodrich, supporting Theissen's analysis.[331]

> The administrative rank of Erastus is integral to the ongoing dispute about the social and economic composition of the early Pauline churches. In this article I have argued for the correlation between

---

329. See Bruce, *Acts*, p. 372; Marshall, *Acts*, p. 314. Strangely, this Erastus is omitted from Barclay's translation of Romans: see Barclay, *Romans*, p. 240.

330. Bruce, *Romans*, pp. 280-1. A photograph of the pavement referred to by Bruce is found on 'The Search for the Historical Erastus', *Corinthian Matters, https://corinthianmatters.org/2011/08/17/the-search-for-the-historical-erastus/*

331. J. K. Goodrich, 'Erastus, Quaestor of Corinth: The Administrative Rank of ὁ οικονόμος της πόλεως (Rom. 16:23) in an Achaean Colony', *NTS* 56, no. 1 (2009); pp. 90-115. G. Theissen, *The Social Setting of Pauline Christianity: Essays on Corinth*, trans. J. H. Schutz (Philadelphia: Fortress Press, 1982).

> Erastus' position as ὁ οικονόμος της πόλεως (Rom. 16.23) and the municipal office of *quaestor*, a thesis originally advanced at length by Gerd Theissen some thirty-five years ago and never since given fuller defence. I have attempted both to defend this reading from its recent critics as well as to offer in its support important new data from the Achaean colony of Patras. While I make no claims about the identity of Erastus the Corinthian *aedilis* (*IKorinthKent* p. 232), it has been my contention that the new evidence presented here is far weightier than any other comparative text bearing the title οικονόμος previously advanced in the Erastus Debate. Admittedly, since evidence still exists which suggests that some municipal οικονόμοι were public slaves (*arcarii*), the case that Erastus occupied the quaestorship is not certain. But, as Dale Martin explains, 'normal historiography need not demonstrate what must be the case. It need only show what *probably* is the case – which is *always* accomplished by cumulative and complicated evidence.'[61] Indeed, after one considers the colonial status of Patras, its proximity to Corinth, as well as the political and structural similarities between the two cities, preference should be given to the Neikostratos inscription (*SEG* 45.418) when drawing parallels with Erastus' office in Corinth. NT scholars should consider it highly probable, then, that Erastus served as the *quaestor* of Corinth and was a man of considerable wealth.[332]

The insertion of Erastus and his occupation in Romans is a critical confirmation of 1 Corinthians 1:26, where Paul describes the church as comprising 'not many wise according to the flesh, not many mighty, not many noble': but there were some! Erastus is one of the people from the social elite of Corinth and helps to explain the literary style of that book.[333] Haldane makes the important point that Erastus 'shows us that Christians may hold offices even

332. Goodrich, *Erastus, Quaestor of Corinth*, pp. 114-15. Subsequent criticism of this article was responded to in J. K. Goodrich, 'Erastus of Corinth (Rom. 16:23): Responding to Recent Proposals on his Rank, Status, and Faith', *NTS* 57, no. 4. (2011): pp. 90-115. The conclusions concerning Erastus' position remain murky but I accept the conclusions of Theissen and Goodrich. The reference to footnote 61 in the quotation is to, D. B. Martin, 'Review Essay: Justin J. Meggitt, Paul, Poverty and Survival,' *JSNT* 24: no. 2 (2001): pp. 51-64, p. 62 (original emphasis).

333. See Mitchell, *Paul and the Rhetoric of Reconciliation*.

under heathen governments, and that to serve Christ we are not to be abstracted from worldly business'.[334] Joseph (*Genesis*) and Daniel (*Daniel*) in the OT are exemplary examples.

The rank of city treasurer was the Roman office of *quaestor*, the next position above *aedile*. This suggests a man of mature years, who would have laid the pavement earlier in his career. 'If the Erastus here in Romans and the Erastus of the inscription are the same person, then he would be a Christian of unusually high social and political standing within the Pauline circle.'[335] Other than Aquila's occupation, this is the only instance where Paul describes the 'worldly office' of a Christian.[336]

> Why Paul places this reference to Erastus the city administrator at the emphatic conclusion of a carefully constructed series of five greetings must have a significant bearing on the project that the entire letter seeks to advance. My suggestion is that this greeting from a Roman official implies his support for the mission project that Paul wishes to organize from Rome. The introduction above to the situation in Spain offers a probable explanation, namely, that Spain was the most sensitive colony in the empire, not only because of its frequent rebellions but also because its silver mines and other economic resources were under the direct control of the government and were essential for the financial viability of the empire as a whole. A mission to convert the barbarians in Spain to a religion whose subversive qualities had already come to the attention of imperial authorities might endanger the congregations in Rome. There was no more effective way to allay such concerns than by sending greetings from Erastus, a Roman official in Corinth. It was not merely his eminent social status but, more important, his public office held despite his Christian identity that carried the rhetorical force in this situation.[337]

EUBULUS

2 TIMOTHY 4:21

[21] *Make every effort to come before winter. Eubulus greets you, also Pudens, Linus, Claudia, and all the brethren.*

---

334. Haldane, *Romans*, p. 647.

335. Thielman, *Romans*, p. 744. See also Jewett, *Romans*, pp. 981-3.

336. See Theissen, *Social Setting*, pp. 75-6.

337. Jewett, *Romans*, pp. 982-3.

This is a common Greek name meaning 'well-advised'.[338] He was a faithful Christian who remained with Paul when he was imprisoned in Rome (2 Tim. 4:6, 17) and was obviously known to Timothy. He is not mentioned in Romans 16.

> Since Paul passes on their greetings to Timothy, one wonders why they did not support Paul at his trial (v. 16). Perhaps they lacked social standing to make any difference in such a situation, or perhaps it would have exposed them to inordinate danger to appear to stand at Paul's side. Paul does not feel it necessary to account for these details to Timothy .... The Greek verb is singular because in a series, the verb usually takes its number from the nearest subject nominative.[339]

Eunice

Acts 16:1

[1] Now Paul also came to Derbe and to Lystra. And a disciple was there, named Timothy, the son of a Jewish woman who was a believer, but his father was a Greek,

2 Timothy 1:5

[5] For I am mindful of the sincere faith within you, which first dwelled in your grandmother Lois and your mother Eunice, and I am sure that it is in you as well.

2 Timothy 3:15

[15]... and that from childhood you have known the sacred writings which are able to give you the wisdom that leads to salvation through faith which is in Christ Jesus.

Eunice (meaning 'good victory')[340] was the daughter of Lois and the mother of Timothy. It is a Greek name, 'common among Jews in the Roman Empire'.[341] She was a Jewess and her husband was a 'Greek', a Gentile (Acts 16:1); this marriage suggests that she was not a strictly orthodox Jewess. Nevertheless, she and her mother

338. HSIBD, p. 358. See Thompson, 'Eubulus', in Klauck, *Encyclopaedia of the Bible*, vol. 8, pp. 166-7.

339. Yarbrough, *Letters to Timothy and Titus*, p. 459.

340. HSIBD, pp. 358-9.

341. Yarbrough, *Letters to Timothy and Titus*, p. 352, n. 19.

Lois were devoted to the (OT) Scriptures (2 Tim. 1:5) and had taught them to Timothy since he was a child (2 Tim. 3:15).[342]

The family lived in Lystra, which Paul visited on his first missionary journey. Lystra was a town on the imperial road from Tarsus to Pisidian Antioch, near the middle of modern Turkey. In response to Paul's preaching, Eunice, Lois, and Timothy became committed Christians. This reflects the benefits for children growing up in families where grandparents and/or parents are Christians. 'The most formative influence on each of us has been our parentage and our home. … True, no man can inherit his parents' faith in the way that he inherits facets of their personality. But a child can be led to faith by his parents' teaching, example and prayers.'[343]

It is possible that, by the time of writing, Timothy's grandmother (and perhaps also his mother) had died.[344] We know nothing of Timothy's father except that he was a Gentile.[345]

Paul refers to the continuation of his ancestors' faith in the God of Judaism in 2 Timothy 1:3 (cf. 1 Tim. 5:4). During Paul's second imprisonment he reminds Timothy that he should continue in the same faith strongly held by his grandmother Lois and mother (2 Tim. 3:15). 'At such times a look back at the godly people who have influenced us and the duties that do with our spiritual heritage may provide a stabilising perspective.'[346]

See also the entry for Lois.

Euodia and Syntyche

Philippians 4:2-3

[2] I urge Euodia and I urge Syntyche to live in harmony in the Lord.

[3] Indeed, true companion, I ask you also, help these women who have shared my struggle in the cause of the gospel, together with Clement as well as the rest of my fellow workers, whose names are in the book of life.

---

342. See the entry for Lois concerning the faith of Timothy's grandmother.

343. Stott, *The Message of 2 Timothy*, p. 27.

344. Yarbrough, *Letters to Timothy and Titus*, p. 353.

345. Keener, *Acts*, vol. 3, pp. 2312-17, provides a lengthy discussion about intermarriage between Jews and Gentiles.

346. Towner, *1-2 Timothy and Titus*, p. 158.

It is unusual for two different people to be part of only one entry but the circumstances in which Paul writes about these women makes this the most convenient means of discussing them.

Euodia (meaning 'good journey')[347] and Syntyche (meaning 'fortunate')[348] were women in the church at Philippi and personally known to Paul. He commends them as women 'who have shared my struggle' (συνήθλησάν μοι μετὰ – *sunēthlēsan moi meta*) for the work of the gospel. Note the use of συν with the underlying Greek verb ἀθλέω (*athleō*) from which we derive the English word 'athlete'. The implication is clear that Euodia and Syntyche have made great exertions to contend for the gospel (against opponents?) with Paul.

However, disharmony has occurred between them and Paul, using a strong Greek word, 'pleads with' (παρακαλῶ – *parakalō*, cf. 2 Cor. 12:8) each woman to be reconciled to the other. An important point is Paul's dual use of this word: '*I plead with* Euodia *and I plead with* Syntyche.' Paul urges them to 'agree together and live in harmony' with one another.[349]

We know nothing more about either woman but Paul's specific urging of them personally in a letter to their church indicates that they were prominent members of the Christian community in Philippi, whose dissension must have been known and could not but cause disruption among their fellow believers.

Paul asks an unnamed 'loyal yokefellow' (see Syzygus as a possibility) to assist in bringing about reconciliation.[350] Motyer provides an excellent analysis of resolving such issues with which, of course, all of us have to contend.

> In summary, then, this why Paul sees disunity as such a solemn and disastrous thing: it is contrary to the apostolic mind; it is a denial of the nature of the church; and it is a flaw in the church's armour against the world. In the light of all this, how noteworthy

347. HSIBD, p. 359.

348. ibid., p. 1021.

349. Zerwick and Grosvenor, *Grammatical Analysis*, vol. 2, p. 601.

350. Various people have been nominated as the mediator but all suggestions are speculative.

that Paul (who apparently knew all about the differences between the two women in question) neither specifies the problem nor tries to act as mediator. He does not sum up their rival claims; he does not say to the one or the other, 'You are wrong; you must apologise.' He does not sit on the fence with 'There are two sides to every story; you are both partly right and partly wrong. So kiss and make up.' It is not a matter of who is right and who is wrong or what rightness and wrongness exists on each side. The plea *I entreat* is made to each contestant alike. No doubt each said, 'I am right, she is wrong'; but to Paul each was under the same obligation to make the first move.

Relationships can be atrociously tangled, and Christian relationships are no exception. Starting, however, where things are fairly simple, there is the situation where one believer has wronged another. Maybe it was this for Euodia and Syntyche. Neither is to wait for the other. The one is not to say, 'I am perfectly ready to make an apology when I have a hint that it will be accepted.' Each must make the first move.

More difficult is the case where each believes the other to be in the wrong and where no amount of 'talking the thing through' can make sense of it. Yet even here there is no need to allow a breakdown of Christian love and communication. 'Conditional' apologies are in order: 'I do not see where I have wronged you, but it is plain that you feel I have hurt you, so please forgive me' – and all the realities of grace and power, forbearance and gentleness available *in the Lord* can be brought to our aid; the place of prayer is open, and even though the past cannot be resolved it need no longer be an open sore.

Worst of all are cases where a breakdown in trust is involved: perhaps one Christian has betrayed a confidence and the other, the betrayed, has to say, 'How can I ever trust him again?' And, sadly, the answer sometime has to be that the old trust cannot be recovered, that from now on all serious communication be with a third party present to vouch, if necessary, for what was said, and that where there was once frankness, now there must be wariness. It is sad when things are so, but fellowship is not foolishness and we need to be aware of each other's strengths. Nevertheless, *in the Lord* we can find strength to eradicate bitterness of heart, and even though we cannot speak of the past again, never mind mend it, we can understand one another, express practical concern and pray for each other.

> While we may thank God that the first and easiest of our three examples is more common that the others, it is in itself no matter for thanksgiving but rather for action. The matter of dispute between Euodia and Syntyche is not described and we may each fill in our own details. Likewise, the *true yokefellow* is left anonymous: here also we may put our own names, ever alert to discern and then to heal the cancer of disunity in the fellowship of the church.[351]

This advice is quite relevant when applied to the disagreement between Paul and Barnabas over Mark (Acts 15:39) as well as Paul's differences with Cephas and Barnabas following the incident in Galatians 2:13.

Fortunatus

1 Corinthians 16:15-18

[15]Now I urge you, brethren (you know the household of Stephanas, that they were the first fruits of Achaia, and that they have devoted themselves for ministry to the saints),

[16]that you also be in subjection to such men and to everyone who helps in the work and labours.

[17]I rejoice over the coming of Stephanas and Fortunatus and Achaicus, because they have supplied what was lacking on your part.

[18]For they have refreshed my spirit and yours. Therefore acknowledge such men.

Unsurprisingly, the name Fortunatus means 'fortunate'.[352] It is a common Latin name and he was probably a slave or freed man from Achaia, which, in Paul's time, was a Roman province of Greece whose capital was Corinth. Notwithstanding whatever connotation his name once had and his circumstances, there can be no doubt that, after his conversion, Fortunatus regarded his name with special affection. He was fortunate indeed because, whatever else he was, he was now a slave of Jesus Christ. Moffatt assumed that he and Achaicus belonged to the household of Stephanas (either as slaves or freed men) and this seems likely.[353] They were members of the

---

351. Motyer, *Philippians*, pp. 203-4.

352. HSIBD, p. 395.

353. See Moffatt, *The First Epistle of Paul to the Corinthians*, p. 279; Ciampa and Rosner, *1 Corinthians*, p. 859.

Corinthian church. The mention of the 'household of Stephanus' implies that he was a person of some means.

Corinth is nearly 900 miles (1,450 km) from Ephesus by land. These three may have walked the journey but it is much more likely that they crossed the Aegean Sea in about two weeks during Paul's extended stay in Ephesus (A.D. 53 to 55). Scripture suggests that they brought with them a letter with questions for the apostle to answer (1 Cor. 7:1). Paul urges the Corinthian church 'to submit to such people and to everyone who joins in the work and labours at it'.

> Thus we may have here people, including two of relatively low social standing, who are to be honoured for their 'serving' of the people, characterised in part by their refreshing of both Paul's spirit and that of others. The anomaly of 'servant' figures being 'respected' for their labouring is made all the more stark by Paul's insistence that these figures be submitted to precisely because of their labour (1 Cor. 16:16). This verb implies the attribution of authority – an unexpected command in the wider Graeco-Roman context given the social status of the individuals concerned.[354]

The NASB translates τοῖς ἁγίοις (*tois hagiois*) as 'of the Lord's people', but the Greek text refers to 'the saints' (of Corinth and Achaia). 'The military echoes in the imperatives of 1 Cor. 16:13 have probably inspired Paul's use of τάσσω [ἔταξαν] and ὑποτάσσω here (1 Cor. 16: 15, 16), both of which also have military connotations.'[355] The use of συν- (*sun-*) in συνεργοῦντι (*sunergounti*) in this context indicates that 'certain ones are worthy of more exceptional regard than others'.[356]

The three men visited Paul in Ephesus while he was writing this letter to the Corinthians. It is possible that they took the letter back to Corinth on their return journey. Paul writes to the Corinthians

---

354. Clarke, 'Refresh the Hearts of the Saints,' pp. 277-300, esp. p. 288. See Fee, *1 Corinthians*, pp. 918-20, for a detailed analysis of the relationship between Stephanas, Achaicus, and Fortunatus, reflecting Paul's new Christian society in practice.

355. Brookins and Longenecker, *1 Corinthians 1–9*, p. 202.

356. ibid., pp. 202-3.

that he rejoiced over their visit because 'they have supplied what was lacking on your part'. There is no implied criticism that these men did something that the Corinthian church could not (or would not) do. The sense of the words is that, by coming to Paul personally, they have brought a little bit of Corinth with them.[357]

Paul tells the Corinthian church that their visit 'refreshed my spirit and yours'. The word for 'refreshed' (ἀναπαύω – *anapauō*) is the same as that used by Jesus in Matthew 11:28 when He talks about giving 'rest' to those who labour and are heavy-laden.[358] Perhaps their presence lifted a burden of concern from Paul's shoulders about the state of the Corinthian church. Morris also comments about the end of 1 Corinthians 16:18 that '*And yours* is an interesting addition. Not only was it good for Paul to receive news from Corinth; it was good for the Corinthians to send the messages to Paul that they had done through these three men. The believers should acknowledge people like this; i.e. know them for what they are, and ascribe to them their true worth.'[359]

In 1 Corinthians 16:18 Paul concludes that Fortunatus and his companions should be highly esteemed by the Corinthian Christians, only reinforcing his commendation in verse 15. The use of ἐπιγινώσκω (*epiginōskō*) should be understood as meaning 'appreciate (or recognise) these men for what they are'.[360]

Gaius Titius Justus

Acts 18:7

[7]Then he [Paul] left the synagogue and went to the house of a man named Titius Justus, a worshipper of God, whose house was next door to the synagogue.

Romans 16:23

[23]Gaius, host to me and to the whole church, greets you. Erastus, the city treasurer, greets you, and Quartus, the brother.

---

357. Moffatt, *1 Corinthians*, 280. See Brookins and Longenecker, *1 Corinthians 10–16*, p. 203.

358. Compare this with the use of ἀναψύχω – *anapsuchō* regarding Onesiphorus (2 Tim. 1:16).

359. Morris, *1 Corinthians*, p. 245 (original emphasis).

360. Zerwick and Grosvenor, *Grammatical Analysis*, vol. 2, p. 533.

1 Corinthians 1:13-15

[13] *Has Christ been divided? Paul was not crucified for you, was he? Or were you baptized in the name of Paul?*

[14] *I am thankful that I baptized none of you except Crispus and Gaius,*

[15] *... so that no one would say you were baptized in my name.*

Gaius was a very common Latin name and was a Roman *gens* name.[361] He lived in Corinth. It is quite unlikely that he is the same person as those named in Acts 19:29 (from Macedonia); 20:4 (from Derbe); 3 John 1 (location unknown).[362] The more important reference to this man is Romans 16:23, where Paul greets the Roman Christians. Gaius is the possessor of some wealth because he is able to show hospitality both to Paul and 'the *whole* church' (ὅλης τῆς ἐκκλησίας – *holēs tēs ekklēsias*). Cranfield suggests that the reference to 'the whole church' is meant to indicate that 'he gave hospitality to travelling Christians passing through Corinth (ὅλης τῆς ἐκκλησίας – [*holes tēs ekklēsias*], denoting the Church as a whole)'.[363] The implication from this verse is that Paul is staying with Gaius as he writes his letter to the Romans.

> The term translated 'host' was used to refer both to a foreigner (e.g. Eph. 2:19) and to someone willing to extend hospitality to a foreigner. Plato, for example, could describe the custom by which a distinguished person might travel to another country, present himself to people of similar social standing there, and 'believing himself to be a proper guest [ξένος] for such a host [ξένῳ]' expect to receive a warm welcome (*Laws* 953d [G Bury, LCL]).
>
> Gaius was not merely a host to the foreigner Paul but to 'the whole church' (ὅλης τῆς ἐκκλησίας). This phrase probably does not mean that Gaius accommodated in his supposedly large house an occasional plenary assembly of all the different, smaller house churches in Corinth. Since the term 'host' indicates that he was

361. There are four men named Gaius in HSIBD; however, there is no reference there to the Gaius of Romans 16:23; Cranfield, *Romans*, vol. 2, p. 807.

362. ibid., pp. 806-7.

363. ibid., p. 807. Jewett, *Romans*, pp. 980-1 notes that most commentaries support this inference.

> hospitable to foreigners, 'the whole church' describes the wide extent of his hospitality to believing foreigners. Paul may have especially had in mind the delegates from Macedonia, Asia, and Galatia who had assembled in Corinth to go with Paul and the collection to Jerusalem (cf. Acts 20:4). The term 'church' (ἐκκλησία), therefore, has the sense here of the worldwide fellowship of believers (cf. 1 Cor. 10:32; Gal. 1:13) rather than, as in Romans 16:1, 4, 5, and 16, the local 'assembly' of believers.[364]

Acts 18 describes Paul's attempts to speak to the Jews and Greeks (i.e. Gentiles) in the synagogue in Corinth on several Sabbath days, but they resisted his attempts to proclaim the gospel and he departed from them. Acts 18:7 notes that Paul 'went to the house of a certain man named Titius Justus, a worshipper of God, whose house was next to the synagogue'. However, the leader of the synagogue, Crispus, was converted to belief in Christ and Paul confirms in 1 Corinthians 1:14 that he baptised Crispus and a person called Gaius. It was not Paul's usual practice to baptise converts, but given the absence of Christian leaders in Corinth during the city's initial evangelisation, Paul probably had little alternative.

Brookins and Longenecker make the following comments regarding 1 Corinthians 1:13 about the nature of this baptism.

> **εἰς τὸ ὄνομα.** Not 'in the name', but 'into the name'. Harris (pp. 228-9) identifies 'three principal views' about the meaning of this phrase, arranged 'in descending order of probability': (1) It may denote 'the establishment of a relationship of belonging and possession, and so a transference of ownership'; (2) it may mean 'with respect to', denoting the 'fundamental reference or purpose of some thing, rite, or action', in such a way as to distinguish it from other rites or actions; or, (3) especially when the context pertains to baptism, it may indicate that a person is endowed with the benefits of the salvation accomplished therein. The first option seems best, but this could be stated in a manner more resonant with Paul's notion of 'being in Christ'. To be 'baptised into the name of Christ' means to

364. Thielman, *Romans*, p. 743. For a contrary view, see Dunn, *Romans 9-16*, pp. 910-11.

> be united with or incorporated into the One to whom the baptised person gives his/her allegiance. Cf. εἰς τὸν μωϊσῆν ἐβαπτίσθησαν in [1 Cor.] 10:2; see also Rom. 6:3; Gal. 3:27.[365]

Since Crispus was a leading Jew, his baptism by the apostle himself would have confirmed the sincerity of his conversion. It would have been convenient for Gaius to be baptised at the same time.

> Paul repeats the idea expressed in the third question of verse 13 in a different way. The conj. *hina* expresses result (ZBG ʃ352; BDF ʃ391.5). Paul thus insists that no matter what relationship the Paul-group of Corinth might be claiming to him, it does not stem from him as their baptiser. Some interpreters have argued that this was the nature of the rival groups, that Corinthians who had been baptised by a certain preacher developed a bond of allegiance to him. Now Paul would be countering that claim.[366]

It has been suggested that this Corinthian, Gaius, is the same person as Titius Justus in Acts 18:7; his full name being Gaius Titius Justus. This remains an uncertain proposition but, in my view, is highly likely, as argued by Goodspeed.[367] The insertion of Gaius in Romans 16:23 is a critical confirmation of 1 Corinthians 1:26, where Paul describes the church as comprising 'not many wise according to the flesh, not many mighty, not many noble': but there were some! This verse was also important in the description of Erastus.

An often-overlooked aspect of Gaius Titius Justus is that he clearly has a Roman name. Yet he was 'a worshipper of God' (σεβομένου τὸν θεόν – *sebonemou ton Theon*). This was not unusual. 'God-fearers', as Gentiles converted to Judaism were called, were found all across the Roman Empire and there are many cases of such people recorded in the NT. Having been called to convert from polytheism to monotheism (Judaism), it was probably less of a mental hurdle to see Jesus Christ as the culmination of Judaistic belief; whereas Jews were inherently

365. Brookins and Longenecker, *1 Corinthians 1-9*, p. 19.

366. Fitzmyer, *First Corinthians*, p. 147.

367. See E. J. Goodspeed, 'Gaius Titius Justus,' *JBL* 69, no. 4 (1950): pp. 382-3; Dunn, *Romans 9-16*, 910-11.

imbued with a sense of religious superiority in their own beliefs. We see examples of God-fearers in Acts 13:43, 50; 16:14; 17:4, 17 before the mention of Gaius Titius Justus.

> Some in Corinth may have thought it to be personally advantageous to be associated with Paul, Apollos or Peter via the administration of baptism. This type of thinking was rife in Corinth, where personality-centred politics and status-seeking 'hangers-on' were the norm in secular society. If so, Paul's comments in these verses would have given such Corinthian Christians no encouragement. In what must be the greatest disappointment in Paul's otherwise impressive history of giving thanks, the apostle is grateful that he performed so few baptisms in Corinth! He wants no part in petty rivalries, even if indirectly, and is happy not to have unwittingly played into anyone's hands. In the context of his arguments in the unit, not having baptised many of the Corinthians contributes to Paul's depiction of the nature of Christian ministry as a 'shared partnership'. (Thistleton, p. 140)
>
> The only two that Paul does admit to baptising, at least initially (see v. 16), are *Crispus* and *Gaius*, presumably early converts in the city. ... *Gaius* may be the Gaius of Romans 16:23, whose 'hospitality' Paul, along with the 'whole church', enjoyed in Corinth. Since Gaius was a common name (cf. Acts 19:29; 20:4; 3 John 1; Martyrdom of Polycarp 22:2), this identification is not certain.[368]

However, Paul concedes in 1 Corinthians 1:14 that he baptised Crispus and Gaius.

> **εἰ μὴ**. An idiom meaning 'but', 'except' (= πλήν). To say, 'I baptised no one except', rhetorically downplays Paul's involvement in baptisms more than if he said, 'I baptised only'.[369]

Since Crispus was a leading Jew, it is quite possible that, given his seniority in Judaism and his conversion to Christianity, he baptised the new converts mentioned in the latter part of Acts 18:8. The other baptisers may have been Stephanas, the first convert in Corinth, and Gaius Titius Justus.

---

368. Ciampa and Rosner, *1 Corinthians*, pp. 83-4 express some doubt.
369. Brookins and Longenecker, *1 Corinthians 1-9*, p. 20.

From 1 Corinthians 1:15, it may appear that Paul was not particularly concerned who baptised who.[370] He wrote that he had not come to baptise but to preach the gospel (1 Cor. 1:17). However, in 1 Corinthians 1:15, the phrase εἰς τὸ ἐμὸν ὄνομα (***eis to emon*** *onoma* – ***into my*** name) is similar to εἰς τὸ ὄνομα in verse 13 above it. Therefore, this fact might be quite important to Paul in the light of the divisions within the Corinthian church. The literal meaning '*into my* name' may be important in the light of 1 Corinthians 1–3 where one group of believers is 'the Paul group'. Paul never baptised anyone *into his* name. *All were baptised, not into any person, but into Christ.* Paul is emphasising that *his* baptism of people is not the significant issue.[371]

Hermas

Romans 16:14

[14]Greet Asyncritus, Phlegon, Hermes, Patrobas, Hermas, and the brethren with them.

Hermas is a Greek name, meaning unknown, but probably related to Hermes (see below). Ἑρμᾶς can be either a dialect form of Ἑρμῆς or an abbreviation for several names beginning with Ἑρμ'.[372] He is greeted with Asyncritus, Phlegon, Hermes, and Patrobas. All of these are masculine names of Gentile slaves or freed men. Given the common greeting afforded to them, it is most likely that they worked in the same household or were members of a particular house church in Rome. This possibility is supported by Paul's addition of 'and the brethren with them'.[373] It was clearly a larger group whom Paul knew to be associated with one another and who were committed Christians. However, they had not worked with Paul, only being described as 'brothers'.

---

370. See Ciampa and Rosner, *1 Corinthians*, p. 84.

371. For a technical discussion of the alternative interpretations of εἰς τὸ ἐμὸν ὄνομα, see Brookins and Longenecker, *1 Corinthians 1-9*, pp. 19, 21.

372. Cranfield, *Romans*, vol. 2, p. 795. This paragraph has also been used to describe Asyncritus, Phlegon, Hermes and Patrobas to avoid unnecessary cross-referencing.

373. ibid., p. 795.

Jewett notes that Hermas 'belongs with a group of other persons whose servile status is indisputable lead[ing] me to concur with Lampe that he is probably a slave or freed man.'[374]

> Here a number of brethren are selected without distinction. This mark of brotherly attention would gratify those whom the Apostle here names, beside the brethren who were with them. The Lord's people are not equally distinguished, but they are all brethren equally related to Him who is the Elder Brother of His people. Some of them are eminent, and others are without peculiar distinction. They are all, however, worthy of love. A Church is not to consist of the most eminent believers, but of believers, though some be of the lowest attainments. A church of Christ is a school in which their education is to be perfected. And all the saints which are with them – that is the believers in their families and neighbourhood. These might not be personally known to the Apostle, but as believers they were worthy of his notice.[375]

Hermes

Romans 16:14

[14]Greet Asyncritus, Phlegon, Hermes, Patrobas, Hermas, and the brethren with them.

Hermes was the name of the Greek god of commerce (Mercury is the Roman equivalent), who served as the messenger of the other gods. It was a very common slave name. Hermes is greeted with Asyncritus, Phlegon, Patrobas, and Hermas. All of these are masculine names of Gentile slaves or freed men. Given the common greeting afforded to them, it is most likely that they worked in the same household or were members of a particular house church in Rome. This possibility is supported by Paul's addition of 'and the brethren with them'.[376] It was clearly a larger group whom Paul knew to be associated with one another and who were committed Christians. However, they had not worked with Paul, only being described as 'brothers'. Jewett notes that Hermes 'belongs with a group of other persons whose servile

374. Jewett, *Romans*, p. 970.
375. Haldane, *Romans*, p. 640.
376. Cranfield, *Romans*, vol. 2, p. 795.

status is indisputable lead[ing] me to concur with Lampe that he is probably a slave or freed man'.[377]

> Here a number of brethren are selected without distinction. This mark of brotherly attention would gratify those whom the Apostle here names, beside the brethren who were with them. The Lord's people are not equally distinguished, but they are all brethren equally related to Him who is the Elder Brother of His people. Some of them are eminent, and others are without peculiar distinction. They are all, however, worthy of love. A Church is not to consist of the most eminent believers, but of believers, though some be of the lowest attainments. A church of Christ is a school in which their education is to be perfected. And all the saints which are with them – that is the believers in their families and neighbourhood. These might not be personally known to the Apostle, but as believers they were worthy of his notice.[378]

Hermogenes

2 Timothy 1:15

[15] *You are aware of the fact that all who are in Asia turned away from me, among whom are Phygelus and Hermogenes.*

This Greek Gentile name means 'offering of Hermes'.[379] Not everything went in Paul's favour. In this verse he recalls to Timothy that '[Y]ou are aware of the fact that all who are in Asia turned away from me, among whom are Phygelus and Hermogenes.' Paul also uses the verb ἀποστρέφω (*apostrephō*) in Romans 11:26, 2 Timothy 4:4, and Titus 1:14. It is a strong verb (cf. Luke 23:14, NIV). This verb can 'denote decisive rejection (as in 2 Tim. 4:4; Titus 1:14; Heb. 12:25). ... Believers and even ministers today may recast or abandon the core gospel message because of various pressures, but from Phygelus and Hermogenes we learn that such moves have a hoary heritage (see also 1 Cor. 4:9-13; 2 Cor. 4:7-12; 1 John 2:19).'[380] The sense

377. Jewett, *Romans*, p. 970.
378. Haldane, *Romans*, p. 640.
379. HSIBD, p. 475.
380. Yarbrough, *Letters to Timothy and Titus*, p. 367.

of the verse is that these people are still residing in the province of Asia.[381]

The claim that this turning away from the apostle refers to 'all who are in Asia' is clearly 'hyperbolic',[382] given the loyalty of Onesiphorus. Guthrie, quoting White, describes it as 'the sweeping assertion of depression',[383] which reflected Paul's imprisonment and the likelihood of his death. Paul's strong statement confirms his desire that Timothy does not turn away from him. The naming of Phygelus and Hermogenes may suggest that they were the driving force in this withdrawal of support from Paul.

Herodion

Romans 16:11

[11]Greet Herodion, my kinsman. Greet those of the household of Narcissus, who are in the Lord.

In this list of names 'the fact that Paul next mentions someone called Herodion, a name which naturally suggests a connexion (probably a slave or freed man) of the Herod family, may perhaps be some support for the suggestion that the Aristobulus of Rom. 16:10 belonged to the family of Herod.'[384] It may be the case that Herodion was a slave in the house of Aristobulus. 'Again, the fact that Paul adds no commendation indicates that he knows of Herodian's role by hearsay. As an indisputably Jewish Christian, Herodion is honoured by Paul with the request that all other converts greet him as a member of their family.'[385]

Commentators have varied in their interpretation of τὸν συγγενῆ μου – *ton sungenē mou*, 'my kinsman' (NASB). Some prefer that this description means that he was a relative of Paul;[386]

381. Guthrie, *Pastoral Epistles*, p. 135; Yarbrough, *Letters to Timothy and Titus*, p. 367.

382. Collins, *1 & 2 Timothy and Titus*, p. 215.

383. Guthrie, *Pastoral Epistles*, p. 135. For a completely contrary view, see Oden, *First and Second Timothy and Titus*, p. 170.

384. Cranfield, *Romans*, vol. 2, p. 792. See the entry for Aristobulus.

385. Jewett, *Romans*, p. 967.

386. See Hodge, *Romans*, p. 449; Haldane, *Romans*, p. 637.

others that, as in Romans 9:3, Paul is referring to fellow Jews.[387] It is clear that he was not part of Paul's family, but a fellow Jew.

Hymenaeus

1 Timothy 1:18-20

[18] This command I entrust to you, Timothy, my son, in accordance with the prophecies previously made concerning you, that by them you fight the good fight,

[19] ... keeping faith and a good conscience, which some have rejected and suffered shipwreck in regard to their faith.

[20] Among these are Hymenaeus and Alexander, whom I have handed over to Satan, so that they will be taught not to blaspheme.

2 Timothy 2:16-18

[16] But avoid worldly and empty chatter, for it will lead to further ungodliness,

[17] ... and their talk will spread like gangrene. Among them are Hymenaeus and Philetus,

[18] ... men who have gone astray from the truth, claiming that the resurrection has already taken place; and they are jeopardising the faith of some.

Hymenaeus (whose name was also that of the mythological Greek god of marriage) lived in Ephesus,[388] where Timothy was then residing. Paul wrote 1 Timothy from Macedonia after being released from his first imprisonment in Rome (see Acts 28:30-31).[389]

Paul warns Timothy that some people 'have turned their backs' (ἀπωθέω – *apōtheō*) on the faith.[390]

> 'Rejected' translates a word (*apōtheō*) used six times in the NT, three of those in Acts, where it refers to a literal pushing aside of Moses ([Acts] 7:27) in a physical scuffle and then a rejection of his spiritual leadership by the wayward children of Israel in the exodus

---

387. See Murray, *Romans*, p. 229, Bruce, *Romans*, p. 272; Cranfield, *Romans*, vol. 2, p. 788. See the entry for Andronicus, which discusses this point.

388. Yarbrough, *Letters to Timothy and Titus*, p. 135.

389. See Stott, *The Message of 2 Timothy*, pp. 16-18, for a summary of Paul's possible travels between his first and second imprisonments in Rome.

390. Zerwick and Grosvenor, *Grammatical Analysis*, vol. 2, p. 629.

> ([Acts] 7:39). Paul and Barnabas dramatically charge their synagogue audience with rejecting God's word ([Acts] 13:46), resulting in a historic shift in their mission so that they will henceforth target the Gentiles. Paul used the same word twice in Romans 11, once in the historical question 'Did God reject his people?' (v. 1) and again with the insistence 'God did not reject his people', adapting words from the LXX. Usage in Josephus and Philo indicates the word often connotes a rash and violent dispersal of something or putting someone to flight. Paul may be understood as describing, not a less-than-perfect faith or a spiritual outlook not completely congruent with his own, but a determined or even vehement blockage. His implied critique in this verse is by no means petty.[391]

They rejected it so completely that Paul describes their fate as a 'shipwreck' (ἐναυάγησαν – *enauagēsan*). By this time, Paul was well aware of the outcome of being in a shipwreck (2 Cor. 11:25; Acts 27:9-44)!

> These misunderstandings are in fact culpable and wilful distortions that wreak havoc on what believers affirm and confess to their salvation – indicating that to follow their mistaken lead would be fatal betrayal of the means of grace embodied in the truth of the gospel (see Col. 1:5). Paul refers to people like someone who receives the keys to an impressive new car and then promptly takes it out and wrecks it. The reckless driver may live to drive again, but the car is totalled. Timothy is up against persons at Ephesus whose religious bent – whose bogus belief and unredeemed conscience – would result in total wreckage of the apostolic conviction Paul and Timothy champion, were that possible.[392]

Hymenaeus and Alexander were among the casualties. Perkins notes that 'the expression ναυαγεῖν περί (*nauagein peri*) + accusative in the majority of cases refers to geographical locations'.[393]

> Although these examples are not plentiful, they suggest that in 1 Tim. 1:19 'the faith' may be the element against which the shipwreck occurs. The writer may be saying that these believers

391. Yarbrough, *Letters to Timothy and Titus*, p. 389.

392. ibid., p. 134.

393. Perkins, *Pastoral Letters*, p. 27.

> have been wrecked on the rock of the faith. If this is a correct reading of the metaphor, then 'the faith' – i.e., the gospel teaching – in this setting becomes the shoal on which these people's lives are foundering because they are pursuing a false gospel and placing themselves in danger of God's judgment.[394]

With his authority as an apostle, Paul 'handed [them] over' (NIV) (παραδίδωμι – *paradidōmi*) to Satan.[395] Paul uses exactly the same verb to describe their fate as he uses to describe the judgment of God (Rom. 1:23), where he writes that people 'exchanged the glory of the incorruptible God for an image in the form of corruptible man and of birds and four-footed animals and crawling creatures'. As a consequence, Romans 1:24 says that 'God gave them over' (παραδίδωμι – *paradidōmi*). Both verbs are in the aorist tense, reflecting the finality of the matter.[396] Paul's purpose was so that they might 'be taught' (παιδευθῶσιν – *paideuthōsin*) not to blaspheme (about what we do not know). This word is more forceful than 'taught' (NASB); it relates more to discipline.[397]

> The verb translated 'be taught' (from *paideuō*) is used elsewhere by Paul to refer to restorative instruction rather than blind punishment or vengeance. (See 1 Cor. 11:32; 2 Tim. 2:25; Titus 2:12.) Paul's action is intended to bring or restore them to saving faith rather than allowing them to continue to misrepresent that

---

394. Perkins, *Pastoral Letters*, p. 28. See Köstenberger, *Commentary on 1–2 Timothy and Titus*, p. 89, n. 103.

395. This is a passage subject to various interpretations but the general conclusion revolves around excommunication. See H. Towner, *1-2 Timothy and Titus*, pp. 59-60. Perkins, *Pastoral Letters*, p. 29, provides lengthy comments about παιδευθῶσιν and βλασφημεῖν.

396. See the use of the same verb in Ephesians 5:2, 25 where Christ 'gave Himself up' for the Church. There is a finality about this.

397. See NASBEC, p. 1554, ref. *3860*. Perkins, *Pastoral Letters*, p. 29, suggests that the sense is 'so they might discipline/train themselves not to defame [the faith] profanely'. He notes that '[T]he verb as well as the cognate noun and adjective occur frequently within the PE [Pastoral Epistles] (seven times) to describe actions and roles that profane the faith.'

> faith, slander it, or otherwise speak evil of it, the sorts of meanings that attach to NT occurrences of 'blaspheme'.[398]

Paul uses this same expression in 1 Corinthians 5:5; see also Job 2:6 (LXX) for a similar action. No one seems to be sure of its meaning and implications for the offender. Nevertheless, it is an extreme form of discipline in the Christian community.

> It apparently signifies excommunication (see 1 Cor. 5:2, 7, 13). The idea underlying this is that outside the Church is the sphere of Satan (Eph. 2:12; Col. 1:13; 1 John 5:19). To be expelled from the Church of Christ is to be delivered into that region where Satan holds sway. It is a very forcible expression for the loss of all Christian privileges.[399]

I assume that this is the man referred to in 1 Timothy 1:18-20.[400] It appears that Hymenaeus continued to sin because of his mention in 2 Timothy 2:17-18. Hymenaeus and Philetus taught that the second resurrection of Christ had already occurred.

> The false assertion of Hymenaeus and Philetus that 'the resurrection has already taken place' is not a statement about Jesus' resurrection itself. It is about the meaning of the resurrection for His followers. Some in the early decades of church life illegitimately applied the Bible's end-time teaching (eschatology) in a manner called 'acute realised eschatology' .... It is possible that Hymenaeus and Philetus were also denying the bodily nature of believers' final resurrection, which was an absurd if not revolting notion in some Hellenistic understanding (cf. Acts 17:32) .... Hymenaeus and Philetus were not just misdirected doctrinally but were functioning as a two-man wrecking crew of the fragile faith of first-generation believers under Timothy's care.[401]

---

398. Yarbrough, *Letters to Timothy and Titus*, p. 135.

399. Morris, *1 Corinthians*, p. 88. See Guthrie, *The Pastoral Epistles*, pp. 68-9; Köstenberger, *1–2 Timothy and Titus*, p. 90. Prior, *The Message of 1 Corinthians*, pp. 72-9, provides a fuller discussion of church discipline regarding this matter.

400. Köstenberger, *1–2 Timothy and Titus*, pp. 244-5.

401. Yarbrough, *Letters to Timothy and Titus*, p. 389.

JAMES

ACTS 15:13

[13] *After they had stopped speaking, James answered, saying, 'Brethren, listen to me'.*

ACTS 21:18

[18] *And the following day Paul went in with us to James, and all the elders were present.*

1 CORINTHIANS 15:7

[7] *... then He appeared to James, then to all the apostles;*

GALATIANS 1:18-19

[18] *Then three years later I went up to Jerusalem to become acquainted with Cephas, and stayed with him for fifteen days.*

[19] *But I did not see another one of the apostles except James, the Lord's brother.*

GALATIANS 2:9, 12

[9] *... and recognising the grace that had been given to me, James and Cephas and John, who were reputed to be pillars, gave to me and Barnabas the right hand of fellowship, so that we might go to the Gentiles, and they to the circumcised.*

[12] *For prior to the coming of some men from James, he [Cephas] used to eat with the Gentiles; but when they came, he began to withdraw and separate himself, fearing those from the circumcision.*

James (Hebrew: Jacob, meaning 'a supplanter') was a brother of Jesus.[402] He had become the leader of the early church in Jerusalem, hence his priority over Cephas and John in Galatians 2:9. In 1 Corinthians 15:5-8, Paul provides some chronology as to Jesus' appearance to people after His resurrection. In this account, Christ appeared to Cephas, the Twelve, and more than five hundred brothers and sisters (in Christ) simultaneously, 'then he appeared to James' (v. 7).[403] A great deal could be written about James, but this

402. HSIBD, p. 531; It is not being pedantic to note that, if Jesus' virgin birth is given credence, all of His siblings were technically half-brothers and half-sisters whose parents were Joseph and Mary.

403. See Fitzmyer, *First Corinthians*, p. 551, who seems to regard this James as neither one of the Twelve nor the Lord's blood brother. This interpretation is rejected.

entry focuses on his being referred to in Paul's letter to the Galatians and what a few verses in Acts say about their interaction together.

Notwithstanding his leadership of the Jerusalem church, James apparently exercised his influence in a quiet way. In Acts he is only mentioned by name twice (Acts: 15:13; 21:8). He is mentioned in Galatians concerning two meetings with Paul in Jerusalem.

In Galatians 1:18-19, Paul notes his meeting with Cephas, when he stayed for fifteen days. This occurred three years after his conversion. During that time, he did not meet 'any other of the apostles, except James, the Lord's brother'. It is noteworthy that Paul includes James as an apostle, reflecting his faith in the risen Christ. This stands in stark contrast to his initial unbelief (John 7:5).

Fourteen years after his conversion, Paul, Barnabas, Titus, and other believers went to Jerusalem to meet the leaders of the Jerusalem church to discuss the issue of whether circumcision was necessary for Gentile believers. In Galatians 2:4, the pressure to circumcise Titus was compounded 'because of the false brethren secretly brought in, who had sneaked in to spy out our liberty'. Note the use of the verbs παρείσακτος (*pareisaktos* –'secretly brought in'[404]) and παρεισέρχομαι (*pareiseschomai* – 'sneaked in').[405] But, having described their experiences, the Jerusalem leaders were convinced that the Holy Spirit rested on the brothers from Antioch. The sentence in Galatians needs careful examination because of the particular words chosen by Paul.

Given what he writes in Galatians 2:1-6, Paul gives the impression that he is not fully convinced (*as he wrote that letter*) of the standing attributed to James (the Lord's brother), Cephas (Peter) and, to a lesser extent, John (the apostle) by the Jerusalem church. Paul acknowledged that they recognised him as a fellow-believer (note the use of – *koinōnia*); however, he uses 'who were reputed to be pillars' (οἱ δοκοῦντες στῦλοι εἶναι – *hoi dokountes stuloi einai*) to describe their positions

404. Zerwick and Grosvenor, *Grammatical Analysis*, vol. 2, p. 565, suggest 'brought in surreptitiously'.

405. Jude faced the same problem with the church(es) to whom he wrote. See Manuell, *The Letter of Jude*, pp. 97-8, for the use of παρεισδύω in Jude 4.

of authority in the Jerusalem church. In the NT the verb for 'reputed' (δοκέω – *dokeō*) is often used with an air of scepticism about the authenticity of the claim (cf. Luke 22:24; Phil. 3:4; James 1:26). Although the Jerusalem leaders had confirmed Paul's understanding of the gospel, it may be the case that, within his own spirit, Paul was yet to be completely convinced of the Jerusalem leaders' complete repudiation of the Law of Moses for the gospel of grace alone, given the tricky tactics of the Judaisers in Jerusalem. How committed to their cause was James? Yet it was James who pronounced the declaration of the Jerusalem Council (Acts 15:13-29), which recognised that there was no need for Gentiles to be circumcised before they became Christians.

> Paul is somewhat sarcastic about James, Peter and John, speaking of them as those who 'appeared' to be the pre-eminent ones ([Gal.] 2:2, 6, 9); the reference to 'pillars' probably being ironic.[21] Prophet-like, Paul attaches infinitely more importance to the 'call' of God than the endorsement of men. Nonetheless, he does point to that endorsement.[22] Accordingly the 'go[ing]' to Galatia was first and foremost in obedience to the 'call' of God to Paul, but also – if secondarily – with the endorsement of the 'pillars' of Jerusalem.[406]

In Galatians 2:9 Paul writes,

> 'And having recognised (γνόντες – *gnontes*) the grace having been given to me, James and Cephas and John, the ones having the reputation of being pillars (οἱ δοκοῦντες στῦλοι εἶναι – *hoi dokountes stuloi einai*), gave the right hand of fellowship (κοινωνίας – *koinōnias*) to me and Barnabas, that we should go to the Gentiles

---

406. Barnett, *Galatians and Earliest Christianity*, p. 123. Reference 21 in this quotation is to R. Aus, 'Three Pillars and Three Patriarchs: A Proposal Concerning Gal. 2:9,' *ZNW* 70 (1979): pp. 252-61, who argues that 'pillars' had a positive connotation in the Jerusalem church pointing to these three men as 'patriarchs' of the messianic community. Paul, however, is less than enthusiastic about applying this reverential term to these men. Reference 22 is to J. D. G. Dunn, 'The Relationship Between Paul and Jerusalem According to Galatians 1–2,' *NTS* 28 (1982), pp. 461-78, who argues that Galatians 1–2 may be read to suggest that prior to the 'incident in Antioch' Paul's attitude to the Jerusalem apostles was more deferential than appears in Galatians.

(τὰ ἔθνη – *ta ethnē*) and they to the circumcised (τὴν περιτομήν – *tēn peritomēn*).'

Subsequently, 'men came from James' to Antioch (Gal. 2:12), which caused Cephas to refrain from table fellowship with Gentile believers. Much has been written about these men from James.[407]

> Peter changed his habits in Antioch when 'some men from James arrived' (ἐλθεῖν τινας ἀπὸ ἰακώβου – *elthein tinas apo Iakōbou*) and 'because he feared the people of the circumcision' (φοβούμενος τοὺς ἐκ περιτομῆς – *phoumenos tous ek peritomēs*; the participle is causal). Three major questions arise with respect to these clauses. What was the relationship between James himself and the envoys from James? What is the relationship between these two groups of people? And what was it specifically about these groups or their message that led Peter to change his behaviour? We take these questions in order.
>
> It is unclear whether ἀπὸ ἰακώβου modifies τινας – 'some men belonging to, or representing, James came'; or modifies the verb ἐλθεῖν – 'some men came from James' (so most of the translations) .... In either case, the text indicates some kind of relationship between these people who arrived in Antioch and James, one of the 'pillars' of the Jerusalem church (v. 9). Interpreters have often tended towards opposite poles in assessing this relationship. Some think the envoys accurately conveyed James's own message (e.g., R. Longenecker, 1990: p. 73; Martyn 1997: p. 233; Bockmuehl 2000: pp. 71-3; Schnabel 2004: pp. 1003-4; Elmer 2009: pp. 104-5). Others, however, insist that the envoys only claimed to be representing the apostle and were in reality seeking authority for their message by a bogus appeal to James (e.g., Lightfoot 1881: p. 112; Barnett 1999: pp. 285-6). Our text does not allow us to make a clear decision between these two options (Silva 2003: p. 101). But what we can be sure of is that on the two occasions when James is called on to make a decision about the inclusion of Gentiles *as Gentiles* within the Messianic community, he sides with those who insist that Gentiles should not be required to 'Judaise' (Acts 11:1-18 [James is not mentioned, but we can assume he was involved] and Acts 15). ...

---

407. See Keener, *Galatians*, pp. 139-58; Moo, *Galatians*, pp. 147-9; Schreiner, *Galatians*, p. 140; Morris, *Galatians*, pp. 76-82.

If it is possible, then, that the people who came from James really were representing his own view, were these the same as 'those from the circumcision' whom Peter feared? The designation of people as ἐκ [τῆς] περιτομῆς occurs five other times in the NT: Acts 10:45; 11:2; Rom. 4:12; Col. 4:11; Titus 1:10. In this last text, the reference seems to be to people from 'a circumcision party', that is, as the NLT puts it, 'those who insist on circumcision for salvation'. This could be the meaning in our text (e.g., R. Longenecker 1990: p. 73; Martyn 1997: pp. 236-40). ...

With these identifications in place, we can now answer our third question and suggest that each group is important in understanding why Peter withdrew from the Gentiles. Although we cannot be certain, the following scenario makes good sense of the text and what we know of the larger and specific background. The envoys from James were probably sent to investigate and convey concern about the degree to which Jewish believers were associating with Gentiles. From James's perspective, nothing in the agreement hammered out between the 'pillars' and Paul suggested that Jewish believers would be free to put aside the traditional torah-based barriers to fellowship (and potential moral contamination) with Gentiles. And fueling his concern was the larger social-political situation. Persecution (esp. at the time of the Maccabees) and exile (the Diaspora) led many Jews to erect or insist on careful barriers between themselves and the Gentiles as means of preserving their religious identity .... This background explains why Peter – and James – would be fearful of 'the circumcision'. Outright persecution was perhaps part of the issue, but perhaps even more important was concern about how Jews in Jerusalem would perceive this new messianic movement (this is explicitly a concern that James expresses on a later occasion [Acts 20:21-24]). The envoys from James would, on this reading of the situation, have urged Peter and other Jewish Christians in Antioch to refrain from close contact with Gentiles, out of fear that their behaviour would bring disrepute to Christians in Jerusalem and elsewhere. For James and Peter, then, separating from the Gentile believers would have been perceived as an accommodation to facilitate Jewish evangelism. But Paul rightly sees that such an accommodation cannot be allowed because of what it would say about the Gentiles' status within the community.[408]

408. Moo, *Galatians*, pp. 147-9.

There is an argument that these 'men from James' did not represent his view but only pretended that they had received James' endorsement. Acts 15:23-29 records the letter sent by the Jerusalem Council to the Christians at Antioch. Verse 24 notes that 'we have heard that *some of our number to whom we gave no instruction have disturbed you with their words*, unsettling your souls' (emphasis added). This suggests that the 'men from James' were part of this dissenting group, who would not abandon their prejudices. By this interpretation, these men, then, were the party of whom Cephas was afraid, not James' followers in Jerusalem.

However, if the conclusion is that Paul's underlying thoughts regarding James' (see separate entry regarding Cephas) disquietude about circumcision of Gentiles is correct, those thoughts may have been vindicated by the occurrence of his meeting with James in Jerusalem recorded in Acts 21:17-26. Bruce provides an excellent summary.[409] Acts 21:18 records that: 'And the following day Paul went in with us [Gentiles from Galatia] to *James, and all the elders were present'* (emphasis added). Verse 20 records that '*they* said to him' [Paul] (emphasis added) that there were rumours that Paul was 'teaching apostasy against Moses' (ἀποστασίαν διδάσκεις ἀπὸ μωϊσέως – *apostasian didaskeis apo Mōiseōs*, v. 21).

Bruce comments: 'James and the elders evidently regarded these rumours as false.'[410] The account in Acts 21:17-26 does not give this impression. *James and the elders* presented these accusations to Paul that he was 'teaching all the Jews who are among the Gentiles to forsake Moses' and ignore Jewish customs, especially circumcision. They would not have done so if they were confident that Paul had abided by the agreement *proposed by James* in Acts 15:20 and repeated in Acts 21:25.

Indeed Acts 21:22, 23 records the alarm of James and the elders that Jews outside Jerusalem may become aware of Paul's visit to Jerusalem. *James and the elders* instruct Paul: 'Therefore, do this that we tell you' (v. 24). In the event, Paul did as they asked, which

409. See Bruce, *Acts*, pp. 403-8.

410. Bruce, *Acts*, p. 405.

would eventually lead to his arrest and journey to Rome. A more conciliatory analysis is provided by Cole.[411]

> Acts 15 shows a puzzled but loyal James accepting the palpable differences of approach and method in a kind of 'interim agreement'; but his real embarrassment is manifest in Acts 21:17-26. The irony of the situation is seen in the fact that it was this attempted compromise that, humanly speaking, caused Paul's arrest, imprisonment, and ultimate death, although to Paul this had a deeper explanation and meaning in the purposes of God.[412]

This understanding of the events in Acts 21 suggests that Paul's underlying scepticism of James' complete renunciation of the Mosaic Law (including circumcision) in favour of justification by faith (through grace) alone was vindicated and that, when under pressure from the circumcision party of the Jews in Jerusalem, James (like Cephas) wavered. As in the case of Cephas, it must be said in James' defence that he was only human. Just because he was the leader of the Jerusalem church did not place him beyond fault. With the benefit of hindsight, James and the elders should have supported Paul with more vigour. But we must understand that:

> God moves in a mysterious way,
> His wonders to perform; ...
>
> Judge not the Lord by feeble sense,
> But trust Him for His grace; ...
>
> Blind unbelief is sure to err,
> And scan His work in vain;
> God is His own interpreter,
> And He will make it plain.[413] (cf. Rom. 8:28)

See entries for John and Cephas for further analysis of this issue regarding each of them.

---

411. Cole, *Galatians*, pp. 64-70.

412. ibid., p. 69.

413. Extracts from the hymn by William Cowper (1731–1800), 'God moves in a mysterious way', *The Methodist Hymn Book with Tunes, No. 503*, 34th ed. 1962 (London: Methodist Conference Office, 1933).

Jason

Acts 17:5-9

[5] But the Jews, becoming jealous and taking along some wicked men from the marketplace, formed a mob and set the city in an uproar; and they attacked the house of Jason and were seeking to bring them out to the people.

[6] When they did not find them, they began dragging Jason and some brothers before the city authorities, shouting, 'These men who have upset the world have come here also;

[7] ... and Jason has welcomed them, and they all act contrary to the decrees of Caesar, saying that there is another king, Jesus.'

[8] They stirred up the crowd and the city authorities who heard these things.

[9] And when they had received a pledge from Jason and the others, they released them.

Romans 16:21

[21] Timothy, my fellow worker, greets you, and so do Lucius, Jason, and Sosipater, my kinsmen.

In Acts 17 we have a description of Paul's ministry in Thessalonica, the capital city of the province of Macedonia. Paul and Silas had travelled in a south-westerly direction on the Via Egnatia, about 160 miles (265 km) from Philippi. Thessalonica was made a free city by the Romans in 42 B.C. and had the Greek style of self-government. It was a port on the north-western end of the Aegean Sea. In what appears to have been a relatively short time, some Jews were converted, along with 'a great multitude of the God-fearing Greeks and a number of the leading (πρώτων – *prōtōn*: prominent) women' (Acts 17:4).

Jason, a Greek name meaning 'healing',[414] would have been one of the converted Jews (see below) rather than one of the God-fearing Greek converts.[415] 'The name was common among Jews,

414. HSIBD, p. 537.

415. It is Luke's custom to use 'Greeks' for any reference to Gentiles, but it is likely that most of the God-fearing converts were Macedonians because this occurred in Thessalonica.

being used as a pure Greek substitute for *Ἰησοῦς*, which was simply a transliteration of *Yēšûa*'.[416]

> Though the name for Jews was not so uncommon that we must suppose that a Jewish-Christian Jason in Corinth must be the same person as the Jason here, some secondary support points in this direction. In a letter written during Paul's stay in Corinth in Acts 20:2-3, Paul mentions him next to Sosipater (Rom. 16:21), who is probably the Sopater of Beroea who was there at the same time (Acts 20:4).[417]

However, the Jews became enraged by the number of converts and caused a riot. They may have been encouraged by news from Philippi regarding Paul's adverse treatment there (Acts 16:22-39).

Apparently, Paul and Silas were staying at Jason's house and the crowd came to apprehend them so that they could be brought before the people's assembly (δῆμος – *dēmos*). When they could not be found, Jason and some of the newly converted 'brethren' (ἀδελφοί – *adelphoi*) were apprehended and dragged before the city rulers. Luke describes them as 'politarchs' (πολιτάρχης – *politarchēs*), a very unusual word for magistrates. But see the footnote concerning the accuracy of Luke's nomenclature.[418] Then there is that famous accusation shouted out by the crowd in Acts 17:6. From the KJV onwards, most translations are: 'these men have turned the world upside down.' The NASB more accurately says: 'These men who have upset the world [the inhabited earth] have come here also [οἱ τὴν οἰκουμένην ἀναστατώσαντες οὗτοι καὶ ἐνθάδε πάρεισιν – *hoi tēn*

416. Cranfield, *Romans*, vol. 2, pp. 805-6.

417. Keener, *Acts*, vol. 3, p. 2550.

418. 'The 'politarchs' of Thessalonica, Acts 17:6, 8 (Greek text: τοὺς πολιτάρχας, i.e., τοὺς ἄρχοντας τῶν πολιτῶν, praefectos civitatis, the rulers of the city). This was a very rare title for magistrates, and might easily be confounded with the more usual designation 'poliarchs'. But Luke's accuracy has been confirmed by an inscription still legible on an archway in Thessalonica, giving the names of seven 'politarchs' who governed before the visit of Paul. From P. Schaff and D. S. Schaff, *History of the Christian Church* (New York: Charles Scribner's Sons, 1910), vol. 1, p. 735. A photograph of the stone is found at Leon Mauldin, 'Thessalonian Politarch Inscription & its Bearing on Acts 17:6,8,' *Leon's Message Board, https://leonmauldin.blog/2018/02/21/Thessalonian-politarch-inscription-its-bearing-on-acts-1768/*

oikoumenēn anastasōsantes outoi kai enthade pareisin]. In Luke 2:1 and Acts 11:28 the NIV translates τὴν οἰκουμένην (*tēn oikoumenēn*) as 'the Roman world'. Clearly, Paul's preaching had a major impact on the traditional Jewish Thessalonians, who must have been of a sizeable number in that city. The NIV translates the Greek ἀναστατώσαντες (*anastatōsantes*) as 'caused trouble', which considerably tones down the word's underlying meaning. See the use of ἀναστατώσαντες in Acts 21:38 ('stirred up a revolt'); Galatians 5:12 ('would mutilate themselves'). A serious civic disturbance was underway.

It is clear that, given the absence of Paul and Silas, Jason and his companions were accused of serious crimes against the state: they said that there was another god besides Caesar, called Jesus (Acts 17:7). The authorities in Thessalonica would face serious trouble from the Romans if disloyalty to Caesar was suspected.[419] Jason was right at the centre of this imbroglio because it was alleged that 'Jason has welcomed them'. In the event, the matter was settled by Jason being released after being required to offer a financial pledge to keep the peace, and the removal of Paul and Silas from the city. The use of ἱκανος (*hikanos*) suggests a large sum of money (cf. Matt. 28:12; Luke 8:32; Acts 14:3).

Because Jason was able to accommodate Paul and Silas in his house and pay a large bond to the authorities, we can presume that he was a person of some means and known in the community.

Thielman suggests that Jason 'may well have been one of the Thessalonians, in addition to Aristarchus and Secundus, who functioned as delegates from Macedonia for conveying the collection to Jerusalem' (Acts 20:4).[420]

Jason is one of those who greet the Roman church in Paul's letter from Corinth.[421] No doubt, the trouble aroused in Thessalonica caused him to move to another city. At the conclusion of Romans 16:21, Paul makes it clear that Jason, Lucius, and Sosipater were Jews.

---

419. See Keener, *Acts,* vol. 3, pp. 2551-8 for a detailed examination of the legal issues involved.

420. Thielman, *Romans*, pp. 741-2.

421. Cranfield, *Romans*, vol. 2, pp. 805-6; Jewett, *Romans*, pp. 977-8.

> Jason could be Paul's host from Thessalonica (Acts 17:5-7, 9); the implication of the distinction between Timothy on the one hand (a coworker = one of Paul's 'team') and the group in verse 23 (residents from Corinth) may be that the three mentioned here were delegates from other churches travelling with Paul to deliver the collection (Schmidt; Georgi, *Geschichte*, p. 80; Ollrog, *Paulus*, p. 58). This probability is strengthened since Sosipater could be a longer form of Sopater (BGD; the name is common under both forms [MM]), who is mentioned in Acts 20:4 as one of the delegates of the Pauline churches travelling with him (so e.g., Lietzmann, Cranfield).[422]

For comments on the phrase οἱ συγγενεῖς μου (*hoi suggeneis mou*), a term already used in Romans 16:7, 11 to denote fellow Jews, see the entry on Andronicus.

> By explicitly identifying these persons as his fellow Jews [Rom. 16:21], he [Paul] makes plain that although he identified himself with the 'strong' Gentile majority in Rome, he maintains respectful, collegial relationships with Jewish Christian leaders. Moreover, these Jewish Christian leaders had been entrusted with the Jerusalem offering donated by churches with Gentile majorities, which means that their greetings to all of the congregations in Rome embodies the mutuality that derives from their common life in Christ (Rom. 15:26-27).[423]

Jesus Justus

Colossians 4:10-11

[10]Aristarchus, my fellow prisoner, sends you his greetings; and also Barnabas' cousin Mark (about whom you received instructions; if he comes to you, welcome him);

[11]... and also Jesus who is called Justus; these are the only fellow workers for the kingdom of God who are from the circumcision, and they have proved to be an encouragement to me.

Justus was a common name amongst the Jews, meaning 'the just' or 'the righteous'.[424] So a parallel to 'Jesus called Justus' is a man in Acts 1:23: 'Joseph called Barsabbas, who was also

422. Dunn, *Romans 9-16*, p. 909.

423. Jewett, *Romans*, p. 980. See Peterson, *Romans*, p. 548.

424. HSIBD, p. 610.

called Justus.' This Jew was a faithful Christian remaining with Paul when he was imprisoned in Ephesus. In this verse, along with Aristarchus and Mark, the three men are given a unique description in the NT: 'fellow-workers for the kingdom of God' (οὗτοι μόνοι συνεργοὶ εἰς τὴν βασιλείαν τοῦ θεοῦ – *outoi monoi sunergoi eis tēn basileian Theou*). The reference to only three Jews (ἐκ περιτομῆς – *ek peritomēs*, 'from the circumcision') helping Paul in his imprisonment again raises the constant reminder that Judaisers presented a constant threat and harassment to Paul's gospel work among Jews. It is apparent from Romans 16 that some Jews in Rome strongly supported Paul's gospel of grace; however, there also seems to have been ongoing opposition from Jews (even in Rome) not wishing to renounce historical habits (e.g. Acts 15:1). However, the Jews Aristarchus, Mark, and Jesus Justus were faithful companions.

They were also the only Jews with Paul (if in Ephesus) when he wrote Colossians. Given the number of Jews in Rome favourably disposed towards Paul (e.g. Romans 16), why are none of them mentioned in Colossians? This is further evidence for an Ephesian imprisonment for the writing of Colossians. Paul notes that they were 'an encouragement' (NASB), 'a comfort' (NIV) (παρηγορία – *parēgoria*) to him. This is its only occurrence in the NT. 'Comfort' is preferred by Scott.[425]

> About this man (not mentioned in Philemon) we have no other authentic item of information than that which is given here in Col. 4:11. However, the little that is said about him, as he joins others in sending greetings to the believers in the church of Colosse, is very favourable. We are told that of *Jewish* Christians the three persons just mentioned – Aristarchus, Mark and Jesus Justus – were the only fellow-workers who had been of *comfort* – that shade of meaning of the word παρηγορία predominates here – to Paul. For the term *fellow-workers*: see on Philem. 1. Note the striking modifier after the word *fellow-workers*: 'fellow-workers *for the kingdom of God*.' Did the

425. Scott, *Colossians*, p. 89, provides a helpful explanation of verse 11, but I quote from Hendriksen on the same issue. (Hendricksen implies a Roman provenance for Colossians.) See also the entry for Aristarchus.

apostle thus qualify the term in order to convey the idea, 'Especially among the Jews with their great emphasis upon *the kingdom* I should have received more co-operation?' Besides, had he not preached 'the kingdom of God' among these very people almost from the moment of his arrival in Rome? See Acts 28:31. In that passage and also here in Col. 4:11 the term 'kingdom of God' obviously has reference to the divine realm as a *present* reality. It indicates the dispensation of salvation which in its present phase began with the coming of Christ. God is using Paul and others as his agents in the establishment of this reign of God in the hearts of men. See also on Col. 1:13.

It must not escape our attention that the apostle's statement with reference to these three men as the *only* Jewish-Christian fellow-workers who had been a comfort to him implies deep disappointment with other people of his own race. Paul was painfully aware of his estrangement from his own people (Rom. 9:1-5). And he was not insensitive to the fact that the Judaists (Jews who confessed Jesus but over-emphasised the law) regarded him with suspicion (Acts 15:1, 2, 24; 21:20, 21; Gal. 2:12; Phil. 3:23). It cannot be wrong to regard Phil. 1:14-17; 2:20, 21; 2 Tim. 4:16 as shedding further light on the apostle's feelings anent this matter. All the more, therefore, does he appreciate the co-operation he is receiving from Aristarchus, Mark and Jesus Justus![426]

John

Galatians 2:9

[9]*... and recognising the grace that had been given to me, James and Cephas and John, who were reputed to be pillars, gave to me and Barnabas the right hand of fellowship, so that we might go to the Gentiles, and they to the circumcised.*

John, the son of Zebedee (Matt. 4:18-22), was a fisherman and one of Jesus' disciples: 'the disciple whom Jesus loved' (John 13:23). He was the author of the Gospel of John, 1, 2, 3 John, and Revelation. However, he is rarely mentioned by name in Acts. After the resurrection he was with the other disciples in the upper room (Acts 1:13). His powerful and courageous testimony with Cephas is recorded in Acts 3–4, but after these episodes (see also Acts 5:40),

426. Hendriksen, *Philippians*, pp. 189-90 (original emphases).

he fades from the scene. A great deal could be written about John but this entry focuses on his being referred to in Galatians 2:9 at the Jerusalem Council. This episode is described by Luke in Acts 15 and by Paul in Galatians 2.

Paul, Barnabas, Titus, and other believers went to Jerusalem to meet the leaders of the Jerusalem church to discuss the issue of whether circumcision was necessary for Gentile believers. Having described their experiences, the Jerusalem leaders were convinced that the Holy Spirit rested on them. The sentence above needs careful examination because of the particular words chosen by Paul.

> And recognizing (γνόντες – *gnontes*) the grace that had been given to me, James and Cephas and John, who were reputed to be pillars (οἱ δοκοῦντες στῦλοι εἶναι – *hoi dokountes stuloi einai*), gave to me and Barnabas the right hand of fellowship (κοινωνίας – *koinōnias*), so that we might go to the Gentiles and they to the circumcised (τὴν περιτομήν – *tēn peritomēn*).

Given what he writes in Galatians 2:11-16, my impression is that Paul was not fully convinced (*as he wrote this letter*) of the standing attributed to James (the Lord's brother), Cephas (Peter), and John (the apostle). Paul acknowledged that they recognised him as a fellow believer (note the use of κοινωνία); however, he uses οἱ δοκοῦντες στῦλοι εἶναι to describe their positions of authority in the Jerusalem church. In the NT the verb for 'reputed' (δοκέω – dokeō) is often used with an air of scepticism about the authenticity of the claim (cf. Luke 22:24; Phil. 3:4; James 1:26). Although the Jerusalem leaders had confirmed Paul's understanding of the gospel, it may be the case that, within his own spirit, Paul was yet to be completely convinced of the Jerusalem leaders' repudiation of the Mosaic Law for grace. However, it must be said that Scripture gives no warrant for any criticism of John himself. He is simply included in the leadership group. A more conciliatory analysis is provided by Cole.[427]

427. Cole, *Galatians*, pp. 64-70.

See entries for James and Cephas for further analysis of this issue.

JULIA

ROMANS 16:15

[15] Greet Philologus and Julia, Nereus and his sister, and Olympas, and all the saints who are with them.

Julia (meaning unknown) is a common female name among the *gens* Julius; however, there is nothing to link her as a member of this prominent Roman family. It was also a common slave name. It is much more relevant that Paul's greeting is addressed to 'Philologus *and* Julia'. This most likely indicates husband and wife, or perhaps brother and sister. Cranfield surmises that, if husband and wife, Nereus and his sister are their children.[428] There is no evidence to support this suggestion and it is regarded as unlikely. Paul also greets Olympas and 'all the saints who are with them' (καὶ τοὺς σὺν αὐτοῖς ἀδελφούς – *kai tous sun autois adelphous*). It is most likely that all of these people were members of a particular house church in Rome. It was clearly a larger group whom Paul knew to be associated with one another and were committed Christians.[429] See a similar greeting to a number of men in Romans 16:14. Whereas they were greeted as 'brothers', being all men, this greeting is to 'the saints', perhaps reflecting the combination of men and women. Both are genuine Christian descriptions.

JUNIAS see also ANDRONICUS

ROMANS 16:7

[7] Greet Andronicus and Junias, my kinsmen and my fellow prisoners, who are outstanding among the apostles, who also were in Christ before me.

There has been much discussion on whether the person linked with Andronicus has the name Junia (f.) or Junias (m.).[430] There

---

428. Cranfield, *Romans*, vol. 2, p. 795.

429. See Murray, *Romans*, p. 232.

430. See E. Y. L. Ng, 'Was Junia(s) in Rom. 16:7 a Female Apostle? And So What?' *JETS* 63, no. 3 (2020): 517-33. This article is of particular importance regarding the sex of Junia(s).

are strong arguments supporting both views, which are discussed below. The gender of this name has assumed importance for those who wish to argue for egalitarianism or complimentarianism regarding the roles to be undertaken by women in the church.[431] Especially in the light of E. Y. L. Ng's article in 2020, I am persuaded that the correct name is Junias (*Ἰουνίαν*), derived from a masculine Hebrew name.[432]

The article-noun-και-noun construction τοὺς συγγενεῖς μου καὶ συναιχμαλώτους (*tous suggeneis mou kai sunaichmalōtous*) ['*my kinsmen and my fellow prisoners*'] applies both descriptors to Andronicus and Junias and is an example of the Granville Sharp Rule.[433] Commentators have varied in their interpretation of Andronicus and Junia(s) as 'my kinsmen' (ὅι συγγενοι μου – *hoi suggenoi mou*). Some suggest that they were relatives of Paul;[434] others that, as in Romans 9:3, Paul is referring to fellow Jews.[435] The NIV always translates συγγενής as referring to a familial relative, with the exception of Romans 9:3 where the alternative of 'my race' is clear. This word is used by Paul only in Romans 16:7, 11, 21: he refers to six people with this word. It seems highly unlikely to imagine that so many members of Paul's personal family would be in Rome. Importantly, Strong regards the singular (συγγενίς – *suggenis*) as referring to a personal relative but the plural (συγγενής – *suggenēs*) as referring by extension to a fellow-countryman (i.e. for Paul, a Jew).[436] It seems clear that Paul uses this word not to refer to part of his personal family but to fellow members of the family of Abraham through faith in

---

431. My book, *Gender Wars in Christianity* (Brisbane: Connor Court, 2018) strongly argues the case for complementarianism but this belief has not affected my conclusions concerning Junias. Indeed, before considering Ng's article, I thought it likely that Junia was female.

432. Ng, 'Was Junia(s) in Rom. 16:7 a Female Apostle?', 520.

433. J. D. Harvey, *Exegetical Guide to the Greek New Testament*, p. 379. For a full explanation of the rule and this issue, see the entry for Andronicus.

434. See Hodge, *Romans*, p. 449; Haldane, *Romans*, p. 637.

435. See Murray, *Romans*, p. 229; Bruce, *Romans*, p. 272; Cranfield, *Romans*, vol. 2, p. 788.

436. Strong, *Greek Dictionary of the New Testament*, p. 67, ref. *4772*, *4773*.

Christ. The Pauline use of this word is to refer to fellow Jews. The necessity of this description may reflect the fact that, even though they were Jews, Andronicus and Junia(s) had what looked like Hellenistic and Roman names, respectively.

If feminine, Junia, a Jewess with a Latin name (meaning 'pertaining to Juno'),[437] was the wife of Andronicus, although Hodge suggested the unlikely possibility of her being a sister.[438] Her husband's name was associated with slaves in the imperial household.[439] Duff, arguing from an egalitarian position, makes the following point about the name itself.

> Never mind that while the female name 'Junia' occurs over 250 times in sources outside the Bible, the supposed male version of the name, Junias, cannot be found anywhere. There is undeniably a certain subjectivity involved in all efforts at translation. But here *the assumption that women could not – and should not – assume leadership roles in biblical times or now,* led to a completely unjustified change in the well-established female apostle, Junia, to a make-believe male character, Junias.[440]

The 1977 NASB translation of Romans 16:7 has 'Junia' but, surprisingly, the 1995 edition uses 'Junias' with the marginal note that the name could be 'Junia (fem)'. The 2020 edition reverts to 'Junia'; and 'kinsmen' to 'kinsfolk'.

Those favouring egalitarianism for women's roles in the church regard the identification of Junia as feminine as a step forward in their attempt to make women in the Bible 'equal with men'.[441] More than forty years ago before this became an issue in

437. HSIBD, p. 609.

438. Hodge, *Romans*, p. 449.

439. Cranfield, *Romans*, vol. 2, p. 788.

440. N. J. Duff, 'The ordination of women: Biblical perspectives', *Theology Today* 73, no. 2 (2016): p. 102 (emphasis added). See also D. J. Preato, 'Junia, a Female Apostle: An Examination of the Historical Record', *Priscilla Papers* 33, no. 2 (2019): pp. 8-15.

441. Such 'equality' is never defined except in so far as roles in the church are concerned. This book accepts a complementarian view of women's roles as described in Piper and Grudem, *Recovering Biblical Manhood and Womanhood.* See also Manuell, *Gender Wars in Christianity.*

Christian theology, Cranfield decisively quashed this thought of women being somehow inferior to men in earliest Christianity.

> That Paul should not only include a woman (on the view taken above) among the apostles but actually describe her, together with Andronicus, as outstanding among them, is highly significant evidence (along with the importance he accords in this chapter to Phoebe, Prisca, Mary, Tryphaena, Tryphosa, Persis, the mother of Rufus, Julia and the sister of Nereus) of the falsity of the widespread and stubbornly persistent notion that Paul had a low view of women and something to which the Church as a whole has not yet paid sufficient attention.[442]

However, notwithstanding Junia's apparent apostleship, both Belleville and Duff (like so many feminist commentators on Scripture) feel compelled to make the unwarranted claim that this woman was a *leader* (of equivalent standing to men) in the early church. Being husband and wife, Andronicus and Junia would have lived in a manner according to Paul's teaching about family relationships as per Jewish customs and, particularly, Ephesians 5 – otherwise he would not have praised them so highly. It can be concluded that, if Junia was an apostle, this gave her no authority over men but she would have been most influential amongst female Christians. See the entries for Prisca and Phoebe for relevant comparisons.

Paul describes Andronicus and Junia(s) as '*my* fellow prisoners' (συναιχμαλώτους μου – *sunaichmalōtos mou*), reflecting their preparedness to suffer for Christ (cf. Rom. 7:23). This word is also used in relation to Aristarchus (Col. 4:6) and Epaphras (Philem. 23). Although there is no mention of their imprisonment in the NT, two possibilities arise. First, it is possible that they were imprisoned with Paul in some unreported incident. This is likely to be an imprisonment in Ephesus.[443] The inclusion of μου *(mou* = 'my') may indicate this. Second, it is less likely that they were

442. Cranfield, *Romans*, vol. 2, p. 789.

443. See *Letters From Prison: Ephesians, Philippians, Colossians and Philemon* in the introduction, p. 36.

imprisoned on their own for their gospel work. In either case, Paul's comment must be taken as an authentic statement that, at some time, they were in custody. The entries for Aristarchus and Epaphras support the argument that their (actual) imprisonment was most likely in Ephesus. In my judgment, imprisonment with Paul in Ephesus seems more likely.[444]

Then comes the controversial statement that this couple were 'outstanding among the apostles' (ἐπίσημοι ἐν τοῖς ἀποστόλοις – *episēmoi en tois apostolois*).[445] No one else in the NT is accorded such high praise regarding their relationship with the apostles. There are two alternatives: they were themselves to be accorded the distinctive title 'apostle', or they were highly regarded by that group known as '*the* apostles'.

> Some would claim that, while ἐπίσημοι may mean 'well-known, acknowledged,' had Paul wished to say that Andronicus and Junia were well-known to the apostles, he would have used the Greek preposition ὑπο followed by the genitive τῶν ἀποστόλων, and not ἐν followed by the dative τοῖς ἀποστόλοις. Moreover, the phrase ἐπίσημοι ἐν τοῖς ἀποστόλοις has consistently been interpreted by Church Fathers in an inclusive sense. Thus there is no valid reason not to translate the phrase as 'prominent among the apostles.' Some of these scholars go on to claim that the attempt to interpret the phrase as 'well known to, and acknowledged by, the apostles' stems from a theological bias in order to deny or downplay the fact that women once served as apostles.[(1)] However, in two subsequent scholarly articles published in 2009 and 2015 by David Huttar and M. H. Burer respectively,[(2)] the authors cited further extrabiblical texts that used similar words and similar grammatical constructions and made a strong case that it is plausible to render ἐπίσημοι ἐν τοῖς ἀποστόλοις in Rom. 16:7 as 'well known to the apostles.' The paper by Burer also demonstrated that Paul would have said ἐπίσημοι τῶν ἀποστόλων had he wanted to say that Andronicus and Junia were themselves prominent among the apostles. Here I will make no

444. See Jewett, *Romans*, pp. 962-3.

445. The only other use of ἐπίσημος in the NT is the description of Barabbas (Matt. 27:16).

attempt to adjudicate between the two views. My objective is merely to point out that the common rendering of 'prominent among the apostles' is not unassailable truth.(3)

(1) Thus Belleville concludes by saying, 'The sole basis is a theological and functional predisposition against the naming of a woman among the first-century cadre of apostles.' See her 'Re-examination,' 248. It is nonetheless noteworthy that neither Bauckham, nor Belleville, nor Epp could deny that there were indeed instances cited by Burer and Wallace that can support the non-inclusive view. Belleville merely discounted the evidence as too early (!) to be relevant (247).

(2) David Huttar, 'Did Paul'; M. H. Burer, '"ΕΠΙΣΗΜΟΙ 'ΕΝ ΤΟΙΣ 'ΑΠΟΣΤΟΛΟΙΣ in Rom. 16:7 as "Well Known to the Apostles": Further Defense and New Evidence,' JETS 58.4 (2015): 731–55. In his article, Burer broadened his search of similar Greek constructions in extrabiblical texts, answered the rebuttals of his critics, and laid an even stronger foundation for the 'non-inclusive' view. He also cited other scholars who agreed with his position.

(3) In my opinion, the following extrabiblical texts cited by Huttar and Burer strongly support the non-inclusive view: Euripides, Hipp. 103 (Huttar, 'Did Paul,' 750); inscription Asia Minor FdXanth VII 76.6 (Burer, 'Further Defense,' 741); Lucian, Harm. 1.17 (Burer, 'Further Defense,' 742–43); Ephraem Syrus Theol. Ad imitationem proverbiorum, p. 187, line 6 (Burer, 'Further Defense,' 749); Prolegomena de Comoedia, De comoedia, line 22 (Burer, 'Further Defense,' 750).[446]

Paul then acknowledges that 'they were in Christ before me'.

Paul's description of Andronicus and Junia as before him in Christ is not an afterthought, tacked on merely as further praise. Paul adds this clause because he has named other apostles, and in doing so he never fails to return to his own role as the last and the 'least'. In fact, the only other time Paul uses προ ἐμοϋ is in Gal. 1:17, in reference to other apostles: 'nor did I go up to Jerusalem to those who were already apostles before me, but I went away at once into Arabia, and afterwards I returned to Damascus'.[447]

This places them amongst the earliest Christians and raises the possibility that they may have been among the 500 to whom Christ appeared before His ascension, referred to in

446. Ng, 'Was Junia(s) in Rom. 16:7 a Female Apostle?', 526.
447. Y-J. Lin, 'Junia: An Apostle before Paul,' *JBL* 139, no. 1 (2020): p. 208.

1 Corinthians 15:6.[448] They were probably two of those Hellenistic Jews who believed after Pentecost: see Acts 6:1. Given the early date of their conversion, we cannot exclude the possibility (even likelihood) that, like Paul's self-reference in 1 Corinthians 9:1, Andronicus and Junia(s) were regarded by Paul as apostles.

> As Andronicus and Junia were Christians before Paul, who was converted (on a reasonable chronology) not more than two or three years after the Crucifixion, we must connect them with the primitive church at Jerusalem. As they were Jews bearing Greek or Graeco-Latin names, they would naturally belong to the Hellenistic group whose leaders were Stephen, Philip and their associates. Like others of this group (Acts 8:4-5; 11:21), they became missionaries, or 'apostles' in the wider sense. In the stricter sense 'the Apostles' were the Twelve appointed by Christ Himself; or the Eleven of them who remained faithful, together with Matthias who was appointed in place of Judas. But the Acts of the Apostles gives the title also to Paul and Barnabas (14:14). Paul (1 Cor. 15:5-7) seems to distinguish 'the twelve' from 'all the apostles' as a wider body. He gives the title also to delegates of churches (2 Cor. 8:23). … It seems clear, therefore, that the title was widely given to persons properly commissioned by the Church to preach the Gospel.[449]

The consensus view up to 2008 assumed that *Junia* was derived from a Latin name and that its accusative case would be Junian (*Ἰουνίαν*) as a Greek transcription of a Latin name. Had the person been male, the Latin would be *Ἰουνίος* (nominative) with *Ἰουνίον* as the accusative case. Since Junius was a common Latin *nomen gentilicum* (hereditary surname), women (belonging to this family whether by heredity or as a slave or freedwoman) often bore the personal name Junia..[450] The general consensus that Junia was a woman was challenged in 2008 by A. M. Wolters.[451] An argument for masculinity, based on Wolters' research, and not

448. Bruce, *Romans*, p. 272; Cranfield, *Romans*, vol. 2, p. 789; Thielman, *Romans*, pp. 719-20.

449. Dodd, *Romans*, pp. 237-8.

450. Ng, 'Was Junia(s) in Rom. 16:7 a Female Apostle?', 520.

451. A. Wolters, '*IOYNIAN* (Rom. 16:7) and the Hebrew Name Yĕḥunnī', *JBL* 127, no. 2 (2008): 397-408.

driven by gender issues in the church, was presented by E. Y. L. Ng. Against Lin's position, Ng notes:

> In a recent article, Yii-Jan Lin challenges Wolters's argument in an attempt to reinforce the consensus view that 'Junia' was a well-attested Latin feminine name. See Yii-Jan Lin, 'Junia: An Apostle before Paul,' *JBL* 139.1 (2020): pp. 191–209, esp. pp. 193–94. Here we may note that Lin has made three assumptions: (1) Junia was a woman; (2) she adopted a Latin feminine name while in Rome; and (3) a Jewish man would not adopt a Latin or Greek name nearly identical with a feminine Roman name. The first assumption is the very point to be established, and the other two are simply unproven assumptions.

Interested readers are encouraged to consider Ng's article. Her four lines of investigation were: (1) the etymology of the name Junia(s); (2) the frequency of the name in the Greco-Roman world of the first century; (3) Paul's use of the term 'apostle'; and (4) references to, and discussions of, Junia(s) in church history. One of the key issues is the use of accents in Greek documents in the ninth century and the translation of Greek documents into Latin, where errors may have occurred.

Wolters' article raised the possibility that this name reflected a masculine Hebrew name. (Of course, it must be remembered that Paul describes Andronicus and Junia(s) as Jews.)

> His [Wolters'] argument may be summed up in three steps: (1) A Hebrew name *yḥwny*, meaning "may he be gracious," is attested during Paul's time inscribed on ossuaries. (2) This name would most likely be pronounced *yĕḥunnī*. (3) In biblical Greek, this name would be Hellenised as the first declension masculine noun *Ἰουνίας* and its accusative form would be *Ἰουνίαν*. If so, the fact that accented Greek manuscripts read *Ἰουνίαν* in Rom. 16:7 does not prove that people of that generation understood the name to be feminine. In the end, Wolters does not insist that *Ἰουνίαν* was derived from a masculine Hebrew name but thinks that his view is as persuasive as the common view of a Latin derivation of the name.[452]

452. Ng, 'Was Junia(s) in Rom. 16:7 a Female Apostle?', 520.

It is now apparent that Dunn was incorrect in his comment: 'We may firmly conclude, however, that one of the foundation apostles of Christianity was a woman and wife.'[453] 'In situations like this, it seems prudent to turn to the oldest Greek commentators on Romans, who spoke as their native tongue the language in which Paul was writing. All who comment on the passage assume without debate that Andronicus and Junia were apostles.'[454]

> All we can say with certainty is that this couple had functioned as Christian apostles for more than two decades before Paul wrote this letter to Rome requesting that they be greeted by other believers in Rome who evidently were not inclined to acknowledge their accomplishments and status.[455]

'The fact that we know nothing more of such significant figures shows how fragmentary is our knowledge of this whole period.'[456]

My conclusion is that Junias (*Ἰουνίας*) is a masculine name. He was one of the earliest Christians and an apostle. Alternatively, he was highly regarded by 'the apostles'. He was obviously well known to, and highly regarded by, Paul.

Justus, see **Jesus Justus**

Linus

2 Timothy 4:21

[21]*Make every effort to come before winter. Eubulus greets you, also Pudens, Linus, Claudia, and all the brethren.*

Linus (meaning unknown) was a faithful Gentile Christian with a Latin name (from the Greek *Linos*) who remained with Paul when he was imprisoned in Rome (2 Tim. 4:6, 17) and was obviously known to Timothy.

> Irenaeus says that Linus served as the first bishop of Rome, followed by Anacletus and Clement (*Against Heresies* 3.3.3). If Linus here

453. Dunn, *Romans 9-16*, p. 895. See also Schreiner, *Romans*, pp. 770-1. A more detailed analysis is provided in the entry for Junia.

454. Thielman, *Romans*, p. 719.

455. Jewett, *Romans*, p. 964.

456. Dunn, *Romans 9-16*, p. 895.

> in the text is this bishop, Paul shows no signs of recognising such prominence but simply includes him in a list of names.[457]

He is not mentioned in Romans 16.

> Since Paul passes on their greetings to Timothy, one wonders why they did not support Paul at his trial (v. 16). Perhaps they lacked social standing to make any difference in such a situation, or perhaps it would have exposed them to inordinate danger to appear to stand at Paul's side. Paul does not feel it necessary to account for these details to Timothy .... The Greek verb is singular because in a series, the verb usually takes its number from the nearest subject nominative.[458]

Lois

2 Timothy 1:5

[5]For I am mindful of the sincere faith within you, which first dwelt in your grandmother Lois and your mother Eunice, and I am sure that it is in you as well.

2 Timothy 3:15

[15]... and that from childhood you have known the sacred writings which are able to give you the wisdom that leads to salvation through faith which is in Christ Jesus.

Lois (a Greek name meaning 'desirable') was the mother of Eunice and grandmother of Timothy.[459] She was a devout Jewess. Lois and her daughter Eunice were devoted to the (OT) Scriptures (2 Tim. 1:5) and had taught them to Timothy since he was a child (2 Tim. 3:15). The family lived in Lystra, which Paul visited on his first missionary journey. Lystra was a town on the imperial road from Tarsus to Pisidian Antioch, near the middle of modern Turkey. In response to Paul's preaching, Eunice, Lois, and Timothy became committed Christians. This reflects the benefits for children growing up in families where grandparents and/or parents are Christians. 'The most formative influence on each of us has been our parentage and our

---

457. Yarbrough, *Letters to Timothy and Titus*, p. 459.

458. ibid., p. 459.

459. HSIBD, p. 652; Yarbrough, *Letters to Timothy and Titus*, p. 352, n. 19, regards Lois as a name which was 'common among Jews in the Roman Empire'; while Perkins, *Pastoral Letters*, p. 160, notes that Lois 'is rare in Greek sources of this era'.

home.... True, no man can inherit his parents' faith in the way that he inherits facets of their personality. But a child can be led to faith by his parents' teaching, example and prayers.'[460] We know nothing of Timothy's father except that he was a Gentile.[461]

Paul refers to the continuation of his ancestors' faith in the God of Judaism in 2 Timothy 1:3 (cf. 1 Tim. 5:4). When Paul endured his second imprisonment, he reminded Timothy that he should continue in the same faith strongly held by his grandmother Lois and his mother Eunice. 'At such times a look back at the godly people who have influenced us and the duties that go with our spiritual heritage may provide a stabilising perspective.'[462] Lois' commitment to the OT Scriptures was vindicated by her coming to faith in Jesus Christ. There is affection in Paul's use of τῇ μάμμῃ σου (*tē mammē sou*) (not often found in ancient Greek sources); as Spicq writes: '*un mot affectueux d'enfant* (cf. *l'anglais grannie*).'[463]

> Another clue to the quality of Timothy's faith may lie in Paul's statement that it 'lived' in his grandmother (perhaps mentioned first out of respect for age) and mother. The word translated 'lived' (from Greek *enoikeō*) is found only in Paul in the New Testament. Paul uses it to speak of the Spirit indwelling believers (Rom. 8:11; 2 Tim 1:14). God living in the midst of His people (2 Cor. 6:16, adapted from Lev. 26:12), and 'the message of Christ' dwelling lavishly among the Colossians (Col. 3:16). In Paul, *enoikeō* describes divine, dynamic and transforming presence. The faith of Timothy's maternal forebears was not passive, merely external, or pro forma but deep and alive. 'Lived in' (NIV) is accurate though perhaps a little bland. No wonder Timothy's appropriation of this faith (not shared, it seems, by his father; Acts 16:1, 3) resulted in a fidelity and fervour that Paul found matched by few if any even among his distinguished coworkers (Phil. 2:20).[464]

See also the entries for Eunice and Timothy.

---

460. Stott, *The Message of 2 Timothy*, p. 27.

461. Yarbrough, *Letters to Timothy and Titus*, p. 353.

462. Towner, *1–2 Timothy and Titus*, p. 158.

463. C. Spicq, 'Loïs, ta grand'maman (2 Tim. 1:5),' *Revue Biblique*, 84, no. 3 (1977): pp. 362-3.

464. Yarbrough, *Letters to Timothy and Titus*, p. 353. See Köstenberger, *Commentary on 1–2 Timothy and Titus*, p. 212, n. 24.

Lucius

Romans 16:21

[21]Timothy, my fellow worker, greets you, and so do Lucius, Jason, and Sosipater, my kinsmen.

Lucius is a Latin name meaning luminous.[465] He is one of Paul's colleagues in Corinth, who, with Timothy, Jason, and Sosipater send greetings to the Christians in Rome. Notwithstanding their non-Jewish names, Paul refers to Lucius, Jason, and Sosipater as 'my kinsmen' (τούς συγγενεῐς μου – *tous sungeneis mou*), a term already used in Romans 16:7, 11 to denote fellow Jews.[466] We cannot tell whether these men in Corinth personally knew any of the Christians in Rome, but for them to be included in the letter suggests some degree of familiarity, even if only by reputation. It also needs to be understood that by the time Romans was composed some Jews would have already returned to Rome from Corinth. Lucius, Sosipater, and Jason send greetings to the Roman churches.

This name also appears in Acts 13:1 for a person named 'Lucius of Cyrene', but Cranfield correctly concludes that there is no basis for assuming that the two men are one and the same. 'Lucius is unlikely to be the man of the same name in Acts 13:1, since someone associated with Paul so long ago in the leadership of the church at Antioch would probably have been given a fuller description.'[467] Although Cranfield and Dunn concede the possibility that Lucius (λούκιος) is a variation of Luke (λουκᾶς),[468] this is improbable because Doctor Luke (a Gentile) would not be included amongst Jewish brethren.

> While it is possible that he [Lucius] was a leader in the Corinthian church despite his not having been mentioned in the Corinthian correspondence itself, his mention in a series of four names of which two are definitely delegates for the Jerusalem offering makes it more likely that he was a representative of other Pauline churches.[469]

---

465. HSIBD, p. 657.
466. For further information on this term, see the entry for Andronicus.
467. Dunn, *Romans 9-16*, p. 909.
468. Cranfield, *Romans*, vol. 2, p. 805; Dunn, *Romans 9-16*, p. 909.
469. Jewett, *Romans*, p. 77, n. 19.

Jewett explains that: By explicitly identifying these persons as his fellow Jews [Rom. 16:21], he [Paul] makes plain that although he identified himself with the 'strong' Gentile majority in Rome, he maintains respectful, collegial relationships with Jewish Christian leaders. Moreover, these Jewish Christian leaders had been entrusted with the Jerusalem offering donated by churches with Gentile majorities, which means that their greetings to all of the congregations in Rome embodies the mutuality that derives from their common life in Christ (Rom. 15:26-27).[470]

Luke

Colossians 4:14

[14]*Luke, the beloved physician, sends you his greetings, and also Demas.*

2 Timothy 4:11

[11]*Only Luke is with me. Pick up Mark and bring him with you, for he is useful to me for service.*

Philemon 23-24

[23]*Epaphras, my fellow prisoner in Christ Jesus, greets you,*

[24]*... as do Mark, Aristarchus, Demas, and Luke, my fellow workers.*

The verses above are the only occasions on which Luke (λουκᾶς – *Loukas*) is mentioned by name. His name means 'light-giving'. His humility is reflected by the fact that more than a quarter of the NT was written by him (Gospel of Luke and Acts), yet he never mentions himself by name. However, the 'we' passages in parts of Acts signify his eye-witness accounts of some events in Paul's life. He was the only Gentile to have contributed to the NT. See the entry on Titus regarding his possible family relationship to Luke (which is regarded as unlikely).

Before commenting on Luke generally, one of the few facts that we know about him was that he was a Gentile. Colossians 4:10-11 names the Jewish Christians with Paul. In verses 12 and 14 Paul names three Gentile believers, Epaphras, Luke, and Demas. In verse 12 Paul describes Luke as 'the beloved physician' (ὁ ἰατρὸς ὁ ἀγαπητὸς – *ho iatros ho agapētos*). Special mention should be made of Paul's use of ἀγαπητὸς here. This word appears sixty-one

---

470. Jewett, *Romans*, p. 980. See Peterson, *Romans*, p. 548.

times in the NT. It is meant to be a sign of genuine brotherly and sisterly affection between those who are committed to and love Christ. For this word, the NASB uses 'beloved'. Note how many times it is used in 1 John. It is used by Jude (vv. 3, 17) in his letter. The NIV disappointingly translates this word as 'friend'.

The word Ἀγαπητοί (*Agapētoi*) 'is most frequently used in the NT with reference to the love of Christians for their fellow Christians'.[471] There is a seriously disturbing tendency in the twenty-first century church (carried on from the second half of the twentieth century) to water down the strong language of the Bible to a weak and wimpy version that lacks the force and intention of the Greek terms used by the writers of the NT. Jude's greeting to these believers is 'Beloved!' It now suffers the same fate in the NIV as it does in the Australian version of the Anglican Book of Common Prayer. Compare these two greetings: 'Dearly beloved brethren' (Jude 3)[472] and 'Dear friends'.[473] The first is a Christian greeting full of meaning to the hearers: brothers and sisters in Christ who are dearly loved by Jude. The second would not be out of place at a meeting of the Country Women's Association or any social gathering.

Jude's deeply meaningful and heartfelt 'beloved' has been reduced to a greeting that has no Christian context whatsoever and is as much at home in the secular world as it is in church on Sunday. These weak forms of Christian greeting reflect an attempt (probably well meant) to make Christianity more acceptable to a broader audience and to remove from its liturgy terms that outsiders might find 'threatening' – although it is difficult to see how calling people 'beloved' would put them ill at ease. We are who we are. Let us not be ashamed of it (Rom. 1:16) or weaken the theology of our status before God. Let Christians then greet one another in a manner and form befitting the One who caused us to be loved in the first place.[474]

---

471. Cranfield, *Romans*, vol. 1, p. 69.

472. 'The Order for Morning Prayer' in *The* [Anglican] *Book of Common Prayer*; NASB, NKJV, NRSV, KJV.

473. 'Morning and Evening Prayer' in *A Prayer Book for Australia*, The Anglican Church of Australia (Mulgrave, Victoria: Broughton Books, 1999), p. 4. Schreiner, *1, 2 Peter, Jude*, p. 433, regards 'dear friends' as 'a remarkably weak translation'.

474. Manuell, *The Letter of Jude*, pp. 87-8.

There are a limited number of individuals (*nine men and one woman*) to whom Paul ascribes his dearly felt fellowship with them in his letters. They are Ampliatus (Rom. 16:8), Epaenetus (Rom. 16:5), Epaphras (Col. 1:7), Luke (Col. 4:14), Onesimus (Col. 4:9; Philem. 16), Persis (Rom. 16:12), Philemon (Philem. 1), Stachys (Rom. 16:9), Timothy (1 Cor. 4:17; 2 Tim. 1:2), and Tychicus (Eph. 6:21; Col. 4:7). The closeness in Christian fellowship with Paul of some of these people may surprise us in view of how little we know about them. How true this may be of our own fellowship groups where someone of apparent insignificance is nevertheless 'mighty in the Lord' (cf. 2 Cor. 10:17, 18).

In his letter to Philemon, Paul describes Luke, along with others, as 'my fellow workers' (οἱ συνεργοί μου – *hoi sunergoi mou*). Near the end of his life, Paul writes in 2 Timothy 4:11, 'Only Luke is with me' (λουκᾶς ἐστιν μόνος μετ' ἐμοῦ – *Loukas estin monos met' emou*). I include an excellent summary of Luke's life from HSIBD.

> A bit more of Luke's life and personality can be pieced together with the aid of his writings (Luke and Acts) and some outside sources. Tradition records that he came from Antioch in Syria. This is possible, because Antioch played a significant role in the early Gentile mission which Luke described in Acts (Acts 11; 13; 14; 15; 18). Luke was a Gentile (Col. 4:10-17) and the only non-Jewish author of a New Testament book. A comparison of 2 Cor. 8:18 and 12:18 had led some to suppose that Luke and Titus were brothers, but this is a guess.
>
> Luke accompanied Paul on parts of his second, third, and final missionary journeys. At three places in Acts, the narrative changes to the first person ('we'). This probably indicates that Luke was personally present during those episodes. On the second journey (A.D. 49-53), Luke accompanied Paul on the short voyage from Troas to Philippi (Acts 16:10-17).
>
> On the third journey (A.D. 54-58), Luke was present on the voyage from Philippi to Jerusalem (Acts 20:5-21:18). Whether Luke had spent the intervening time in Philippi is uncertain, but his connection with Philippi has led some to favour it (rather than Antioch) as Luke's home.

> Once in Palestine, Luke probably remained close by Paul during his two-year imprisonment in Caesarea. During this time, Luke probably drew together material, both oral and written, which he later used in the composition of his gospel (Luke 1:1-4). A third 'we' passage describes in masterful suspense the shipwreck during Paul's voyage to Rome for his trial before Caesar. Each of the 'we' passages involves Luke on a voyage, and the description of the journey from Jerusalem to Rome is full of observations and knowledge of nautical matters.
>
> Luke was a humble man, with no desire to sound his own horn. More than one-fourth of the New Testament comes from his pen, but not once does he mention himself by name. He had a greater command of the Greek language and was probably more broad-minded and urbane than any other New Testament writer. He was a careful historian, both by his own admission (Luke 1:1-4), and by the judgment of later history.
>
> Luke's gospel reveals his concern for the poor, sick, and outcast, thus offering a clue to why Paul called him 'the beloved physician' (Col. 4:14). He was faithful not only to Paul, but to the greater cause which he served – the publication of 'good tidings of great joy' (Luke 2:10).[475]

Barnett provides an interesting aside about Luke:

> It was at the time of Paul's first visit to Troas that the anonymous diarist (Luke?) – apparently already a believer – first attached himself to Paul's group, though only from Troas to Philippi, where he seems to have remained from A.D. 49 to 56 (Acts 16:10, 40; 20:5-6).Were the believers that Paul found in Troas in *c.* A.D. 55 connected with the anonymous believer who seven years earlier left Troas with Paul for Philippi?[476]

Lampe provides an unusual assessment of Luke's personality when he comments: 'If Luke had known anything about a socially elevated status of Prisca, he would have loved to mention it, distinguished women being a preferred subject for him: e.g., Luke 8:3; Acts 17:4, 12; cf. 16:14; 17:34.'[477]

475. HSIBD, pp. 657-8.

476. Barnett, *2 Corinthians*, p. 20, n. 20.

477. Lampe, *The Roman Christians*, p. 223.

Of all the beloved fellow workers with Paul, it is difficult to find someone more praiseworthy in Christian character than Luke.

Mark

Acts 12:12, 25

[12] *And when he realised this, he went to the house of Mary, the mother of John, who was also called Mark, where many were gathered together and were praying.*

[25] *And Barnabas and Saul returned from Jerusalem when they had fulfilled their mission, taking along with them John, who was also called Mark.*

Acts 13:13

[13] *Now Paul and his companions put out to sea from Paphos and came to Perga in Pamphylia; but John left them and returned to Jerusalem.*

Acts 15:37-39

[37] *Barnabas wanted to take John, called Mark, along with them also.*

[38] *But Paul kept insisting that they should not take him along who had deserted them in Pamphylia and had not gone with them to the work.*

[39] *And there occurred such a sharp disagreement that they separated from one another, and Barnabas took Mark with him and sailed away to Cyprus.*

Colossians 4:10

[10] *Aristarchus, my fellow prisoner, sends you his greetings; and also Barnabas' cousin Mark (about whom you received instructions; if he comes to you, welcome him);*

2 Timothy 4:11

[11] *Only Luke is with me. Pick up Mark and bring him with you, for he is useful to me for service.*

Philemon 23, 24

[23] *Epaphras, my fellow prisoner in Christ Jesus, greets you,*

[24] *... as do Mark, Aristarchus, Demas, and Luke, my fellow workers.*

1 Peter 5:13

[13] *She who is in Babylon, chosen together with you, sends you greetings, and so does my son, Mark.*

Mark, whose full name was John Mark, was a Jew born in Jerusalem. It was to his mother's house (another Mary) that Cephas fled when he was miraculously freed from prison (Acts 12:3-17).

Her house was large enough for 'many' to gather there for prayer, so Mark was raised in affluent surroundings. 'It was certainly spacious, for it had an outer entrance or vestibule where Cephas knocked, and presumably a courtyard between this and the main house.'[478] Mark is far better known for his Gospel of Mark than for personal incidents in his life. Marshall suggests the possibility that Mark was one of Luke's sources of information about the early church, especially before the resurrection.[479] Who but Mark could inform Luke that his mother's servant was called Rhoda (Acts 12:13)? A great deal could be written about Mark but this entry focuses on his being referred to in relation to Paul. He is generally associated in a lesser role with Cephas or Paul. He was the cousin of Barnabas (Col. 4:10).

When Paul and Barnabas returned to Antioch from their visit to Jerusalem, 'John who was also called Mark' accompanied them (Acts 12:25). They visited many towns in Cyprus and sailed to Perga, the capital city of Pamphylia (now south-eastern Turkey). At that time it was a major city about 7 miles (12 km) from the sea, reached via the river Cestrus from the port at Attalia. Paul did not preach the gospel there but did so on his return journey (Acts 14:25). Suddenly, it was at Perga that 'John' (Mark) left (ἀποχωρήσας – *apochōrēsas*) Paul and Barnabas and returned to Jerusalem (Acts 13:13).[480] No reason is given, although various commentators have speculated on the reason(s). Stott's analysis is the most expansive:

> Why then did he desert? A variety of conjectures has been made. Was he homesick and missing his mother, her spacious Jerusalem home, and the servants? Did he resent the fact that the partnership of 'Barnabas and Saul' (Acts 13:2, 7) had become 'Paul and Barnabas' (Acts 13:13, 46, etc.), since Paul was now taking the lead and eclipsing his cousin? Did he, as a loyal member of Jerusalem's

---

478. Stott, *Acts*, p. 210.

479. Marshall, *Acts*, pp. 209-10.

480. A word used only two other times in the NT: Matthew 7:23 and Luke 9:39. It is a severe word: 'I never knew you. ***Away from*** me, you evildoers!' (Matt. 7:23).

> conservative Jewish church, disagree with Paul's bold policy of Gentile evangelism? Was it even he, who on his return to Jerusalem, provoked the Judaisers into opposing Paul (Acts 15:1f.)? Or did Mark simply not relish the stiff climb over the Taurus mountains which were known to be infested with brigands (cf. Paul's 'in danger from bandits' – 2 Cor. 11:26)? We do not know.
>
> Or was it that Paul was sick and that Mark thought it foolhardy that he was determined to go north over the mountains? We do know that, when Paul reached the cities of the south Galatian plateau, he was suffering from a debilitating illness ('it was because of an illness that I first preached the gospel to you' – Gal. 4:13).[481]

After some time in Antioch Paul encouraged Barnabas to accompany him to the churches visited on their first missionary journey. Barnabas was keen to take Mark with them but Paul was not (Acts 15:37-39). Luke provides the reason for Paul's reluctance to take Mark, being the fact that 'he had deserted (ἀποστάντα – *apostanta*) them' in Pamphylia. This word is a strong description of Mark's departure. Luke uses it ten times in his Gospel and Acts, usually with quite negative connotations. He is clearly on Paul's side regarding this matter. Paul uses it in 1 Timothy 4:1, which the NIV translates as 'abandon', reflecting the firmness of its meaning. The issue over Mark was so serious that Paul and Barnabas 'parted company' (NIV) (ἀποχωρισθῆναι – *apochōristhēnai*, closely related to the word used in Acts 13:13). See also the entry for Barnabas concerning his involvement in this major dispute. Paul chose Silvanus for his next missionary journey. Mark went to Cyprus with Barnabas and disappears from the scene in Acts.

Many years later, Mark appears in a Pauline letter. In Colossians 4:11, along with Aristarchus and Jesus Justus, they and Mark are given a unique personal description in the NT: 'fellow-workers for the kingdom of God' (οὗτοι μόνοι συνεργοὶ εἰς τὴν βασιλείαν τοῦ θεοῦ – *outoi monoi sunergoi eis tēn basileian Theou*). See also 2 Thessalonians 1:5. These three were also the only Jews with Paul when he wrote to the Colossians. Clearly,

481. Stott, *Acts*, p. 221. See also Bruce, *Acts*, pp. 250-1.

by this time, Paul had lost his ambivalence towards Mark, who was now with the apostle in (most likely) Ephesus. Mark is now acknowledged for his steadfast devotion to duty. He also sends greetings to Philemon (Philem. 24) and it is possible that he met Philemon in Colosse in his travels with Barnabas.

What factors or agencies did the Holy Spirit use in bringing about this favourable change in the life of John Mark? In all probability one or more of the following:

a. The kindly tutelage of Barnabas, that 'true son of encouragement'. Not *entirely* was it due to this but 'no doubt in great measure' (F. F. Bruce, *Colossians*, NICOT, 305).

b. The stern discipline of Paul, shown in refusing to take Mark with him on the second journey. Perhaps Mark needed exactly that seeming harshness.

c. The influence of Peter who calls Mark 'my son' (1 Pet. 5:13). A consistent early tradition links these two men. Peter knew *by experience* that there was hope for those who had fallen into the sins of disloyalty and cowardice.

The Holy Spirit may well have used all three factors and others also to perform His marvellous work in the mind and conscience of 'the man who came back'.[482]

Near the end of his life Paul wrote to Timothy about Mark (2 Tim. 4:11): 'Only Luke is with me. Pick up Mark and bring him with you, for he is useful [εὔχρηστος – *euchrēstos*] to me for service [διακονία – *diakonia*].'[483] διακονία is better translated 'ministry', the general NT use of this word.

Cephas also mentions Mark in 1 Peter 5:13, where the aging apostle calls him, 'my [spiritual] son Mark' (μᾶρκος ὁ υἱός μου – *Markos ho huios mou*).[484] Paul and Cephas had had their

---

482. Hendriksen, *Colossians*, p. 188.

483. See its use in 2 Timothy 2:21 and especially Philemon 11 in reference to the latter usefulness of Onesimus.

484. See M. Dubis, *1 Peter: A Handbook on the Greek Text*, BHGNT (Waco, TX: Baylor University Press, 2010), p. 177.

differences. Paul had past reservations about Mark. But in the combination of 2 Timothy 4:11, 1 Peter 5:13, and 2 Peter 3:15, we see unity between brothers in Christ (particularly regarding Mark), all seeking the expansion of God's kingdom and the praise of His glory – a fulfilment of Psalm 133.

MARY, see **MIRIAM**

MIRIAM

ROMANS 16:6

[6] Greet Mary, who has worked hard for you.

Although we cannot determine this woman's ethnic origin with complete certainty, hers is a commonly occurring name in the NT. It is difficult to determine whether this name is the Hellenised form of the Hebrew name Miriam, meaning 'bitterness'.[485] If it is, the woman was Jewish; otherwise, she was either a Greek or, less likely, a Roman.

In Greek, Paul names this woman as μαρίαν (*Marian*). An explanation of Miriam's name and identity is provided by Cranfield.

> In the NT Mariam and Maria both occur frequently, and in many places there is variation in them in the textual tradition. The former is, of course, a transliteration of the Hebrew 'Miriam'. In all its other occurrences in the NT the latter is naturally assumed to be the Hellenised form of the Hebrew name; (2) but in the present verse it is possible that it (3) is a Roman name, the feminine form of 'Marius'. Whether the woman referred to was a Jewish Christian or a Gentile is therefore uncertain. (4) On the significance of ἐκοπίασεν see on verse 3 (συνεργούς). That the reading ὑμᾶς is to be preferred to ἡμᾶς is hardly to be doubted: her much labouring was for the good of the Roman Christians, not a service rendered specially to Paul and his companions.[486]

---

485. HSIBD, p. 718.

486. Cranfield, *Romans*, vol. 2, p. 787. He has made detailed comments in his footnotes:

2: According to Nestlé, Luke uses Mariam for the nominative in Luke 1:27, 34, 38, 39, 46, 56, but Maria in 2:19; Mariam for the vocative in 1:30, for the accusative in 2:16 and 34, and for the dative in 2:5; but Maria – so *tēs Marias* – for the genitive in 1:41.

The more important issue is that, regardless of her actual identity, no English translation of this verse really does justice to this woman's efforts on behalf of the Christians in Rome. Paul writes 'who has worked hard for you' (ἥτις πολλὰ ἐκοπίασεν εἰς ὑμᾶς – *hētis polla ekopiasen eis humas*).[487] The important addition of *polla* (meaning 'again and again' or 'many times')[488] has been widely underestimated. Zerwick and Grosvenor note that this word intensifies the verb.[489] The NASB states that she 'has worked hard for you'. The NIV better states that she 'worked very hard

---

3: That is assuming that we should read Marian here rather than the Mariam supported by P[46] ℵ K D G pm. Mariam is read by UBS, but Marian should perhaps on the whole be preferred.

4: If the name is Roman, the woman will naturally have been a Gentile; but, if Mariam is read or if Marian is the Hellenisation, she will have been Jewish. It has been argued, but with little cogency, both (i) that the woman was probably a Gentile since Paul has not described her as his kinswoman (see vv. 7, 11, 21 – but Aquila was a Jew, according to Acts, and Paul does not call him his 'kinsman', and the case of Herodion in verse 11 is different from that of Mary in that nothing else but the fact of his Jewishness occurs to Paul as something to say about him here, whereas, in the case of Mary, Paul has her much labouring for the good of the Roman Christians to mention); and also (ii) that Paul did not call Mary his kinswoman, though she was a Jewess, because (forgetting the fact that 'Maria' was also a Roman name?) he thought that her Jewishness was clear enough from her name. The Roman name 'Maria' interestingly occurs in a pagan inscription from Rome combined with the feminine form of 'Ampliatus', another name in Paul's list (see v. 8), 'D M Mariae Ampliatae ...' (CIL 6. 22223).

487. While the following comments relate to Persis, they are equally applicable to the verb used to describe Miriam's work. I support Schreiner's analysis: 'Some commentators observe that in verse 12 the present participle (*kopiōsas*, labouring) is used to designate the labour of Tryphaena and Tryphōsa, while an aorist indicative (*ekopiasen*, she laboured) describes the toil of Persis. They speculate that the latter may now be old or have completed her labours, since the aorist tense is used (so Murray 1965: p. 231; Cranfield 1979: p. 93; Morris 1988: p. 536.) Such a view reads too much precision into the aorist tense, which is used to describe generally the labours of Persis' (Schreiner, *Romans*, p. 767) [The attribution to Cranfield above is incorrect. It should be 1979: p. 793.]

488. See NASBEC, p. 1559, ref. *4178*, *4183*. See the entry for Persis. For the opposite end of the spectrum, see the entry for Alexander (2 Tim. 4:14).

489. Zerwick and Grosvenor, *Grammatical Analysis*, vol. 2, p. 496. Few commentators emphasise the significance of πολλὰ.

for you'. The real sense of Paul's commendation is that, 'over and over again, she worked really hard for you'. See also the entries for Persis, Tryphaena and Tryphōsa.[490]

Miriam is greeted and recognised by Paul as one who has laboured much for the Roman Christians as a whole, rather than specifically helping Paul and his colleagues.

> Mary is another instance of a woman labouring on behalf of the church. There is no validity to the objection that Paul could not have had such intimate knowledge of affairs at Rome so as to be able to particularise thus. He must have received much information from Aquila and Prisca who had just come from Rome when Paul first arrived at Corinth. The 'much labour' suggests that Mary was one of the earliest members of the church at Rome and its organisation could have been largely due to her influence.[491]

Her early commendation in Paul's list in Romans 16 speaks strongly of the apostle's regard for her service to Christ. Matthew Henry noted: 'True love never sticks at labour, but rather takes a pleasure in it; where there is much love, there will be much labour.'[492] Thielman provides more background on this woman's name and is certain of her Jewish background.[493] Her name, Miriam, was derived from the name of Moses' sister (Exod. 15:20).

Dunn notes that Miriam's hard work reflects

> tasks voluntarily taken at their [believers'] own initiative – that is, devoting a sensitivity to needs within a new congregation and willingness to expend energy and time in meeting them (cf. the Roman inscription *CIG* 9592, cited by Deissmann, *Light*, p. 313). Thus it does not denote a leadership function as such (cf. 1 Thess. 5:17); Paul's point elsewhere is that those who do so devote themselves to working for the good of the church ought to be given recognition (1 Cor. 16:16; 1 Thess. 5:12; for προϊσταμένους there, see on

490. Barclay, *Romans*, has overemphasised his praise for Tryphaena and Tryphosa to the detriment of Paul's (relatively) stronger commendation of Miriam and Persis.

491. Murray, *Romans*, p. 229. cf. Acts 2:10.

492. Henry, *Commentary on the Whole Bible*, p. 1799.

493. Thielman, *Romans*, p. 718.

[Rom.] 12:8). Nevertheless, it is noticeable here that Mary is picked out first for such commendation, confirming that women played a not insignificant part in the emerging roles of leadership within the infant Christian communities – the weightier the significance of κοπιάω (Harnack), the more significant their role.[494]

Narcissus

Romans 16:11

[11] Greet Herodion, my kinsman. Greet those of the household of Narcissus, who are in the Lord.

Narcissus (meaning unknown) was not a Christian and is not greeted, only those of his household who are 'in Christ'.[495] Because they only receive this brief acknowledgement by Paul without comment, it seems likely that he knew of these believers by reputation rather than personal association. Cranfield summarises the commentators in these words:

> The suggestion, supported by J. B. Lightfoot, (6) that the Narcissus referred to is the notorious freed man of the Emperor Claudius, whose wealth was proverbial (cf. Juvenal, 14.329) and whose influence with Claudius had been practically unlimited, but who had been forced to commit suicide by Agrippina shortly after Nero's accession and only a year or two before Paul was writing, seems to us quite probable. After his death his household most probably passed into the possession of Nero, its members still forming a distinct group within the imperial household, Narcissiani, as they would be called. That Narcissiani should be represented in Greek by οἱ Ναρκίσσου would be natural enough. Here, in contrast with v. 10b, Paul indicates explicitly by the words τοὺς ὄντας ἐν κυρίῳ that those members of the group who are to be greeted are those who are Christians.[496]

---

494. Dunn, *Romans 9-16*, p. 894.

495. See Lampe, *The Roman Christians*, p. 222.

496. Cranfield, *Romans*, vol. 2, pp. 792-3. See Murray, *Romans*, p. 231; Bruce, *Romans*, p. 273, Jewett, *Romans*, pp. 967-8. The footnote reference for Lightfoot numbered (6) is this: 'op. cit., p. 175. cf. Calvin, p. 323; Sanday and Headlam, pp. 425f.; Dodd, p. 16; Barclay, pp. 233f. Others repeat the suggestion without indicating definitely that they are inclined to accept it: e.g. Lagrange, p. 368; Black, p. 182.'

Barclay comments that 'If Aristobulus (Rom. 16:10) really is the Aristobulus who was the grandson of Herod, and if Narcissus really is the Narcissus who was Claudius' secretary, then this means that many of the slaves at the imperial court were already Christians. The leaven of Christianity had reached the highest circles in the Empire.'[497]

Nereus and his sister

Romans 16:15

[15]Greet Philologus and Julia, Nereus and his sister, and Olympas, and all the saints who are with them.

In Greek mythology Nereus was the eldest son of *Gaia* (the Earth) and *Pontus* (the Sea). This name definitely precludes Nereus and his sister from being Jews. Cranfield surmises that, if Philologus and Julia were husband and wife (quite probable), Nereus and his sister were their children.[498] There is no evidence to support this suggestion and I regard it as more likely that they were adults. 'The sister of Nereus is not known by Paul and his associates, but she is reputed to have played a leading role in the church, so Paul mentions her. He has evidently not heard her name mentioned, except that she is Nereus' sister.'[499] Paul also greets Olympas and 'all the saints who are with them' (καὶ τοὺς σὺν αὐτοῖς ἀδελφούς – *kai tous sun autois adelphous*). It is most likely that all of these people were members of a particular house church in Rome. It was clearly a larger group whom Paul knew to be associated with one another and were committed Christians.[500]

Nympha

Colossians 4:15

[15]Greet the brethren who are in Laodicea and also Nympha and the church that is in her house.

---

497. Barclay, *Romans*, pp. 233-4. See the entry on Aristobulus.

498. Cranfield, *Romans*, vol. 2, p. 795. Dumbrell, *Romans*, p. 142, raises the same possibility.

499. Jewett, *Romans*, p. 972.

500. See Murray, *Romans*, p. 232.

This is a Greek female name meaning 'gift of the nymphs'.[501] This Gentile woman lived in Laodicea and was a person of some means because a church (ἐκκλησία – *ekklēsia*) met in her house.[502] Paul sends his greetings to her via the Colossian church. She was probably a convert of Epaphras' ministry in the Lycus Valley. Since the church was in *her* house, it is likely that she was a widow.[503]

Olympas

Romans 16:15

[15] Greet Philologus and Julia, Nereus and his sister, and Olympas, and all the saints who are with them.

Olympas is a shortened form of a Greek masculine name like Olympiodorus, Olympianus, etc., meaning unknown but obviously associated with Greek mythology. As well as Philologus, Julia, Nereus, and his sister, Paul also greets Olympas and 'all the saints who are with them' (καὶ τοὺς σὺν αὐτοῖς ἀδελφούς – *kai tous sun autois adelphous*). It is most likely that all of these people were members of a particular Christian group in Rome. It was clearly a larger group whom Paul knew to be associated with one another and were committed Christians.[504]

> This congregation, like that mentioned in the preceding verse, fits the profile of a tenement church. Instead of a patron there is collective leadership by five persons. This group probably meets for its love feasts somewhere in an insula [apartment] building where the majority of Rome's underclass lived. In lieu of a patron who could provide the means for the common meal, this group, like many others in the early church, would have to rely on 'agapaic communalism' by pooling resources from the earnings of the members. Although its structure and ethos were very different from a standard house church such as that led by Prisca and Aquila, Paul asks for them to be greeted and welcomed as equals.[505]

---

501. HSIBD, p. 766. In Greek mythology, nymphs were semi-divine spirits regarded as maidens and associated with aspects of nature, especially rivers and woods.

502. See Bruce, *Colossians*, p. 183; Dunn, *Colossians*, p. 284.

503. See Witherington, *Colossians*, p. 205.

504. See Murray, *Romans*, p. 232.

505. Jewett, *Romans*, p. 972.

Onesimus

Colossians 4:8-9

[8] *For I have sent him [Tychicus] to you for this very purpose, that you may know about our circumstances and that he may encourage your hearts;*

[9] *... and with him Onesimus, our faithful and beloved brother, who is one of your number. They will inform you about the whole situation here.*

Philemon 10-21

[10] *I appeal to you for my child Onesimus, whom I have begotten in my imprisonment,*

[11] *... who formerly was useless to you, but now is useful both to you and to me.*

[12] *I have sent him back to you in person, that is, sending my very heart,*

[13] *whom I wished to keep with me, so that on your behalf he might minister to me in my imprisonment for the gospel;*

[14] *... but without your consent I did not want to do anything, so that your goodness would not be, in effect, by compulsion but of your own free will.*

[15] *For perhaps he was for this reason separated from you for a while, that you would have him back forever,*

[16] *... no longer as a slave, but more than a slave, a beloved brother, especially to me, but how much more to you, both in the flesh and in the Lord.*

[17] *If then you regard me a partner, accept him as you would me.*

[18] *But if he has wronged you in any way or owes you anything, charge that to my account;*

[19] *I, Paul, am writing this with my own hand, I will repay it (not to mention to you that you owe to me even your own self as well).*

[20] *Yes, brother, let me benefit from you in the Lord; refresh my heart in Christ.*

[21] *Having confidence in your obedience, I write to you, since I know that you will do even more than what I say.*

Onesimus (ὀνήσιμον – *onēsimon*) was the name of a slave, whose master was Philemon. His name meant 'useful' or 'profitable'.[506] He worked in the household of Philemon at Colosse but eventually ran away. He may have stolen some of Philemon's possessions

506. HSIBD, p. 784.

(Philem. 18) but ended up in Ephesus, about 100 miles (160 km) to the west of the Lycus Valley.[507] By divine providence he found his master's friend, Paul, and became a Christian.

> There is no way of deciding how in fact Onesimus made his way to Paul. Perhaps Epaphras of Colossae, who was on a visit to Paul at the time, came across Onesimus in the city, recognised him, and brought him to Paul because he knew that Paul would help him in his predicament. One cannot be sure. It may even be outrunning the evidence to conclude that Onesimus was a runaway slave in the usual sense of the term. It could be argued that his master had sent him to fulfil some commission, and that he had overstayed his leave and required a note of excuse from Paul begging pardon for his unduly long absence. In view of our ignorance of so many details, the possibilities are numerous. ...
>
> Paul had no means of compelling Onesimus to go back to Philemon: if Onesimus had refused to go, or had changed his mind on the way back to Phrygia, Paul could have done nothing about it. (The idea of reporting Onesimus to the authorities, as a fugitive slave, was out of the question.) That Onesimus agreed to go back, and presumably did so, must be seen as evidence that the grace of Christ which worked so powerfully in Paul, and which (Paul hoped) would work in Philemon, was also at work in Onesimus. It would help Onesimus, no doubt, to have the congenial and encouraging companionship of Tychicus on his way back: it may well have been Tychicus's departure for the Lycus valley that provided Paul with a suitable opportunity for sending Onesimus back.[508]

---

507. See the entry for Epaphras regarding the geographical details of Colosse.

508. Bruce, *Epistles to the Colossians, to Philemon, and to the Ephesians*, p. 197. The mention of Tychicus by Bruce undoubtedly incorporates his assumption that Tychicus delivered both letters at the same time (p. 191). That assumption, however, is incorrect. See *Letters to the Colossians and Philemon* in the introduction. If anyone accompanied Onesimus (highly probable), it would likely have been Tychicus because Epaphras was, at that time, Paul's fellow prisoner (Philem. 23). This would have protected Onesimus from an initially hostile 'welcome'. See Witherington, *Letters to Philemon, the Colossians, and the Ephesians*, pp. 22-36, 84-90, for a comprehensive examination of the issues facing Paul, Onesimus, and Philemon, including the issue of slavery.

Paul describes Onesimus as 'my child, whom I have "begotten" (v. 10, NASB) (ἐγέννησα – *egennēsa*) in my imprisonment'.[509] It is as if Paul has given birth to Onesimus, *and he has* to the extent that the slave was 'born again' with faith in Christ. Regarding verse 12, '[T]he relative ὃν is virtually repeated in αὐτόν, which is thus emphatic ("Onesimus himself").'[510] Verse 16 expresses a deep bond between Paul and Onesimus, who is called 'a beloved brother, *especially to me*' (ἀδελφὸν ἀγαπητόν, μάλιστα ἐμοί – *adelphon agapēton, malista emoi*). The NIV translation says: 'who became my son.' Apparently, he was most useful to Paul while he was in prison in Ephesus but, despite this closeness, the time had come for him to return to his master as Paul knew he must. There is no suggestion in the text that Onesimus was imprisoned with Paul, otherwise he could not have demonstrated his usefulness.[511]

In verse 11 there is a pun regarding the slave's name, 'who formerly was *useless* to you, but now is *useful* both to you and me.' In verse 20 Paul writes, 'Let me benefit from you in the Lord' (ἐγώ σου ὀναίμην ἐν κυρίῳ – *egō sou onaimēn en kuriō*). There is clearly a word play between ὀναίμη (*onaimē*) (whose root is the verb ὀνίνημι (*oninēmi*) – to benefit) and the name of the slave, ὀνήσιμον (*Onēsimon*). The use of this pun is a useful demonstration that, like most humans, Paul had a sense of humour.[512] By using this verb, it is as if Paul is saying: I now want you (Philemon) to be useful to me by accepting him as a brother in Christ.[513]

What was the outcome? It seems needless to say that the existence of this precious letter (and its incorporation into Scripture) answers the question. This is confirmed by Paul's

---

509. ἐγέννησα (*egennēsa*) is derived from γεννάω (*gennaō*), the verb used throughout the NT for 'giving birth' or 'being the father of …' (cf. Matt. 1:16). See Titus 1:4 where Paul uses τίτῳ γνησίῳ τέκνῳ κατὰ κοινὴν πίστιν (*titō gnēsiō teknō kata pistin* – 'To Titus, my true child in a common faith').

510. Bruce, *Epistles to the Colossians, to Philemon, and to the Ephesians*, p. 210.

511. ibid., p. 196.

512. For the possibility of a similar pun, see the entry for Syzygus.

513. See E. M. Blaiklock, *Commentary on the New Testament* (London: Hodder and Stoughton, 1977), p. 210.

mentioning Onesimus in Colossians 4:9. Since Colossians was written some time after Philemon, the former slave had been sent back to Paul, where he vindicated the apostle's confidence in his potential usefulness. He is subsequently described as 'the faithful and beloved brother' (τῶ πιστῶ καὶ ἀγαπητῶ ἀδελφῶ – *tō pesto kai agapētō adelphō*).

About fifty years after this letter was written, the bishop of Ephesus was named Onesimus. Was it the same man? No one knows for sure, but the issue is examined by Bruce.[514] See also the entry for Philemon.

Onesiphorus

2 Timothy 1:16-18

[16] The Lord grant mercy to the household of Onesiphorus, for he often refreshed me and was not ashamed of my chains;

[17]... but when he was in Rome, he eagerly searched for me and found me –

[18]... the Lord grant to him to find mercy from the Lord on that day – and you know very well what services he rendered at Ephesus.

2 Timothy 4:19

[19] Greet Prisca and Aquila, and the household of Onesiphorus.

Onesiphorus, meaning 'profitable',[515] was probably a Gentile of some wealth in Ephesus. He had 'refreshed' (ἀναψύχω – *anapsuchō*) Paul on numerous occasions, clearly offering his home for the apostle's benefit (2 Tim. 1:16). This is the only use of ἀναψύΧω in the NT but see ἀναπαύω – *anapauō* in 1 Corinthians 16:17 regarding Stephanas, Achaicus, and Fortunatus. The inclusion of πολλάκις (*pollakis*) in 2 Timothy 1:16 means that this happened 'again and again' (cf. 2 Cor. 11:23).

His household (ὁ ὀνησιφόρου οἶκος – *ho Onēsiphoros oikos*) is mentioned by Paul at the beginning and end of the letter. They, too, were believers. In the first instance (2 Tim. 1:16), Paul asks

---

514. See Bruce, *Epistles to the Colossians, to Philemon, and to the Ephesians*, pp. 201-2, 221.

515. HSIBD, p. 784.

that 'the Lord grant mercy' (δῴη ἔλεος ὁ κύριος – *dōn eleos ho Kurios*) to his household.

16 Paul commends Onesiphorus (mentioned also in 4:19), who rose to the occasion, despite Paul's chains as he languished in Rome (for Paul as a prisoner, see v. 8 above). Prisoners relied on help from relatives or friends. Onesiphorus provided it, the word order perhaps stressing the frequency of this assistance. Paul prays for God's 'mercy' on his behalf as a result. (For 'mercy' in Paul, see Titus 3:5.) If Onesiphorus was the head of this 'household', he may have been a man with a residence large enough to host Christian meetings in Ephesus, where Paul had earlier contact with him (v. 18). Perhaps, though, he was just a household member, whether family or slave, in which case Paul's prayer is for those who permitted Onesiphorus to act on his benevolent impulses towards Paul. His refusal to be 'ashamed' of Paul's incarceration models for Timothy the courage to transcend any tendency he may have to lie low because of being 'ashamed' (v. 8) or feeling 'shame' (v. 12). By 'refreshed', Paul may refer to hospitality. But Onesiphorus's encouragement might also have been a non-tangible nature. Visits, friendship, and the ministry of prayer can mean a great deal to a wizened Christian worker in captivity. Paul had learned to flourish with or without his physical needs being met (see Phil. 4:11-13). In any case, Onesiphorus furnished repeated, laudable relief ('relief' being a prominent word in the discussion in BDAG 75 of the word translated 'refreshed').

17 These gestures of assistance were possible because Onesiphorus 'searched hard' and found Paul in Rome. 'Hard' implies zeal, determination, persistence, which Siebenthal sees as borne out also by Paul's use of a durative verb form here. Further details are unknown. Perhaps he was a man of means on business travel to the imperial capital city and sought out Paul while he was there. Or he may have been an underling of the household doing something of his master's bidding. He might have traced Paul's whereabouts via the network of local Christians (see the many names of Roman believers listed in Romans 16; these were known to Paul although he had never been in Rome, indicating that Christians in various population centres knew of each other by report).

> **18** Paul repeats his call for God's mercy on Onesiphorus, this time with an eye to 'that day' (see discussion at v. 12 above and esp. n. 66 on p. 364). Paul has no doubts about the full sufficiency of Christ's work to deliver from judgment those who trust in Him (in addition to v. 12 and 2 Tim. 4:8, see Rom. 8:1 and Phil. 1:6). But he is also conscious that the working of divine grace impels the faithful to faithfulness until the end. So Paul's plea for divine mercy does not seek to ward off an unpredictable bitter end for Onesimus [sic] but rather to see him fortified in the present in ways that will sustain his valuable ministrations (including outreach to Paul) to such an extent that they will enjoy even eschatological validation (cf. 1 Cor. 3:10-15).[516]

Paul sends a greeting to his household (2 Tim. 4:19), as well as to Prisca and Aquila. In neither greeting is Onesiphorus named personally. We then have the strange clause by Paul in 2 Timothy 1:18: 'the Lord grant to him to find mercy from the Lord on that day.' It has been presumed by some commentators that this implies that Onesiphorus had died.[517] Stott provides a vigorous comment about 2 Timothy 1:16, 18:

> Various commentators, especially Roman Catholics, have argued from the references to the household of Onesiphorus (mentioned again in 4:19) and to 'that Day' that Onesiphorus himself was now dead, and that we have therefore in verse 18 a petition for the departed. This is an entirely gratuitous assumption, however. The fact that Paul keeps distinct his allusions to Onesiphorus on the one hand and to his household on the other could equally well mean that they were separated from each other by distance as by death, Onesiphorus still being in Rome, while his family were home in Ephesus. 'I take it to be a prayer for them separately, the man and

---

516. Yarbrough, *Letters to Timothy and Titus*, pp. 358-60. Two of my conclusions differ a little from Yarbrough's. There is more likelihood that Onesiphorus was wealthy and that his hospitality in Ephesus was greater than that in Rome.

517. See Zerwick and Grosvenor, *Grammatical Analysis*, vol. 2, p. 640. They were Roman Catholic scholars and commented on verse 16: 'was Onesiphorus then dead? His exclusion here and the separate prayer in verse 18 leave us with this impression.' This, of course, raises the Roman Catholic theological claim that there can be prayers for the dead, which must be rejected.

> his family', writes Bishop Handley Moule, 'because they were for the time separated from one another by lands and seas ... There is no need at all to assume that Onesiphorus had died. Separation from his family by a journey quite satisfies the language of the passage.'[518]

Patrobas

Romans 16:14

[14]Greet Asyncritus, Phlegon, Hermes, Patrobas, Hermas, and the brethren with them.

Patrobas is a Greek name meaning 'having life from father'.[519] It is an alternative form of Patrobios.[520] What an appropriate name for one who has been given new life in Christ! He is greeted with Asyncritus, Phlegon, Hermes, and Hermas. All of these are masculine names of Gentile slaves or freed men. 'He was a Gentile Christian whose family stemmed from the east, although he had never met Paul and very well may have been a slave or freed man who resided in Rome all his life.'[521] Given the common greeting afforded to them, it is most likely that they worked in the same household and/or were members of a particular house church in Rome. This possibility is supported by Paul's addition of 'and the brethren with them'.[522] It was clearly a larger group whom Paul knew to be associated with one another and were committed Christians. However, they had not worked with Paul, only being described as 'brothers'. Jewett notes that Patrobas 'belongs with a group of other persons whose servile status is indisputable lead[ing] me to concur with Lampe that he is probably a slave or freed man'.[523]

> Here a number of brethren are selected without distinction. This mark of brotherly attention would gratify those whom the Apostle

518. Stott, *2 Timothy*, pp. 45-6. The comment by Moule is from H. C. G. Moule, *The Second Epistle to Timothy, The Devotional Commentary* series (London: Religious Tract Society, 1905), pp. 67-8.

519. HSIBD, p. 805.

520. Cranfield, *Romans*, vol. 2, p. 795.

521. Jewett, *Romans*, p. 971.

522. Cranfield, *Romans*, vol. 2, p. 795.

523. Jewett, *Romans*, p. 970.

> here names, beside the brethren who were with them. The Lord's people are not equally distinguished, but they are all brethren equally related to Him who is the Elder Brother of His people. Some of them are eminent, and others are without peculiar distinction. They are all, however, worthy of love. A Church is not to consist of the most eminent believers, but of believers, though some be of the lowest attainments. A church of Christ is a school in which their education is to be perfected. And all the saints which are with them – that is the believers in their families and neighbourhood. These might not be personally known to the Apostle, but as believers they were worthy of his notice.[524]

PERSIS

ROMANS 16:12

[12] Greet Tryphaena and Tryphosa, workers in the Lord. Greet Persis the beloved, who has worked hard in the Lord.

Persis is a common Greek female slave name, originally meaning 'Persian woman',[525] although it occurs in Latin as the name of a freed woman.[526] Such names became common and, eventually, had no reference to the person's place of origin.[527] Paul had particular affection for Persis because of her work in the church calling her '***the*** beloved' (**τὴν** ἀγαπητήν – ***tēn*** *agapētēn*). Murray grasps Paul's sensitivity to propriety in his comment on this. 'Epaenetus, Ampliatus, and Stachys he calls "my beloved", Persis he calls "the beloved". It might have been indelicate to call her *my* beloved.'[528]

> She may be a Gentile or believer of ethnic Persian origin, or perhaps a believer of Jewish background whose family had lived in the large Persian-Babylonian diaspora ... Paul had met her in the eastern mission area, and her current location indicates that she was probably among the exiles whom Paul met after A.D. 49. That Persis 'had laboured much in the Lord' indicates a very intensive involvement in congregational and missionary leadership.[529]

---

524. Haldane, *Romans*, p. 640.
525. HSIBD, p. 823. She is not even mentioned in Moffatt's commentary.
526. Cranfield, *Romans*, vol. 2, p. 793.
527. Hodge, *Romans*, p. 449.
528. Murray, *Romans*, p. 231.
529. Jewett, *Romans*, p. 968. See Thielman, *Romans*, p. 724.

However, Paul's description of her efforts on behalf of the gospel are understated in all translations of the Greek because of the lack of emphasis on Paul's use of πολλὰ (*polla*), which emphasises the extent of her effort.[530] She is described as one 'who laboured much in the Lord' (KJV, ASV), 'who has worked hard in the Lord' (NASB, RSV), 'who has worked very hard in the Lord' (NIV, HCSB), 'who toiled in his service so long' (NEB). Given her degree of service to Christian work, she may, by this time, be a free woman. Matthew Henry noted: 'True love never sticks at labour, but rather takes a pleasure in it; where there is much love, there will be much labour.'[531] The past tense of ἐκοπίασεν (*ekopiasen*) may indicate that she is now of elderly years but, more likely, it is an indication of her length of service for the Lord.

> Three times in this list of greetings Paul uses a certain Greek word for Christian work and toil. He uses it of Mary (Rom. 16:6), and of Tryphaena and Tryphosa and of Persis in this passage. It is the verb *kopian*, and kopian means to toil to the point of exhaustion; it means to give to the work all that one has got; it means to work to the stage of utter weariness.[532]

To put these women's work in perspective, it must be noted that of the four noted above by Barclay, only Mary (see the entry on Miriam) and Persis have the added Greek emphasis of *polla* (πολλὰ). The important addition of *polla* reflects an even greater effort (perhaps over a longer period of time) than Tryphaena or Tryphosa.[533] The efforts of Persis are comparable to those of

---

530. See the entry for Miriam. For the opposite end of the spectrum, see the entry for Alexander (2 Tim. 4:14).

531. Henry, *Commentary on the Whole Bible*, p. 1799.

532. Barclay, *Romans*, pp. 234-5. In W. Barclay, *The New Testament: A New Translation* (Glasgow: William Collins, 1968), p. 337, Romans 16:12 says, 'Give my good wishes to my dear Persis, who has toiled so hard in the Lord's service.' Relatively speaking, Barclay fails to give πολλὰ its full weight in this description. See also the entry for Miriam in Morris, *Romans*, p. 536, regarding this phrase.

533. See Peterson, *Commentary on Romans*, p. 542, for recognition of Persis' 'intensive involvement' in Christian work. This recognition also appears in the translation of Romans 16:12 in R. N. Longenecker, *The Epistle to the Romans*, NIGTC (Grand Rapids: Eerdmans, 2016), p. 970: 'Greet my dear friend Persis, another woman who has worked very hard in the Lord.'

Miriam. As with her, (and in contrast to Tryphaena and Tryphosa), Paul uses **πολλὰ** ἐκοπίασεν to describe Persis' persistent efforts for the gospel 'in the Lord' (ἐν κυρίῳ – *en kuriō*).

Peter see **Cephas**

Philemon

Philemon 1-25

[1] Paul, a prisoner of Christ Jesus, and Timothy our brother,

To Philemon our beloved brother and fellow worker, …

[2]… and to Apphia our sister, and to Archippus our fellow soldier, and to the church in your house:

[3] Grace to you and peace from God our Father and the Lord Jesus Christ.

[4] I thank my God always, making mention of you in my prayers,

[5] because I hear of your love and of the faith which you have toward the Lord Jesus and toward all the saints; …

[6]… and I pray that the fellowship of your faith may become effective through the knowledge of every good thing which is in you for Christ's sake.

[7] For I have come to have much joy and comfort in your love, because the hearts of the saints have been refreshed through you, brother.

[8] Therefore, though I have enough confidence in Christ to order you to do what is proper, …

[9]… yet for love's sake I rather appeal to you – since I am such a person as Paul, the aged, and now also a prisoner of Christ Jesus –

[10] I appeal to you for my child Onesimus, whom I have begotten in my imprisonment, …

[11]… who formerly was useless to you, but now is useful both to you and to me.

[12] I have sent him back to you in person, that is, sending my very heart,

[13]… whom I wished to keep with me, so that on your behalf he might minister to me in my imprisonment for the gospel; …

[14]… but without your consent I did not want to do anything, so that your goodness would not be, in effect, by compulsion but of your own free will.

[15] For perhaps he was for this reason separated from you for a while, that you would have him back forever, …

[16]… no longer as a slave, but more than a slave, a beloved brother, especially to me, but how much more to you, both in the flesh and in the Lord.

[17] If then you regard me a partner, accept him as you would me.

[18] But if he has wronged you in any way or owes you anything, charge that to my account; ...

[19] I, Paul, am writing this with my own hand, I will repay it (not to mention to you that you owe to me even your own self as well).

[20] Yes, brother, let me benefit from you in the Lord; refresh my heart in Christ.

[21] Having confidence in your obedience, I write to you, since I know that you will do even more than what I say.

[22] At the same time also prepare me a lodging, for I hope that through your prayers I will be given to you.

[23] Epaphras, my fellow prisoner in Christ Jesus, greets you, ...

[24] ... as do Mark, Aristarchus, Demas, Luke, my fellow workers.

[25] The grace of the Lord Jesus Christ be with your spirit.

Paul's letter to Philemon is sufficiently short that it is repeated in full above. One chronological issue needs to be dealt with first to put the letter in context. Paul's letters to Philemon and the Colossians are closely associated. However, Philemon was written before Colossians, which was delivered to the church in Colosse some time later.[534]

Philemon (meaning 'loving'), his wife Apphia, and son Archippus lived in Colosse. Paul's letter to Philemon is the smallest of his letters in length and the only surviving example of his personal correspondence of which there must have been many letters. Paul clearly had a deep sense of affection for Philemon because he is described in verse 1 as τῶ ἀγαπητῶ καὶ συνεργῶ ἡμῶν – *tō agapētō kai sunergō hēmōn*: 'the beloved and our fellow worker.' Nowhere else in the Pauline letters is this phrase used.[535]

To better understand Paul's letter to Philemon, it is necessary to be aware of the geography of these towns' locations. About 100 miles (160 km) east of Ephesus there were the towns of Hieropolis,

534. See *Letters to the Colossians and Philemon* in the introduction.

535. Witherington, *Letters to Philemon, the Colossians, and the Ephesians*, p. 53, n. 2.

Laodicea, and Colosse (Col. 4:13). They were located in the Lycus Valley in the Roman province of Asia (now western Turkey). Through this valley flows the Lycus River, an offshoot to the right of the larger Maeander (now Menderes) River. Hieropolis was located on the northern side of the river, Laodicea was on the southern side of the river about 6 miles (10 km) south and Colosse was a small town that lay on both sides of the river about 12 miles (20 km) to the south-east of Laodicea. They were cities known for dyeing cloth. The general area was very fertile.[536]

Philemon was a businessman of some wealth, having a house large enough to accommodate the Colossian church (Philem. 2) and owning (probably some) slaves, one of whom was called Onesimus (Philem. 10). Although Paul never visited Colosse (Col. 2:1),[537] he probably became acquainted with Philemon during one of his business trips to Ephesus and a warm friendship developed. Philemon may have been accompanied by Onesimus, who would then be able to recognise his master's friend in later years.

The gospel was brought to the three towns by Epaphras, one of Paul's early converts in Ephesus (Col. 1:7). Philemon was probably one of his converts.

We need to understand this letter in full by considering the personality and faith of Philemon. However, we can say briefly here that Onesimus (meaning 'useful') ran away, found his way to Ephesus and was returned (with Tychicus?) to Philemon. See the entry for Onesimus concerning his activities. The letter to Philemon is primarily about his reception of Onesimus as an escaped slave, who had become a Christian.

---

536. For a comprehensive description of this region, see Bruce, *Colossians*, 3-13; Hendriksen, *Philippians, Colossians and Philemon*, 6-14. For an accurate (and moving) description of first-century Colosse and its history, see H. C. G. Moule, *Colossian and Philemon Studies*, pp. 18-20. 'But by the Christian era Colossae was small and obscure; a place which hovered between town and village, a townlet, a *polisma* (p. 18).' See also the entries for Apphia and Archippus.

537. This is the subject of scholarly dispute, but I favour the arguments of Hendriksen, *Colossians*, 9-15, that Paul never visited Colosse.

Paul is most gracious in his letter to Philemon (v. 14), giving him a free choice about what to do with the runaway slave. We cannot express the sincerity of Paul's request any better than by reading verses 17-21.

> In verse 11 there is a pun using the slave's name, 'who formerly was useless to you, but now is useful both to you and me.' In verse 20 Paul writes, 'Let me benefit from you in the Lord' (ἐγώ σου ὀναίμην ἐν κυρίῳ – *egō sou onaimēn en kuriō*). There is clearly a word play between ὀναίμην (*onaimēn*) (whose root is the verb ὀνίνημι (*oninēmi*) – to benefit) and the name of the slave, ὀνήσιμον (*Onēsimon*). By using this verb, it is as if Paul is saying: I now want you (Philemon) to be useful to me by accepting him as a brother in Christ.[538]

The relationship between these brothers in Christ is so close that Paul can humorously discuss the financial implications of returning Onesimus (v. 18). Although penniless in prison, Paul suggests that he will be responsible for any financial expenses that the escape of Onesimus cost Philemon. An impossibility! Yet Paul claims: 'I will repay it', although he notes that Philemon owes his life (in Christ) to Paul and the gospel (v. 19). Such is the closeness of their personal relationship and the sincerity which Paul knows resides in the heart of Philemon that he can say this without offence.

What was the outcome? It seems needless to say that the existence of this precious letter (and its incorporation into Scripture) answers the question. To fully understand the relationship between Paul and Philemon, it is necessary to read the letter (twenty-five verses) in full. Paul did not need to call for the abolition of slavery. That would have fallen on deaf ears in the Roman Empire. Rather, through love (*agapē*), one slave at a time would be freed if the gospel was obeyed.[539]

Of course, whole commentaries have been written on this sensitive letter but verses 8-10 best reflect the pastoral skill of

---

538. See Blaiklock, *Commentary on The New Testament*, p. 210.

539. See Witherington, *Letters to Philemon, the Colossians, and the Ephesians*, pp. 22-36, 84-90 for a comprehensive examination of the issues facing Paul, Onesimus, and Philemon, including a discussion on slavery.

Paul and the faithfulness to the gospel of Philemon. Using his apostolic authority, Paul could 'order'[540] (ἐπιτάσσειν – *epitassein*) Philemon to release Onesimus but, instead, (vv. 9, 10) the loving pastor 'would rather make an appeal' (μᾶλλον παρακαλῶ – *mallon parakalō*) to his brother in Christ. This is the essence of the grace shown by Christ to those He might have ordered about (e.g. His disciples); instead, He showed mercy (cf. Matt. 26:36-41).[541]

Several commentators have presumed that the inclusion of greetings to the church meeting in Philemon's house implies that this letter would have been read in public. Bruce has a far wiser understanding of the social implications of the receipt of this letter, notwithstanding his (incorrect) presumption that this letter and Colossians were delivered together.

> But one thing is certain: after the extraordinary delicacy with which Paul makes his plea for Onesimus in the letter to Philemon, it would be an incredibly flat-footed action to put pressure on Onesimus's owner by name in another letter which was to be read aloud at a church meeting where the owner would presumably be present. The reference to Onesimus in Col. 4:9, on the other hand, is unobtrusive: 'Along with Tychicus I am sending Onesimus, my trusty and well-loved brother, who is one of yourselves.' No one could take exception to that, although doubtless it would add just a little more weight to Paul's plea in the letter to Philemon. But there was no need to put on the spot a man to whom Paul was writing separately and saying, 'I know you will do more than I say', any attempt to put him on the spot before the church of Colossae would go far to neutralise the effect of Paul's diplomacy in the letter to Philemon.
>
> And it would if anything be still more disastrous for Paul to direct that the letter to Philemon should be read aloud to the assembled church at Colossae. True, in the letter to Philemon Paul sends greetings to 'the church that meets in your house' as well as to Philemon, Apphia and Archippus – but that does not mean that

540. Zerwick and Grosvenor, *Grammatical Analysis*, vol. 2, p. 652, translate the word as 'command'.

541. See Bruce, *Epistles to the Colossians, to Philemon, and to the Ephesians*, pp. 210-11, for an excellent analysis of verses 8-20.

> the private contents of verses 4-22 were to be divulged even to the household church with which these three were associated, let alone the city church of Colossae.[542]

Although imprisoned in Ephesus at the time of writing this letter (Philem. 23), Paul is optimistic that he can eventually travel to Colosse and stay with Philemon (v. 22). This seems a more likely request if the letter was written in Ephesus rather than Rome.[543] Unfortunately, this never eventuated, making this sole physical contact from Paul even more valuable. From this we can learn that there is nothing wrong with our human desires to be reacquainted with our loved ones (especially brothers and sisters in Christ) and our praying that this might occur. But, as in the case of Paul, there is no guarantee that God will grant every request. See also the entry for Onesimus.

> The epistle ends (22-25) on notes of intimacy. There was something truly Greek about Paul. The great Greek orators never placed the climax of their speech in the closing words. The oration closed on a minor note designed to bring the excited audience back to normality and rest. So here.[544]

PHILETUS

2 TIMOTHY 2:16-18

16 But avoid worldly and empty chatter, for it will lead to further ungodliness, ...

17 ... and their talk will spread like gangrene. Among them are Hymenaeus and Philetus, ...

18 ... men who have gone astray from the truth, claiming that the resurrection has already taken place; and they upset the faith of some.

Philetus is a Greek name meaning 'beloved'.[545] He lived in Ephesus, where Timothy was then residing. Paul wrote 1 Timothy

---

542. Bruce, *Paul: Apostle of the Free Spirit*, p. 405. For a contrary view, see Witherington, *Letters to Philemon, the Colossians, and the Ephesians*, p. 54.

543. Bird, *Colossians and Philemon*, p. 143.

544. Blaiklock, *Commentary on The New Testament*, p. 210.

545. HSIBD, p. 832.

from Macedonia after being released from his first imprisonment in Rome (see Acts 28:30-31).[546]

I assume that Hymenaeus is the man referred to in 1 Timothy 1:18-20. It appears that Hymenaeus continued to sin because of his mention in 2 Timothy 2:17-18. Hymenaeus and Philetus taught that the second resurrection of Christ had already occurred. The 1997 NASB translated ἀνατρέπουσιν (*anatrepousin*) in verse 18 as 'jeopardising' but in the 1995 edition the verb is (better) translated as 'upsetting' (or 'overturning'[547]) the faith of some.

> The false assertion of Hymenaeus and Philetus that 'the resurrection has already taken place' is not a statement about Jesus' resurrection itself. It is about the meaning of the resurrection for His followers. Some in the early decades of church life illegitimately applied the Bible's end-time teaching (eschatology) in a manner called 'acute realised eschatology'. In this view the future is *now*. Believers *already* enjoy the full benefit of God's eternal forgiveness. So live however you wish! Your soul is already saved forever, so what you do with your body doesn't matter. Some think this outlook was a factor at Corinth, causing Paul to write sarcastically, 'Already you have all you want! Already you have become rich! You have begun to reign – and that without us! How I wish that you had already begun to reign so that we might also reign with you!' (1 Cor. 4:8). This outlook might help explain the involvement of Corinthian church members in incest (1 Cor. 5:1-5) and prostitution (1 Cor. 6:12-20). It is possible that Hymenaeus and Philetus were also denying the bodily nature of believers' final resurrection, which was an absurd if not revolting notion in some Hellenistic understanding (cf. Acts 17:32).
>
> An understanding of the resurrection this twisted is tantamount to a denial of it. No wonder 'the faith of some' is being destroyed. NIV's 'destroy' translates a form of *anatrepō*. The same word is used in Titus 1:11, also of the disastrous results of false teaching. The only other NT use is in John 2:15, when Jesus 'overturns' the tables of the money changers. Hymenaeus and Philetus were not just misdirected

546. See *Time Between Two Roman Imprisonments* in the introduction. Stott, *The Message of 2 Timothy*, pp. 16-18 provides a summary of Paul's possible travels between his first and second imprisonments in Rome.

547. See Zerwick and Grosvenor, *Grammatical Analysis*, vol. 2, p. 642.

> doctrinally but were functioning as a two-man wrecking crew of the fragile faith of first-generation believers under Timothy's care.[548]

See also the entry for Hymenaeus.

Philologus

Romans 16:15

[15]Greet Philologus and Julia, Nereus and his sister, and Olympas, and all the saints who are with them.

Philologus was a common Greek slave name, meaning 'talkative'.[549] It is quite relevant that Paul's greeting is addressed to Philologus *and* Julia. This probably indicates husband and wife, or brother and sister. Cranfield surmises that, if husband and wife, Nereus and his sister are their children.[550] Paul also greets Olympas and 'all the saints who are with them' (καὶ τοὺς σὺν αὐτοῖς ἀδελφούς – *kai tous sun autois adelphous*). It is most likely that all of these people were members of a particular house church in Rome. It was clearly a larger group whom Paul knew to be associated with one another and were committed Christians.[551]

See a similar greeting to a number of men in Romans 16:14. Whereas they were greeted as 'brothers', being all men, this greeting is to 'the saints'. Both are genuine Christian descriptions, but this notation may reflect Paul's greeting of both men and women by this specifically Christian emphasis on 'true believers'.

Phlegon

Romans 16:14

[14]Greet Asyncritus, Phlegon, Hermes, Patrobas, Hermas, and the brethren with them.

Phlegon is a Greek name meaning 'zealous'.[552] He is greeted with Asyncritus, Hermes, Patrobas, and Hermas. All are masculine

---

548. Yarbrough, *Letters to Timothy and Titus*, p. 389.

549. HSIBD, p. 837.

550. Cranfield, *Romans*, vol. 2, p. 795. There is no evidence to support this suggestion and I regard it as unlikely.

551. See Murray, *Romans*, p. 232.

552. HSIBD, p. 838. Cranfield, *Romans*, vol. 2, p. 795 notes: 'Φλέγων is the name of a dog in Xenophon, Cyn. 7.5, but occurs later as a slave name.'

names of Gentile slaves or freed men. Given the common greeting afforded to them, it is most likely that they worked in the same household and/or were members of a particular house church in Rome. This possibility is supported by Paul's addition of 'and the brethren with them'.[553] It was clearly a larger group whom Paul knew to be associated with one another and were committed Christians. However, they had not worked with Paul, only being described as 'brothers'. Jewett notes that Phlegon 'belongs with a group of other persons whose servile status is indisputable lead[ing] me to concur with Lampe that he is probably a slave or freed man'.[554]

> Here a number of brethren are selected without distinction. This mark of brotherly attention would gratify those whom the Apostle here names, beside the brethren who were with them. The Lord's people are not equally distinguished, but they are all brethren equally related to Him who is the Elder Brother of His people. Some of them are eminent, and others are without peculiar distinction. They are all, however, worthy of love. A Church is not to consist of the most eminent believers, but of believers, though some be of the lowest attainments. A church of Christ is a school in which their education is to be perfected. And all the saints which are with them – that is the believers in their families and neighbourhood. These might not be personally known to the Apostle, but as believers they were worthy of his notice.[555]

Phoebe

Romans 16: 1-2

[1] I commend to you our sister Phoebe, who is a servant of the church which is at Cenchrea; …

[2]… that you receive her in the Lord in a manner worthy of the saints, and that you help her in whatever matter she may have need of you; for she herself has also been a helper of many, and of myself as well.

This entry for Phoebe is quite lengthy because it is necessary to determine who and what she actually was as per the text of

553. Cranfield, *Romans*, vol. 2, p. 795.

554. Jewett, *Romans*, p. 970.

555. Haldane, *Romans*, p. 640.

Scripture, rather than (as time goes by) the increasingly fictional person of feminist imagination, who bears no resemblance to the woman briefly mentioned in Romans 16:1-2.[556]

Phoebe is a female Greek name meaning 'radiant',[557] derived from Greek mythology. It is certain that a Jewess would not use such a name, thus indicating that Phoebe was a Gentile Christian, who was a resident of Cenchrea, the eastern port of Corinth. In NT times it was common to introduce strangers with a letter of commendation. Quite naturally, Paul commends Phoebe and, as the person who is carrying the letter from Corinth to Rome, Phoebe is mentioned first in Romans 16.[558] Being mentioned first in the long list of names in Romans 16 has no implication for her role in her home church. Paul commends Phoebe to the Christians in Rome as 'our sister': not only a sister in Christ of Paul and her own congregation but also a sister of the Christians in Rome.

> [t]he designation of a woman fellow-Christian as 'sister' seems to have been particularly characteristic of Christianity (1 Cor. 7:15; 9:5; Philem. 2; James 2:15; Ign. *Pol.* 5:1; *2 Clem.* 12:5; 19:1; 20:2; Herm. *Vis.* 2.2.3; 2.3.1). The ἡμῶν [*hemon*] must denote Christians as a whole (Cranfield): the concept of a universal, or at least fully international brotherhood and sisterhood is already well established.[559]

She is part of their family too. Paul asks the Romans to welcome her in a manner befitting her role at Cenchrea and as Paul's personal representative. The word (προσδέξησθε – *prosdexēsthe*)

---

556. It appears to be only women, not men, who require detailed analysis of Greek words in the NT to determine their activities in earliest Christianity. This reflects both increasing liberalism with regard to doctrine and the increasing extent to which current worldly views are accepted. Hebrews 13:8 seems to have been completely forgotten, because we now see God changing His mind from generation to generation.

557. HSIBD, p. 838. Like Quartus, Phoebe has received much more attention than her brief reference in Romans initially appears to warrant.

558. Cranfield, *Romans*, vol. 2, p. 780; J. R. W. Stott, *The Message of Romans*, TBST (Leicester: InterVarsity Press, 1994), p. 392; Morris, *Romans*, p. 528.

559. Dunn, *Romans 9-16*, p. 886.

was 'commonly used for welcoming an envoy'.[560] She is to be treated with respect as someone for whom Christ died and, therefore, to be given whatever assistance she needs, especially in the light of her personal assistance to Paul (see below concerning the use of παραστῆτε, *parastēte*).

> Paul bespeaks a welcome for Phoebe in the Roman Church. He asks the people at Rome to welcome her as God's dedicated people ought to welcome each other. There should be no strangers in the family of Christ; there should be no need for formal introductions between Christian people, for surely, they are sons and daughters of the one father, and therefore brothers and sisters of each other. And yet a church is not always the welcoming institution that it ought to be. It is possible for Churches, and still more possible for Church organisations, to become little cliques, almost little closed societies which are not really interested in welcoming the stranger. When a stranger comes amongst us, Paul's advice still holds good – welcome such a one as God's dedicated people ought to welcome each other.[561]

Phoebe is described as 'a servant of the church in Cenchrea' (οὖσαν [καὶ] διάκονον τῆς ἐκκλησίας τῆς ἐν κεγχρεαῖς – *housan (kai) diakonon tēs ekklēsias tēs en kenchreais*).

> The fact that ἐκκλησία appears for the first time in the letter is striking, since its casual use in reference to Cenchreae makes its absence hitherto all the more noticeable (see further *Introduction* §2.4.3). It was a peculiarly suitable title for the Christian congregations, because it drew heavily on the LXX use of ἐκκλησία to denote the assembly of Yahweh (e.g. Deut. 23:1-2; 1 Chron. 28:8; Neh. 13:1; Mic. 2:5; BGD, 3: *TDNT* 3:P527), while using a concept which was sufficiently widespread and noncontentious to avoid comment ('assembly' = regularly summoned political body – LSJ; occasionally for business meetings of clubs – Meeks, *Urban Christians*, p. 222, n. 24). It is noteworthy that Paul uses the word consistently for the local assembly of Christians and never for 'the church universal' (for the first time in Ephesians): hence the plurals

560. Thielman, *Romans*, p. 711.
561. Barclay, *Romans*, p. 227.

> (16:16; 1 Cor. 7:17; 16:1, 19; 2 Cor. 8:18-19, 23-24; etc.; see e.g. those cited in Dunn, *Jesus*, p. 429, n. 17; also Beker, *Paul*, pp. 314-6). But since he also uses it for groups of Christians meeting in homes, 'home churches' (see further on [Rom.] 16:5 and [Rom. 16:] 23), the meaning is more precisely Christians in one place gathered to share their common life of worship and discipleship (Dunn, *Jesus*, pp. 262-3; Banks, *Community*, pp. 35-7, Beker, *Paul*, p. 317).[562]

The word διάκονον has been subjected to much analysis and is best translated into English as 'deaconess' for females.[563] See *The Role of διάκονος (diakonos)* in the introduction for more detailed descriptions of the meaning and role of διάκονος in the NT generally and the churches in particular. 'Deacons functioned as servants instead of leaders.'[564]

> The office of deacon, however, must be distinguished from that of overseer/elder (see discussion in Schreiner 1991c: pp. 219-21). One should not conclude from Phoebe's role as a deacon that she functioned as a leader of the congregation (against Jewett 1988: pp. 149-50; 2007: pp. 944-5). Mathew (2013: pp. 66-74) rightly notes the official role of Phoebe, but she goes beyond the evidence in claiming that she has as much authority as Timothy.[565]

This indicates that Phoebe was not a leader, especially not *the* leader, in Cenchrea.

> Her role as a deacon must have involved some sort of practical service to the Christian assembly in Cenchrea and may well have entailed a lot of running around, since a deacon was most basically a go-between, messenger or courier. Part of her duties, then, may have been to act as a human connection between her own assembly in Cenchrea and other groups of Christians, such as the various assemblies of believers in Rome.[566]
>
> Probably she was not a deaconess in the later formal sense of the word, for *diakonos* is a functional term ([Rom. 16:] 2) for a

---

562. Dunn, *Romans 9-16*, p. 887.
563. Zerwick and Grosvenor, *Grammatical Analysis*, vol. 2, p. 495.
564. Schreiner, *Romans*, p. 760, n. 6.
565. ibid., p. 760, n. 7.
566. Thielman, *Romans*, p. 710.

> helper. She seems to have been a benefactress who exercised social and pastoral care.[567]

As well as being a deaconess, Paul notes in Romans 16:2: '*for she herself has also been a helper of many, and of myself as well* (καὶ γὰρ αὐτὴ προστάτις πολλῶν ἐγενήθη καὶ ἐμοῦ αὐτοῦ – *kai gar autē prostatis pollōn egenēthē kai emou autou*'). The critical (and controversial) word here is προστάτις (*prostatis*), which is the feminine of προστάτης (*prostatēs*). In Hellenistic culture, a προστάτης (m.) was a patron of 'clients'. In Hellenistic society 'it is a highly honourable title'.[568] There was a distinct and legal relationship between a patron (either male or female) and their client involving mutual obligations.[569] Generally, the patron was a person of wealth, prestige, or high social standing whose position would enable him or her to do favours for clients, who would in some way be under obligation to reciprocate the benefit received. Paul's use of *prostatis* suggests that Phoebe was a free woman of some means.[570]

A critically important examination of Paul's financial relationships with a variety of churches and individuals is provided by Witherington. It provides essential background material to fully appreciate their complexity; however, Paul himself never used financial or obligatory relationships that would compromise the gospel of grace.[571]

The following two extracts are from commentators who fail to appreciate the huge cultural differences between Hellenistic society and earliest Christianity.

> Paul's use of προστάτις to describe Phoebe was to bestow a prestigious and flattering appellation upon her, and it was a status that, as far as we know, Paul did not furnish upon anyone else. So while προστάτις

567. Dumbrell, *Romans*, p. 141.

568. Hodge, *Romans*, p. 448.

569. J. Adelman, E. Pollard and R. Tignor, *Worlds Together, Worlds Apart*, concise edition. vol. 1 (New York: W. W. Norton, 2015), p. 253. Meeks, *The First Urban Christians*, pp. 60, 79 misinterprets the relationship between Paul and Phoebe as that of patron/client.

570. Cranfield, *Romans*, vol. 2, p. 781.

571. Witherington, *Philippians*, pp. 266-70.

> did not have the same necessary connotations of wealth that 'patron' would have had, it does imply that Phoebe's help was substantial – and that it was especially appreciated by Paul. *We should still expect that their relationship would have operated within the reciprocal dynamic that so trenchantly governed the ancient mindset.*[572]

The sentiment in MacGillivray's last sentence above contradicts all of Paul's teaching about personal relationships among Christians (e.g. Rom. 12:2-3; Col. 3:12-17) and the practical examples in the NT of sharing resources (e.g. Acts 2:45; 1 Cor. 16:1; 1 Thess. 4:10).

> The fact that Paul mentions Phoebe as a patroness 'to many, and also to me' indicates the level of material resources that would support this kind of leadership role. In light of her high social standing, and Paul's relatively subordinate social position as her client, it is mistaken to render προστάτις as 'helper' or to infer some kind of subordinate role.[573]

Paul turned the culture of the world upside down. Why should it be thought that social norms of Hellenistic culture would not be exempt from the gospel's transformative power (1 Cor. 1:25)? MacGillivray and Jewett apply a Hellenistic analysis of Phoebe where wealth automatically endues one with authority and leadership. As to Paul being a 'client' of Phoebe in some socially subordinate role where he 'owes' her some benefit, this view demonstrates that neither author understands that earliest Christianity's culture completely rejected all those secular ideas, especially the relationships between rich and poor; men and women.[574]

A correct understanding of Phoebe's role as προστάτις in a *Christian* context is provided by Ng. The term *prostatis* ...

---

572. E. D. MacGillivray, 'Romans 16:2, προστάτις/προστάτης, and the Application of Reciprocal Relationships to New Testament Texts', *NTest* 53, no. 2 (2011): p. 198 (emphasis added). This conclusion is strongly rejected. See Dunn, *Romans 9-16*, pp. 888-9.

573. Jewett, *Romans*, p. 974, but see p. 980. Given his assessment of earliest Christian culture in the entry for Tertius, it is difficult to reconcile Jewett's comments there with the προστάτις relationship he postulates between Paul and Phoebe.

574. See Manuell, *Gender Wars in Christianity.*

> can hardly have here any technical legal sense such as the masculine form προστάτης could bear; for Paul himself is not likely to have stood in need of such formal legal protection as is sometimes indicated by the use of the masculine form of προστάτης, and it is doubtful whether Phoebe, as a woman, would have been able to fulfil the formal legal functions involved. However, while it is possible that the word is here used in its most general sense of 'helper', it seems quite probable that its choice implies that Phoebe was possessed of some social position, wealth and independence.[575]

It is most unlikely that Phoebe's description as προστάτις has any relevance to Paul's use of ὁ προϊστάμενος (*ho proistamenos*) in Romans 12:8, where it is possible that this word could refer to 'leadership' (NASB) but, as is noted in the margin, could simply mean 'gives aid', although the word can be used in the sense of taking the lead or ruling in a non-Christian environment.[576] More relevant, however, is Paul's use of παραστῆτε (*parastēte*) earlier in the same verse, where the word refers to the assistance that the Roman Christians can provide to Phoebe. It is as if Paul justifies his request by saying that, in like manner, Phoebe herself has helped other people and me; so please help her in the same way.[577] Verse 2 indicates that Phoebe was a benefactor of many people, including Paul.[578]

Ng's article concerning Phoebe's role as *prostasis* clarifies a number of issues. She correctly rejects any notion that the Hellenistic social understanding of the patron/client relationship has any connection with early Christian culture

---

575. See Ng, 'Phoebe as Prostatis', pp. 517-33.

576. Zerwick and Grosvenor, *Grammatical Analysis*, vol. 2, p. 487.

577. See T. R. Schreiner, 'The Valuable Ministries of Women in the Context of Male Leadership: A Survey of Old and New Testament Examples and Teaching' in *Recovering Biblical Manhood and Womanhood: A Response to Evangelical Feminism*, eds. J. Piper and W. Grudem (Wheaton IL: Crossway Books, 2006), pp. 219-20.

578. See MacGillivray, *Romans 16:2*, p. 197, n. 50, where Banks notes that 'we can single out as many as forty sponsors in the New Testament active in providing hospitality and financial support for the larger Christian community'.

and practice.[579] Contrary to his assertion above, MacGillivray comments that 'we should not expect that either Paul or Phoebe received the sort of financial/economic assistance envisaged and sustained by the patron-client relationship or an acceptance of its implicit asymmetrical demands'.[580] We should particularly note the use of προΐστασθαι by Paul in Titus 3:8 and Calvin's substantial comment on the word, which has the meaning of 'take the lead, rule' *in the context of generously giving aid*.[581] 'Nor should the concept of leadership be read into the term here.'[582]

> There is no mention of honour here. Indeed, Phoebe's role as a 'deacon' in the church in Cenchraea involved lowly service by Greco Roman standards and contrasts with her ability to serve as a 'patron' to others. This may reflect the transforming effect that the gospel had on the systems of honour and status that were so prevalent in the cultures where it first flourished.[583]

However, Osiek completely misunderstands this use of the word and produces the conclusion that this (Hellenistic) form of patronage was commonplace throughout early Christianity. Indeed, as noted below, Paul is pictured as manipulating Phoebe through this supposed patron/client relationship!

> The passage [Rom. 16:2-3] is a crux for understanding how patronage functioned among early followers of the NT church.[584]
>
> Here we see *the more obvious exercise of patronage by Paul in order to get the results he wishes.* Paul considers Phoebe a patron

579. See Ng, *Phoebe as Prostatis*, pp. 7-9. 'Paul's insistence that *social distinctions lost their relevance within the Christian fellowship* was not peculiar to him: it inhered in the logic of Christian faith and life', in Bruce, *Pauline Circle*, p. 45 (emphasis added).

580. MacGillivray, *Romans 16:2*, p. 197.

581. Calvin, 'Commentaries on the Epistle to Titus', *Calvin's Commentaries*, vol. 21, pp. 337-8. See Zerwick and Grosvenor, *Grammatical Analysis*, vol. 2, pp. 650-1.

582. Schreiner, *Romans*, p. 761.

583. Thielman, *Romans*, p. 712.

584. C. Osiek, 'The Politics of Patronage and the Politics of Kinship: The Meeting of the Ways', *BTB* 39, no. 3 (2009), p. 148.

> and a leader of some kind in the assembly of Cenchrae [sic] but especially as provider of the goods and services expected in such a role for him personally and for many others, as he says (Rom. 16:1-2): hospitality, *protection, and access to social networks*. In this case we see better the reciprocal nature of the relationship, whereby Paul enhances Phoebe's status by calling her his *prostatis*, while *she will enhance his status* by association with her upon her arrival in Rome bearing his letter.[585]

There is also the issue of the extent of Phoebe's wealth. If we discount the possibility of her financial assistance to Paul and others, which can be justified both by the text and Paul's refusal of financial assistance (1 Cor. 9:18; 2 Cor. 11:9-10), Phoebe's wealth was probably significant.[586] Undoubtedly, she was a woman of independent means; otherwise she could not have provided as much assistance as she did. But her assistance was to individuals, not to the church at Cenchrea.[587] Nor can it be claimed that the church met in her house.

Many feminist commentators have attempted to inflate the role and status of Phoebe. For a rather extreme example, Branch concludes that 'Finger quite rightly sees Phoebe as a businesswoman, theologian, and diplomat'.[588] There are many more examples of this type of unwarranted distortion of the plain meaning of the text.[589]

To summarise, Phoebe was a free woman of considerable financial independence, who was a deaconess in the church at Cenchrea. No doubt, there were many opportunities for her to

---

585. ibid., p. 150 (emphasis added).

586. See Schreiner, *The Valuable Ministries of Women*, pp. 219-20.

587. D. J. Moo, *The Epistle to the Romans*, NICNT (Grand Rapids: Eerdmans, 1996), p. 916.

588. R. H. Finger, 'Phoebe: Role model for leaders', *Daughters of Zion* 14, no. 2 (1988): pp. 5-7. R. G. Branch, 'Female leadership as demonstrated by Phoebe: An ***interpretation*** of Paul's words introducing Phoebe to the saints in Rome', *In die Skriflig* 53, no. 2 (2019). (emphasis added).

589. Murray, *Romans*, p. 227, n. 1, provides a much earlier example in R. C. Prohl, *Woman in the Church* (Grand Rapids: Eerdmans, 1957), p. 70.

show Christian service to a wide variety of people in a busy port. She used her wealth to help others in the church (we know not how) and also assisted Paul as a benefactor 'without strings attached'. Her assistance was sufficiently generous and widespread that Paul complemented her with the acclamation of her work for Christ as a προστάτις *within Christian culture.*

PHYGELUS

2 TIMOTHY 1:15

[15] You are aware of the fact that all who are in Asia turned away from me, among whom are Phygelus and Hermogenes.

This Greek Gentile name means 'fugitive',[590] perhaps referring to his background as a slave; 'there is even dispute about the spelling of this rare name.'[591] Not everything went in Paul's favour. In this verse he recalls to Timothy that '[Y]ou are aware of the fact that all who are in Asia turned away from me, among whom are Phygelus and Hermogenes'. Paul also uses the verb ἀποστρέφω (*apostrephō*) in Romans 11:26; 2 Timothy 4:4 and Titus 1:14. It is a strong verb (cf. Luke 23:14, NIV). This verb can

> denote decisive rejection (as in 2 Tim. 4:4; Titus 1:14; Heb. 12:25) .... Believers and even ministers today may recast or abandon the core gospel message because of various pressures, but from Phygelus and Hermogenes we learn that such moves have a hoary heritage (see also 1 Cor. 4:9-13; 2 Cor. 4:7-12; 1 John 2:19).[592]

The sense of the verse is that these people are still residing in the province of Asia.[593]

The claim that this turning away from the apostle refers to 'all who are in Asia' is clearly 'hyperbolic',[594] given the loyalty of Onesiphorus and others in Ephesus. Guthrie, quoting White,

---

590. HSIBD, p. 840.

591. Yarbrough, *Letters to Timothy and Titus,* p. 367.

592. ibid., p. 367.

593. Guthrie, *Pastoral Epistles*, p. 135; Yarbrough, *Letters to Timothy and Titus*, p. 367.

594. R. F. Collins, *1 & 2 Timothy and Titus,* New Testament Library (Louisville: Westminster John Knox, 2002), p. 215.

describes it as 'the sweeping assertion of depression',[595] but that does not seem consistent with Paul's underlying confidence in God's support despite his imprisonment and the likelihood of his death (cf. 2 Tim. 4:7). Paul's strong statement confirms his desire that Timothy does not turn away from him. The naming of Phygelus and Hermogenes may suggest that they were the driving force in this withdrawal of support from Paul.

Pontius Pilate

1 Timothy 6:13

[13]I charge you in the presence of God, who gives life to all things, and of Christ Jesus, who testified the good confession before Pontius Pilate,

Pontius Pilate (*Pilatus*) is best known for his role in the condemnation to death by crucifixion of Jesus of Nazareth (Matt. 27:11-26; Mark 15:2-15; Luke 23:2-25; John 18:28-19:22). He was the prefect (*praefectus*), not 'procurator' of Judea from A.D. 26-36.[596] This entry concerns Pilate himself, not the biblical narrative. Vermes provides an overview of Pilate from contemporary sources and some extracts are provided below.

> There exist two very different portraits of Pilate, one drawn by the first-century C.E. Jewish writers, Philo and Josephus, and the other by the evangelists and the early church.
>
> The Pilate of Josephus is a harsh, insensitive and cruel official who fully deserved his dismissal from office by his regional superior Vitellius, the Roman governor of Syria in 36/37 C.E. Apparently, soon after his arrival in Judea, Pilate broke with the custom of his predecessors, who respected the religious sensitivities of the Jews, and commanded his soldiers to march into Jerusalem carrying Roman standards bearing the image of the emperor, thus unnecessarily causing provocation and offence. Next he gave

595. Guthrie, *Pastoral Epistles*, p. 135.

596. See Vermes, *Who's Who in the Age of Jesus*, p. 213, which provides a copy of an inscription concerning Pilate, found in Caesarea in 1961. The remaining inscription reads: '... *TIBERIEVM ... [PON]TIVS PILATVS ... [PRAEF]ECTVS IVDA[EA]A*'. He also portrays two very different Pilates, according to contemporary secular and Christian sources.

rise to a popular upheaval when he unlawfully appropriated the money called *Corban* (offering) from the Temple treasury and used it for the construction of an aqueduct bringing water to Jerusalem. Crowds of Jews protested. Though unarmed, many were slaughtered by the legionaries on Pilate's order, while others were trodden to death in the ensuing tumult. The so-called *Testimonium Flavianum*, Josephus' notice on Jesus, inserted in the context of these calamities ... A further act of cruelty, unrecorded in Josephus but attested in the Gospel of Luke (13:1), relates to the massacre of Galilean Jewish pilgrims travelling to Jerusalem with their sacrificial offerings.

Philo, a contemporary of Pilate, has no personal testimony to offer, but quotes at length a letter of the Jewish king Agrippa I (37–41 C.E.) to the emperor Caligula, in which Pilate is described as a stubborn, irascible and vindictive man. He is said to have been naturally inflexible, a blend of self-will and obduracy. As a governor he was guilty of insults, robberies, outrage and wanton injuries, in addition to accepting bribes; he was also responsible for numerous executions without trial as well as for numerous acts of grievous cruelty. It would be hard to paint a darker picture.

In contrast, the Pilate of the New Testament is a totally different person. He appears as a fair-minded weakling, who found Jesus innocent of the charges levelled against Him by the Jewish leaders ...

As far as the respective characterisations go, the Pilate of Josephus and Philo is irreconcilable with the Pilate of the evangelists ...

Another detail in the Gospel account which is intended to show Pilate's sympathetic attitude towards Jesus is the anecdote of the so-called paschal privilege (*privilegium paschale*) connected with the Barabbas episode. ... However, the historicity of the story is debateable. No ancient document, narrative or legal, Jewish or Roman, attests a Passover amnesty ...

However, the most convincing evidence for Pilate's disregard for the law is the fact that it was on account of his cruelty that he was demoted from his office by the emperor and sent into exile.[597]

---

597. Vermes, *Who's Who in the Age of Jesus*, pp. 213-4. Vermes' sources were Josephus, *War* 2:169-177; *Ant.* 18:35-89; Philo, *Legatio* 299-305; Tertullian, *Apologeticum* 21:24; Eusebius, *Eccl. Hist.* 2:2.

The role of Pontius Pilate in Jesus' death confirms that it occurred publicly and is a matter of historical fact.[598] Perkins also reflects Paul's technical description of Jesus' trial as being an official trial.

> **ἐπὶ ποντίου πιλάτου.** Spatial. BDAG (363-364.3) indicates that in legal proceedings ἐπὶ + genitive case indicates 'involvement in an official proceeding' before a judge or other official (see Matt. 28:14; Mark 13:9). The writer refers to Jesus' Roman trial before Pontius Pilate. In 2 Tim. 4:16 he alludes to his own imminent trial before the emperor.[599]

Prisca and Aquila[600]

Acts 18:1-3

[1] *After these things he left Athens and went to Corinth.*

[2] *And he found a Jew named Aquila, a native of Pontus, having recently come from Italy with his wife Priscilla, because Claudius had commanded all the Jews to leave Rome. He came to them, ...*

[3] *... and because he was of the same trade, he stayed with them and they were working, for by trade they were tent-makers.*

Acts 18:18, 19, 26

[18] *Paul, having remained many days longer, took leave of the brethren and put out to sea for Syria, and with him were Priscilla and Aquila. In Cenchrea he had his hair cut, for he was keeping a vow.*

[19] *They came to Ephesus, and he left them there. Now he himself entered the synagogue and reasoned with the Jews.*

[26] *... and he [Apollos] began to speak out boldly in the synagogue. But when Priscilla and Aquila heard him, they took him aside and explained to him the way of God more accurately.*

Romans 16:3-5

[3] *Greet Prisca and Aquila, my fellow workers in Christ Jesus, ...*

[4] *... who for my life risked their own necks, to whom not only do I give thanks, but also all the churches of the Gentiles; ...*

---

598. See Yarbrough, *Letters to Timothy and Titus*, p. 327.

599. Perkins, *Pastoral Letters*, p. 145.

600. This entry reflects the detailed analysis of Prisca and Aquila in G. Manuell, 'Prisca and Aquila: Exemplary Models of Gospel Obedience,' *RTR* 80, no. 3 (2021): pp. 218-41.

[5]... also greet the church that is in their house. Greet Epaenetus, my beloved, who is the first convert to Christ from Asia.

1 Corinthians 16:19

[19]The churches of Asia greet you. Aquila and Prisca greet you heartily in the Lord, with the church that is in their house.

2 Timothy 4:19

[19]Greet Prisca and Aquila, and the household of Onesiphorus.

1. Introduction

Prisca (a Latin name meaning 'ancient') and her husband, Aquila, are two of the most prominent Christians in the NT.[601] They are certainly its most famous married couple. 'Aquila is a frequent Roman name [meaning eagle], regularly Hellenised in the inscriptions as Ἀκύλας or Ἀκυίλας. It merits a brief note as being interestingly attested in contemporary Pontus, the stated origin of our character.'[602] There appears to be a strong temptation for modern biblical commentators to mould Prisca (especially) and Aquila into whatever personae suit their social and/or political biases or doctrinal presuppositions. Resisting this urge, this article concentrates on this couple's identity *as described by Scripture in its historical environment* to confirm their position as exemplars of Paul's new society for believers in Jesus.[603]

This article addresses one secular cultural issue, given the non-status nature of early Christianity: that Prisca is sometimes mentioned before her husband in Scripture. Bruce notes that '*in the secular society of the time*, when one finds a wife being named before her husband, the reason usually is that her social status was higher than his'.[604] However, Jewett insists that 'a mixed marriage

601. NT references to Prisca and Aquila are Acts 18:2-3, 18-19, 26; Romans 16:3-5; 1 Corinthians 16:19; and 2 Timothy 4:19. For ease of reference, this couple is always named 'Prisca and Aquila'.

602. Hemer, *The Book of Acts*, pp. 232-3.

603. The historical work of fiction, B. Witherington III, *Priscilla: The Life of an Early Christian* (Downers Grove: IVP Academic, 2019), has not been used as a reference for this article.

604. Bruce, *Pauline Circle*, p. 45 (emphasis added).

between a Roman noblewoman and a Jewish Christian freed man is the only circumstance that explains all the evidence about this couple'.[605] 'If Luke had known anything about a socially elevated status of Prisca, he would have loved to mention it, distinguished women being a preferred subject for him: e.g., Luke 8:3; Acts 17:4, 12; cf. 16:14; 17:34.'[606] Analysis suggests that the reason for her distinction was non-secular: it was an event in Acts 18. This chapter is also relevant to the dating of 1 Corinthians.

As should be expected in ancient historical analysis, some opinions cannot be asserted categorically; nevertheless, this entry is intended to form a stronger foundation for future analysis of Prisca and Aquila. It considers their personal origins, occupation, secular social status, travels, and roles in assisting Paul's ministry in Corinth, Ephesus, and Rome. It attempts to clarify their role in educating Apollos (Acts 18:26), seeking to counter errant ideas about Prisca (and Aquila) emanating from feminist theology, and a lack of appreciation of the radical Christian culture taught by Jesus and Paul.

2. The New Society

A foundation stone of this analysis must be the theological and sociological patterns described by Paul for the early NT churches established throughout the Roman Empire. As well as providing factual and theological information to these new communities, Paul was establishing a manner of personal and community living that was singularly distinct from the cultural and societal norms of the first century A.D. The new Christian culture established by Paul involved specific instructions for Christian women and men generally and for the conduct of married couples in particular, as stated in Ephesians 5:21-33. 'Paul's insistence that *social distinctions lost their relevance within the Christian fellowship* was not peculiar to him: it inhered in the logic of Christian faith and life.'[607] All aspects of secular social status were to be subsumed

605. Jewett, *Romans*, p. 956.
606. Lampe, *The Roman Christians*, p. 223.
607. Bruce, *Pauline Circle*, p. 45 (emphasis added).

under one goal: 'all of you who were baptised into Christ have clothed yourselves with Christ. There is neither Jew nor Greek, there is neither slave nor free man, there is neither male nor female; for you are all one in Christ Jesus' (Gal. 3:27-28, NASB). The only qualification for membership of this new Christian community was faith in Jesus Christ.

The new society that Paul was establishing did not reject secular society or its institutions out of hand (e.g. slavery). The only measuring stick used was: is this or that activity compatible with being 'in Christ'? To the extent that it was, it was acceptable in the *ekklēsia*, otherwise it was rejected (John 17:14-18). It was a new community formed *ab initio* without reliance on current secular practices. The comparative use of Hellenistic social constructs can obscure the manner in which Prisca and Aquila behaved in the *ekklēsia* in their homes and their evangelistic ministry.

3. Personal Origins

The more intimate, affectionate form of Prisca is Priscilla. Paul always refers to her as 'Prisca' in his letters but Luke uses 'Priscilla' in Acts. This is consistent with Paul's use of formal names and Luke's habit of using more familiar forms.[608] We do not know Prisca's place of birth. Although having a Latin name, Aquila was a Jew, born in the region of Pontus on the southern coast of the Black Sea, as noted in Acts 18:2. Aquila migrated from Pontus to Rome but we do not know when or where he met his wife.

> I suggest that 'Pontic' does have a significant function in the narrative, because the gentilic would have invited associations entirely opposite to those of 'Alexandrian'. While the stereotype concerning the latter was one of learning and cultural sophistication, the common

---

608. Examples where Paul uses the person's formal name and Luke uses the more familiar version are Sosipater/Sopater (Rom. 16:21 *vs* Acts 20:4) and Silvanus/Silas (2 Cor. 1:19; 1 Thess. 1:1; 2 Thess. 1:1 *vs* Acts 15:22-40; 16:19-40; 17:1-16; 18:5). 1 Pet. 5:12 uses Silvanus. It is interesting that Sydney's Moore Theological College chose the more familiar name for its 'Priscilla and Aquila Centre'.

> prejudice about people from Pontus was that they were uneducated and dim-witted barbarians. When Acts tells the story of how people connected to this region 'took aside' the learned Alexandrian 'and explained the Way [of God] to him more accurately' (προσελάβοντο αυτόν και ἀκριβέστερον αὐτω ἐξέθεντο την ὁδὸν [του θεοὺ], 18:26), this would likely have seemed very surprising to an ancient audience familiar with these common stereotypes. The fact that this interpretation fits the way ethnic designations function elsewhere in Luke-Acts strengthens its plausibility.[609]

Suetonius may provide a clue to the fact that this Jewish couple had Latin names. Just before his famous comment about the expulsion of Jews from Rome, he notes that it had become illegal for foreigners to adopt the names of Roman families.[610] It could be that the Jew from Pontus and his wife adopted Roman names to enhance their business prospects in the Roman capital (social acceptability seems a likely ambition if they were then not Christians). Since her husband was a Jew, it is highly likely that Prisca was too.[611] This conclusion is supported by her attendance

---

609. den Dulk, *Aquila and Apollos*, p. 180. This article provides ancient perceptions of 'Pontus' as a region. In p. 179, n. 7, den Dulk comments: 'One of the few scholars who does accord significance to the Pontic background of Aquila is William O. Walker Jr. "The Portrayal of Aquila and Priscilla in Acts: The Question of Sources." *NTS* vol. 54, no. 4. 2008.'

610. Suetonius, *Life of Claudius*, trans. J. Rolfe, p. 25, in A Digital Library of Classical Antiquity, *https://lexundria.com/suet_cl/25/r*: '3. He forbade men of foreign birth to use the Roman names so far as those of the clans were concerned. … 4. Since the Jews constantly made disturbances at the instigation of Chrestus, he expelled them from Rome.' Whether the edict referred to by Suetonius is the same one that applied to this couple is uncertain. A full analysis of the issue is provided in Keener, *Acts*, vol. 3, pp. 2697-711. Keener nominates A.D. 49 for the expulsion. See also A. D. Clarke, 'Rome and Italy', *The Book of Acts in its First Century Setting*, vol. 2, eds. D. W. J. Gill and C. Gempf (Grand Rapids: Eerdmans, 1994), pp. 469-71. Barclay, *The Letter to the Romans*, p. 228, suggests that the edict affecting Prisca and Aquila was issued in A.D. 52 but gives no explanation for this dating. Keener, *Acts*, is the most comprehensive analysis of the Book of Acts.

611. See D. L. Bock, *Acts* (Grand Rapids: Baker, 2007), p. 578; Cranfield, *Romans*, vol. 2, p. 783; Meeks, *First Urban Christians*, p. 59.

at the synagogue in Ephesus with Aquila (Acts 18:26). If the couple were known to be part of the *Chrestus* group, their expulsion from Rome is more understandable. Meeks notes that 'Both have good Roman names, but in Rome that was quite common for Jews, Greek- as well as Latin-speaking, especially for women', concluding '*They are* eastern provincials and Jews besides, but assimilated to Greco-Roman culture'.[612] Gill comments that 'Many of the people of Roman Corinth have Latin names. These include Aquila and Priscilla (Prisca) who were clearly Jews'.[613] As Paul demonstrated, it was possible to be a Jew and a Roman citizen. However, their expulsion from Rome mitigates against the possibility of Prisca and Aquila possessing Roman citizenship.[614]

Notwithstanding the possibility raised in the previous paragraph, Acts 18:1-3 suggests that Prisca and Aquila were Christians before Paul met them, otherwise Luke would have recorded their conversion.[615] They may have been Christians for some time – even foundation members of the church in Rome[616] – because we know that the gospel reached Rome soon after Pentecost (Acts 2:10), many years before Paul's first meeting with this couple. Their meeting seems to have been a matter of divine providence because Paul, like Aquila, was familiar with tentmaking and they also happened to be Jews as well as Christians. When, or the means by which, either of the couple became Christians is not known. It is noteworthy that Prisca and Aquila are always mentioned together in Scripture and much controversy has attached to the fact that Prisca is mentioned first, other than in Luke's introduction of the couple in Acts 18:2-3 and Paul's salutation in 1 Corinthians 16:19. This is considered below.

---

612. Meeks, *First Urban Christians*, p. 59 (emphasis added), but this is too definitive for Prisca.

613. D. W. J. Gill, *Macedonia*, in Gill and Gempf, *Book of Acts*, p. 451.

614. See Keener, *Acts*, vol. 3, pp. 2711-12.

615. Keener, *Acts*, vol. 3, p. 2711; Marshall, *Acts*, p. 293. Thielman, *Romans*, p.714, suggests that they were most likely believers before leaving Rome.

616. Bruce, *Pauline Circle*, p. 46.

4. Tentmaking and the Meaning of σκηνοποιός

Prisca and Aquila are described as σκηνοποιός, which is translated 'tentmakers' in most Bibles.[617] The only reference to the practice of tentmaking in the NT is Acts 18:3. 'Tentmaker' is the most common translation since σκηνος means 'tent'. In the first century A.D. some tents were made of leather (and all tents required leather accessorics), but many were also made from a coarse woollen cloth woven from black goats' hair. The most famous cloth of this type was called *cilicium* because it originated from Paul's native region of Cilicia. It is equivalent to today's felt. The *Theological Dictionary of the New Testament* says that 'tents of antiquity were usually made of leather'.[618] On the other hand, *The Illustrated Bible Dictionary* says that 'In biblical times tents were frequently made of a cloth woven out of black goat's [sic] hair.'[619]

In his detailed study of tentmaking around the first century A.D., Hock concludes that an average artisanal shop in Corinth comprised about six to twelve artisans.[620] He suggests that the context of Acts 18:3 could see Paul joining a business that was sufficiently large to cope with the arrival of an additional worker. Given Paul's family business in Tarsus as tentmakers, he would

617. e.g. ASV, ESV, HCSB, ISV, J. B. Phillips, KJV, NASB 1995, NIV, NKJV, NREV, RSV. However, Barclay's translation of the NT records that 'they were leather-workers'. See W. Barclay, *The New Testament* (Glasgow: William Collins, 1969), p. 280, well before that view was more generally accepted. HCSB has a marginal note re 'leatherworker' as an alternative.

618. *Theological Dictionary of the New Testament*, ed. G. Kittel, vol. 7 (Grand Rapids: Eerdmans, 1964–1976), p. 393.

619. HSIBD, p. 780.

620. R. F. Hock, *The Social Context of Paul's Ministry: Tentmaking and Apostleship* (Philadelphia: Fortress Press, 1980), pp. 32-3. See also R. F. Hock, 'Paul's Tentmaking and the Problem of His Social Class', *JBL* 97, no. 4 (1978): pp. 555-64. G. Theissen, *Social Setting*, p. 90. Keener, *Acts*, vol. 3, p. 2725 notes that Hock's 'study of Paul's labour has proved invaluable information'. However, Hock, pp. 66-7, asserts that 'Paul's view of his trade and of work in general was not as positive as is often assumed'. This opinion is strongly (and correctly) rejected in T. D. Still, 'Did Paul Loathe Manual Labour? Revisiting the Work of Ronald F. Hock on the Apostle's Tentmaking and Social Class,' *JBL* 125, no. 4 (2006): pp. 781-95.

have been familiar with both *cilicium* and leather.[621] This view is supported if, in Acts 18:3, Luke uses ἠργάζετο (*hēgazeto*) to mean that Paul 'worked *for*' Prisca and Aquila, rather than 'worked *with*' them as equals in the business.[622]

Hock concluded that 'To identify the nature of Paul's trade as leatherworking is correct';[623] 'We may thus picture Paul as making tents and other products from leather';[624] However, 'the thesis that Paul wove tentcloth from the goats' hair (*cilicium*) of his native province should once and for all be dropped.'[625] Thus, Paul's occupation is better described as a leatherworker, an occupation only requiring portable tools, which aided the mobility of its exponents. Thus it is a reasonable starting point to conclude from Scripture that Prisca and Aquila were primarily engaged in a tentmaking business with all the paraphernalia associated with leather in that activity. All tents required leather components.

> As a missionary travelling lightly (Luke 9:3; 10:4), Paul may not have always taken his tools with him; on occasions when he was abruptly driven from a city (as in the case of his flight from Thessalonica shortly before his arrival in Achaia), he likely could not have done

621. This conclusion reflects the normal Jewish custom of sons following their father's trade in the same way that Jesus followed Joseph's occupation as a carpenter. Given that Paul's father was both a Pharisee (Acts 23:6) and a Roman citizen (Acts 16:37 implies this), he would not have been a menial labourer, but a person of some wealth and social standing, owning a business. See Keener, *Acts*, vol. 3, pp. 2734-5.

622. Various Bible versions translate this as Paul working with Prisca and Aquila, not for them: 'they carried on business together' (NEB); 'he stayed with them and worked with them' (Barclay, *New Testament*); 'he stayed with them and they worked' (RSV); 'he stayed with them and they were working' (NASV); 'he abode with them and wrought' (KJV). The KJV may be closest to the sense of the Greek here if it implies that Paul stayed with Prisca and Aquila and worked in their shop – but not necessarily doing the same things that they did. He was a worker and they were managers.

623. Hock, *Social Context*, p. 21. On the other hand, Hemer, *The Book of Acts*, p. 233, regards 'the arguments for σκηνοποιοί = "leather workers" are inconclusive at best'.

624. Hock, *Social Context*, p. 21.

625. ibid., p. 66.

> so. It seems nevertheless significant that he settled especially in cities with many tradesmen whom he could evangelise and through whose numerous contacts his message would be widely spread. Paul could have borrowed tools when coming to a new town, or perhaps he worked for those who would have supplied them.[626]

An article by Neuhaus attempts to minimise the factual description of the occupation of Aquila and Paul by turning the facts into a primarily spiritual expression of Paul's ministry but this thesis is rejected.[627]

5. Travels and Activities

The itinerant lifestyle of Prisca and Aquila is examined in its chronological order. Their movements provide an impression of the world in which they lived and their relationship with various churches. They moved from Rome to Corinth, to Ephesus, back to Rome and then travelled to Ephesus for Paul. It was not uncommon for people to move from place to place in NT times, particularly Jews, who were a constant target for harassment. Blaiklock comments that, in people like Prisca and Aquila, 'we see a feature of the first century which marks the twentieth – habits of travel, immigration and change of residence, all of which propagated and spread the gospel. Can this be harnessed again?'[628]

5.1 Corinth

Paul first met Prisca and Aquila in Corinth (Acts 18:1-2). Luke's use of προσφάτως (meaning 'recently') in Acts 18:2 implies that Prisca and Aquila arrived in Corinth a little before Paul did around A.D. 49/50. Their destination of Corinth may have reflected 'the dominance of Greek [language] among Roman Jews who were not Roman citizens' as well as the fact that 'Corinth held

626. Keener, *Acts,* vol. 3, p. 2736.

627. D. M. Neuhaus, 'Paul: A Tentmaker' in *Saint Paul: Educator to Faith and Love*, eds. M. Ferrero and R. Spataro (Jerusalem: Studium Theologicum Salesianum, 2008): pp. 147-66.

628. E. M. Blaiklock, *Romans* (Grand Rapids: Eerdmans, 1971), p. 90.

Achaia's most significant Jewish population'.[629] It also had 'the most obvious ties with Italy'.[630] Their early fellowship in Corinth must have been a great encouragement to Paul in the face of constant Jewish opposition to his preaching (Acts 18:6).

The arrival of Silas and Timothy from Macedonia (Acts 18:5) enabled Paul to cease his occupation and concentrate on preaching, which then caused considerable opposition and conflict at the synagogue. The outcome was that Paul 'left there [the synagogue] and went to the home of a man named Titius Justus, a worshipper of God, whose house was next to the synagogue' (Acts 18:7). There have been suggestions that, after these incidents at the synagogue, Paul no longer resided with Prisca and Aquila but now dwelt in the house of Titius Justus.[631] This interpretation is completely contrary to Paul's preference that, wherever possible, he supported himself (1 Cor. 9:17-18; 1 Thess. 2:9; 2 Thess. 3:8-9). Keener has the correct understanding of Paul's decision.[632] Paul continued to live with Prisca and Aquila until his departure from Corinth to Ephesus but changed his *locus operandi* from the synagogue to the house next door to it.

To move from the house of Prisca and Aquila to that of Titius Justus would have completely contradicted and undermined Paul's stated intention to be independent of patrons (see Section 5.2). It would have also contravened Jesus' instructions to travelling evangelists as per Mark 6:10; Luke 10:7. Some commentators refer to the church in Prisca and Aquila's house in Corinth. Ellis describes them as 'having homes used by the church in one way or another in Corinth, Ephesus and Rome'.[633]

---

629. Keener, *Acts*, vol. 3, p. 2712.

630. C. S. Keener, *Paul, Women & Wives* (Massachusetts: Hendrickson, 1993), p. 241.

631. Marshall, *Acts*, 294. Theissen, *Social Setting*, p. 90, asks: 'That he [Paul] stopped work is understandable, but why did he not stay on with Priscilla and Aquila?'

632. Keener, *Acts*, vol. 3, pp. 2744-7. See also Bruce, *Acts*, p. 50.

633. E. E. Ellis, *Pauline Theology: Ministry and Society* (Grand Rapids: Eerdmans, 1989), p. 142.

However, his Corinthian house church assumption is not supported by the evidence.

5.2 Prisca and Aquila as προστάτης in Corinth?

Although Paul did not want to be a burden on anyone, he had to obtain food and shelter. A most important principle adopted by Paul was the acceptance of assistance only when necessary. This raises a critical issue in Paul's varying policy about reliance on assistance from others. Paul began to engage in full-time evangelism (Acts 18:5) after the arrival of Timothy and Silas in Corinth with a gift from Philippi (2 Cor. 11:8-9; Phil. 4:15). Also, Paul lived in the home of Prisca and Aquila until his departure with them for Ephesus.

To consider Prisca and Aquila's relationship with Paul, we should briefly examine the role undertaken by Phoebe in Cenchrea[634] as described in Romans 16:2. Paul describes Phoebe as having 'been a helper of many, and of me myself' (NASB).

The critical word describing Phoebe is προστάτις, the female form of προστάτης, which in first century Greco-Roman society meant 'patron', reflecting some form of subservience or obligation by the donee to the donor. Many attempts have been made to force a meaning on this *hapax legomenon* in the NT, which is quite incompatible with both tradition and practice in the early Christian communities and Paul's own preference (where possible) to be independent for the sake of preaching the gospel, unconstrained from worldly shackles. Luke never mentions this issue in Acts. An important article reflecting Luke's use of προστάτις in a first-century *Christian* setting is provided by Ng.[635] Phoebe's role was to provide practical (possibly including monetary) assistance to Paul's ministry activities. Any implication that Paul was in any way indebted to, or subject to the dictates of, Phoebe cannot be sustained.

---

634. Cenchrea was a port of Corinth, about 11 km (8 miles) south of the city. A Christian church was established there, of which Phoebe was a member (Rom. 16:1). See Keener, *Acts*, vol. 3, pp. 2787-9 for details on Cenchrea.

635. Ng, *Phoebe as Prostatis*.

Although not mentioned in Acts or Paul's letters, it seems likely that Prisca and Aquila acted as προστάτης (in a Christian context as per the example of Phoebe) by providing Paul with food and lodging at their home.[636] Paul was determined that he would not rely on financial assistance from the Corinthian church. Although he changed this policy when it came to the Philippian church, he reverted to his earlier Corinthian policy with the Thessalonians (1 Thess. 2:9).

> The Macedonian church helped Paul when he was in Corinth (2 Cor. 11:8-9), and later he hoped that the Corinthian church might help him evangelise other regions (probably the meaning of 10:15-16; also the Roman church, Rom. 15:24). Yet to be one church's missionary elsewhere differed from depending on local support where the missionary could be viewed as *becoming a client of the supporters*; Paul refused the Corinthian Christians' support when he was among them (2 Cor. 12:13) and would also refuse it on his future trip (12:14-15). He did so not because he doubted that support for apostolic labours was the ideal (1 Cor. 9:4-14) but because he sacrificed this (9:15-18). Rather, he apparently would not submit to *local ideas of patronage* or did not want to be compared too closely to begging Cynics.[637]
>
> But Paul may well have wished to resist becoming so closely tied to one particular household, not least to avoid the furtherance of party division (1 Cor. 1:10-13). ... What was particularly offensive to some of the Corinthians was Paul's insistence upon working at a trade to support himself ... Paul insists on working with his hands. This was not only a sign of continued independence, but also of lowly status which would hardly have made Paul seem an impressive leader to the relatively few well-to-do Corinthians.[638]

---

636. Some articles on Phoebe reflect a self-admitted feminist bias, leading to positions unsupportable by Scripture (e.g. Eph. 5:22-33; 1 Tim. 1:11-12), as in the case of Osiek, *The Politics of Patronage* (which dismisses Ng's conclusions without any analysis). See also Branch, *Female leadership*. See Section 9 below.

637. Keener, *Acts*, vol. 3, p. 740. See also Ciampa and Rosner, *The First Letter to the Corinthians*, pp. 400-20, for their comments on Paul's arguments concerning 1 Corinthians 9:3-18 regarding his refusal of payment from the Corinthians for preaching the gospel.

638. D. G. Horrell, *The Social Ethos of the Corinthian Correspondence* (Edinburgh: T. and T. Clark, 1996), p. 214. See also pp. 203, 215. This would

5.3 Ephesus

When Paul finally left Corinth (Acts 18:18-19), Prisca and Aquila accompanied him but no reason is given. Paul's intention was to journey to Syria and Judaea, so they departed from Cenchrea, the port for sailing east from Corinth. Prisca and Aquila only travelled as far as Ephesus. Their prominence in early Christianity suggests that their exposure to Paul's preaching and example encouraged them to move to Ephesus more for gospel work than for the expansion of their tentmaking business. The gospel imperative seems a far more probable motivation in view of the increasing praise they subsequently received about their role with Paul as 'fellow-workers in Christ' and providing assistance to Gentile churches (Rom. 16:4). This was their first experience in this missionary role. Before Paul's arrival in Ephesus (Acts 19:1), Prisca and Aquila must have been active in Christian evangelism.

Paul's first letter to the Corinthians was written from Ephesus. In 1 Corinthians 16:9 he sends greetings from Aquila and Prisca (note the order) and 'the church that is in their house'. At this time, Christians did not have buildings specifically set aside for worship and the church relied on wealthier people to use their larger homes as meeting places. The success of their business activities apparently afforded Prisca and Aquila a home suitably large enough to accommodate Christian gatherings.[639]

Welborn's analysis of the extent of 'democracy' in house churches in Corinth is probably applicable to the groups that met in the home of Prisca and Aquila in Ephesus and Rome.[640]

---

have reflected the large variances in wealth of the Corinthian congregation (1 Cor. 1:26).

639. For studies on house churches, see R. W. Gehring, *House Church and Mission: The Importance of Household Structures in Early Christianity* (Peabody, MA: Hendrickson, 2004); E. Adams, *The Earliest Christian Meeting Places: Almost Exclusively Houses?* Library of New Testament Studies 450 (London: Bloomsbury T. and T. Clark, 2016).

640. L. L. Welborn, 'How "Democratic" Was the Pauline *Ekklēsia*? An Assessment with Special Reference to the Christ Groups of Roman Corinth', *NTS* 65, no. 3 (2019): p. 289.

The problem with this type of analysis is that it uses institutions in secular society as the base model for interpreting Christian activities. For example, Welborn uses the Roman model of προστάτης (*prostatēs*) to determine the responsibilities and leadership role of the home-owner.[641]

> The conclusion that the household was the organisational unit of the Christ groups at Corinth has consequences for our conception of the nature and function of leadership in the *ekklēsia*. In a hierarchical society such as Roman Corinth, the head of the household would have exercised authority over the group to which he extended hospitality. In the most concrete sense, the householder would have functioned as the patron of the group, and may have been expected to provide beneficia, such as legal help, a loan, advice on domestic matters, and so forth. The householder also probably supplied food and drink for the believers who gathered in his or her house to eat the Lord's Supper.
>
> The role of the leader of a household *ekklēsia* of Christ-believers seems to find its closest analogy in the Greco-Roman cubic associations in which a single patron provided hospitality for the group which met in his or her house.[642]

The exemplary behaviour of Prisca and Aquila is reflected in Welborn's observation.

> For even if the household was the organisational unit of the Christ groups, and even if the householders functioned as de facto patrons, Paul never explicitly acknowledges their role as leaders, and the case of the Corinthian women prophets demonstrates that some members were unwilling to be subordinate.[643]

This couple practised hospitality from the first time that Paul met them – first to Paul and then to other Christian brothers and sisters. Their participation in house church activities in non-status roles must have been exemplary for them to receive Paul's ongoing praise over the years.

641. See the entry for Phoebe concerning the use of προστάτης.
642. Welborn, 'How "Democratic" Was the Pauline *Ekklēsia*?', p. 298.
643. ibid., p. 302.

5.4 Rome

By the time Paul returned to Corinth and penned his letter to the Roman Christians, Prisca and Aquila had moved back to Rome.

> They were now back in Rome heading a house church, perhaps wealthy as their constant travels may indicate. Their initial position in the greeting list attests to their prominence (v. 5). By the time of 2 Tim. 4:19 they were back in Ephesus.[644]

There has been a good deal of academic speculation as to whether the final chapter of Romans was actually a letter to Ephesus because that is where Prisca and Aquila were last mentioned (1 Cor. 16:19). Blaiklock comments on this point but also a broader, more important issue concerning our reading of the Pauline letters. It is a refreshingly frank view.

> Since Aquila and Prisca were last heard of in Ephesus, the bold suggestion has been made that this chapter (Romans 16) was a letter, or part of a letter to Ephesus which somehow became attached to the epistle to Rome. This suggestion is typical of the nonsense which sometimes invades NT studies. The only basis for such a theory is someone's inability to accept the mobility of ancient populations. There is no evidence to support it. Irresponsible conjecture, rashly rushed into print, has been for a century a feature of Biblical studies which would not be tolerated in any other branch of literary criticism and exegesis.[645]

Verses 3-5 in Romans 16 are the first of many greetings in the last chapter of that letter. A number of points can be made. First, and most obviously, the mention of Prisca and Aquila (note the order) first in this long list reflects Paul's close personal association with them in Corinth and Ephesus. It would have also signalled their eminence to the Roman churches.

Secondly, Paul describes them as 'my fellow-workers in Christ Jesus' (v. 3). The word for fellow-worker is συνεργος. The Greek preposition συν (*sun*) means 'with, in company with, along with, together with'. It denotes a much closer relationship than

644. Dumbrell, *Romans*, p. 141.
645. Blaiklock, *Romans*, p. 90.

would μετά (*meta*) or παρά (*para*). The addition of συν to the otherwise normal descriptions (in Greek) of Paul's colleagues in the gospel is a consistent reminder (throughout Paul's letters) of the strong bonds of fellowship that existed amongst the early Christians.[646] Paul's description of Prisca and Aquila as 'my fellow-workers' reminds us that, despite his apostleship, Paul did not take his rank too seriously although, if the need arose, he was prepared to defend it (e.g. 1 Corinthians 9).[647] Paul equates their work with his. Surely Prisca and Aquila must have been much more heavily involved in gospel work than tentmaking or leatherworking for their efforts to warrant equal status with Paul's labours. The couple are also described as being ἐν χριστῷ (*en Christō* – in Christ). For Paul, this is a significant acknowledgement of their contribution to the early church and the state of their marriage.[648]

Thirdly, we have some new information not otherwise mentioned in the NT. In Romans 16:4 Paul notes that Prisca and Aquila τὸν ἑαυτῶν τράχηλον ὑπέθηκαν 'risked their own necks' to save his life. (See Section 8.3.) Paul's salutation extends to the church in their home, reflecting their relative affluence. The phrase is the same as that used in 1 Corinthians 16:19. It is quite unlikely that all the people greeted in the remainder of Romans 16 were people from this house church.[649]

---

646. Other Pauline uses of συνεργος (or comparable verb) are Romans 16:9, 21; 1 Corinthians 3:9; 2 Corinthians 1:24; 8:23; Philippians 2:25; 4:3; Colossians 4:11; 1 Thessalonians 3:2; Philemon 1:1; 24. It is also used in 3 John 1:8. See *Paul's Use of σύν (sun)* in the introduction.

647. See Cranfield, *Romans*, vol. 2, p. 785.

648. Paul uses ἐν χριστῷ in many letters to signify the relationship between a congregation and Christ (1 Cor. 1:30; 2 Cor. 12:2; Eph. 1:1; Phil. 1:1; 4:21; Col. 1:2; Philem. 23). However, Paul only personalises this description in Romans 16:3, 7, 9, 10 and, even then, it is used to acknowledge relatively few people. From Paul's perspective, Prisca and Aquila are clearly among an elite group in the Pauline Christian communities. Stewart, *A Man in Christ*, pp. 154-5, describes the significance of ἐν χριστῷ for Paul. See *Paul's Use of ἐν χριστῷ (en Christō – in Christ)* in the introduction.

649. See Moo, *Romans*, p. 936.

5.5 *Ephesus*

Paul's second letter to Timothy in Ephesus[650] (probably his last and written in Rome) greets Prisca and Aquila (2 Tim. 4:19). They must have again travelled from Rome to be active on Paul's behalf as συνεργοι in that city when this letter was penned. One of the final greetings from the aged apostle, who now regarded death as imminent (2 Tim. 4:6), was for two of his best-loved associates. Once again, they are placed first in the list of those greeted by Paul. There is no mention of their house church on this occasion, probably because Prisca and Aquila were moving too frequently between churches in their missionary activities to have established a domicile on this occasion.

6. Their Secular Social Status

First-century society was quite stratified, with most people belonging to positions of low status. Those of lowest status 'such as the hired menials and *dependent handworkers*; the poorest of the poor, peasants, agricultural slaves, and hired agricultural day labourers are absent [from Acts and the Pauline correspondence] because of the urban setting of the Pauline groups'.[651] Meeks notes that Paul, in pursuing the occupation of σκηνοποιός, 'would have placed him among the lowest of the free poor'.[652] This is consistent with Paul's self-description in 1 Corinthians 9:19.

One of the critical questions is whether Prisca and Aquila were actually tentmakers or not. This is an important determinant of their social status. No doubt, this is the trade which Aquila learnt and practised as a young man.

An initial clue to their social status lies in Luke's description of the couple in Acts 18:3: 'for by trade *they* were tentmakers' (NASB, emphasis added). Although it is possible that Aquila might have been an artisan, it seems less likely that Prisca would have engaged in this dirty and exhausting work. My interpretation is that Luke's use of σκηνοποιός for both of them (rather than for Aquila alone)

650. Guthrie, *Pastoral Epistles*, pp. 12-52; 212-28.

651. Meeks, *First Urban Christians*, p. 73 (emphasis added).

652. ibid., p. 52. See also Hock, *Paul's Tentmaking*.

is a reference to the nature of their (jointly-owned) business rather than their joint involvement in manual labour. A comparable example is the use of the occupation 'banker'. When people speak of J. P. Morgan as a banker, they do not picture him behind a teller's cage but as one of the most powerful men in world finance in his day. Prisca and Aquila always inhabited large cities, which provided a natural base for their tentmaking business and for meeting people. That would have also given them the opportunity for the attainment of higher social status if that was their aim.

Prisca and Aquila were relatively wealthy owners of a tentmaking business, which was sufficiently large to enable them to assist Paul's ministry at Corinth (*on Paul's terms*) by offering him employment as a σκηνοποιός until Silas and Timothy arrived from Macedonia. Their travels were financed by the expansion of their tentmaking businesses in Rome, Corinth, and Ephesus; however, they subordinated their business activities to their gospel ministry. Their lives have prompted the formulation of a modern description of evangelism known as 'tentmaking ministries'.[653]

The fact that, in Ephesus and Rome, Prisca and Aquila owned a dwelling sufficiently large to accommodate a house church suggests a degree of wealth well in excess of that attributable to factory workers. They are also recorded as travelling extensively: from Rome to Corinth to Ephesus to Rome and back to Ephesus *at least*. Again, they would need reasonable financial resources to afford these journeys. 'Prisca and Aquila are apparently (as their travels also suggest) a fairly wealthy couple; thus they are able to provide a decent-sized meeting room for a group of Christians in Rome.'[654]

---

653. J. R. W. Stott, *The Message of Acts* (Leicester: IVP, 1990), p. 297, describes it as a twentieth-century term used to describe 'cross-cultural messengers of the gospel, who support themselves by their own professional or business expertise, while at the same time being involved in mission'. See modern exponents in Tentmaker, *https://tentmaker.org/* and *https://www.biblicalministries.org/serve/opportunities/tentmaking/*.

654. Moo, *Romans*, p. 936.

They possessed significant material wealth. Meeks provides the following summary of the *secular* social level of Prisca and Aquila.

> We may summarise their known indicators of status as follows: wealth: relatively high. They have been able to move from place to place, and in three cities to establish a sizable household; they have acted as patrons for Paul and for Christian congregations. Occupation: low, but not at the bottom. They are artisans, but independent, and by ancient standards they operate on a fairly large scale. Extraction: middling to low. They are eastern provincials and Jews besides, but assimilated to Greco-Roman culture. One thing more: the fact that Prisca's name is mentioned before her husband's once by Paul and two out of three times in Acts suggests that she has higher status than her husband.[655]

The evidence broadly supports Meeks' conclusions although he affords a *secular* 'higher status' to Prisca. But Prisca's secular social standing (relative to her husband – or anyone else!) seems irrelevant if she came from Pontus, as Meeks argues.[656] It seems an oxymoron to say that Prisca was a Jewess from Pontus and had high social status in secular terms.

Although Paul was willing to be regarded as among the lowest of the free poor, did Prisca and Aquila belong to this very low stratum of society? The answer is that they did not. Given their type of business activity, their Jewishness and their Christian beliefs, a socioeconomic analysis of first-century society would place them at the low (but wealthy) end of the middle classes.

7. Their Marriage and Relationship with Apollos

It seems clear that Paul commended this married couple as highly as he did because they not only carried on an extensive evangelistic ministry in different places but also followed his clear teaching on marital relationships (and behaviour generally) in the Christian community. This is demonstrated in their interaction with Apollos.

---

655. Meeks, *First Urban Christians*, p. 59.

656. ibid., p. 212, n. 264: 'The names of Prisca and Aquila are also Latin, but *they are* from Pontus via Rome' (emphasis added).

It is instructive that these Christian Jews attended the synagogue in Ephesus (Acts 18:26), not because of their Jewish background but as Christians. They were trying to offer the gospel to the Jewish community in Ephesus. Otherwise, they may have never met Apollos. This supports the earlier suggestion of an evangelistic emphasis in their move from Corinth to Ephesus because they followed Paul's strategy of preaching to Jews first and then Gentiles (e.g. Acts 13:14; 14:1; 17:2). No doubt Prisca and Aquila were discipling the Christian gathering in their house.

When Apollos began his preaching ministry at the synagogue in Ephesus, Prisca and Aquila heard him (Acts 18:26). They were concerned that his message had some shortcomings, particularly because he only knew about the baptism of John the Baptist. Baptism in the name of Jesus (Acts 2:38) was apparently unknown to him. Prisca and Aquila 'took him aside and explained to him the way of God more accurately'. The verb for 'took aside' (προσελάβοντο – *proselabonto*) indicates that the faithful couple gently spoke to Apollos without causing him embarrassment.[657] The context in which this verb is used suggests that it may not be going too far to propose that they invited Apollos home for a meal and a discreet chat about the essence of the gospel (cf. Romans 14:1).

> Name sequence can be important, especially when it diverges from the anticipated ancient norm of naming the husband first (see fuller discussion at Acts 18:3). Luke normally mentions first the dominant member of a pair; the mention of Priscilla's name first suggests 'her primary role as Apollos' tutor' [Spencer, *Acts*, p. 184].[658] Some scholars suggest that they did this at home, which is possible, but all that is clear from what Luke says is that they did not confront him publicly in the synagogue. Private reproof was always considered more honourable than public confrontation, especially among Jewish people.[659]

---

657. See Zerwick and Grosvenor, *Grammatical Analysis*, vol. 1, p. 414.

658. F. S. Spencer, *Journeying through Acts: a literary-cultural reading* (Peabody, MA: Hendrickson, 2004), p. 184. The author is self-described as a 'male feminist biblical scholar'.

659. Keener, *Acts*, vol. 3, p. 2809.

This reason for Prisca being named first is rejected from a lack of scriptural evidence and because another more likely reason is discussed in Section 8.3. Here is a lesson for those who see the need to correct public statements by Christians. Bruce reminds us 'how much better it is to give such private help to a teacher whose understanding of his subject is deficient than to correct or denounce him publicly.'[660] Undoubtedly, Paul's tutoring of Prisca and Aquila in the gospel of Jesus would have strongly influenced their instruction of Apollos, both in content and manner of instruction. They had sufficient knowledge and authority to gain his respect and accept the correctness of their message. The successful results of their knowledgeable instruction of Apollos are evidenced by his activities in Ephesus (Acts 18:27-8). The text clearly presents Prisca and Aquila teaching Apollos together. Yet the occurrence of her name before her husband's in the description of this incident has nothing to do with her leadership in the marriage.

On the contrary, Paul's praise of the couple reflected inter alia their adherence to his principles for marriage. This also would have been a practical demonstration of practical Christian living for Apollos. Unsustainable claims about the roles of Prisca and Aquila within their marriage relationship are now prominent among feminist commentators, without any supporting evidence (see Section 9).

8. Was Prisca's Prominence Based on Faith?

There are various theories as to why Prisca is generally mentioned before her husband, which was contrary to common practice in the first century A.D. A convenient stepping-off point *from a secular perspective* concerns the issue of her social superiority over her husband. It has revolved around Prisca possessing a Latin name and the claim that she was an aristocratic Roman lady, being a member of the prominent Roman *gens* Acilia (with its 'Rome' connotation). Cranfield provides a detailed explanation of the evidence for linking Prisca with the *gens* Acilia. However,

660. Bruce, *Acts*, p. 360.

he concludes that 'The suggestion that Prisca was actually an aristocratic Roman lady, and it was for this reason that she was named before her husband, while it can scarcely be ruled out as impossible, seems unlikely.'[661] This possibility should be rejected. The early Christians were prepared to overthrow contemporary social conventions and replace them with one criterion for prominence in their community: love of the Lord Jesus (cf. Philippians. 3:8; Philemon 10, 16).

> Meeks, *First Urban Christians*, p. 59, assumes that Prisca occupied a higher social position than Aquila and was therefore mentioned before him. Our source (Rom. 16), however, is not secular but Christian. It stands in the wider context of Gal. 3:28 and hardly cares about a person's significance in Roman society. It cares about a person's significance for the church: see e.g., Rom. 16:3b, 4, 5a. Also the passage Rom. 16:21-23 does not list the socially elevated first (Erastus with his municipal office and Gaius with his spacious habitation). It first mentions five other Christians. One of them is a missionary coworker, another functions as Paul's secretary. If Luke had known anything about a socially elevated status of Prisca, he would have loved to mention it, distinguished women being a preferred subject for him: e.g., Luke 8:3; Acts 17:4, 12; cf. 16:14; 17:34.[662]

There are three favoured explanations for Prisca's prominence over her husband, all based on faith.

8.1 Her Faith?

The first is that Prisca was converted before Aquila or, as Cranfield conjectures, was instrumental in leading her husband to faith in Christ.[663] Either of these hardly seem to be of such moment as to warrant Prisca achieving major prominence across the broad spectrum of the Gentile churches (Rom. 16:4). These are unlikely reasons.

---

661. Cranfield, *Romans*, vol. 2, p. 784, n. 1. See also Jewett, *Romans*, pp. 955-9.

662. Lampe, *The Roman Christians*, p. 223, n. 29.

663. Cranfield, *Romans*, vol. 2, p. 784.

8.2 Contribution to Gentile Ministry?

The second possibility, discussed by Schreiner, is not in vogue in recent years. He acknowledges that Prisca was more prominent but the following comment does not suggest why this is so.

> As coworkers with Paul, they functioned as missionaries .... Paul adds that the remaining Gentile churches are also grateful for Prisca and Aquila. Are they grateful for them because they helped preserve Paul's life and thereby sustained the Gentile mission? Or were they also grateful because their own ministry was of significant benefit to the Gentiles? Certainty is impossible, but the latter seems more credible.[664]

8.3 Conspicuous Bravery?

The third explanation is that Prisca played a more prominent role in the early church than Aquila. There is support for this view in Acts and Paul's letters. It is reasonable to assume that, in the absence of any pressing reason or special Christian custom(s), the early Christian writers would conform to accepted social conventions (e.g. naming husbands before wives). In Acts, Luke complied with accepted social conventions by introducing a married couple with the husband named first; e.g. Ananias and Sapphira (Acts 5:1) and Aquila and Priscilla (Acts 18:2).[665] Thereafter (Acts 18:18-19, 26), he used a more 'Christian' style of naming the spiritually more prominent partner (if that language is not too pretentious) first. It is argued that Paul does not give Prisca prominence in his letters until the occasion meriting recognition occurs.

In the case of Paul's letters, there is one reference to 'Aquila and Prisca' (1 Cor. 16:19) and two to 'Prisca and Aquila' (Rom. 16:3-5; 2 Tim. 4:19). It is important to note that 1 Corinthians was written before Romans and 2 Timothy, a clue as to Paul's change of emphasis in the latter two letters. Paul's choice of using the order of 'Aquila and Prisca' in his first mention of this couple

---

664. Schreiner, *Romans*, p. 768. See Moo, *Romans*, p. 935, n. 216, for various possibilities; however, he does not discuss Prisca's prominence, only referring to other scholarly conclusions.

665. See also Acts 24:24; 25:13; 26:30.

may provide another clue to the dating of 1 Corinthians. It is generally agreed that 1 Corinthians was written near the end of Paul's second stay in Ephesus because of his comment that he would leave Ephesus at Pentecost (1 Cor. 16:8); presumably a time not too long after the letter was written.[666] Clearly, the event that marked out Prisca for attention had not yet occurred.

Commentators give little or no emphasis to the *sudden change of order by Luke in Acts 18*. One of the historical deficiencies of Acts is that Luke provides little information about Ephesus, which must have come from other sources. Activity in Ephesus is not one of the 'we' passages in Acts (e.g. Acts 20:9). From Acts 18:18 onwards, something important (and unstated) has happened because Luke now refers to 'Priscilla and Aquila' *regarding their time in Ephesus*. Acts 18:24-26 describes the couple's conversation with Apollos and eventually the riot in Ephesus involving Paul, Gaius, and Aristarchus (Acts 19:23–20:1).

> Interpreters commonly understand the phrase 'laid down their own neck [sic] for my life' to mean that Prisca and Aquila had risked their lives for Paul, perhaps in Ephesus, where Paul encountered much social and political opposition (Acts 19:23-41; 1 Cor. 6:9; 2 Cor. 1:8). This may well be correct, but the examples interpreters often give of the use of the phrase in this way are not an exact match to Paul's phrase. 'To lay down one's neck' (ὑποτιθέναι τὸν τρᾴχηλον – *hupotithenai ton trachēlon*) typically referred simply to placing one's self under a burden or submitting one's self to some duty (1 Clem. 63:1; Epictetus, *Diatr.* 4.1.77). Whether Prisca and Aquila risked their own lives for Paul or not, their efforts involved great personal sacrifice and, from Paul's perspective, saved his life.[667]

Therefore, the sequence of events seems likely to have been:

a. Paul writes to the Corinthians that he will stay in Ephesus until Pentecost (1 Cor. 16:8).

---

666. S. E. Porter, *The Apostle Paul: His Life, Thought, and Letters* (Grand Rapids: Eerdmans, 2016), p. 57, suggests a date for 1 Corinthians of spring A.D. 55, nearer the end of Paul's stay in Ephesus.

667. Thielman, *Romans*, pp. 716-77.

b. Paul mentions 'Aquila and Prisca' in a (secular) conventional manner to the Corinthians, naming the husband before his wife (1 Cor. 16:19). He is well aware of their contribution to the Corinthian church.

c. Some time later, the riot occurs at Ephesus, just before Paul's departure from that city (Acts 20:1). The Greek text of Romans 16:4 οἵτινες ὑπὲρ τῆς ψυχῆς μου τὸν **ἑαυτῶν** τράχηλον ὑπέθηκαν(*hoitines huper tēs phuchēs mou ton* ***eautōn*** *trachēlon* – who for my life risked ***their*** own necks) indicates that Prisca ***and*** Aquila were both involved. If this is the incident to which Paul refers, Prisca must have played a dominant role.[668] Paul was an eye-witness to their heroism but does not describe it. If Luke had witnessed the event himself, surely it would have been described in Acts.

d. Prisca's fame (especially) becomes widespread throughout all the *churches of the Gentiles* (Rom. 16:4), although that description gives no precision to the Ephesus hypothesis. Accordingly, Paul places Prisca first when subsequently writing Romans and 2 Timothy. Paul writes that both he and the Gentile churches 'give thanks' (εὐχαριστῶ – *eucharistō*) for such (Jewish) friends (Rom. 16:4). This is the only occasion in the NT where humans are the object of thanks using this word.[669]

e. This act of (unrecorded) heroism in Ephesus appears to be the reason for Prisca's being named before Aquila by Paul subsequent to Acts 18:2.

---

668. For the view that Romans 16:4 is a literary exaggeration, and not a description of a near-death incident, see Moo, *Romans*, p. 936, n. 30. For Jewett, *Romans*, pp. 957-8, it is a 'colloquialism', adding that 'the expression provides additional confirmation of the high social status of Prisca and Aquila'. Dunn, *Romans 9-16*, p. 893, regards the language as 'hyperbolic'. However, Thielman, *Romans*, p. 716, is less certain, conceding that it involved 'great personal sacrifice'. Cranfield, *Romans*, vol. 2, p. 784, suggests a literal interpretation of the text. It is impossible to discern the precision of these opinions, but the views of Thielman and Cranfield are favoured.

669. Morris, *Romans*, p. 532.

9. The Danger of Both Ancient and Modern Social Concepts

The intrusion of ancient social constructs into biblical analysis is discussed above. Similarly, commentators can also place modern sociological ideas in Paul's mind, none of which existed in the first century A.D. Although absent in Scripture, they are creeping into Christianity, both in scholarship and practice (cf. Jude 4). For example, Keener postulates that Paul is particularly anxious to commend women in Romans 16.

> It appears that Paul is aware of the prejudice against women's contributions in his society, and therefore works all the harder to make sure that the praiseworthy among them receive their due.[670]

There is no evidence in the Pauline correspondence or Acts to support this type of assertion. The most likely reason for Paul to commend women is that they deserved it. Paul was equally willing to criticise women when necessary (e.g. Philippians 4:2). Another issue is the attribution to Prisca of unrealistic historical claims, such as her authorship of Hebrews.[671]

10. Final Conclusions

Prisca and Aquila were relatively wealthy owners of a leather/tentmaking business, which was sufficiently large to enable them to assist Paul's ministry at Corinth (*on Paul's terms*) by offering him employment as a σκηνοποιός until Silas and Timothy arrived from Macedonia. Having come under Paul's instruction in Corinth, *they* developed a ministry of evangelism and teaching in Corinth, Ephesus, and Rome, including the instruction of Apollos. Their travels were financed by the expansion of their business in Rome, Corinth, and Ephesus; however, their business activities were significantly subordinated to their gospel ministry.

---

670. Keener, *Acts*, vol. 1, p. 240. See Walker, *The Portrayal of Aquila and Priscilla in Acts*, who concludes at p. 495 that 'The Book of Acts reflects a distinctly anti-feminist bias'.

671. See I. L. E. Ramelli, 'Origen, Greek Philosophy, and the Birth of the Trinitarian Meaning of Hypostasis', *HTR* 105, no. 3 (2021): pp. 338-9.

The couple's relatively significant wealth enabled them to host house churches in Ephesus and Rome, which would have been a natural outlet for their gospel teaching skills. Their Jewishness and Christian faith would likely position them as part of the lower middle class in secular society. Nevertheless, they would have enjoyed a secular social status well above that of low-class workers. They certainly would not have been regarded as contemptuously by society as was Paul in his manual labouring job. Of course, their standing in the eyes of secular society was irrelevant, both to their position in the early church and to their effectiveness in ministry. So significant was their work that they were regarded as συνεργοι by the great apostle and among the few individuals who were personally designated by Paul to be ἐν χριστῷ.

Their teaching of Apollos reflected their mutual submission to one another, where their joint teaching was more important than the superiority (whatever that might have meant in earliest Christianity) of one over the other. The positioning of Prisca's name before that of her husband's in some verses of Scripture after the composition of 1 Corinthians is likely to reflect her outstanding courage in acting (even more than her husband) to save Paul's life. The recognition of the unnumbered efforts of this couple were a matter of thanks amongst all the Gentile churches. Undoubtedly, they both deserve the highest praise as evangelists and exemplars of gospel behaviour. Both Prisca *and* Aquila were major figures in earliest Christianity.

PRISCILLA see **PRISCA AND AQUILA**

PUDENS

2 TIMOTHY 4:21

[21] Make every effort to come before winter. Eubulus greets you, also Pudens, Linus, Claudia, and all the brethren.

This man's Latin name means 'modest.'[672] He was a faithful Christian who remained with Paul when he was imprisoned in

672. HSIBC, p. 888.

Rome (2 Tim. 4:6, 17) and was obviously known to Timothy. He is not mentioned in Romans 16.

> Since Paul passes on their greetings to Timothy, one wonders why they did not support Paul at his trial (2 Tim. 2:16). Perhaps they lacked social standing to make any difference in such a situation, or perhaps it would have exposed them to inordinate danger to appear to stand at Paul's side. Paul does not feel it necessary to account for these details to Timothy .... The Greek verb is singular because in a series, the verb usually takes its number from the nearest subject nominative.[673]

However, Marshall notes that the name Pudens 'was used in upper class families'.[674]

Quartus

Romans 16:23

[23] *Gaius, host to me and to the whole church, greets you. Erastus, the city treasurer, greets you, and Quartus, the brother.*

This is a Latin name meaning 'one fourth'. He resided in Corinth and joins Paul in greeting the Roman Christians. He is the last person mentioned in Romans 16, described as 'Quartus the brother' and mentioned nowhere else in the NT. The question must be asked: Why would an apparently inconsequential person conclude this list, if his predecessors in verse 23 were apparently impressive people in Corinth? One suggestion has Quartus as the brother of Erastus.

> Cranfield (*Romans*, vol. 2, p. 808) opposes this view [that Quartus is the brother of Erastus] and argues that the reference is simply to 'brother Quartus'. But this concludes the greetings in verses 21-23 with something of an anticlimax, unless Quartus is well known to the Roman readers in another way.[675]

The opinions of various commentators concerning Quartus are provided below. This unknown person has raised more questions than many other better-known Christians in the NT.

---

673. Yarbrough, *Letters to Timothy and Titus*, p. 459.
674. Marshall, *Pastoral Epistles*, p. 830.
675. See Peterson, *Romans*, p. 550, n. 114.

He is otherwise unknown. Perhaps 'brother' means 'brother in the Lord', 'fellow Christian'; but in that case why is he singled out to receive a designation which was common to them all? If the word means 'brother in the flesh', whose brother was he? Erastus's, since his name immediately precedes? Or, since *Quartus* is Latin for 'fourth', and Tertius for 'third', would it be excessively far-fetched to think of him as Tertius's brother, born next after him?[676]

Quartus is called the brother. It is more likely that this means brother in Christ rather than brother of Erastus or even Tertius. The fact that he is distinguished as 'the brother', when all the others are brethren in Christ, does not require the ordinary use of the term 'brother' any more than does the addition of 'in the Lord' in verse 8 in the case of Ampliatus mean that others mentioned as beloved were not beloved in the Lord as well. All the others mentioned in these greetings (vv. 21-23) are not only mentioned by name but identified by some other addition. To end with no more than the name Quartus would be, stylistically if no more, abrupt.[677]

Nothing is known of Quartus beyond this mention of him. By ὁ ἀδελφός is surely meant 'the fellow Christian', as we might say 'brother Quartus'. To Bruce's question why, if 'brother' simply means 'fellow-Christian', 'is he singled out to receive a designation which was common to them all?', we would reply: (i) that it is quite likely that τὴν ἀγαπητήν in verse 12 and τὸν ἐκλεκτὸν ἐν κυρίῳ in verse 13 are similar cases (see notes on those verses); (ii) that, whereas Paul seems to take considerable pains to find appropriate commendatory descriptions of the people with him who are sending greetings are of a more matter-of-fact kind, so that it is not really surprising that the last person should be called 'brother Quartus'. The suggestion that ὁ ἀδελφός is intended to indicate that Quartus is the brother of Erastus or that he is the brother of Tertius (v. 22) strike us as highly improbable: if the former were meant, αὐτοῦ would surely have been added, and the latter suggestion cannot claim to be more than an exercise of free fancy.[678]

Having said all this (especially Cranfield's comments above), Jewett proposes a completely different interpretation of Quartus

676. Bruce, *Romans*, p. 281.

677. Murray, *Romans*, 239.

678. Cranfield, *Romans*, vol. 2, 808.

being named after Erastus. His lengthy argument follows. The reader will need to decide which arguments are to be preferred.

> The last person to send greetings to the believers in Rome has in some ways been the most puzzling. Quartus is a Latin name meaning 'Fourth', which was common among slaves and freed men, but the identification of him as 'the brother' is quite peculiar. Why should he be thus singled out when all the other male believers were routinely called 'brothers'? And why is the series of greetings concluded on such a note, in which a singular verb of greeting is attached to Erastus, and Quartus's name follows as an afterthought? The same expression appears in 1 Cor. 1:1, *Σωσθένης ὁ ἀδελφός*, usually translated 'Sosthenes our brother', appears as the coauthor of the letter. The article appears in the genitive in 1 Cor. 16:12, employed to raise the topic of *Ἀπολλῶ τοῦ ἀδελφοῦ*, where by the article is routinely translated as 'Apollos our brother'. If these precedents are followed, the most likely translation would be 'Quartus our brother', as in the reference to Phoebe as 'our sister' in 16:1. The problem is that this translation produces an anticlimactic impression that is hardly improved by the theory that Quartus was known in Rome, because the neutral expression *ὁ ἀδελφός* would have been perceived as insufficiently honorific when the appropriate formulation would be something like 'your beloved brother'. If this is merely a reference to 'our brother', the peroration would thereby close with a faintly resounding thud that seems totally out of place in the most rhetorically sophisticated and carefully composed letter in the career of one of the greatest letter writers in history.
>
> There are three clues that lead to a potential resolution of this interpretative anomaly. (1) The preceding reference to Erastus was intended to lend maximum public prestige to Paul's project, especially among those circles in Rome that were within the imperial administration, which leads one to expect that the reference to Quartus in the same sentence must also have been honorific in some way. (2) the connection with καὶ ('and') between the two names is ordinarily understood as linking persons who have a relationship with each other, as in 'Prisca and Aquila' (16:3), 'Andronicus and Junia' (16:7), and 'Nereus and his sister' (16:15). (3) The article between 'Quartus' and 'brother' can readily be translated with the possessive 'his', because the article often functions as a possessive

> in the Greek. For example, Josephus *Ant.* 2.183 refers to 'Judas his brother (Ἰούδας ὁ ἀδελφός)', and *Ant.* 2.279 speaks of 'his brother, Aaron (*ὁ ἀδελφός Ἀαρών)*'.
>
> The translation 'and his brother Quartus [sends greetings]', referring to Quartus as the brother of Erastus, eliminates the impression of an afterthought, because it was natural to mention the office held by Erastus before referring to his sibling. Moreover, this translation satisfies the rhetorical requirement of ending the list of greetings on a positive and honorific note, because if Quartus is Erastus's brother, he shares the same high social status and prestige within the circle of Roman citizens that had colonised Corinth. That both brothers in this Roman family send greetings to the house and tenement churches in Rome, and thereby endorse Paul's project, addresses one of the major barriers that could have been felt to jeopardise the mission that this letter promotes, namely, whether it would threaten the fragile relations between believers and the state, because Spain was so sensitive an area of imperial administration. The tension would have been most acutely felt by the Christian slaves of Narcissus and Aristobulus, if my hypothesis is correct that they were part of the Neronian bureaucracy. The sponsorship by the rich patroness Phoebe at the beginning of chapter 16 and the support of the influential Roman brothers Erastus and Quartus at the end of the chapter are the rhetorical trump cards that finally render Paul's project politically plausible. With this reading, there is nothing lame or awkward about the greeting from the Roman administrator of Corinth and his brother Quartus. For this particular audience in Rome, where public honours were supremely valued, there was no more effective way for Paul to conclude his peroration.[679]

The comments that 'brother Quartus' is a disappointing end to the people greeted in Paul's letter (after the illustrious Erastus) *may* support the suggestion that this conclusion only demonstrates a complete misunderstanding of the revolutionary culture of the Pauline (i.e. Christian) community. As is often demonstrated in this book, Paul envisioned a new community that was 'in Christ', not 'in the world'. The mores, social structures, ethics, customs, and economic realities of first-century Hellenistic and

679. Jewett, *Romans*, pp. 983-4.

Jewish cultures were irrelevant to those who were followers of the Way. Brother Quartus, treasurer Erastus, Persis, and the slaves of Caesar's household were members of a new community where the only personal credential that mattered was faith in Jesus Christ and the only criterion for behaviour was the Word of God. So, questioning the positioning of (lowly?) Quartus' place at the end of Paul's greetings in Romans 16 is as irrelevant as asking why Mariam precedes Andronicus and Junia. Lampe's conclusion best fits this new view of *Christian* society.

> Our source (Romans 16), however, is not secular but Christian. It stands in the wider context of Gal. 3:28 and hardly cares about a person's significance in the Roman society. It cares about a person's significance for the church: see Rom. 16:3b, 4, 5a. Also the passage Rom. 16:21-23 does not list the socially elevated first (Erastus with his municipal office and Gaius with his spacious habitation). It first mentions five other Christians. One of them is a missionary worker, another functions as Paul's secretary.[680]

Rufus and His Mother

Mark 15:21

[21] And they pressed into service a passer-by coming from the country, Simon of Cyrene (the father of Alexander and Rufus), to bear his cross.

Romans 16:13

[13] Greet Rufus, a choice man in the Lord, also his mother and mine.

Rufus is a Latin name meaning 'red-headed'.[681] Rufus and his brother, Alexander, are named in Mark 15:21 as the sons of Simon of Cyrene, a city on the north coast of what is now called Libya. The sons are only mentioned by Mark. Simon, probably a Jew (rather than a Gentile), was in Jerusalem for the Passover and was compelled by the Roman soldiers to carry Jesus' cross on the way to His crucifixion (Matt. 27:32; Mark 15:21; Luke 23:26). Cyrenians were present at Pentecost (Acts 2:10): some would have believed the gospel and taken it home with them.

---

680. Lampe, *The Roman Christians*, p. 223, n. 29.
681. HSIBD, p. 929.

In Romans 16:13 Paul greets 'Rufus, a choice man in the Lord, also his mother and mine' (ῥοῦφον τὸν ἐκλεκτὸν ἐν κυρίῳ καὶ τὴν μητέρα αὐτοῦ καὶ ἐμοῦ – *roufon ton eklekton ev kuriō kai tēn mētera autoukai mou*). There is widespread acceptance of Lightfoot's judgment that this Rufus is the person mentioned by Mark, but certainty is impossible.[682] Paul's use of ἐκλεκτὸν (*elekton*) has nothing to do with predestination because this applies to every believer. It is far more likely to be a reference to his father's service to Jesus.

> There has been a very widespread tendency to explain τὸν ἐκλεκτὸν ἐν κυρίῳ as meaning something like 'that outstanding Christian'[3] on the ground that 'here would be no point' in Paul's using it here in its usual NT sense of 'chosen', 'elect', since that would be applicable to all Christians.[4] But, in spite of the volume of opinion supporting this view, its rightness should not be allowed to go unquestioned; for it is presumably also true that ἀγαπητός, as used in verse 12 (without the limiting μου)[5] would apply to all Christians. We suspect that Paul wanted to attach some commendatory expression to the names he mentioned and found it not easy to avoid repletion. In such a situation there would seem to be nothing very surprising in his specially applying to an individual a commendation equally applicable to all believers. We take it then that ἐκλεκτός probably has here its sense of 'chosen by God', 'elect'.[683]

Rufus' mother is also greeted by Paul.

> It is clear in any case that Paul knew Rufus and his mother well, so well that Rufus's mother had 'mothered' Paul. They had all therefore been together at some point in the eastern Mediterranean area before Rufus and his mother had travelled west to Rome, where Rufus played a special role among Roman Christians.[684]

---

682. Lightfoot, *Philippians*, p. 176. See Cranfield, *Romans*, vol. 2, pp. 793-4; Murray, *Romans*, p. 231; Thielman, *Romans*, p. 725.

683. Cranfield, *Romans*, vol. 2, p. 794. References in this quotation are [3]C. K. Barrett, *A Commentary on the Epistle to the Romans*, Black's NT Commentaries (London: A. and C. Black, 1957), p. 280. [4]Barrett, *Romans*, p. 284. [5]Barrett, *Romans*, p. 280, translates τὴν ἀγαπητήν here 'my beloved', not distinguishing it from τὸν ἀγαπητόν μου in verses 5, 8 and 9.

684. Thielman, *Romans*, p. 725.

That Paul had met Rufus and his mother in the eastern mission area and that they are now back in Rome where they are well known to the audience indicates that they had probably belonged to the exiles resulting from the Edict of Claudius in 49 C.E. To refer to Rufus' mother as 'mine' indicates that she had provided hospitality and patronage in such a manner that Paul at some point in his career became virtually a member of their family. This detail confirms the impression that Rufus was a person of considerable means, because he and his mother were in the position of providing hospitality in their dwelling. If the identification with Simon of Cyrene is correct, there is also considerable evidence of mobility and thus a measure of economic power in their travels between Africa, Jerusalem, Rome, and somewhere in Paul's eastern mission areas.[685]

> Cranfield (*Romans*, vol. 2, pp. 793-4), Dunn (*Romans 9-16*, p. 896), and Jewett (*Romans*, pp. 967-8) consider the possibility that this might be the Rufus mentioned together with Alexander in Mark 15:21, whose father was Simon of Cyrene. If Mark's Gospel was written for the Christians in Rome, it is a reasonable assumption that Alexander and Rufus were well known there.[686]

SILAS or **SILVANUS**

ACTS 15:22-40

[22] *Then it seemed good to the apostles and the elders, with the whole church, to choose men from among them to send to Antioch with Paul and Barnabas – Judas called Barsabbas, and Silas, leading men among the brethren, ...*

[23]*... and they sent this letter by them, ...*

"The apostles and the brethren who are elders, to the brethren in Antioch and Syria and Cilicia who are from the Gentiles, greetings.

[24] *"Since we have heard that some of our number to whom we gave no instruction have disturbed you with their words, unsettling your souls, ...*

[25]*... it seemed good to us, having become of one mind, to select men to send to you with our beloved Barnabas and Paul, ...*

---

685. Jewett, *Romans*, p. 969.

686. Peterson, *Romans*, p. 542, n. 88.

[26]... men who have risked their lives for the name of our Lord Jesus Christ.

[27]"Therefore we have sent Judas and Silas, who themselves will also report the same things by word of mouth.

[28]"For it seemed good to the Holy Spirit and to us to lay upon you no greater burden than these essentials:

[29]... that you abstain from things sacrificed to idols and from blood and from things strangled and from fornication; if you keep yourselves free from such things, you will do well. Farewell."

[30]So when they were sent away, they went down to Antioch; and having gathered the congregation together, they delivered the letter.

[31]When they had read it, they rejoiced because of its encouragement.

[32]Judas and Silas, also being prophets themselves, encouraged and strengthened the brethren with a lengthy message.

[33]After they had spent time there, they were sent away from the brethren in peace to those who had sent them out.

[34][But it seemed good to Silas to remain there.]

[35]But Paul and Barnabas stayed in Antioch, teaching and preaching with many others also, the word of the Lord.

[36]After some days Paul said to Barnabas, "Let us return and visit the brethren in every city in which we proclaimed the word of the Lord, and see how they are."

[37]Barnabas wanted to take John, called Mark, along with them also.

[38]But Paul kept insisting that they should not take him along who had deserted them in Pamphylia and had not gone with them to the work.

[39]And there occurred such a sharp disagreement that they separated from one another, and Barnabas took Mark with him and sailed away to Cyprus.

[40]But Paul chose Silas and left, being committed by the brethren to the grace of the Lord.

Acts 16:19-40

[19]But when her masters saw that their hope of profit was gone, they seized Paul and Silas and dragged them into the market place before the authorities,

[20]... and when they had brought them to the chief magistrates, they said, "These men are throwing our city into confusion, being Jews,

[21]... and are proclaiming customs which it is not lawful for us to accept or to observe, being Romans."

[22] The crowd rose up together against them, and the chief magistrates tore their robes off them and proceeded to order them to be beaten with rods.

[23] When they had struck them with many blows, they threw them into prison, commanding the jailer to guard them securely;

[24]... and he, having received such a command, threw them into the inner prison and fastened their feet in the stocks.

[25] But about midnight Paul and Silas were praying and singing hymns of praise to God, and the prisoners were listening to them; ...

[26]... and suddenly there came a great earthquake, so that the foundations of the prison house were shaken; and immediately all the doors were opened and everyone's chains were unfastened.

[27] When the jailer awoke and saw the prison doors opened, he drew his sword and was about to kill himself, supposing that the prisoners had escaped.

[28] But Paul cried out with a loud voice, saying, "Do not harm yourself, for we are all here!"

[29] And he called for lights and rushed in, and trembling with fear he fell down before Paul and Silas,

[30]... and after he brought them out, he said, "Sirs, what must I do to be saved?"

[31] They said, "Believe in the Lord Jesus, and you will be saved, you and your household."

[32] And they spoke the word of the Lord to him together with all who were in his house.

[33] And he took them that very hour of the night and washed their wounds, and immediately he was baptised, he and all his household.

[34] And he brought them into his house and set food before them, and rejoiced greatly, having believed in God with his whole household.

[35] Now when day came, the chief magistrates sent their policemen, saying, "Release those men."

[36] And the jailer reported these words to Paul, saying, "The chief magistrates have sent to release you. Therefore come out now and go in peace."

[37] But Paul said to them, "They have beaten us in public without trial, men who are Romans, and have thrown us into prison; and now are they sending us away secretly? No indeed! But let them come themselves and bring us out."

[38] *The policemen reported these words to the chief magistrates. They were afraid when they heard that they were Romans,*

[39] *... and they came and appealed to them, and when they had brought them out, they kept begging them to leave the city.*

[40] *They went out of the prison and entered the house of Lydia, and when they saw the brethren, they encouraged them and departed.*

Acts 17:1-16

[1] *Now when they had travelled through Amphipolis and Apollonia, they came to Thessalonica, where there was a synagogue of the Jews.*

[2] *And according to Paul's custom, he went to them, and for three Sabbaths reasoned with them from the Scriptures, ...*

[3] *... explaining and giving evidence that the Christ had to suffer and rise again from the dead, and saying, "This Jesus whom I am proclaiming to you is the Christ."*

[4] *And some of them were persuaded and joined Paul and Silas, along with a large number of the God-fearing Greeks and a number of the leading women.*

[5] *But the Jews, becoming jealous and taking along some wicked men from the market place, formed a mob and set the city in an uproar; and attacking the house of Jason, they were seeking to bring them out to the people.*

[6] *When they did not find them, they began dragging Jason and some brethren before the city authorities, shouting, "These men who have upset the world have come here also;*

[7] *... and Jason has welcomed them, and they all act contrary to the decrees of Caesar, saying that there is another king, Jesus."*

[8] *They stirred up the crowd and the city authorities who heard these things.*

[9] *And when they had received a pledge from Jason and the others, they released them.*

[10] *The brethren immediately sent Paul and Silas away by night to Berea, and when they arrived, they went into the synagogue of the Jews.*

[11] *Now these were more noble-minded than those in Thessalonica, for they received the word with great eagerness, examining the Scriptures daily to see whether these things were so.*

[12] *Therefore many of them believed, along with a number of prominent Greek women and men.*

[13] But when the Jews of Thessalonica found out that the word of God had been proclaimed by Paul in Berea also, they came there as well, agitating and stirring up the crowds.

[14] Then immediately the brethren sent Paul out to go as far as the sea; and Silas and Timothy remained there.

[15] Now those who escorted Paul brought him as far as Athens; and receiving a command for Silas and Timothy to come to him as soon as possible, they left.

[16] Now while Paul was waiting for them at Athens, his spirit was being provoked within him as he was observing the city full of idols.

ACTS 18:5

[5] But when Silas and Timothy came down from Macedonia [**to Corinth**], *Paul began devoting himself completely to the word, testifying to the Jews that Jesus was the Christ.*

2 CORINTHIANS 1:19

[19] For the Son of God, Christ Jesus, who was preached among you by us – by me and Silvanus and Timothy – was not yes and no, but has been yes in him.

1 THESSALONIANS 1:1

[1] Paul, Silvanus, and Timothy, ...

To the church of the Thessalonians in God the Father and the Lord Jesus Christ: Grace to you and peace.

2 THESSALONIANS 1:1

[1] Paul, Silvanus, and Timothy, ...

To the church of the Thessalonians in God our Father and the Lord Jesus Christ:

1 PETER 5:12

[12] Through Silvanus, our faithful brother (for so I regard him), I have written to you briefly, exhorting and testifying that this is the true grace of God. Stand firm in it!

Silvanus (Σιλουανός – *Silouanos*), the Latin name used by Paul, is called Silas (Σίλας – *Silas*) by Luke in Acts. Silas means 'person of the woods'.[687] Because Paul only uses 'Silvanus' in his letters, that is the name used in this book.

687. HSIBD, p. 991.

> Silas in Acts is clearly identical with Paul's 'Silvanus' (2 Cor. 1:19; 1 Thess. 1:1; 2 Thess. 1:1; cf. 1 Pet. 5:12), and the latter Latin name serves as his *cognomen* as a Roman citizen (cf. Acts 16:37). The name Silas is relatively rare, but parallels for it as a Semitic name have been noted in Palmyrene inscriptions, and it has been explained as a Hellenisation of the Aramaic form of 'Saul' (*BDAG*).[688]

Silvanus is only mentioned by Luke in Acts 15–18. In Acts 15:22, Silvanus (and a fellow believer called Judas) were sent by the leaders in Jerusalem to Antioch following the Jerusalem Council. Silvanus is described as a 'prophet'. He was clearly a Jew but, like Paul, had a Roman name and was a Roman citizen. (Acts 16:37).

Following Paul's disagreement with Barnabas over John Mark, Paul chose Silvanus to accompany him on his second missionary journey (Acts 15:36-40). The accounts in Acts vividly describe Silvanus' experiences with Paul and need little commentary. He was as courageous as Paul during the riot at Philippi, but it is surprising that neither of them used their Roman citizenship to avoid a severe beating and jail. But we can see the hand of God in these events. Without that experience, Paul and Silvanus would not have converted the Philippian jailer.

Acts 18:5 may be the key to the end of Paul's labour with Prisca and Aquila. Silvanus and Timothy came to Corinth from their time in Berea (Acts 17:14) and possibly also in Thessalonica. Their arrival (and possible replacement of Paul's work with Prisca and Aquila) enabled Paul to begin 'devoting himself completely to the word'. The verb συνείχετο (*suneicheto*) suggests that 'he began to be engrossed' in this work.[689] It was a full commitment, but he was assisted in preaching and teaching in Corinth by Silvanus and Timothy (2 Cor. 1:19). In due course Silvanus and Timothy remained in Corinth when Paul left that city with Prisca and Aquila (Acts 18:18). This is the last mention of Silvanus in Acts.

Silvanus' early activities with Paul are reflected by the inclusion of both their names in the first verses of 1 and 2

688. Hemer, *The Book of Acts*, p. 230.

689. See Zerwick and Grosvenor, *Grammatical Analysis*, vol. 2, p. 412.

Thessalonians. The final mention of Silvanus is in 1 Peter 5:12, where he is described by the apostle as 'our faithful brother (for so I regard him)' (ὑμῖν τοῦ πιστοῦ ἀδελφοῦ, ὡς λογίζομαι – *humin tou pistou adelphou, hōs logizomai*). He was chosen to deliver Peter's last letter to the Christians scattered throughout modern Turkey. It is presumed that 1 Peter was written in Rome after Paul had been released from his first Roman imprisonment.[690] The destination of the letter is clearly stated in the letter's first verse: 'aliens, scattered throughout Pontus, Galatia, Cappadocia, Asia, and Bithynia.' Silvanus would have another long journey ahead of him.

Silvanus would have rejoiced at his reacquaintance with Peter in Rome. It would have been decades since he probably last saw Peter when he left Jerusalem for Antioch. Although not often mentioned in Scripture, Silvanus was a tireless worker for the kingdom of God over decades. Our inability to know much about Silvanus from the NT reflects the story of most committed and sincere Christians throughout the centuries. They often were (and are) men and women (more women than we might readily admit!) whose life experiences are not vividly recorded like those of a Paul or Barnabas. Nevertheless, they contended for the faith once for all time delivered to them – even to death (Jude 3). We must continue that struggle.

Before the great Three-One
They all exulting stand,
And tell the wonders He hath done,
Through all their land:
The listening spheres attend,
And swell the growing fame;
And sing, in songs which never end,
The wondrous name.[691]

---

690. W. Grudem, *1 Peter*, TNTC (Leicester: IVP, 1988), pp. 36-7.

691. From the hymn by Thomas Olivers (1725–1799), 'The God of Abraham praise'. The Methodist Hymn Book with Tunes, no. 21, 34th ed. 1962 (London: Methodist Conference Office, 1933).

Sopater or **Sosipater**

Acts 20:3-4

[3] And there he spent three months, and when a plot was made against him by the Jews as he was about to set sail for Syria, he decided to return through Macedonia.

[4] And he was accompanied by Sopater of Berea, the son of Pyrrhus, and by Aristarchus and Secundus of the Thessalonians, and Gaius of Derbe, and Timothy, and Tychicus and Trophimus of Asia.

Romans 16:21

[21] Timothy, my fellow worker, greets you, and so do Lucius, Jason, and Sosipater, my kinsmen.

Sopater is a shortened form of Sosipater, meaning 'saving one's father'.[692] Acts 20:4 informs us that Sosipater's father's name was Pyrrhus (both Greek names) and their hometown was Berea. Acts 17:10 informs us that, after leaving Thessalonica in haste, Paul and Silvanus travelled a little further south to Berea and went to 'the synagogue of the Jews' (ἦν συναγωγὴ τῶν ἰουδαίων – *ēn sunagōgē tōn Ioudaiōn*). This is a peculiar phrase. It is generally taken for granted that synagogues are places of worship for Jews, including God-fearers. However, in Acts 13:5 (plural in Salamis, Cyprus), Acts 17:1 (Thessalonica), Acts 17:10 (Berea), Luke uses this phrase rather than simply writing 'synagogue' as is his usual practice. This raises the question as to whether there were also synagogues for (Gentile) God-fearers in these towns. It may also shed new light on Paul's claim that Jews had priority over Gentiles in both grace and judgment as noted in Romans 1:16; 2:9; and 9:24.

It is clear from the context of Acts 20:9 that Sosipater and Pyrrhus were Jews with Hellenised names. By being named in Acts, we can assume that Pyrrhus had also converted to Christianity. But it needs to be asked whether, in any town that had separate synagogues for Jews and Gentile God-fearers, Paul would approach the Jewish synagogue first. The question arises as to how Paul's 'to the Jew first' strategy was put into practice. Brindle makes these comments.

---

692. HSIBD, p. 1005. Hemer, *The Book of Acts*, p. 236 notes that both forms of this name were 'characteristic of Macedonia'.

> Russell suggests that as Paul completed his epistle, he demonstrated to the Romans that he was modelling God's programme by going to the Jews first and then to the Gentiles. For example he stated that he must go first with the collection to the Jews in Jerusalem (Rom. 15:30-32) and then to the Gentiles in Spain by way of Rome (vv. 22-29).[51] The progress of the gospel must include both groups throughout the present church age. True missionary endeavour must take this into account.
>
> *Conclusion*
>
> Paul's phrase 'to the Jew first' is not simply a rhetorical device. It was designed not to deceive readers about his view of Israel, but to emphasise it. Paul's attitude toward Israel, though cautious because of their hardness of heart and constant rejection of the gospel, is based on a thoroughgoing conviction that Israel's election by God is permanent and determinate for salvation history. Nor does the phrase merely depict Paul's missionary pattern or the chronological precedence of Israel as the object of gospel preaching, since the context of Romans 1:16 is primarily theological and is designed to set the stage for Paul's consideration of the relevance of God's promises to both Jews and Gentiles throughout the epistle.[693]

Sosipater's Jewish origin is confirmed by Paul in Romans 16:21 with the Pauline phrase οἱ συγγενεῖς μου – *hoi suggeneis mou*, a term already used in Romans 16:7, 11 to denote fellow Jews.[694]

> By explicitly identifying these persons as his fellow Jews [Rom. 16:21], he [Paul] makes plain that although he identified himself with the 'strong' Gentile majority in Rome, he maintains respectful, Collegial relationships with Jewish Christian leaders. Moreover, these Jewish Christian leaders had been entrusted with the Jerusalem offering donated by churches with Gentile majorities, which means that their greetings to all of the congregations in Rome embodies the mutuality that derives from their common life in Christ (Rom. 15:26-27).[695]

---

693. W. A. Brindle, '"To the Jew First": Rhetoric, Strategy, History, or Theology?' *BS* 159, no. 634 (2002), p. 233. The reference in this quotation is [51]W. B. Russell III, 'An Alternative Suggestion for the Purpose of Romans', *BS* 145, no. 578 (1988): pp. 174-84. See Peterson, *Romans*, p. 548.

694. See the entry on Andronicus.

695. Jewett, *Romans*, p. 980.

Sosipater, Lucius, and Jason send greetings to the Roman churches.

> Jason could be Paul's host from Thessalonica (Acts 17:5-7, 9); the implication of the distinction between Timothy on the one hand (a coworker = one of Paul's 'team') and the group in verse 23 (residents from Corinth) may be that the three mentioned here were delegates from other churches travelling with Paul to deliver the collection (Schmidt; Georgi, *Geschichte*, p. 80; Ollrog, *Paulus*, p. 58). This probability is strengthened since Sosipater could be a longer form of Sopater (BGD; the name is common under both forms [MM]), who is mentioned in Acts 20:4 as one of the delegates of the Pauline churches travelling with him (so e.g., Lietzmann, Cranfield).[696]

SOSTHENES

ACTS 18:17

[17] *And they all took hold of Sosthenes, the leader of the synagogue, and began beating him in front of the judgment seat. But Gallio was not concerned about any of these things.*

1 CORINTHIANS 1:1

[1] *Paul, called as an apostle of Jesus Christ by the will of God, and Sosthenes our brother,*

After Paul arrived in Corinth, he stayed there for about one and a half years (Acts 18:11). The following verses describe a united attack on Paul by the Jews of Corinth, but Gallio (the proconsul for Achaia and brother of Seneca) would hear nothing of it and dismissed their complaint. Reflecting the anti-Jewish sentiment in much of the Gentile world, the (Gentile) crowd responded to Gallio's decision by seizing (ἐπιλαβόμενοι – *epilabomenoi*) Sosthenes (meaning 'of sound strength'),[697] the leader of the synagogue (ὁ ἀρχισυνάγωγος – *ho archisunagōgos*), and beat him up (ἔτυπτον – *etupton*). 'For "synagogue leader" often being an honorary title for significant donors, sometimes Gentile ones, see comment on Acts 13:15.'[698] It would have been a bruising experience. Although the Jews beat

---

696. Dunn, *Romans 9-16*, p. 909.

697. HSIBD, p. 1005.

698. Keener, *Acts*, vol. 3, p. 2779. The reference to Acts 13:15 is found in Keener, *Acts*, vol. 2, pp. 2045-7.

Sosthenes in front of the court, Gallio was unmoved. Sosthenes must have succeeded Crispus (*archisunagōgos* in Acts 18:8), who became a Christian. It is interesting that both leaders of the synagogue, while undoubtedly Jews, had Hellenistic names.

> The identity of the 'all' who beat Sosthenes constitutes the primary obscurity of this text, but Sosthenes's own identity invites some discussion as well. Sosthenes could be, but is probably not, the same person as Crispus ([Acts] 18:8; see comment there). More likely he was simply a fellow synagogue ruler with Crispus or his replacement. It is possible that Paul's Sosthenes in his letter to Corinth (1 Cor. 1:1) is the same person as in Acts 18:17. Against this proposal is the fact that the former is very likely a Pauline Christian whereas the present one at least appears to lead a delegation against Paul. In favor of it is that this is the name's only other occurrence in the NT (though, of course, it occurs elsewhere), in both cases associated with Corinth. If it is the same Sosthenes, there are several possibilities for reconciling the identities of the two:
>
> 1. Sosthenes was a Christian or a sympathizer not yet expelled from the synagogue, against whom the members' anger spilled over when their attempts to punish Paul proved unsuccessful.
>
> 2. Sosthenes retained his previous title but had already been forced out like Crispus; a local Jewish Christian (or possibly Gentile donor), he provided a readier target for the angry synagogue delegation than did Paul, whom Gallio's words now de facto protected.
>
> 3. He was converted after this incident (and hence probably beaten by Gentiles in an anti-Jewish incident here; cf. [Acts] 16:20-21; 19:34) and was with Paul in Ephesus when he authored 1 Corinthians. If they are the same person, Luke's audience might not have access to 1 Cor. 1:1 to know about his conversion; if Luke writes partly for Greece, however, some members of his audience may know of Sosthenes. That the Sosthenes in Paul and the one in Luke are the same person seems more probable than not (though not extremely probable), since the name appears nowhere else in the NT. But at what point Sosthenes becomes a Christ follower we cannot say; in Acts, Paul's opponents sometimes get themselves in trouble (Acts 19:34), but opposition can also hurt his fellow ministers (19:29).[699]

---

699. Keener, *Acts* vol. 3, pp. 2778-9, n. 4829: 'So most commentators (with varying levels of certainty), in the event that it is the same Sosthenes (Bruce,

Perhaps because of his conversion and the ugly reaction to him by the crowd, Sosthenes moved from Corinth to Ephesus, where Paul wrote the letter. Subsequently, when writing 1 Corinthians 1:1, Paul greets the church with Sosthenes, 'our (the) brother' (ὁ ἀδελφός - *ho adelphos*). Sosthenes was the co-sender, not the co-author, of 1 Corinthians. There would be no point in mentioning this brother unless he was well known to the Corinthian church.[700]

> Paul clearly regards him as a fellow worker in Ephesus, but even more as one who is known to the Christians in Corinth. He appears nowhere else in Paul's letters. The plur. verbs in 1:18–31 and 2:6–16, followed by an emphatic *kagō*, 'I myself,' cannot be taken as a sign that Sosthenes was actually involved in writing this letter along with Paul.[701]

One of the critical historical indicators in Paul's chronology is the mention of the proconsul of Achaia, Gallio. The tenure of his office in Corinth can be specifically determined and is a concrete historical event, as was the rule of Aretas IV.

> It seems likely that Claudius ordered provincial officials to leave Rome by April 1 (or, at latest, mid-April), to ensure smooth transitions for their assuming office on July 1. Gallio did not finish his term of office, and so his first (and only complete) year would thus run from July 1 of one year to July 1 of the following year – in the majority view, from July 1, 51 C.E., to July 1, 52.
>
> Gallio (Acts 18:12) Son of Seneca the Elder (ca. B.C. 50 – ca. 40 C.E.). Gallio was born in what is now Cordova, Spain. When the family moved to Rome, his name was changed to Lucius Junius Gallio as he took the name of his new adoptive father in Rome. Lucius Annaeus Seneca, his famous brother (ca. B.C. 3–65 C.E.), naturally enough, thought well of him, and some others also preserve pleasant reports. Paul and others may well have seen a governor's procession in public before; slaves would walk in front of any high aristocrat's procession to announce his titles and keep people out of the entourage's way. Paul uses provincial titles more consistently than Luke (cf. the less formal

Acts 1, p. 348; idem, *Commentary*, p. 375, n. 35; Fitzmyer, *Acts*, p. 630; Hays, *First Corinthians*, p. 15).'

700. See Fee, *1 Corinthians*, p. 27; Fitzmyer, *First Corinthians*, p. 125.

701. Fitzmyer, *First Corinthians*, p. 124.

> 'Greece' in Acts 20:2), but Luke often uses provincial titles (elsewhere including Achaia, Acts 18:27; 19:21), and in this case he must do so to suit the office described.
>
> To most scholars this suggests that he probably left Rome in April of 51 and arrived in Corinth by May .... The later possibility, in 52 C.E., is also reasonable (since he is said to have left 'immediately', whatever this means); some mention this later date as plausible but less likely than the earlier date .... In any case, we must date Paul's appearance before Gallio early in the proconsul's tenure because this was the only part of his tenure he served; he departed before completing his term. He may have become ill because of the Corinthian climate; Seneca reports that the illness was due to the location. In any case, he cut short his tenure in Achaia for health reasons, taking a cruise.
>
> It thus seems likely that Paul's accusers brought the case to Gallio early in his term of office. Some scholars even aver that Gallio held office only between July and October 51 CE, which would require the hearing to be early (but this dating is debated). A secondary, supporting argument in favor of this earlier dating of the case is the desirability of bringing difficult cases to new and potentially open-minded governors (Acts 25:2-3). On this dating, Paul may have arrived in Corinth in February or March of 50 C.E. or, more generally, late 49 to early 50.
>
> Achaia was apparently one of the most desirable posts for proconsuls (cf. Pliny *Ep.* 8.24.2). After Nero executed Gallio's brother Seneca for complicity in the plot against Nero's life, Gallio sought Nero's favor but was publicly denounced; some think that he was forced to commit suicide. 'Proconsul of Achaia' is the appropriate title.[702]

Gallio's mention in this passage is a critical historical marker for the chronology of Paul's life.

STACHYS

ROMANS 16:9

> [9] *Greet Urbanus, our fellow worker in Christ, and Stachys my beloved.*

'"Stachys" is a rare Greek name, though it too is found as the name of a slave in the imperial household (*CIL* 6.8607)'.[703] It means 'ear

702. Keener, *Acts*, vol. 3, pp. 2761-3.

703. Cranfield, *Romans*, vol. 2, p. 791. Jewett, *Romans*, p. 965 also cites the name in *CIL* 6:4452 and 6:26732.

of grain'.[704] Paul addresses Stachys as 'my beloved Stachys' (τὸν ἀγαπητόν μου – *ton agapēton mou*), which Haldane describes as 'an expression of peculiar love for Christ's sake'.[705] This reflects a close personal relationship with Paul, like that of Epaenetus, Ampliatus, and Persis. It is interesting to note that Urbanus (v. 9) is described as '*our* fellow worker in Christ' (τὸν συνεργὸν ἡμῶν ἐν χριστῶ – *ton sunergon hēmōn env Christō*). This may indicate that Urbanus had a broader ministry, with which some Roman Christians would have been familiar. It appears that Stachys was more closely related to Paul's own work in Corinth. Now both men were in Rome. 'In view of his Roman origin, it is likely that Stachys was part of the Gentile majority in the Roman congregations, but his personal acquaintance with Paul indicates that he had travelled in the east, and had perhaps also been banned along with other Christ believers in 49 C.E.'[706]

STEPHANAS

1 CORINTHIANS 1:16

[16] *Now I did baptise also the household of Stephanas; beyond that, I do not know if I baptised any other.*

1 CORINTHIANS 16:15-18

[15] *Now I urge you, brethren (you know the household of Stephanas, that they were the first fruits of Achaia, and that they have devoted themselves for ministry to the saints); ...*

[16] *... that you also be in subjection to such men and to everyone who helps in the work and labours.*

[17] *I rejoice over the coming of Stephanas and Fortunatus, and Achaicus, because they have supplied what was lacking on your part.*

[18] *For they have refreshed my spirit and yours. Therefore acknowledge such men.*

Stephanas (meaning 'crown-bearer'[707]) and his household lived in Achaia, which in Paul's time was a Roman province of Greece

704. HSIBD, p. 1009.

705. Haldane, *Romans*, p. 638.

706. Jewett, *Romans*, p. 965. I am not sure how Stachys' 'Roman origin' is apparent.

707. HSIBD, p. 1011.

whose capital was Corinth, but the province included Athens. The mention of the 'household of Stephanus' implies that he was a person of some means. It is quite possible that his larger home might have become a meeting place for a house church. In 1 Corinthians 1–3 Paul discusses his grave concern over the divisions that had developed in the Corinthian church. This is partly related to the baptism of Stephanas by Paul.

First Corinthians ascribes no blame at all to either Apollos or Cephas for these quarrels and divisions in the church. From 1 Corinthians 1:13-17 it is clear that the issue of a baptiser's name had developed significance in furthering these divisions. It was not Paul's usual practice to baptise converts, but given the absence of other Christians in Corinth during the city's initial evangelisation, Paul had no alternative. In 1 Corinthians 1:14, Paul declared that he had baptised Crispus and Gaius; but this was the exception, not the rule, for Paul. Since Crispus was a leading Jew, his baptism by the apostle himself would have confirmed the sincerity of his conversion. It is quite possible that, given his seniority in Judaism and his conversion to Christianity, he was the one who baptised those new converts mentioned in the latter part of Acts 18:8.

> Paul repeats the idea expressed in the third question of verse 13 in a different way. The conj. *hina* expresses result (ZBG ʃ352; BDF ʃ391.5). Paul thus insists that no matter what relationship the Paul-group of Corinth might be claiming to him, it does not stem from him as their baptiser. Some interpreters have argued that this was the nature of the rival groups, that Corinthians who had been baptised by a certain preacher developed a bond of allegiance to him. Now Paul would be countering that claim.[708]
>
> Paul corrects the sweeping statement made in verse 14, as he recalls what he did for Stephanas and his *oikos*, 'house' (probably household, but 'house church' is not impossible) .... All told, then, Paul admits that he baptised at Corinth Crispus, Gaius, and the household of Stephanas. At least he cannot recall others.[709]

---

708. Fitzmyer, *First Corinthians*, p. 147.
709. ibid., p. 147.

In explaining his role as a preacher of the gospel and not as a baptiser of believers, Paul concedes in 1 Corinthians 1:16 that he did baptise the household of Stephanas in Corinth. Other examples of households being baptised are described in Acts 16:15, 32-33. Concerning 1 Corinthians 1:16:

> **δὲ**. Introduces an additional consideration, but which Paul takes to be of minimal consideration. Lightfoot (p. 156) proposes that the verse is an 'afterthought'; but the effect could be deliberate, calculated to brush aside the fact that Paul did actually perform a few baptisms. Vis-à-vis verse 14, the addition has almost concessive force ('I baptised no one except Crispus and Gaius .... Now, admittedly, I did baptise the household of Stephanas').[710]
>
> Some in Corinth may have thought it to be personally advantageous to be associated with Paul, Apollos or Peter via the administration of baptism. This type of thinking was rife in Corinth, where personality-centred politics and status-seeking 'hangers-on' were the norm in secular society. If so, Paul's comments in these verses would have given such Corinthian Christians no encouragement. In what must be the greatest disappointment in Paul's otherwise impressive history of giving thanks, the apostle is grateful that he performed so few baptisms in Corinth! He wants no part in petty rivalries, even if indirectly, and is happy not to have unwittingly played into anyone's hands. In the context of his arguments in the unit, not having baptised many of the Corinthians contributes to Paul's depiction of the nature of Christian ministry as a 'shared partnership'.
>
> The only two that Paul does admit to baptising, at least initially (see v. 16), are *Crispus* and *Gaius*, presumably early converts in the city.[711]

From 1 Corinthians 1:15, it may appear that Paul was not particularly concerned who baptised whom.[712] Other baptisers may have been Stephanas, the first convert in Corinth, and Gaius Titius

710. Brookins and Longenecker, *1 Corinthians 1-9*, p. 21.

711. Ciampa and Rosner, *1 Corinthians*, pp. 83-4. See Fitzmyer, *First Corinthians*, p. 147.

712. See Ciampa and Rosner, *1 Corinthians*, p. 84.

Justus. Paul wrote that he had not come to baptise but to preach the gospel (1 Cor. 1:17). However, the phrase εἰς τὸ ἐμὸν ὄνομα (***eis to emon*** *omona* – ***into my*** name) is similar to εἰς τὸ ὄνομα in verse 13 above it. This fact would be of importance to Paul in the light of the divisions within the Corinthian church. The literal meaning '*into my* name' may be important in the light of 1 Corinthians 1–3 where one group of believers is 'the Paul group'. All have been *baptised not into any person but into Christ.* Paul is emphasising that his baptism of people is not the significant issue.[713]

> Paul has already mentioned baptising this household (1:16). Now we have the additional information that they were the *firstfruits* of this province. As the province included Athens, where Paul had some converts before preaching in Corinth, this raises a minor problem. It may be that the household of Stephanus was in some way converted before Paul preached at Athens. It may be that while there were earlier conversions of individuals this was the first household to be won. Or, it may be that *firstfruits* indicates those fruits which gave promise of the harvest to come. 'To the Apostle's mind the pledge of a future Church came not in Athens, but in Corinth' (Edwards).[714]

It is generally considered by many commentators that Stephanus and his household held a distinctive position as the *first* Christian converts ('first fruits') *in the province of Achaica.* 'First fruits' is a Jewish term for anything set apart to God before the remainder could be used (Exod. 23:16, 19; 34:24, 26; Num. 15:17-21; cf. 1 Cor. 15:20).[715] However, information in Acts 17:34 and the Greek text of verse 15 contradicts that opinion.

> Acts has Dionysius the Areopagite, Damaris, and apparently others from Athens (also in Achaia) coming to faith before Paul first sets foot in Corinth. Whether these very individuals were in fact 'the first' converts of Achaia, it is well within the range of possibility

713. For a technical discussion of the alternative interpretations of εἰς τὸ ἐμὸν ὄνομα, see Brookins and Longenecker, *1 Corinthians 1-9*, pp. 19, 21.

714. Morris, *1 Corinthians*, p. 244.

715. See Haldane, *Romans*, p. 636; Ciampa and Rosner, *1 Corinthians*, pp. 857-8. The household of Stephanas is regarded as a singular entity. This singular use of ἀπαρχὴ is justified in the case of Epaenetus.

> that, if Paul had already visited elsewhere in Achaia prior to arriving in Corinth, he had indeed already brought others to the faith. **Yet the lack of the article here probably alleviates the difficulty**: the household of Stephanas was not '*the* firstfruit of Achaia', but *a* firstfruit', an indication (in either an indefinite or, through its nature as a metaphor, a qualitative sense) of the kind of yield Paul was to expect in that region.[716]

Therefore, it seems likely that Stephanas and his household were the first converts *in Corinth*. It then seems obvious that Paul would baptise these new believers (1 Cor. 1:16) as well as Crispus and Gaius (1 Cor. 1:14) because there was no other Christian to do so! Paul praises the *whole household* (τὸν ... οἶκον – *ton oikon* – cf. 1 Cor. 16:19) who 'have devoted themselves for ministry to the saints'. From this brief comment we cannot estimate the size of Stephanas' household. In considering ἑαυτων – *eautōn* (meaning 'devoted'), Moffatt, using a 'trade metaphor' from Plato, describes their commitment as 'addicted themselves to the ministry'.[717]

Moffatt assumed that Achaicus and Fortunatus (common Latin names for slaves or freed men) belonged to the household of Stephanas and this seems likely.[718] Corinth is nearly 900 miles (1,450 km) from Ephesus by land. These three may have walked the journey but it is much more likely that they crossed the Aegean Sea in about two weeks during Paul's extended stay in Ephesus (A.D. 54 to 55). Scripture suggests that they brought with them a letter with questions for the apostle to answer (1 Cor. 7:1). Paul urges the Corinthian church 'to submit to such people and to everyone who joins in the work and labours at it'.

> Thus we may have here people, including two of relatively low social standing, who are to be honoured for their 'serving' of the people, characterised in part by their refreshing of both Paul's spirit and

716. Brookins and Longenecker, *1 Corinthians 10-16*, pp. 201-2. Original emphasis in italics; bold added.

717. Moffatt, *The First Epistle of Paul to the Corinthians*, p. 278.

718. See Moffatt, *The First Epistle of Paul to the Corinthians*, p. 279; Ciampa and Rosner, *1 Corinthians*, p. 859.

> that of others. The anomaly of 'servant' figures being 'respected' for their labouring is made all the more stark by Paul's insistence that these figures be submitted to precisely because of their labour (1 Cor. 16:16). This verb implies the attribution of authority – *an unexpected command in the wider Graeco-Roman context given the social status of the individuals concerned.*[719]

The NASB translates τοῖς ἁγίοις as 'of the Lord's people' but the Greek text refers to 'the saints' (of Corinth and Achaia). Given the strength of the verbs in v. 13, 'the military echoes in the imperatives of 1 Corinthians 16:13 have probably inspired Paul's use of τάσσω [ἔταξαν] and ὑποτάσσω here (1 Corinthians 16:15, 16), both of which also have military connotations.'[720] The use of συν- in συνεργοῦντι in this context indicates that 'certain ones are worthy of more exceptional regard than others'.[721]

The three men visited Paul in Ephesus while he was writing this letter to the Corinthians. It is likely that they took the letter back to Corinth on their return journey. Paul writes to the Corinthians that he rejoiced over their visit because 'they have supplied what was lacking on your part'. There is no implied criticism that these men did something that the Corinthian church could not (or would not) do. The sense of the words is that, by coming to Paul personally, they have brought a little bit of Corinth with them.[722]

Paul tells the Corinthian church that their visit 'refreshed my spirit and yours'. The word for 'refreshed' (ἀναπαύω – *anapauō*) is the same as that used by Jesus in Matthew 11:28 when He talks about giving 'rest' to those who labour and are heavy-laden.[723] Perhaps their presence lifted a burden of

---

719. Clarke, *Refresh the Hearts of the Saints*, p. 288 (emphasis added). See Fee, *The First Epistle to the Corinthians*, pp. 918-20.

720. Brookins and Longenecker, *1 Corinthians 10-16*, p. 202.

721. ibid., pp. 202-3.

722. See Moffatt, *1 Corinthians*, p. 280; Ciampa and Rosner, *1 Corinthians*, pp. 858-60; Brookins and Longenecker, *1 Corinthians 10-16*, p. 203.

723. Compare this with the use of ἀναψύχω (*anapsuchō*) regarding Onesiphorus (2 Tim. 1:16).

concern from Paul's shoulders about the state of the Corinthian church. Morris also comments about the end of verse 18 that:

> *And yours* is an interesting addition. Not only was it good for Paul to receive news from Corinth; it was good for the Corinthians to send the messages to Paul that they had done through these three men. The believers should acknowledge people like this; i.e. know them for what they are, and ascribe to them their true worth.[724]

In verse 18 Paul concludes that Stephanus and his companions should be highly esteemed by the Corinthian Christians, only reinforcing his commendation in verse 15. The use of ἐπιγινώσκω (*epiginōskō*) should be understood as meaning 'appreciate (or recognise) these men for what they are'.[725]

SYNTYCHE see EUODIA AND SYNTYCHE

SYZYGOS

PHILIPPIANS 4:3

[3] *Indeed,* **true companion,** *I ask you also to help these women who have shared my struggle in the cause of the gospel, together with Clement also and the rest of my fellow workers, whose names are in the book of life.* **(Emphasis added.)**

Whether a person of this name Σύζυγος (*Syzygos*, meaning 'companion' (NASB) or 'yokefellow' (NIV)[726] existed in the church at Philippi is a matter of conjecture, but he is mentioned here as a person for the sake of completeness. This verse is translated, 'Indeed, true companion, I ask you also to help these women who have shared my struggle in *the cause of* the gospel.' It is a reference to the lack of harmony between Euodia and Syntyche. There are two possible understandings of the Greek γήσιε σύζυγε (*gnēsie Syzyge*). γνήσιος (*gnēsios*) means loyal or true. The first (and generally accepted) translation is 'loyal yokefellow'; an unnamed person in the Philippian

---

724. L. L. Morris, *The First Epistle of Paul to the Corinthians*, TNTC (Leicester: InterVarsity Press, 1983), p. 245 (original emphasis).

725. Zerwick and Grosvenor, *Grammatical Analysis*, vol. 2, p. 533.

726. NASBEC, p. 1567, ref. *4805*.

church. The second possibility is 'loyal Syzygos'. If an actual person, his name implies that he was a (probably Gentile) slave or freed man.

> Who is the person singled out by the expression γνήσιε σύζυγε ('true yokefellow')? Clearly it was unnecessary to name the person (unless Σύζυγε is itself a proper name), since everyone at Philippi, including the one so addressed, would know who was intended. The list of answers is lengthy and includes Timothy, who 'genuinely' cared for the Philippians; Epaphroditus as the bearer of the letter; Silas, Paul's colleague in the evangelisation of the city of Philippi; and Luke, of whom it may be inferred that he was in Philippi for most of the time between the founding of the church and Paul's brief visit to it prior to his last journey to Jerusalem (cf. Acts 16:17 with 20:5). Apart from a number of fanciful guesses, a suggestion that enjoys considerable support among commentators is that Σύζυγος is a proper name. In favour of this it is argued that Paul nowhere else makes use of this term to describe his official colleagues and that if it were a common noun here it would imply that the person stood in a special relation to him. If Σύζυγος is a proper name, then the adjective γνήσιε indicates that the colleague is rightly named; Paul is punning as he does with Onesimus (Philem. 11; cf. the later Chrestos), and in effect saying: 'You who are Σύζυγος (lit. "yokefellow") are a comrade not in name only but also in deed'. To date, however, σύζυγος has not been found as a proper name. This is not a conclusive argument against its existence, the advocates claim, and similar compounds such as Συμφέρων do turn up.
>
> It is no longer possible to determine with certainty just whom Paul has in mind; 'faithful partner' suggests a coworker in the apostolic mission who was no doubt well known to the Philippians. He was probably some prominent and influential member of the congregation, perhaps a person of tact as well as influence.[727]

Clearly, this person was trusted by Paul to resolve the differences between these women and restore harmony. See the entry for Euodia and Syntyche regarding the manner in which the dispute could be resolved *in the Lord*.

727. O'Brien, *Philippians*, pp. 480-1.

Tertius

Romans 16:22

[22] I, Tertius, who write this letter, greet you in the Lord.

Tertius is a Latin slave name meaning 'third'.[728] He was the secretary (amanuensis) who wrote Paul's letter to the Romans. Paul often used an amanuensis to write his letters because we see him taking the scribe's pen and adding a personal comment (1 Cor. 16:21; Gal. 6:11; Col. 4:18; 2 Thess. 3:7; Philem. 19). It is obvious that Tertius was a Christian from the nature of his greeting (ἐν κυρίῳ – *en Kuriō)*: 'in the Lord', a phrase he would have heard from Paul. Since Paul was staying at the house of Gaius Titius Justus in Corinth, Tertius may have been one of his slaves.[729] Paul agreed that he should note his participation in the letter. 'Whether he was an independent secretary or a slave, the self-introduction of Tertius reveals the remarkable equality "in Christ" characteristic for the first generation of Pauline Christianity.'[730]

Articles about Tertius by Richards and Elmer suggested that Tertius was more than an amanuensis, he was one of the contributors to the contents of Romans.[731]

> *Some scholars have speculated* that Tertius would have been the 'number three,' and Quartus, who is also mentioned here, would have been the 'number four' servant in the household of Gaius. If this is correct, *then we might speculate* that the availability of a professional secretary may have afforded Paul an 'offer too good to be refused'.[732]

---

728. HSIBD, p. 1042.

729. A. H. Cadwallader, 'Tertius in the Margins: A Critical Appraisal of the Secretary Hypothesis', *NTS* 64, no. 3 (2018), p. 387, suggests that Tertius could have been a slave in the house of Phoebe, Stephanas, or Chloe.

730. Jewett, *Romans*, p. 980. Given this assessment of earliest Christian culture, it is difficult to understand Jewett's comments about the προστάτις relationship between Paul and Phoebe.

731. E. R. Richards, *The Secretary in the Letters of Paul* (Tübingen: Mohr Siebeck, 1991); E. R. Richards, *Paul and First-century Letter Writing: Secretaries, Composition and Collection* (Downers Grove, IL: InterVarsity Press, 2004); I. J. Elmer, 'I, Tertius: Secretary or Co-author of Romans', *Australian Biblical Review* 56 (2008): pp. 45-60. These arguments are completely rejected.

732. I. J. Elmer, *I, Tertius,* p. 49 (emphasis added).

Note the emphasis on 'speculate'. Their evidence is based on the practices involved in letter-writing in the first century and there is no historical evidence to support their conclusions regarding Romans.

Cadwallader's analysis of Romans 16:22 correctly rejects this assumption:

> Tertius' name and greeting are entirely self-initiated and without parallel in the morphology of greetings: not even Paul uses the form ἀσπάζομαι.[29] The argument that an author stood behind the final product is special pleading, somehow to imply Paul's knowledge and approval before the letter was sent. In any case, this initiative subverts the argument about Tertius' co-authorship (more on this below), especially given that the other supposed secretary references in the Pauline letters (Gal. 6.11; 1 Cor. 16.21; 2 Thess. 3.17; Col. 4.18; Philem. 19) are quite different from that provided here in Romans 16, precisely because the initiative is Paul's.[733]

When considering Romans 16, the use by Tertius of ἀσπάζομαι (*aspazomai* – 'greet') is unique in contrast to Paul's use of ἀσπάσασθε (*aspasasthe* – 'greet') throughout the chapter.

> Whatever function we may want to confer on Tertius from this evidence, he designates himself the writer of the letter (ὁ γράψας την ἐπιστολήν (ἐν κυρίω)), that is, putting himself at the end of the production line, not in the prior stages. This increases the probability of Tertius being a slave, in part because there is evidence that his creative ability in relation to expression, as distinct from letter-forming, is limited – the ambiguity caused by the syntactical placement of ἐν κυρίω does not inspire confidence that Tertius was responsible for chapter 16 or any other part of the letter.[734]

---

733. Cadwallader, *Tertius in the Margins*, p. 382. The details concerning his reference 29 are 'This alone makes it improbable that Tertius was responsible for putting chapter 16 together (contra Richards, *First-century*, p. 152). The unusual descriptors added to many of those greeted hardly befits the secretary's invention – note especially the first-person possessives in verses 3, 4, 5, 7, 8, 9, 11, 13, 21. See, generally, S. Mathew, *Women in the Greetings of Romans 16.1-16: A Study of Mutuality and Women's Ministry in the Letter to the Romans* (London: Bloomsbury, 2013), pp. 21-45.'

734. Cadwallader, *Tertius in the Margins*, pp. 386-7.

In conclusion, it appears that Tertius was a skilled Christian amanuensis in Corinth and probably a slave in the house of one of the (few) wealthy members of the Corinthian church, more likely Gaius.[735] He clearly knew some of the church members who had returned to Rome prior to the writing of this letter.

Timothy

Acts 16:1-3

[1] *Paul came also to Derbe and to Lystra. And a disciple was there, named Timothy, the son of a Jewish woman who was a believer, but his father was a Greek, ...*

[2] *... and he was well spoken of by the brethren who were in Lystra and Iconium.*

[3] *Paul wanted this man to go with him; and he took him and circumcised him because of the Jews who were in those parts, for they all knew that his father was a Greek.*

Acts 17:14-15

[14] *Then immediately the brothers [in Berea] sent Paul out to go as far as the sea; and Silas and Timothy remained there.*

[15] *Now those who escorted Paul brought him as far as Athens; and receiving a command for Silas and Timothy to come to him as soon as possible, they left.*

Acts 18:5

[5] *But when Silas and Timothy came down from Macedonia* [**to Corinth**], *Paul began devoting himself completely to the word, testifying to the Jews that Jesus was the Christ.*

Acts 19:22

[22] *And having sent into Macedonia two of those who ministered to him, Timothy and Erastus, he himself stayed in Asia for a while.*

Acts 20:3-4

[3] *And there he spent three months, and when a plot was made against him by the Jews as he was about to set sail for Syria, he decided to return through Macedonia.*

---

735. Jewett, *Romans*, pp. 978-80 suggests that Tertius may have been in Phoebe's household.

[4] And he was accompanied by Sopater of Berea, the son of Pyrrhus, and by Aristarchus and Secundus of the Thessalonians, and Gaius of Derbe, and Timothy, and Tychicus and Trophimus of Asia.

ROMANS 16:21

[21] Timothy, my fellow worker, greets you, and so do Lucius, Jason, and Sosipater, my kinsmen.

1 CORINTHIANS 4:16-17

[16] Therefore I exhort you, be imitators of me.

[17] For this reason I have sent to you Timothy, who is my beloved and faithful child in the Lord, and he will remind you of my ways which are in Christ, just as I teach everywhere in every church.

1 CORINTHIANS 16:10-11

[10] Now if Timothy comes, see that he is with you without cause to be afraid, for he is doing the Lord's work, as I also am.

[11] So let no one despise him. But send him on his way in peace, so that he may come to me; for I expect him with the brethren.

2 CORINTHIANS 1:1, 19

[1] Paul, an apostle of Christ Jesus by the will of God, and Timothy our brother,

To the church of God which is at Corinth with all the saints who are throughout Achaia:

[19] For the Son of God, Christ Jesus, who was preached among you by us – by me and Silvanus and Timothy – was not yes and no, but is yes in Him.

PHILIPPIANS 1:1

[1] Paul and Timothy, bond-servants of Christ Jesus,

To all the saints in Christ Jesus who are in Philippi, including the overseers and deacons:

PHILIPPIANS 2:19

[19] But I hope, in the Lord Jesus, to send Timothy to you shortly, so that I also may be encouraged when I learn of your condition.

COLOSSIANS 1:1

[1] Paul, an apostle of Christ Jesus by the will of God, and Timothy our brother, ...

1 THESSALONIANS 1:1

[1] Paul, Silvanus, and Timothy,

To the church of the Thessalonians in God the Father and the Lord Jesus Christ: Grace to you and peace.

1 THESSALONIANS 3:2, 6

[2]... and we sent Timothy, our brother and God's fellow worker in the gospel of Christ, to strengthen and encourage you as to your faith,

[6] But now that Timothy has come to us from you, and has brought us good news of your faith and love, and that you always think kindly of us, longing to see us just as we also long to see you,

2 THESSALONIANS 1:1

[1] Paul, Silvanus, and Timothy,

To the church of the Thessalonians in God our Father and the Lord Jesus Christ:

1 TIMOTHY 1:1-3, 18

[1] Paul, an apostle of Christ Jesus according to the commandment of God our Saviour, and of Christ Jesus, who is our hope, ...

[2] To Timothy, my true child in the faith: Grace, mercy, and peace from God the Father and Christ Jesus our Lord.

[3] As I urged you upon my departure for Macedonia, remain on at Ephesus so that you may instruct certain men not to teach strange doctrines, ...

[18] This command I entrust to you, Timothy, my son, in accordance with the prophecies previously made concerning you, that by them you fight the good fight,

2 TIMOTHY 1:1-2, 5

[1] Paul, an apostle of Christ Jesus by the will of God, according to the promise of life in Christ Jesus,

[2] To Timothy, my beloved son: Grace, mercy, and peace from God the Father and Christ Jesus our Lord.

[5] For I am mindful of the sincere faith within you, which first dwelt in your grandmother Lois and your mother Eunice, and I am sure that it is in you as well.

2 TIMOTHY 4:9, 11, 13, 14, 15, 21, 22

[9] Make every effort to come to me soon;

[11] Only Luke is with me. Pick up Mark and bring him with you, for he is useful to me for service.

[13] When you come bring the cloak which I left at Troas with Carpus, and the books, especially the parchments.

[14] Alexander the coppersmith did me much harm; the Lord will repay him according to his deeds.

[15] Be on guard against him yourself, for he vigorously opposed our teaching.

[21] Make every effort to come before winter. Eubulus greets you, also Pudens, Linus, Claudia, and all the brethren.

[22] The Lord be with your spirit. Grace be with you.

PHILEMON 1

Paul, a prisoner of Christ Jesus, and Timothy our brother,
To Philemon our beloved brother and fellow worker, ...

HEBREWS 13:23

[23] Take notice that our brother Timothy has been released, with whom, if he comes soon, I will see you.

Timothy is the person most mentioned in Paul's letters. Timothy is a Greek name meaning 'honoured of God'.[736] He came from the town of Lystra, which Paul had evangelised during his first missionary journey and revisited on his second journey. Lystra was a town on the imperial road from Tarsus to Pisidian Antioch, near the middle of modern Turkey. Timothy's mother Eunice (Acts 16:1; 2 Tim. 1:5) was a Jewess and her husband was a Gentile ('Greek' in Acts 16:1). This marriage suggests that she was not a strictly orthodox Jewess. Nevertheless, she and her Jewish mother, Lois (2 Tim. 1:5), were devoted to the (OT) Scriptures (2 Tim. 1:5) and taught them to Timothy since he was a child (2 Tim. 3:15).

The first reference to Timothy in Acts 16:1 indicates that he, his mother, and grandmother had become Christians after Paul's first visit to Lystra (Acts 14:8). We know nothing of his father's beliefs. After having been 'well spoken of by the brothers who were in Lystra and Iconium' (Acts 16:2), Paul was sufficiently impressed with the young Timothy to want him to join Paul's travelling party and it appears that he was now old enough to do that.

From the outset, it seems that Paul had a deep affection for, and confidence in, this young disciple. As well as describing Timothy in terms afforded to many others such as:

---

736. HSIBD, p. 1053.

- 'my fellow worker' (ὁ συνεργός μου – *ho sunergos mou*) (Rom. 16:21)
- 'the brother' (ὁ ἀδελφός – *ho adelphos*) (2 Cor. 1:1; Philem. 1)
- 'our brother' (τὸν ἀδελφὸν ἡμῶν – *ton adelphon hēmōn*) (1 Thess. 3:2)
- 'slaves of Christ Jesus' (δοῦλοι χριστοῦ ἰησοῦ – *douloi Christou Iēsou*) (Phil. 1:1)

Paul goes so far as to call him:

- 'my beloved and faithful child in the Lord' (ὅς ἐστίν μου τέκνον ἀγαπητὸν καὶ πιστὸν ἐν κυρίῳ – *hōs estin mou teknon agapēton kai piston en kuriō*) (1 Cor. 4:17)
- '[my] true son in grace' (ἀγαπητῷ τέκνῳ· χάρις – *agapētō tekvōn charis*) (1 Tim. 1:2)
- '[my] son' (τέκνον – *teknon*) (1 Tim. 1:18)

Such a deep feeling is only reserved for Onesimus (Philem. 10) and Titus (Titus 1:4). The writer of Hebrews also calls Timothy 'our brother' (τὸν ἀδελφὸν ἡμῶν – (*ton adelphon hēmōn*) (Heb. 13:23).

However, Acts 16:3 notes that Paul 'took him and circumcised him because of the Jews who were in those parts, for they all knew that his father was a Greek'. This requires comment given the events of the Jerusalem Council regarding Titus and the incident at Antioch concerning Cephas.[737] The Jerusalem Council had decided that Titus (a Gentile) need not be circumcised to be regarded as a Christian (Gal. 2:3). Paul had argued strongly that this was not necessary for Gentiles. There had also been the incident in Antioch where Paul rebuked Cephas for differentiating between Jews and Gentiles (Gal. 2:11-16). However, in his text, Luke introduces Paul's circumcision of Timothy. Did some inconsistency arise? In Timothy's case, his mother was a Jew and he had been taught the Hebrew Scriptures. Regardless of his father's ethnicity, Timothy was a Jew.

> Paul here does not in principle oppose circumcision of a person of Jewish descent. Even here, however, Luke supplies missionary

737. Keener, *Acts,* vol. 3, pp. 2311-20 provides a detailed commentary on ethnic intermarriage around Lystra as to how it would have affected Timothy's ethnic status (Jew or Gentile?), acceptability for Paul's mission, and the need for his circumcision. I have provided extracts from Keener's comments, which capture the essence of the issues at hand.

> strategy rather than theology as the reason; this seems to fit the epistolary Paul, who sees circumcision as spiritually neutral (1 Cor. 7:19; Gal. 5:6; 6:15) and warns against making foods or holy days a stumbling block to Jewish Christians (Rom. 14).[738]

Paul clearly differentiates between Jewish customs for Jews (e.g. circumcision) and his gospel insistence of salvation by faith alone. Timothy's ethnicity is completely different from Titus' case. Paul himself identifies his own circumcision as inherently part of his Jewishness in Philippians 3:4-5. I agree with Keener's interpretation of Luke's juxtaposition of Acts 15 with Acts 16 that shows that Paul had no objection to Jews participating in Jewish practices so long as they did not undercut faith in Christ and that Gentiles were exempt from them.[739] The fundamental issue for all Christian believers always remained justification by faith alone.

> Timothy was probably a Pauline convert from Paul's earlier visit; Paul calls him his 'son', and although this could simply involve imitation (1 Cor. 4:16), the context also suggests evangelism (4:15). This also fits the tradition of the Pastoral Epistles that Timothy knew firsthand Paul's sufferings in Antioch, Iconium, and Lystra (2 Tim. 3:11-12), which, so far as we may infer from Acts, were limited, or mainly limited, to his previous journey. But Paul had not spent long enough in Lystra to observe firsthand the maturation of all his converts; he might therefore have solicited reports of Timothy's maturity. The concern that he was well spoken of, however, might be less for Paul's benefit than for that of the group's testimony, as Timothy's circumcision (Acts 16:3) is.
>
> That Timothy was 'attested' by others, in this case the brothers and sisters in Lystra, fits an interest not only of Luke (6:3; 10:22; 22:12) but of others as well (e.g., Col. 4:13; 1 Tim. 3:7; 3 John 12). Good reputation was a matter of great importance (see Tob 10:13; Sir 34:23-24; comment on Acts 6:3). …
>
> Although later Jewish tradition assigned the task of circumcision to a *mohel*, in this period anyone was able to perform

738. Keener, *Acts*, vol. 3, p. 2320.

739. Keener, *Acts*, vol. 3, p. 2321.

it, though one would hope that whoever did so was skillful and careful (cf. Gal. 5:12). For a grown man, however, circumcision would always be painful (Gen. 34:25). That Paul circumcises Timothy here coheres with Timothy's being regarded in Paul's letters as a son in the faith (1 Cor. 4:17; Phil. 2:22). Mentoring younger men was considered a virtuous activity.

It can be no coincidence that Luke reports this event soon after describing the Jerusalem Council; just as Jerusalem believers, when led together by the Spirit, affirmed Gentile converts' freedom from circumcision, Paul here does not in principle oppose circumcision of a person of Jewish descent. Even here, however, Luke supplies missionary strategy rather than theology as the reason; this seems to fit the epistolary Paul, who sees circumcision as spiritually neutral (1 Cor. 7:19; Gal. 5:6; 6:15) and warns against making foods or holy days a stumbling block to Jewish Christians (Rom. 14).

Scholars, however, often debate this difference as a serious incongruity. How could Paul battle circumcisionists in Acts 15:1-2 (on the Lukan literary level) and struggle with Barnabas and contend for Titus's freedom (Gal. 2:3-5, 13, on the historical level), then circumcise Timothy afterward? ... Luke deliberately juxtaposes this notice with Acts 15, providing an apologetic against those who claimed that Paul opposed Jewish circumcision (refuting the slander of 21:21 in advance). Whether everyone regarded Timothy as Jewish or not (see discussion above), Luke plainly treats him as Jewish enough not to contradict his own account in Acts 15. Acts may be irenic as well as apologetic, showing that Paul posed no threat to the true Jewish message and heritage. ...

Many scholars counter, however, that Timothy's case differs substantially from Titus's because Timothy has a Jewish mother and was raised with Jewish faith; he merely lacked circumcision. As Luke's Paul opposes only Gentile, not Jewish, circumcision, the same may be said for the epistolary Paul (1 Cor. 7:18-19; Gal. 5:6; 6:15). Further, Timothy's circumcision is here explicitly a missionary strategy, not a concession to others' mistaken standards of salvation or holiness. Paul specifically says that he practiced Jewish customs and submitted to Jewish law to reach Jewish people (1 Cor. 9:20). It is difficult to believe that this submission to Jewish customs excluded circumcision where it was not a matter of Gentiles' salvation, especially when Paul lists circumcision as among his own

> Jewish 'qualifications' (Phil. 3:5). Ethnicity studies suggest that if Paul defined his primary identity as in Christ, he could adapt some elements of his identity to relate to Gentiles, while under normal circumstances maintaining his own Jewish identity. …
>
> The Pastorals later report the beginning of Timothy's ministry, presumably a sending off by church elders (Acts 14:23) in prayer similar to what is described for Paul and Barnabas in 13:3. When the elders laid hands on Timothy (1 Tim. 4:14), prophecies were given about him (1:18; 4:14). He also received on this occasion a spiritual gift (4:14) that was from the Spirit (2 Tim. 1:7) and came through Paul's laying on of hands (1:6), presumably along with those of the elders. In conclusion, Luke's depiction of Timothy highlights in one person the intersection of Jewish and Greek cultures treated elsewhere more broadly in his narratives. Moreover, Luke's depiction of Timothy's circumcision, coming on the heels of the Jerusalem Council, portrays Paul as continuing to approve Jewish practices so long as they are not imposed on Gentiles (see similarly 21:20-26).[740]

Timothy accompanied Paul and others on their long journey to Troas (Acts 16:6-8) where Paul received a vision to go to Macedonia. He was accompanied by (at least) Luke – note the 'we' sentences in Acts 16 – Silvanus and Timothy. The dramatic events in Philippi described in Acts 16 would have been witnessed by Timothy. Unlike Luke and Timothy (because they were perceived as Gentiles?), the Jews, Paul and Silvanus,[741] were beaten and imprisoned (note Acts 16:20); notwithstanding that they were also Roman citizens! No doubt, the young Timothy was becoming quickly aware that those who spoke for the name of Jesus might receive harsh treatment in large pagan cities. On this occasion he was spared. The party then travelled to Thessalonica, an important city in the region, named after the sister of Alexander the Great. Once again, Luke described the mayhem caused by the *Jews* over the preaching of the gospel (including the resurrection) but excludes any mention of Timothy.

---

740. Keener, *Acts*, vol. 3, 2310-22.

741. In Acts Luke prefers 'Silas' to 'Silvanus', which emphasises his Jewishness.

Paul and his companions were hustled out of the city by those who had been converted and moved to Berea where, initially, they received a more favourable hearing (Acts 17:11). However, *Jews* came from Thessalonica to continue their opposition to Paul. Accordingly, Paul was quickly whisked from the city to the sea where he caught a ship to Athens. However, Silvanus and Timothy remained in Berea. In due course Silvanus and Timothy joined Paul in Corinth. The gap between Acts 17:14 and 18:5 seems to suggest that Paul's stay in Athens was so brief that Silvanus and Timothy never went there but straight to Corinth from Berea, an overland journey of approximately 200 miles (330 km). Their arrival in Corinth enabled Paul to concentrate on full-time ministry (Acts 18:5). Is it possible that the new arrivals assisted Prisca and Aquila in their business in place of Paul as well as contributing to the gospel ministry? We hear no more of Timothy until Acts 20:4. Presumably, he remained in Corinth with Paul.

Acts 19 describes Paul's activities in Ephesus and verse 21 notes his intention to travel to Jerusalem after he had passed through Macedonia and Achaia. Prior to doing so, he sent Timothy and Erastus ahead of him to Macedonia.

> Timothy was part of the group that assembled at Corinth from Macedonia, Asia and Galatia and that travelled with Paul to Jerusalem, a journey that Paul's correspondence indicates was for the purpose of conveying the collection for the poor among the Jewish Christians in Jerusalem (Rom. 15:25-27; 1 Cor. 16:34; 2 Cor. 8:19-21 (cf. Acts 24:17)).[742]

In 1 Corinthians 16:10 Paul reiterates what he wrote in 4:17: that Timothy will visit Corinth on his way via Macedonia, but no mention is made of Erastus, probably because he was unknown to the Corinthians. 2 Corinthians 1:19 records Timothy's efforts in teaching and preaching in Corinth with Paul and Silvanus.

> Timothy has been sent already, and so he is not the bearer of this letter [1 Corinthians]; he is already on his way to Corinth. Timothy will be mentioned again in 16:10 ('If Timothy comes'). That seems

742. Thielman, *Romans*, p. 741.

> to mean that this letter may reach Corinth before Timothy arrives; he may have been sent by an indirect route through Macedonia (see Acts 19:21-22).[743]

Timothy and Erastus are described by Paul as 'two of those who ministered to him' (δύο τῶν διακονούντων αὐτῷ – *duo tōn diakonountōn auto*). The use of the verb related to the noun διακονος underscores the relative lowliness of this term, whereas there seems to be attempts to elevate the term into one of leadership. The underlying meaning of the term is that of service and help.[744]

Paul sends greetings to the Roman Christians from colleagues in Corinth, the first being from his closest companion, Timothy (Rom. 16:21), 'my coworker' (ὁ συνεργός μου – *ho sunergos mou*). 'This introductory epithet suggests that Paul feels Timothy may be unknown to the Roman congregations.'[745] The frequency with which Paul enjoins Timothy in his initial greetings to churches (2 Cor. 1:1; Phil. 1:1; Col. 1:1; 1 Thess. 1:1; 2 Thess. 1:1) demonstrates the extent to which Timothy travelled with Paul. His greeting to Philemon (v. 1) indicates his presence in Ephesus during one of Paul's imprisonments there.

Doole raises the interesting question: Was Timothy in prison with Paul?[746] The prison letters, Philippians, Colossians, and Philemon, are sent from Paul and Timothy. There is no need to consider Timothy as a part author of these letters. It is possible that the evangelist Apollos may have met Timothy in Corinth. But Apollos also travelled to, and stayed in, Ephesus (1 Cor. 16:12). If it is the case that Apollos composed the Letter to the Hebrews, this might explain the greeting to Timothy by the author of Hebrews 13:23: 'Take notice that *our brother Timothy has been released, with whom, if he comes soon, I will see you*' (emphasis added). The author of Hebrews will visit his readers with Timothy. This may be further evidence of an Ephesian imprisonment for Timothy and/or Paul.

---

743. Fitzmyer, *First Corinthians*, p. 223.

744. See *The Role of διάκονος (diakonos)* in the introduction.

745. Jewett, *Romans*, p. 977.

746. Doole, *Was Timothy in Prison with Paul?*

From Doole's article we might presume that Timothy was not in prison at the same time as Paul (if the Ephesus occurrences are true), but that he was nearby to render such assistance as he could to the apostle.

> The *tone* of the prison epistles and the lack of *content* concerning Timothy however are the strongest indicators that Timothy's life and well-being were not at risk. The focus remains firmly on Paul, his situation (τα κατ' εμέ in Phil. 1.12; τα περί εμέ in Phil. 2.23) and his relationships with Philemon and the Philippian Christians. And Paul writes in the first person singular where a plural would surely have been appropriate: Epaphras is *my* (not *our*) fellow prisoner (ὁ συναιχμάλωτός μου in Philem. 23), both thanksgivings are written in the singular (Philem. 4-7 and Phil. 1.3-11), and Paul reflects on the support he received during his mission as though he had been working alone (Phil. 4.15-16).
>
> Regardless of whether Paul expected his letter to be read by censors, accusers or governors, his choice of vocabulary and style – in stark contrast to the petitions for clemency and release in other ancient letters from prison – must surely reveal to some extent his aims in writing at all. Neither Philemon nor Philippians is an appeal for release or for assistance. In writing a letter from prison Paul sought to appeal on behalf of Onesimus; in writing a letter (or three letters) from prison he sought to reassure his sponsors that he was doing well.
>
> Timothy is clearly with Paul as he writes. Yet there is apparently no need to discuss his welfare, his fate or his views on the matter(s) at hand. The correspondence limits itself to the circumstances, relationships, life, career, authority and vulnerability of *Paul*. Paul's letters from prison are exceptionally personal. They show no influence from Timothy at all. It is therefore most likely that Paul is the only one in chains.[747]

Near the end of his life in Rome Paul wrote to Timothy (2 Tim. 4:9, 21) that he should do his best (σπούδασον – *spoudason*; cf. Titus 3:12; Heb. 4:11; 2 Pet. 3:14) to come to Paul 'quickly' (ταχέως – *taxeōs*). There is an urgency in his request;

747. Doole, *Was Timothy in Prison with Paul?*, p. 77.

the verb is in the aorist imperative, indicating that it is more of an order than request, followed by 'quickly'.

> The first request is verbally identical with that in Titus 3:12, but is strengthened by the addition of ταχέως (1 Tim. 5:22). Commentators differ here, as there, whether σπουδάζω means 'to hasten' or 'to make an effort' (so most translations; cf. 2:15; Knight, 463), but the effort is surely in order that he may set off as soon as possible, and the added adverb conveys the urgency and need for haste.[748]

The reason is provided in the next verse: 'For Demas has deserted me and gone to Thessalonica.'

> The last chapter of the second letter is packed with notes that are matters of intimate personal knowledge and Timothy. The words of any dying man are memorable to those who love him. But the words of an innocently condemned are especially treasure. Such is the treasure of this chapter.
>
> Come soon! At last we are able to grasp the main personal reason why Paul was writing this letter. He urgently appealed to Timothy to come to Rome as soon as possible. Recall that in 2 Timothy 1:4 Paul had longed ('day and night'!) to see Timothy. Now we know why, and hear the matter openly stated.
>
> By now everyone else had left Paul, except Luke and perhaps Onesiphorus. There was an urgency in his appeal to 'come soon' because he knew he would die soon. Time, always limited, is now drastically foreshortened.
>
> We meet a very human figure – alone in prison, feeling the most fundamental human needs: for friendship, warmth, and spiritual discernment. Are there not times when nothing is better than having an old companion to talk with? This may have been such a time for Paul. The appeal to Timothy to come soon is best viewed in the light of the departures, for various reasons, of Demas, Titus,

---

748. Marshall, *Pastoral Epistles*, p. 814. See also Perkins, *Pastoral Letters*, pp. 229-30: 'However, assigning the meaning "make haste, hurry" to this imperative may create redundancy with the dependent infinitive + adverb; i.e. "come quickly". The same structure (σπούδασον ἐλθεῖν), without the adverb ταχέως, occurs in Titus 3:12. The time reference in 2 Tim. 4:21 (πρὸ χειμῶνος) may tip the scales toward the meaning "make haste, hurry".'

and others. There is a deep craving for companionship among those who have shared rigorous struggles. Timothy was the one whom Paul most wanted with him in those last days.

Some interpreters have painted Paul at this point as demoralized, lonely, cold, self-pitying, afraid, alienated. Nonsense! There is no evidence in the text itself of demoralization, depression, or anxiety. There is hardly a hint of self-pity or depression. Instead it soars with triumph and anticipation of the completion of the race.

There is no contradiction between the certain expectation of impending death and the urgent summons to come. The case for pseudepigraphy has been argued in part on the basis of the supposed disjunctiveness of this passage with the rest of the letter. But the conditions of impending death are precisely those in which the urgency of final communications are most seriously required. There is no extended opportunity for further communication. No delay is thinkable. Come soon. Before winter. The fact that Paul expresses a sense of urgency implies that he is not sure that Timothy can reach him before it is too late. That is precisely all the more reason for urgency. The length of time for the delivery of the letter and Timothy's return would surely have been three or four months under the best of conditions. He hoped that he might live at least a few months to see Timothy.[749]

It is beyond me why some interpreters insist that the last section of Second Timothy is disjunctive with the rest of the letter. More than personal addendum, it reveals a central motivation for writing the letter. This main point was mercifully saved by Paul to the last, to ready Timothy for the sharp sting it contained – the signaling of Paul's impending death, and the direct summons to Timothy to come soon. Everything had been leading up to this point; all preceding injunctions were deepened by it and made more poignant and urgent. This is the most intensely personal paragraph in the letter. First person pronouns abound (either 'I', 'me', or 'my' occurs twenty-two times in thirteen verses, 4:6-18). Two metaphors predominate: sacrifice and departure. Paul was in effect saying: I have done what was necessary in my time; now you must do what is necessary in your time.[750]

749. Oden, *First and Second Timothy and Titus*, p. 170.
750. ibid., p. 166.

We do not know whether Timothy reached Paul before his execution. The contents of Paul's letters to Timothy are not discussed because there are already many commentaries on these books of Scripture.

One interesting point is the mention of Timothy in Hebrews 13:23. The writer uses ἀπολελυμένον (*apolelumenon*), which means 'to release' or 'set free'. This suggests that Timothy, too, had been imprisoned somewhere. There seems to be broad agreement among commentators that it was probably in Ephesus.

In summary, Timothy was Paul's hope for the future of his evangelical and teaching ministry. The growth of the church in subsequent decades vindicated Paul's confidence, which has been carried forward over the centuries by the key instruction of 2 Timothy 3:14-17.

Titius Justus see Gaius Titius Justus

Titus

2 Corinthians 2:13

[13]*I had no rest for my spirit, not finding Titus my brother; but taking my leave of them, I went on to Macedonia.*

2 Corinthians 7:6-7, 14

[6]*But God, who comforts the depressed, comforted us by the coming of Titus; ...*

[7]*... and not only by his coming, but also by the comfort with which he was comforted in you, as he reported to us your longing, your mourning, your zeal for me; so that I rejoiced even more.*

[14]*For if in anything I have boasted to him about you, I was not put to shame; but as we spoke all things to you in truth, so also our boasting before Titus proved to be the truth.*

2 Corinthians 8:6, 16-17, 23

[6]*So we urged Titus that as he had previously made a beginning, so he would also complete in you this gracious work as well.*

[16]*But thanks be to God who puts the same earnestness on your behalf in the heart of Titus.*

[17]*For he not only accepted our appeal, but being himself very earnest, he has gone to you of his own accord.*

[23] As for Titus, he is my partner and fellow worker among you; as for our brethren, they are messengers of the churches, a glory to Christ.

2 Corinthians 12:18

[18] I urged Titus to go, and I sent the brother with him. Titus did not take any advantage of you, did he? Did we not conduct ourselves in the same spirit and walk in the same steps?

Galatians 2:1, 3

[1] Then after an interval of fourteen years I went up again to Jerusalem with Barnabas, taking Titus along also.

[3] But not even Titus, who was with me, though he was a Greek, was compelled to be circumcised.

2 Timothy 4:10

[10] ... for Demas, having loved this present world, has deserted me and gone to Thessalonica; Crescens has gone to Galatia, Titus to Dalmatia.

Titus 1:4-5

[4] To Titus, my true child in a common faith: Grace and peace from God the Father and Christ Jesus our Saviour.

[5] For this reason I left you in Crete, that you would set in order what remains and appoint elders in every city as I directed you,

Titus 3:12-15

[12] When I send Artemas or Tychicus to you, make every effort to come to me at Nicopolis, for I have decided to spend the winter there.

[13] Diligently help Zenas the lawyer and Apollos on their way so that nothing is lacking for them.

[14] Our people must also learn to engage in good deeds to meet pressing needs, so that they will not be unfruitful.

[15] All who are with me greet you. Greet those who love us in the faith. Grace be with you all.

Titus, a Roman name meaning 'pleasant',[751] was one of Paul's most longstanding partners in the work of the gospel. He is mentioned in several of Paul's letters, especially 2 Corinthians, but never in Acts.

Because Paul mentions Titus in a separate construction, συμπαραλαβὼν καὶ Τίτον (*symparalabōn kai Titon*, taking along also

751. HSIBD, p. 1058.

> Titus) [Gal. 2:1], Titus is given special prominence here (Mussner 1988: p. 101). We do not know when Paul first encountered Titus (not mentioned in Acts), but in Titus 1:4 Paul's calling him 'my true son in our common faith' may imply that Paul was instrumental in his conversion. Titus had an especially important role with the Corinthian church on Paul's third missionary journey (2 Cor. 2:13; 7:6, 13-14; 8:6, 16, 23; 12:18), but he may also have been known to the Galatians (R. Longenecker 1990: 47). Paul's reason for highlighting his presence at this meeting becomes clear as the narrative progresses: he was a Greek, and the fact that he was not compelled to be circumcised is powerful evidence that Paul's law-free gospel was acknowledged to be correct ([Gal. 2:] 3). In fact, it is possible that Paul brought Titus along to Jerusalem precisely for the purpose of forcing the issue (e.g., Hays 2000: p. 222; Garlington 2003: p. 71).[752]

Titus' relationship with Paul covered several decades, reflected in Paul's descriptions of him as 'my brother' – τὸν ἀδελφόν μου (*ton adelphon mou*) – (2 Cor. 2:13); 'my partner and fellow worker' – κοινωνὸς ἐμὸς καὶ εἰς ὑμᾶς συνεργός (*koinōnos emos kai eis humas sunergos*) – (2 Cor. 8:23)[753]; 'my true child in a common faith' – γνησίῳ τέκνῳ κατὰ κοινὴν πίστιν (*gnēsinō teknō kata koinēn pistin*) – (Titus 1:4). His conduct was beyond reproach (2 Cor. 12:18).[754] It has been argued (see below) that his omission from Acts reflects him being a relative of that book's author, Luke. There is no evidence to confirm this. Like Luke, Titus was a Gentile (Gal. 2:3).

> Thus it may very well have happened that Luke was a relative of one of the early Antiochian Christians; and this relationship was perhaps the authority for Eusebius's carefully guarded statement. Further, it is possible that this relationship gives the explanation of the omission of Titus from *Acts*, an omission which everyone finds so difficult to understand. Perhaps Titus was the relative of Luke; and Eusebius found this statement in an old tradition, attached to 2 Cor. 8:18; 12:18, where Titus and Luke (the latter not named by

---

752. Moo, *Galatians*, p. 122.

753. See R. P. Martin, *2 Corinthians*, pp. 456-8.

754. See Harris, *2 Corinthians*, pp. 890-1; Kruse, *2 Corinthians*, p. 273.

> Paul, but identified by an early tradition) are associated as envoys to Corinth. Luke, as we may suppose, thought it right to omit his relative's name, as he did his own name, from his history.[755]

Chronologically, Titus is first mentioned by Paul in Galatians 2:1-3 when he accompanied the apostle to Jerusalem for the Council concerning the need for circumcision by Gentile believers. Titus was not compelled to be circumcised (Gal. 2:3).[756] Titus was clearly a close companion of Paul, as we see from 2 Corinthians 2:13. Paul had travelled to Troas (north-western Turkey) in the Roman province of Mysia expecting to meet Titus, who was travelling there with news of the Corinthian church. So great was Paul's desire to see Titus that he reluctantly left the infant church formed in Troas and travelled to Macedonia. When they met in Macedonia Titus was able to encourage Paul with a favourable report about affairs in Corinth (2 Cor. 7:6-7; cf. 2 Cor. 11:28).

> The agitation that troubled Paul's spirit and made his ministry at Troas less than it might have been is clear from this text. When pastoral concerns weighed heavily on him, he could not put his heart in evangelistic opportunity. In the event it was better for him to quit Troas and press on to meet his colleague on his return from Corinth. No good purpose is served, we learn, in any Christian's attempting a piece of service when his or her interests lie elsewhere; and pastoral responsibility stood high on Paul's agenda at this time.[757]

Paul's comments about meeting Titus are interrupted by a lengthy discourse in 2 Corinthians 2:14–7:4. Paul then resumes his comments about Titus, who was clearly of considerable influence in the Corinthian church as described in 2 Corinthians 7–8. One word used several times by Paul to describe his fellow worker is 'earnest' (σπουδή – *spoudē* and its derivatives), defined in the Oxford English Dictionary as 'sincere and serious about one's

---

755. Ramsay, *St Paul the Traveller and Roman Citizen*, pp. 389-90.

756. Duncan, *Galatians*, pp. 42-8 argues strongly that Titus *was* circumcised in Jerusalem but his conclusion is rejected.

757. R. P. Martin, *2 Corinthians*, p. 180. See Kruse, *2 Corinthians*, pp. 116-17; Barnett *2 Corinthians*, pp. 134-6.

intentions'. Such was Titus' attitude towards the Corinthian church.[758] However, the use of σπούδασον (*spoudason*) also brings a sense of making haste to undertake this journey.[759] Paul had sent Titus to Corinth with the responsibility to deliver a severe letter to the church, calling it to repentance (2 Cor. 7:8-9). Paul had led Titus to believe that he would be welcomed by the Corinthian congregation and this indeed was the outcome.

> Paul also rejoiced when he saw how Titus' own heart now went out to the Corinthians: *And his affection for you is all the greater when he remembers that you were all obedient, receiving him with fear and trembling.* As Titus recalled their obedience (to the demands made in Paul's 'severe letter') and the fear and trembling with which they received him (evidence of the respect in which they held Paul and his apostolic team), his affection for them increased. Their *fear and trembling* may also be evidence of an awareness of their failed responsibility before God, to whom they would have to give an account for the way they had acted during the crisis in Corinth. Informing the Corinthians of Titus' growing affection for them would predispose them to welcome him when he made his upcoming visit in the administration of the collection for the poor believers in Jerusalem.[760]

Titus' journey to Corinth (alluded to in 2 Corinthians 12:18) is difficult to determine chronologically. The letter to Titus was penned in A.D. 63 from Macedonia.[761]

> Paul urged Titus (παρεκάλεσα (*parekalesa*), aorist tense of παρακαλέω (*parakaleō*), 'urge') and sent with συναπέστειλα

758. See Harris, *2 Corinthians*, pp. 599-600. Matthew Henry used Titus' 'earnestness' as an exemplar in his *Sermon Preached at Haberdashers' Hall, 13 July 1712 on the Occasion of the Death of the Rev. Richard Stretton, M.A*. The word 'earnest' is used seventy-two times. See M. Henry, *The Complete works of Matthew Henry: Treatises, Sermons, and Tracts* (Grand Rapids: Baker Books, reprinted 1979), vol. 2: pp. 384-402.

759. See the use of σπούδασον in 2 Timothy 4:9, 21 where urgency is emphasised.

760. Kruse, *2 Corinthians*, p. 195 (original emphasis).

761. See *Time Between Two Roman Imprisonments* in the introduction.

> (*sunapesteila*), aorist tense of συναποστέλλω (*sunapostellō*), 'send with') him a brother (τὸν ἀδελφόν – *ton adelphon*). We note that παρακαλέω, 'urge', is found in both [2 Cor.] 8:6 and 12:18, and may be grounds for connecting the two verses mentioned as describing the same visit. Also it appears that the aorist tenses of 12:18 are genuine (as they are in 8:6), and thus we see another link between 8:6 and 12:18. What must remain a mystery is, if 8:6 and 12:18 describe the same visit, why did not Paul mention the brother in 8:6? Possibly at the time of writing of 8:6, Paul did not deem it important to mention the other brother. This is possible in that Paul was not defending his action toward the offering when he composed chapters 1–9, while he was having to defend it in chapter 12. Whatever the reason, it seems more logical to equate 8:6 and 12:18. Moreover, the person of Titus is more important to Paul's argument. For one, Titus was a Gentile (no doubt an important item with the Corinthians). Furthermore, Titus had the confidence of the Corinthians. He had started the collection in Corinth and had been the one to deliver the 'severe letter'. Whatever one's conclusion about 12:18*a*, Titus must be seen as playing a vital role in Paul's self-defence.[762]

The letter to Titus contains few references to Titus personally and is more in the form of written instructions about how Titus is to behave as a Christian in a difficult location (Crete) and build up the church there by appointing elders and teaching the believers how to behave. Gundry helpfully interprets Paul's instructions and provides a clue about Paul's movements after his release from his first Roman imprisonment.

> 'I left you behind in Crete' implies that Paul had been in Crete. 'That you might set straight the remaining matters' implies that he had done some work there but left before finishing it, and that the work consisted in setting straight some matters that were threatening, or indeed were corrupting, the churches located there. Titus had the job of appointing elders so that they might help in setting straight those matters, for by virtue of their status and appointment they'll have authority to help. 'City by city' implies the existence of a number

762. R. P. Martin, *2 Corinthians*, p. 645; see Barnett, *2 Corinthians*, pp. 589-90.

> of local churches on Crete. 'As I ordered you' indicates that before Paul left he told Titus to appoint elders. So Paul is reminding Titus of that order, and this reminder of the order evolves into a reminder of qualifications for eldership.[763]

The Cretans were given opportunities to show hospitality:

> Titus was asked to equip for further journeys Zenas the jurist and Apollos (v. 13), the eloquent and learned teacher from Alexandria to whom Priscilla and Aquila had given instruction at Ephesus (Acts 18:24-25); a party of Corinthians also claimed him as their leader (Acts 19:1; 1 Cor. 1:12; 3:4-6, 22; 4:6; 16:12). These were important officials for whom Titus was responsible in greeting and resourcing. They were to be warmly received and outfitted for their continued journey. By such acts of hospitality the Cretans were to make themselves useful in relation to the church's worldwide mission. By such acts we let our people learn to apply themselves to good deeds, and help cases of urgent need (Titus 3:14). By being responsive in such occasions, the Christian community is being given opportunity to grow in grace and thereby to welcome the reconciling power of the Spirit in their lives.[764]

The final mention of Titus was written during the apostle's second imprisonment in Rome. Paul simply notes: 'Titus [has gone] to Dalmatia' (2 Tim. 4:10). Dalmatia was a Roman province located on the eastern Adriatic Sea in the southern part of Illyricum, where Paul had preached the gospel (Rom. 15:19). Nicopolis is a town in that region.[765] There are two quite different descriptions of Nicopolis as a winter location. Towner writes, 'Nicopolis was a busy port town on the western coast of Greece. It was actually known for its harsh winters.'[766] Yet Kostenberger writes, 'Nicopolis, the preeminent location for trade with Rome in western and northern Greece, was known for its mild climate ....

---

763. Gundry, *Commentary on First and Second Timothy, Titus*, p. 62.

764. Oden, *First and Second Timothy and Titus*, p. 165.

765. Barclay, *The Letters to Timothy, Titus and Philemon*, p. 265 notes that Nicopolis was in Epirus and was 'the best centre for work in the Roman province of Dalmatia'.

766. Towner, *1-2 Timothy & Titus*, p. 263.

Nicopolis was more than 300 miles from Crete, a five-to-ten-day journey by ship.'[767] To add further confusion, Long comments that 'there were several places named Nicopolis; it hardly matters which one is meant here'.[768]

> Nicopolis lay on the northwest coast of Greece opposite the foot of Italy. 'I've decided to spend the winter there [not "here"]' indicates that Paul hasn't yet arrived in Nicopolis. So we don't know where he was at the time of writing this letter (but see Romans 15:19 for his presence, perhaps at this time, in Illyricum, a region north of Nicopolis). He'll send Artemas or Tychicus to replace Titus in Crete. Then Titus is 'to be diligent' to join Paul in Nicopolis. Paul's decision to spend the winter in Nicopolis favours that the commanded diligence includes Titus's coming before winter's onset. For sailing during winter, as Titus would have to do when leaving the island of Crete, was dangerous and usually avoided (see Acts 27 for Paul's recognition of the danger, involving Crete). So the commanded diligence in a sending of Zenas the lawyer and Apollos is also likely to include action taken before winter's onset (compare 2 Tim. 4:9, 21).[769]
>
> In the concluding section of Titus Paul discusses his immediate plans and crisis instructions – Titus 3:12-14. ... Paul urged Titus to make every effort to join him for the winter. Do your best, he wrote, to come to me at Nicopolis (a city founded by Augustus on the site of his camp after his victory over Mark Antony at Actium, 31 B.C.). Paul had decided to spend the winter there (v. 12a). A similar message would be sent to Timothy in Paul's final days (2 Tim. 4:9, 21). Paul may have used his winters to regroup, rethink, reconceive his mission. Apparently Paul's plan was to send either Artemas (not mentioned elsewhere) or Tychicus to replace Titus in Crete, while Titus was temporarily in Nicopolis consulting with Paul.[770]

As is the case with so many faithful saints, we know nothing about Titus' final years.

---

767. Kostenberger, *1-2 Timothy & Titus*, p. 353.
768. Long, *1 & 2 Timothy and Titus*, p. 278.
769. Gundry, *First and Second Timothy, Titus*, p. 71.
770. Oden, *First and Second Timothy and Titus*, p. 165.

Trophimus

Acts 20:3-4

[3]And there he spent three months, and when a plot was made against him by the Jews as he was about to set sail for Syria, he decided to return through Macedonia.

[4]And he was accompanied by Sopater of Berea, the son of Pyrrhus, and by Aristarchus and Secundus of the Thessalonians, and Gaius of Derbe, and Timothy, and Tychicus and Trophimus of Asia.

Acts 21:27-29

[27]When the seven days were almost over, the Jews from Asia, upon seeing him in the temple, began to stir up all the crowd and laid hands on him, ...

[28]... crying out, "Men of Israel, come to our aid! This is the man who preaches to all men everywhere against our people and the Law and this place; and besides he has even brought Greeks into the temple and has defiled this holy place."

[29]For they had previously seen Trophimus the Ephesian in the city with him, and they supposed that Paul had brought him into the temple.

2 Timothy 4:20

[20]Erastus remained at Corinth, but I left Trophimus sick at Miletus.

Trophimus, meaning 'nourishing',[771] was a Gentile Christian living in Ephesus, who accompanied Paul and several Christians from other regions in a lengthy journey to Jerusalem to deliver a collection of money for poor Christians.

> The name is listed as the twelfth commonest Greek *cognomen* in Rome (in *GPR* 2.990-995; 3.1439) with no fewer than 297 occurrences. Horsley points out (*New Docs* 3.91-93, No. 80) that its popularity peaks markedly in the first century AD. Some of the Roman frequencies are very surprising, and may reflect peculiarities of social sampling, in particular a high percentage of possible slaves or freed men. As a slave-name this probably denoted a house-born slave, reared in the family. But in Ephesus it is another of those names attested in the families which provided the Curetes and associated officers .... In fact the name is frequent and indigenous in western Asia Minor, and among Ephesian

771. HSIBD, p. 1075.

> officials in particular, apart from its apparent proliferation as a slave-name in Rome.[772]

The Temple precinct in Jerusalem was strictly policed by the Jews. Desecration of the Temple, e.g. by allowing Gentiles to enter it, was a capital offence.

> The mention of Asian Jews is significant. Having escaped before Passover a plot from members of a Corinthian synagogue he split, Paul now faces members of another synagogue he split in Asia Minor (19:9). Although Asia was an entire province, those who knew Paul by sight would have encountered him in Ephesus (Acts 19:1, 10). This is often how Luke means "Asia" (19:22; 20:16), including in the earlier mention of Trophimus (20:4; 21:29). Many people knew about Paul and hated him, but with tens of thousands of people passing through the temple courts, only recent years' acquaintances might recognize him. More specifically, only those from Ephesus might know that the Ephesian Trophimus (21:29) was a Gentile.[773]

However, some Jews from Ephesus presumed (or concocted the story) that, contrary to Jewish law, Paul had enabled Trophimus to enter the Temple in Jerusalem. Fortunately, for Trophimus, he was absent when Paul was apprehended at the Temple; otherwise, he would surely have met his death at the hands of the enraged Jews. It is noticeable that commentators make no mention of Trophimus' evident involvement in the Ephesian ministry. He would not have been noticed by the Ephesian Jews had he not been a prominent member of the Christian community in that city.

Trophimus clearly accompanied Paul on his final journey to Rome but left the party, being sick at Miletus, on the coast about 37 miles (60 km) south of Ephesus. Trophimus would have heard Paul's farewell speech to the Ephesian elders on the beach at Miletus (Acts 20:17-38).

---

772. Hemer, *The Book of Acts*, pp. 236-7.

773. Keener, *Acts*, vol. 3, pp. 3144-5.

TRYPHAENA AND TRYPHOSA

ROMANS 16:12

[12]Greet Tryphaena and Tryphosa, workers in the Lord. Greet Persis the beloved, who has worked hard in the Lord.

It is an unusual entry when two people are named together. The reason is that exactly the same comments can be made of each of them. There is an obvious similarity in their names when spelt in English and this is even more the case when their Greek names (also used in Latin) are understood. Tryphaena (τρύφαινα – *Tryphaina*) and Tryphosa (τρυφῶσα – *Tryphōsa*) mean 'dainty'and 'delicate', respectively.[774] Some commentators regard them as sisters, if not twins.[775]

However, Paul's description of their efforts on behalf of the gospel are understated in some translations of the Greek. They are described as those 'who labour in the Lord' (KJV, ASV), 'workers in the Lord' (NASB, RSV), those 'who work hard in the Lord' (NIV, HCSB), 'who toil in the Lord's service' (NEB). Paul describes them as τὰς κοπιώσας ἐν κυρίῳ – *tas kopiōsas ev kuriō.* The same word is used by Jesus in Matthew 11:28 when He says, 'Come to me all who *labour and are heavy laden* and I will give you rest'. 'The fact that they had opportunity to work hard (for κοπιάω see on 16:6) suggests they were freedwomen, probably with a fair degree of independence.'[776]

Properly understood, this verse alone confirms that Paul had a sense of humour! Notwithstanding his flowery style, Barclay best expresses Paul's comment:

> When Paul wrote his greetings to Tryphaena and Tryphosa – who were very likely twin sisters – he wrote them with a smile, for the way in which he puts it sounds like a complete contradiction in terms. Three times in this list of greetings Paul uses a certain

774. HSIBD, p. 1076. They are not even mentioned in Moffatt's commentary on Romans. ibid., p. 1076.

775. Barclay, *Romans*, p. 234; Bruce, *Romans*, p. 273; Cranfield, *Romans*, vol. 2, p. 793 is less certain.

776. Dunn, *Romans 9-16*, p. 897.

> Greek word for Christian work and toil. He uses it of Mary (v. 6), and of Tryphaena and Tryphosa and of Persis in this passage. It is the verb *kopian*, and kopian means to toil to the point of exhaustion; it means to give to the work all that one has got; it means to work to the stage of utter weariness. That is what Paul said that Tryphaena and Tryphosa were in the habit of doing; and the point of it all is that the names *Tryphaena* and *Tryphosa* mean respectively *dainty* and *delicate*! It is as if Paul said: 'You two may be called *dainty* and *delicate*; but you belie your names by working like trojans for the sake of the Church and for Christ.' We can well imagine a smile passing across his face as he dictated that greeting.[777]

To put these women's work in perspective, it must be noted that, of the four noted above by Barclay, only Miriam and Persis have the added Greek emphasis of *polla* (πολλὰ). Barclay does not make this point and even omits mention of Mary in his commentary. The important addition of *polla* reflects an even greater effort by Miriam and Persis (perhaps over a longer period of time) than Tryphaena and Tryphosa. But its absence here should in no way detract from the extent of their efforts. Matthew Henry noted that 'true love never sticks at labour, but rather takes a pleasure in it; where there is much love, there will be much labour.'[778] The same Lord for whom they have toiled will, at the end, provide eternal refreshment as He promised.

TYCHICUS

ACTS 20:3-4

[3] *And there he spent three months, and when a plot was made against him by the Jews as he was about to set sail for Syria, he decided to return through Macedonia.*

[4] *And he was accompanied by Sopater of Berea, the son of Pyrrhus, and by Aristarchus and Secundus of the Thessalonians, and Gaius of Derbe, and Timothy, and Tychicus and Trophimus of Asia.*

---

777. Barclay, *Romans*, pp. 234-5. See also Blaiklock, *Romans*, p. 91. In Barclay, *New Testament*, p. 337, Romans 16:12 says, 'Give my good wishes to Tryphaena and Tryphosa, who are such strenuous workers in the Lord's service.'

778. *Matthew Henry's Commentary on the Whole Bible*, p. 1799.

EPHESIANS 6:21-22

[21] *But that you also may know about my circumstances, how I am doing, Tychicus, the beloved brother and faithful minister in the Lord, will make everything known to you.*

[22] *I have sent him to you for this very purpose, so that you may know about us, and that he may comfort your hearts.*

COLOSSIANS 4:7-9

[7] *As to all my affairs, Tychicus, our beloved brother and faithful servant and fellow bond-servant in the Lord, will bring you information.*

[8] *For I have sent him to you for this very purpose, that you may know about our circumstances and that he may encourage your hearts;*

[9] *... and with him Onesimus, our faithful and beloved brother, who is one of your number. They will inform you about the whole situation here.*

2 TIMOTHY 4:12

[12] *But Tychicus I have sent to Ephesus.*

TITUS 3:12

[12] *When I send Artemas or Tychicus to you, make every effort to come to me at Nicopolis, for I have decided to spend the winter there.*

Tychicus, a Gentile name meaning 'fortuitous',[779] was one of Paul's most faithful colleagues, yet mentioned only once in Acts. His name 'is not very common and according to Horsley in *New Docs* 2.109, No. 86, the majority of attestations come from Rome, and often concern men of servile origin'.[780] He was probably born in or near Ephesus, the capital of the Roman province of Asia (Acts 20:4), where he would have been converted by Paul's preaching in that city. His frequent travel means that he was a freed man. Tychicus is mentioned in Paul's Prison Letters (Eph. 6:21; Col. 4:7; 2 Tim. 4:12; Titus 3:12). Accepting that Ephesians and Colossians were penned while Paul was imprisoned in Ephesus (see *Letters From Prison* in the introduction),[781] and Titus and

779. HSIBD, p. 1076.

780. Hemer, *The Book of Acts*, p. 236.

781. See McKnight, *Colossians*, p. 384, n. 13: 'It is worth pausing here to observe that all these people getting to and from Rome in communications between Paul and the churches in Ephesus, Laodicea, and Colossae create a

2 Timothy originated in Macedonia and Rome, respectively, Tychicus must have accompanied Paul for many years.

> Awaiting trial in prison, Paul sends Tychicus, who 'will tell you all the news about me' and supplement the hints found in [Col.] 1:24-2:5. He will say this again in 4:8 and 4:9 (cf. also Phil. 1:12). This alone makes it more than likely that the couriers for communications between Paul and Colossae are not only Epaphras (Col. 1:7-8) but also Tychicus (cf. Eph. 6:21-22) and Onesimus. We can infer that Tychicus was the courier for Ephesians (6:21-22), and we know that Colossae and Laodicea were close to one another and that travel between Ephesus and the Lycus Valley was slow, so we can well imagine that Tychicus and Onesimus delivered two or more letters at the same time. Such couriers delivered and elaborated their letters and even were seen along with the letter as the personal presence of the author; furthermore, they often collected information to relay back to the apostle.[782]

'Later references in Titus 3:12 [Macedonia to Crete] and 2 Timothy 4:12 [Rome to Ephesus] confirm that he performed this humble function throughout Paul's life and ministry.'[783] The words of Ephesians 6:21-22 are almost an exact copy of Colossians 4:7-8, another clue that these letters were composed within a short time of one another.

He was one of several Gentile Christians who accompanied Paul on his lengthy journey (as it turned out to be) from Corinth to Jerusalem via Macedonia (Acts 20:4-21:17). See also the entry

---

considerable challenge of time, expense, and travel, not least for the runaway slave Onesimus. A far simpler solution is that Paul is in prison in Ephesus (cf. 1 Cor. 15:32; 2 Cor. 1:8), not Rome (Acts 28:16-31).'

782. McKnight, *Colossians*, pp. 383-4. See also Talbert, *Ephesians and Colossians*, pp. 171-2. *Letters from Prison: Ephesians, Philippians, Colossians and Philemon* in the introduction discusses the issue as to whether Paul was imprisoned in Ephesus.

783. Hughes, *Colossians*, p. 143. Hughes is probably incorrect in nominating Tychicus as the letter carrier to Titus. It is more likely that Apollos and/or Zenas delivered the letter (cf. Titus 3:13). Oden, *First and Second Timothy and Titus*, p. 165, suggests that Tychicus may have been Timothy's successor in Ephesus (v. 12).

for Archippus. The word most associated with Tychicus is 'faithful' (Eph. 6:2; Col. 4:7). This was a quality much admired by Paul in his fellow Christians. But Tychicus was more than that: he was dependable. The Ephesians and Colossians are informed that Paul regarded him as a 'beloved brother' (ἀγαπητὸς ἀδελφὸς – *agapētos adelphos*) and 'a fellow slave in the Lord' (σύνδουλος ἐν κυρίῳ – *sundoulos en kuriō*). The latter title was only awarded to Tychicus and Epaphras (Col. 1:7). Given the significant ministry of Epaphras, this reflects highly on the trustworthiness of Tychicus. Morris emphasises his ministry of encouragement: 'There was much to discourage the members of the early church, especially the strong opposition they met from so many people who would not trouble to understand their message nor the work they were doing in the Lord's name. An encourager like Tychicus must have been greatly needed.'[784]

Paul wrote his letter to Titus while his colleague was on Crete (Titus 1:5). At its conclusion, Paul asks Titus to join him in Nicopolis, on the western side of Macedonia, north of Corinth, where he was planning to spend the winter. Paul plans to send Artemas or Tychicus to replace Titus. We know nothing more about Artemas; but the fact that Tychicus would be competent enough to minister to the Cretan Christians speaks volumes for his capacity after his long service and Paul's confidence in him.

Space does not permit quoting in full the wonderful description of Tychicus by Hughes but some of it must be included here.

> Tychicus left no writings which survived. He did no feats which were thought worth preserving by Dr Luke in Acts. He was a very common violin. However, God used him as a part of His divine symphony, and the music was beautiful ….[785]
>
> From the beautiful teamwork of Paul and Tychicus we learn some great truths about fullness in service. *There is greatness in the smallest things done for Christ.* …[786]

---

784. L. L. Morris, *Expository Reflections on the Letter to the Ephesians* (Grand Rapids: Baker, 1994), p. 214.

785. Hughes, *Colossians*, p. 143.

786. ibid., 143 (original emphasis).

> The life of this common, not remarkably gifted man who loyally served Christ and Paul graces all of our lives today. We know of Tychicus, but there are thousands who have equally blessed us whom we will only know in glory – common violins with whom the Master has made eternal music.[787]

Urbanus

Romans 16:9

[9]Greet Urbanus, our fellow worker in Christ, and Stachys my beloved.

Urbanus is a Latin name, meaning 'refined', or 'polite'.[788] It is related to the English word 'urbane', and no doubt is the name of a slave or freed man in a city environment like Corinth or Rome. It is interesting to note that Paul describes Urbanus as '***our*** fellow worker in Christ' (τὸν συνεργὸν **ἡμῶν** ἐν χριστῶ – *ton sunergon* ***hēmōn*** *ev Christō*).

> This greeting for Urbanus relates to someone Paul definitely knows personally, because, along with Prisca and Aquila, he is identified as 'our coworker in Christ', that is a missionary colleague. He had worked with Paul somewhere in the eastern mission field ... [this] leads me to believe that this particular Urbanus was likely a freed man of Roman origin .... The details make it likely that the Urbanus greeted by Paul was among the exiles driven out of Rome in 49 after involvement in the synagogue riots. He has now returned to his home city of Rome. The reference to him as 'our coworker' indicates that he had freely cooperated in the Pauline mission, and that this Gentile believer shared a missional and theological outlook congenial to Paul. In this instance the request for greetings would have been particularly hard for the 'weak', who, according to [Rom.] 14:3-4, 10, were inclined to pass judgment on those who like Paul were free from the law. Urbanus is honoured by Paul with the request that all other converts in Rome greet him as an equal.[789]

---

787. ibid., p. 144.
788. HSIBD, p. 1082.
789. Jewett, *Romans*, p. 965.

ZENAS

TITUS 3:13

[13]Diligently help Zenas the lawyer and Apollos on their way so that nothing is lacking for them.

Zenas is a shortened form of Zenodorus, a Greek name meaning 'gift of Zeus'.[790] Having a Greek name with reference to a pagan god implies that Zenas was a god-fearer – a Gentile converted to Judaism. He is described as 'the lawyer' (ὁ νομικός – *ho nomikos*), which can refer to an expert in the Jewish law or an expert in Greek or Roman law. The word is otherwise used in the NT only in the gospels of Matthew and Luke, where the references are to experts in the Law of Moses. However, Paul uses it twice in his letter to Titus. In Titus 3:9 νομικός is used with regard to disputes about the Law of Moses. If Zenas was a Gentile, and given his linkage to Apollos in this verse, it may be the case that Zenas was skilled in Jewish law. However, Scott[791] came to the opposite conclusion, as did Marshall. 'The relation of his name to that of the Greek god Zeus ("Zenas" meaning "a gift of Zeus") favours that he didn't come from Jewish stock and therefore had legal expertise outside Jewish law.'[792] 'The word in itself does not indicate what kind of law is meant, whether Jewish, Greek or Roman law but a Jewish lawyer is unlikely with such a pagan name (*pace* Lock).'[793] Zenas and Apollos 'were probably the bearers of this letter to Titus'.[794]

> What of 'Zenas the lawyer' (3:13)? Otherwise unknown in the NT, he has been variously identified as an expert in Jewish law, or, as his pagan name might suggest, a Roman lawyer. In fact it was common for lawyers to visit Crete in Roman times. The famous stone panels on which were inscribed the Law Code of Gortyn dated from c. 450

---

790. HSIBD, p. 1121.

791. E. F. Scott, *The Pastoral Epistles*, MNTC (London: Hodder and Stoughton, 1936), p. 181.

792. Gundry, *Commentary on First and Second Timothy, Titus*, p. 72.

793. Marshall with Towner, *Pastoral Epistles*, p. 343. See Yarbrough, *Letters to Timothy and Titus*, p. 557; Gundry, *Commentary on First and Second Timothy, Titus*, p. 62, for agreement.

794. Yarbrough, *Letters to Timothy and Titus*, p. 557.

> BCE but had been restored under Roman rule and were prominently displayed to facilitate study. Crete became 'a centre of pilgrimage for legal inspiration'.[795]

Perkins notes that the use of σπουδαίως (*spoudaiōs*) implies that Paul 'urges Titus to carry out these instructions either quickly, diligently, or eagerly'.[796] He also concludes that the use of the aorist imperative tense of πρόπεμψον (*propempson*, from προπέμπω) ('to send on [one's] way') 'indicates a specific instruction, perhaps with a nuance of urgency amplified by the preceding adverb (Wallace, 1996, p. 720)'.[797]

Paul had indicated in verse 12 to Titus that he would be in Nicopolis (a city in north-west Greece on the Adriatic Sea) and hoped to meet him there.

> Nicopolis was noted for its warm climate, which made it a perfect place for Paul to spend the winter. Nicopolis was the most important centre of trade with Rome in northern and western Greece. The city had two excellent harbours that gave travellers access to the coastal cities of the Adriatic Sea. Paul may have had plans to travel north to Dalmatia in the spring. He had previously founded a church in Illyricum, the province of which Dalmatia was a part (Rom. 15:19). He liked to revisit the churches he had established in order to encourage and strengthen them.
>
> His plans to visit Dalmatia were probably revised, however, when he received word of the great struggles Timothy was experiencing in Ephesus. He probably felt he needed to visit Ephesus personally. When Titus was relieved by Artemas in Crete (Titus 3:12; Tychicus was sent to Ephesus [2 Tim. 4:12]) and joined Paul in Nicopolis, Paul may have sent Titus to Dalmatia in his place (2 Tim. 4:10). Perhaps Titus did not arrive in Nicopolis before Paul had to leave, and Paul later sent Titus to Dalmatia from Rome.[798]

---

795. Wieland, *Roman Crete and the Letter to Titus*, p. 353.

796. Perkins, *Pastoral Letters*, p. 285.

797. ibid., p. 285. He comments that 'This is the only occurrence of this verb in the PE [Pastoral Epistles], but it is frequent in the NT'. See Romans 15:24; 1 Corinthians 16:6, 11; 2 Corinthians 1:16.

798. C. L. Quarles, *Illustrated Life of Paul* (Nashville, TN: B&H Publishing, 2014), p. 259.

Given Paul's direct request in verse 13 to 'diligently help Zenas the lawyer and Apollos on their way so that nothing is lacking for them', the logical conclusion is that Zenas and Apollos were visiting Titus on Crete before travelling elsewhere.

> Paul's decision to spend the winter in Nicopolis favours that the commanded diligence includes Titus's coming before winter's onset. For sailing during winter, as Titus would have to do when leaving the island of Crete, was dangerous and usually avoided (see Acts 27 for Paul's recognition of the danger, involving Crete). So the commanded diligence in a sending of Zenas the lawyer and Apollos is also likely to include action taken before winter's onset (compare 2 Tim. 4:9, 21)....
>
> Since Paul addresses Titus alone, at the time of writing Zenas and Apollos have yet to arrive in Crete. They're probably carrying Paul's letter to Titus. But Paul wants them to rejoin him. Titus's sending forward Zenas and Apollos while he himself waits for the arrival of Artemas or Tychicus before going himself to Paul – this sending forward includes supplying Zenas and Apollos with whatever they need for their journey to Paul: food, money, and such like. And for a supply that will leave nothing lacking, Cretan Christians (whom Paul calls 'our [people]') are 'to be engaging in good deeds', which in this case means supplying Zenas's and Apollos's 'essential needs'. These Cretans will be learning by the actual doing (compare 1 Timothy 5:4, 13). 'Also to be learning' seems to mean learning by doing as well as learning by listening to Titus's exhortations.[799]

I am not sure whether Calvin's conclusion (see below) is correct regarding Zenas' financial circumstances, although verse 14 may suggest this. Paul's urging that 'nothing is lacking for them' ('see that they have everything they need', NIV) does not necessarily imply poverty.

> 13 *Zenas a lawyer.* It is uncertain whether 'Zenas' was a Doctor of the Civil Law or of the Law of Moses; but as we may learn from Paul's words that he was a poor man and needed the help of others, it is probable that he belonged to the same rank with Apollo, that is, an expounder of the Law of God among the Jews. It more

799. Gundry, *Commentary on First and Second Timothy, Titus*, pp. 72-3.

frequently happens that such persons are in want of the necessaries of life than those who conduct causes in civil courts. I have said that Zenas's poverty may be inferred from the words of Paul, because the expression, conduct him, means here to supply him with the means of accomplishing his journey, as is evident from what follows.

14 *And let ours also learn to excel in good works.* That the Cretans, on whom he lays this burden, may not complain of being loaded with the expense, he reminds them that they must not be unfruitful, and that therefore they must be warmly exhorted to be zealous in good works. But of this mode of expression we have already spoken. Whether, therefore, he enjoins them to excel in good works, or to assign the highest rank to good works, he means that it is useful for them to have an opportunity afforded for exercising liberality, that they may not 'be unfruitful' on this ground, that here is no opportunity, or that it is not demanded by necessity. What follows has been already explained in the other Epistles.[800]

800. Calvin, 'Commentaries on the Epistle to Titus', *Calvin's Commentaries*, vol. 21, pp. 343-4.

Appendix 1

People in Paul's Letters
By Reference to Their Appearance in Each NT Book

MARK	Rufus 15:21
ACTS	Alexander 19:33ff. Apollos 18:24-19:1 Aquila 18:18, 19, 26 Aristarchus 19:29; 20:4; 27:2 Barnabas 4:36-7; 9:27; 11:22-30; 12:25; 13:1-2, 43, 46, 50; 14:12-14, 20; 15:2, 12, 22, 25, 26, 35-9 Crispus 18:8 Erastus 19:22 Eunice 16:11 Gaius Titius Justus 18:7 James 15:13; 21:18 Jason 17:5-9 Mark 12:12, 25; 13:13; 15:37-9 Prisca 18:18, 19, 26 Silvanus 15:22-40; 16:19-40; 17:1-16; 18:5 Sosipater 20:4 Sosthenes 18:17 Timothy 16:1-3; 17:14-5; 18:5; 19:22; 20:4 Trophimus 20:4; 21:29 Tychicus 20:4
ROMANS	Ampliatus 16:8 Andronicus 16:7 Apelles 16:10

Romans cont.	**Aquila** 16:3-5 **Aristobulus** 16:10 **Asyncritus** 16:14 **Epaenetas** 16:5 **Erastus** 16:23 **Gaius Titius Justus** 16:23 **Hermas** 16: 14 **Hermes** 16:14 **Herodion** 16:11 **Jason** 16:21 **Julia** 16:15 **Junia** 16:7 **Lucius** 16:21 **Miriam** 16:6 **Narcissus** 16:11 **Nereus and his Sister** 16:15 **Olympas** 16:15 **Patrobas** 16:14 **Persis** 16:12 **Philologus** 16:15 **Phlegon** 16:14 **Phoebe** 16:1, 2 **Prisca** 16:3-5 **Quartus** 16:2 **Rufus and his Mother** 16:13 **Sosipater** 16:21 **Stachys** 16:9 **Tertius** 16:22 **Timothy** 16:21 **Tryphaena** 16:12 **Tryphosa** 16:12 **Urbanus** 16:9
1 Corinthians	**Achaicus** 16:17, 18 **Apollos** 1:12; 3:4-6; 3:22; 4:6; 16:12 **Aquila** 16:19

1 CORINTHIANS CONT.	**Barnabas** 9:6 **Cephas** 1:12; 3:22; 9:5; 15:5 **Chloe** 1:11 **Crispus** 1:14 **Fortunatus** 16:17-18 **Gaius Titius Justus** 1 Cor. 1:14 **James** 15:7 **Prisca** 16:19 **Sosthenes** 1:1 **Stephanas** 1:16; 16:15-8 **Timothy** 4:16-17; 16:10-11
2 CORINTHIANS	**Aretas IV** 11:32 **Silvanus** 1:19 **Timothy** 1:1, 19 **Titus** 2:13; 7:6, 14; 8:6, 16-17, 23; 12:18
GALATIANS	**Barnabas** 2:1, 9, 13 **Cephas** 1:18; 2:7-14 **James** 1:18-19; 2:9, 12 **John** 2:9 **Titus** 2:1, 3
EPHESIANS	**Tychicus** 6:21-2
PHILIPPIANS	**Clement** 4:3 **Epaphroditus** 2:25-30; 4:18 **Euodia** 4:2-3 **Suntuche** 4:2-3 **Syzygus** 4:3 **Timothy** 1:1; 2:19
COLOSSIANS	**Archippus** 4:17 **Aristarchus** 4:10-11 **Barnabas** 4:10 **Demas** 4:14

COLOSSIANS CONT.	**Epaphras** 1:7, 8; 4:12, 13 **Justus** 4:10-11 **Luke** 4:14 **Mark** 4:10 **Nympha** 4:15 **Onesimus** 4:19 **Timothy** 1:1 **Tychicus** 4:7-9
1 THESSALONIANS	**Silvanus** 1:1 **Timothy** 1:1
2 THESSALONIANS	**Silvanus** 1:1 **Timothy** 1:1
1 TIMOTHY	**Alexander** 1:19, 20 **Eunice** 1:5 **Hymenaeus** 1:19-20 **Lois** 1:5 **Pontius Pilate** 6:13 **Timothy** 1:3, 18
2 TIMOTHY	**Alexander** 4: 14-15 **Aquila** 4:19 **Carpus** 4:13 **Claudia** 4:21 **Crescens** 4:10 **Demas** 4:9, 10 **Erastus** 4:20 **Eubulus** 4:21 **Eunice** 1:5; 3:15 **Hermogenes** 1:15 **Humenaeus** 2:17-18 **Linus** 4:21 **Lois** 1:5; 3:15 **Luke** 4:11

2 TIMOTHY CONT.	**Mark** 4:11 **Onesiphorus** 1:16-18; 4:19 **Philetus** 2:17 **Phygelus** 1:15 **Prisca** 4:19 **Pudens** 4:21 **Timothy** 1:1-2, 5; 4:9, 11, 13, 15, 21 **Titus** 4:10 **Trophimus** 4:20 **Tychicus** 4:12
TITUS	**Apollos** 3:13 **Artemas** 3:12 **Titus** 1:4; 3:12 **Tychicus** 3:12 **Zenas** 3:13
PHILEMON	**Apphia** 2 **Archippus** 2 **Aristarchus** 23-4 **Demas** 24 **Luke** 23-4 **Onesimus** 10-21 **Philemon** 1 **Timothy** 1
HEBREWS	**Timothy** 13:23
1 PETER	**Mark** 5:13 **Silvanus** 5:12

Appendix 2

People in Paul's Letters
New Testament References to Each Person

Achaicus	1 Cor. 16:15-18
Alexander	1 Tim. 1:19, 20
Alexander	2 Tim. 4: 14-15
Ampliatus	Rom. 16:8
Andronicus	Rom. 16:7
Apelles	Rom. 16:10
Apollos	Acts 18:24-19:1; 1 Cor. 1:12; 3:4-6; 3:22; 4:6, 16:12; Titus 3:13
Apphia	Philem. 2
Aquila	Acts 18:18-19, 26; Rom. 16:3-5; 1 Cor. 16:19; 2 Tim. 4:19
Archippus	Col. 4:17; Philem. 2
Aretas IV	2 Cor. 11:32
Aristarchus	Acts 19:29; 20:4; 27:2; Col. 4:10, 11; Philem. 23-4
Aristobulus	Rom. 16:10
Artemas	Titus 3:12
Asyncritus	Rom. 16:14
Barnabas	Acts 4:36-7; 9:27; 11:22-30; 12:25; 13:1-2, 43, 46, 50; 14:12-14, 20; 15:2, 12, 22, 25, 26, 35-9; 1 Cor. 9:6; Gal. 2:1, 9, 13; Col. 4:10
Carpus	2 Tim. 4:13
Cephas	1 Cor. 1:12; 3:22; 9:5; 15:5; 1:18; Gal. 2:7-14
Chloe	1 Cor. 1:11

Claudia	2 Tim. 4:21
Clement	Phil. 4:3
Crescens	2 Tim. 4:10
Crispus	Acts 18:8; 1 Cor. 1:14
Demas	Col. 4:14; 2 Tim. 4:9, 10; Philem. 24
Epaenetas	Rom. 16:5
Epaphras	Col. 1:7, 8; 4:12, 13
Epaphroditus	Phil. 2:25-30; 4:18
Erastus	Acts 19:22
Erastus	Rom. 16:23; 2 Tim. 4:20
Eubulus	2 Tim. 4:21
Eunice	Acts 16:11; 1 Tim. 1:5; 2 Tim. 1:5; 3:15
Euodia	Phil. 4:2-3
Fortunatus	1 Cor. 16:17-18
Gaius Titius Justus	Acts 18:7; Rom. 16:23; 1 Cor. 1:14
Hermas	Rom. 16:14
Hermes	Rom. 16:14
Hermogenes	2 Tim. 1:15
Herodion	Rom. 16:11
Hymenaeus	1 Tim. 1:19-20; 2 Tim. 2:17-18
James	Acts 15:13; 21:18; 1 Cor. 15:7; Gal. 1:18-19; 2:9, 12
Jason	Acts 17:5-9; Rom. 16:21
John	Gal. 2:9
Julia	Rom. 16:15
Junia	Rom. 16:7
Justus	Col. 4:10-11
Linus	2 Tim. 4:21
Lois	1 Tim. 1:5; 2 Tim. 1:5; 3:15
Lucius	Rom. 16:21
Luke	Col. 4:14; 2 Tim. 4:11; Philem. 23-4
Mark	Acts 12:12, 25; 13:13; 15:37-9; Col. 4:10; 2 Tim. 4:11; 1 Pet. 5:13

Miriam	Rom. 16:6
Narcissus	Rom. 16:11
Nereus and Sister	Rom. 16:15
Nympha	Col. 4:15
Olympas	Rom. 16:15
Onesimus	Col. 4:19; Philem. 10-21
Onesiphorus	2 Tim. 1:16-18; 4:19
Patrobas	Rom. 16:14
Persis	Rom. 16:12
Philemon	Philem. 1
Philetus	2 Tim. 2:17
Philologus	Rom. 16:15
Phlegon	Rom. 16:14
Phoebe	Rom. 16:1-2
Phygelus	2 Tim. 1: 15
Pontius Pilate	1 Tim. 6:13
Prisca	Acts 18:18, 26; Rom. 16:3-5; 1 Cor. 16:19; 2 Tim. 4:19
Pudens	2 Tim. 4:21
Quartus	Rom. 16:2
Rufus and Mother	Rom. 16:13
Silvanus	Acts 15:22-40; 16:19-40; 17:1-16; 18:5; 2 Cor. 1:19; 1 Thess. 1:1; 2 Thess. 1:1; 1 Pet. 5:12
Sosipater	Acts 20:4; Rom. 16:21
Sosthenes	Acts 18:17; 1 Cor. 1:1
Stachys	Rom. 16:9
Stephanas	1 Cor. 1:16; 16:15-18
Syntyche	Phil. 4:2-3
Syzygus	Phil. 4:3
Tertius	Rom. 16:22
Timothy	Acts 16:1-3; 17:14-5; 18:5; 19:22; 20:4; Rom. 16:21; 1 Cor. 4:16-17; 16:10-11;

	2 Cor. 1:1, 19; Phil. 1:1; 2:19; Col. 1:1; 1 Thess. 1:1; 2 Thess. 1:1; 1 Tim. 1:3, 18; 2 Tim. 1:1-2, 5; 4:9, 11, 13, 15, 21; Philem. 1; Heb. 13:23
Titus	2 Cor. 2:13; 7:6, 14; 8:6, 16-17, 23; 12:18; Gal. 2:1, 3; 2 Tim. 4:10; Titus 1:4; 3:12
Trophimus	Acts 20:4; 21:29; 2 Tim. 4:20
Tryphaena	Rom. 16:12
Tryphosa	Rom. 16:12
Tychicus	Acts 20:4; Eph. 6:21-2; Col. 4:7-9; 2 Tim. 4:12; Titus 3:12
Urbanus	Rom. 16:9
Zenas	Titus 3:13

Bibliography

A *Prayer Book for Australia*, The Anglican Church of Australia. Mulgrave, Vic: Broughton Books, 1999.

Adams, E. *The Earliest Christian Meeting Places: Almost Exclusively Houses?* Library of New Testament Studies 450. London: Bloomsbury T. and T. Clark, 2016.

Adelman, J., E. Pollard and R. Tignor. *Worlds Together, Worlds Apart*, Concise edition, vol. 1. New York: W. W. Norton, 2015.

Aldred, T. 'Philippians 4:2-3: An Alternative View of the Euodia-Syntyche Debate.' *Priscilla Papers* vol. 33, no. 44, 2019.

Alexander, L. C. A. 'Chronology of Paul' in *Dictionary of Paul and His Letters*. G. F. Hawthorne, R. P. Martin and D. G. Reid eds. Downers Grove, IL: InterVarsity Press, 1993.

Aus, R. 'Three Pillars and Three Patriarchs: A Proposal Concerning Gal. 2:9.' *ZNW* no. 70, 1979.

Barclay, W. *The Letter to the Romans*. The Daily Study Bible. Edinburgh: St Andrew Press, 1957.

_____ *The New Testament: A New Translation by William Barclay*. Glasgow: William Collins, 1968.

_____ *The Letters to Timothy, Titus and Philemon*. The Daily Study Bible. Revised edition. Edinburgh: St Andrew Press, 1975.

Barnett, P. *The Second Epistle to the Corinthians*. NICNT. Grand Rapids: Eerdmans, 1997.

_____ 'Galatians and Earliest Christianity.' *RTR* vol. 59, no. 3, 2000.

Barrett, C. K. *A Commentary on the Epistle to the Romans*. Black's NT Commentaries. London: A. and C. Black, 1957.

Bauckham, J. R. *Jude, 2 Peter*. WBC. Waco, TX: Word Books, 1983.

_____ 'James and the Jerusalem Church' in *The Book of Acts in its First Century Setting, vol. 4: The Book of Acts in its Palestinian Setting*. B. W. Winter ed. Grand Rapids: Eerdmans, 1995.

Beitzel, B. J. *The Moody Atlas of the Bible*. Chicago: Moody Publishers, 2009.

Belleville, L. 'Ιουνιαν ... επίσημοι έν τοίς άποστόλοις: A Re-examination of Romans 16.7 in Light of Primary Source Materials.' *NTS* vol. 51, no. 2, 2005.

Bennema, C. 'The Ethnic Conflict in Early Christianity: An Appraisal of Bauckham's Proposal on the Antioch Crisis and the Jerusalem Council.' *JETS* vol. 56, no. 4, 2013.

Bernier, J. 'When Paul Met Sergius: An Assessment of Douglas Campbell's Pauline Chronology for the Years 36 to 37.' *JBL* vol. 138, no. 4, 2019.

Bird, M. F. *Colossians and Philemon*. A New Covenant Commentary. Eugene, OR: Cascade Books, 2009.

_____ and N. K. Gupta. *Philippians*. New Cambridge Bible Commentary. Cambridge: Cambridge University Press, 2020.

Blaiklock, E. M. *Romans*. Scripture Union Bible Study Books. Grand Rapids: Eerdmans, 1971.

_____ *Commentary on the New Testament*. London: Hodder and Stoughton, 1977.

Bock, D. L. *Acts*. BECNT. Grand Rapids: Baker Books, 2007.

Bolt, P. and M. Thompson eds. *The Gospel to the Nations: Perspectives on Paul's Mission*. Leicester: Apollos, 2000.

Book of Common Prayer (Anglican).

Bowen, C. R. 'Are Paul's Prison Letters from Ephesus?' *AJT* vol. 24, no. 1, 1920.

_____ 'Are Paul's Prison Letters from Ephesus? (Conclude).' *AJT* vol. 24, no. 2, 1920.

Branch, R. G. 'Female leadership as demonstrated by Phoebe: An interpretation of Paul's words introducing Phoebe to the saints in Rome.' *In die Skriflig* vol. 53, no. 2, 2019.

Brindle, W. A. '"To the Jew First": Rhetoric, Strategy, History, or Theology?' *BS* vol. 159, no. 634, 2002.

Brookins, T. A. and B. W. Longenecker, *1 Corinthians 1–9: A Handbook on the Greek Text*. BHGNT. Waco, TX: Baylor University Press, 2016.

_____ *1 Corinthians 10–16: A Handbook on the Greek Text*. BHGNT. Waco, TX: Baylor University Press, 2016.

Bruce, F. F. *The Epistle of Paul to the Romans*. TDNC. Leicester: InterVarsity Press, 1963.

_____ *Paul: Apostle of the Free Spirit*. revised edition 1980. Exeter: Paternoster Press, 1977.

_____ *Peter, Stephen, James & John: Studies in Non-Pauline Christianity*. Grand Rapids: Eerdmans, 1979.

_____ *1 and 2 Thessalonians*. WBC. Colombia, 1982.

_____ *The Epistles to the Colossians, to Philemon, and to the Ephesians*. NICNT. Grand Rapids: Eerdmans, 1984.

_____ *The Pauline Circle*. Grand Rapids: Eerdmans, 1985.

_____ *The Book of the Acts*. NICNT. Grand Rapids: Eerdmans, 1988.

Burer, M. H. 'ἘΠΙΣΗΜΟΙ ἘΝ ΤΟΙΣ ἈΠΟΣΤΟΛΟΙΣ in Rom. 16:7 as "Well Known to the Apostles": Further Defense and New Evidence,' JETS 58.4 (2015).

Cadwallader, A. H. 'Tertius in the Margins: A Critical Appraisal of the Secretary Hypothesis.' *NTS* vol. 64, no. 3, 2018.

Calvin, J. *Calvin's Commentaries*. 22 volumes. translated by W. Pringle. Grand Rapids: Baker Books, 1979.

Campbell, C. R. *Colossians and Philemon: A Handbook on the Greek Text*. BHGNT. Waco, TX: Baylor University Press, 2013.

Campbell, D. A. 'An Anchor for Pauline Chronology: Paul's Flight from the "Ethnarch of King Aretas".' *JBL* vol. 121, no. 2, 2002.

_____ *Framing Paul: An Epistolary Biography*. Grand Rapids: Eerdmans, 2014.

Capes, D. B., R. Reeves and E. R. Richards. *Rediscovering Paul: An Introduction to His World, Letters and Theology*. Downers Grove, IL: InterVarsity Press Academic, 2017.

Carson, D. A., D. J. Moo and L. L. Morris eds. *An Introduction to the New Testament*. Grand Rapids: Zondervan, 1992.

Ciampa, R. E. and B. S. Rosner. *The first letter to the Corinthians*. PNTC. Grand Rapids: Eerdmans, 2010.

Clarke, A. D. '"Refresh the Hearts of the Saints": A Unique Pauline Context.' *TynBul* vol. 47, no. 2, 1996.

_____ *Secular and Christian Leadership in Corinth: A Socio-Historical and Exegetical Study of 1 Corinthians 1-6*. Leiden: E. J. Bril, 1993.

_____ 'Rome and Italy' in *The Book of Acts in its First Century Setting*. D. W. J. Gill and C. Gempf eds. vol. 2. Grand Rapids: Eerdmans, 1994.

Cockerill, G. L. *The Epistle to the Hebrews*. NICNT. Grand Rapids: Eerdmans, 2012.

Cohick, L. H. *The Letter to the Ephesians*. NICNT. Grand Rapids: Eerdmans, 2020.

Cole, R. A. *The Epistle of Paul to the Galatians*. TNTC. Leicester: InterVarsity Press, reprint 1983.

Coleman-Norton, P. R. *Studies in Roman Economic and Social History*. Princeton: Princeton University Press, 1951.

Collins, R. F. *1 & 2 Timothy and Titus*. New Testament Library. Louisville: Westminster John Knox, 2002.

Cowper, W. 'God moves in a mysterious way.' Methodist Hymn Book with Tunes, No. 503. 34th edition 1962. London: Methodist Conference Office, 1935.

Cranfield, C. E. B. *The Epistle to the Romans*. Vol. 1. ICC. Edinburgh: T. and T. Clark, 1975.

_____ *The Epistle to the Romans*. Vol. 2. ICC. Edinburgh: T. and T. Clark, 1979.

Davids, P. H. *The Letters of 2 Peter and Jude*. PNTC. Grand Rapids: Eerdmans, 2006.

_____ *2 Peter and Jude: A Handbook on the Greek Text.* BHGNT. Waco, TX: Baylor University Press, 2011.

_____ *A Theology of James, Peter and Jude.* Biblical Theology of the New Testament. Grand Rapids: Zondervan, 2014.

Deissmann, A. *Paul: A Study in Social and Religious History.* 2nd edition. Translated by W. E. Wilson. New York: Harper, 1927.

den Dulk, M. 'Aquila and Apollos: Acts 18 in Light of Ancient Ethnic Stereotypes.' *JBL* vol. 139, no. 1, 2020.

Dodd, C. H. *The Epistle of Paul to the Romans*. London: Hodder and Stoughton, 1932.

Donfried, K. P. 'Chronology: New Testament' in *Anchor Bible Dictionary.* D. N. Freedman, G. A. Herion, D. F. Graf & J. D. Pleins eds. New York: Doubleday, 1996.

Doole, J. A. 'Was Timothy in Prison with Paul?' *NTS* vol. 65, no. 1, 2019.

Dubis, M. *1 Peter: A Handbook on the Greek Text*. BHGNT. Waco, TX: Baylor University Press, 2010.

Duff, N. J. 'The ordination of women: Biblical perspectives.' *Theology Today* vol. 73, no. 2, 2016.

Dumbrell, W. J. *Romans.* A New Covenant Commentary. Eugene, OR: Wipf and Stock, 2005.

_____ *Galatians.* A New Covenant Commentary. Blackwood, SA: New Creation Publications, 2006.

Duncan, G. S. *The Epistle of Paul to the Galatians*. MNTC. London: Hodder and Stoughton, 1934.

Dunn, J. D. G. 'The Relationship Between Paul and Jerusalem According to Galatians 1-2.' *NTS* vol. 28, no. 4, 1982.

_____ *Romans 9-16*. WBC. Dallas, TX: Word Books, 1988.

_____ *The Epistles to the Colossians and Philippians: A Commentary on the Greek Text.* NIGTC. Grand Rapids: Eerdmans, 1996.

Eastman, D. L. 'Paul: An Outline of His Life' in *All Things to All Cultures: Paul among Jews, Greeks, and Romans.* Mark Harding and Alanna Nobbs eds. Grand Rapids: Eerdmans, 2013.

Elliott, S. S. '"Thanks, but No Thanks": Tact, Persuasion, and the Negotiation of Power in Paul's Letter to Philemon.' *NTS* vol. 57, no. 1, 2010.

Ellis, E. E. 'Paul and his Co-workers.' *NTS* vol. 17, no. 4, 1971.

_____ *Pauline Theology: Ministry and Society.* Grand Rapids: Eerdmans, 1989.

_____ *Prophecy and Hermeneutic in Early Christianity.* Grand Rapids: Baker, 1993.

Elmer, I. J. 'I, Tertius: Secretary or Co-author of Romans,' *Australian Biblical Review* vol. 56, 2008.

Eusebius Pamphilius, *Ecclesiastical History.* 8th edition. New York: Dayton and Saxton, 1842.

Fee, G. D. *Paul's Letter to the Philippians.* NICNT. Grand Rapids: Eerdmans, 1995.

_____ *1 & 2 Timothy, Titus.* Peabody, MA: Hendrickson, 1998.

_____ *The First and Second Letters to the Thessalonians.* NICNT. Grand Rapids: Eerdmans, 2009.

_____ *The First Epistle to the Corinthians.* NICNT. Grand Rapids: Eerdmans, 2014.

Fellows, R. G. 'Name Giving by Paul and the Destination of Acts.' *TynBul* vol. 67, no. 2, 2016.

Filson, F. V. 'The Significance of the Early House Churches.' *JBL* vol. 58, no. 2, 1939.

Finger, R. H. 'Phoebe: Role model for leaders.' *Daughters of Zion* vol. 14, no. 2, 1988.

Fitzmyer, J. A. *The Letter to Philemon.* New York: Doubleday, 2000.

_____ *First Corinthians: A New Translation with Introduction and Commentary.* The Anchor Yale Bible. New Haven, CT: Yale University Press, 2008.

Foulkes, F. *Ephesians*. TNTC. Leicester: InterVarsity Press, 1956.

Frayer-Griggs, D. 'The Beasts at Ephesus and the Cult of Artemis.' *HTR* vol. 106, no. 4, 2013.

Friberg, T., B. Friberg, and N. F. Miller. *Analytical Lexicon of the Greek New Testament*. Grand Rapids: Baker Books, 2000.

Garland, D. E. *The NIV Application Commentary: Colossians and Philemon*. Grand Rapids: Zondervan, 1998.

Garnsey, P. and R. Saller. *The Roman Empire: Economy, Society and Culture*. Berkeley: California University Press, 1987.

Gehring, R. W. *House Church and Mission: The Importance of Household Structures in Early Christianity*. Peabody, MA: Hendrickson, 2004.

Geldenhuys, N. *Commentary on the Gospel of Luke*. London: Marshall, Morgan & Scott, 1950.

Gill, D. W. J. 'Macedonia' in Gill, D. W. J. and C. Gempf eds. *The Book of Acts in its First Century Setting*. vol. 2. Grand Rapids: Eerdmans, 1994.

_____ and C. Gempf eds. *The Book of Acts in its First Century Setting*. vol. 2. Grand Rapids: Eerdmans, 1994.

Goodman, M. *Rome and Jerusalem: The Clash of Ancient Civilisations*. New York: Vintage Books, 2007.

Goodrich, J. K. 'Erastus, Quaestor of Corinth: The Administrative Rank of ὁ οικονόμος της πόλεως (Rom. 16.23) in an Achaean Colony.' *NTS* vol. 56, no. 1, 2009.

_____ 'Erastus of Corinth (Romans 16.23): Responding to Recent Proposals on his Rank, Status, and Faith.' *NTS* vol. 57, no. 4, 2011.

Goodspeed, E. J. 'Gaius Titius Justus.' *JBL* vol. 69, no. 4, 1950.

Graham, D. 'The Placement of Paul's Composition of 1 Corinthians in Troas: A Fresh Approach,' *Themelios* vol. 46, no. 3, 2021.

Grant, R. M. 'Hellenistic Elements in 1 Corinthians' in *Early Christian Origins: Studies in Honour of Harold R. Willoughby*. A. Wikgren ed. Chicago: Quadrangle Books, 1961.

Graves, D. E. *Biblical Archaeology Volume 1: An Introduction with Recent Discoveries that Support the Reliability of the Bible*. Moncton, NB, Canada: Electronic Christian Media, 2015.

Green, G. L. *The Letters to the Thessalonians*. PNTC. Grand Rapids: Eerdmans, 2002.

_____ *Jude and 2 Peter*. BECNT. Grand Rapids: Baker Academic, 2008.

Grosheide, F. W. *Commentary on the First Epistle to the Corinthians*. Reprinted 1984. Grand Rapids: Eerdmans, 1953.

Grudem, W. *1 Peter*. TNTC. Leicester: IVP, 1988.

Gundry, R. H. *Commentary on First and Second Timothy, Titus*. Grand Rapids: Baker Academic, 2010.

Guthrie, D. *New Testament Introduction*. Downers Grove, IL: InterVarsity Press, 1970.

_____ *The Pastoral Epistles*. TNTC. Reprinted 1983. Leicester: InterVarsity Press, 1957.

Haldane, R. *An Exposition of the Epistle to the Romans*. Reprinted 1958. Grand Rapids: Evangelical Press, 1819.

Harman, A. M. *Isaiah: A Covenant to be Kept for the Sake of the Church*. Fearn: Christian Focus, 2005.

Harris, M. J. *Slave of Christ: A New Testament Metaphor for Total Devotion to Christ*. New Studies in Biblical Theology 8. Downers Grove, IL: InterVarsity Press, 1999.

_____ *The Second Epistle to the Corinthians: A Commentary on the Greek Text*. Grand Rapids: Eerdmans, 2005.

_____ *Colossians and Philemon*. Exegetical Guide to the Greek New Testament. Nashville, TN: B&H Academic, 2010.

Harvey, J. D. *Exegetical Guide to the Greek New Testament*. Nashville, TN: B&H Academic, 2017.

Hawthorne, G. F., R. P. Martin and D. G. Reid eds. *Dictionary of Paul and His Letters*. Downers Grove, IL: InterVarsity Press, 1993.

Hemer, C. J. 'Observations on Pauline Chronology' in *Pauline Studies: Essays presented to F. F. Bruce*. D. A. Hagner and M. J. Harris eds. Grand Rapids: Eerdmans, 1980.

_____ *The Book of Acts in the Setting of Hellenistic History*. WUNT no. 49. Tubingen: J. C. B. Mohr, 1989.

Hempel, C. G. *Philosophy of Natural Science*. Englewood Cliffs, NJ: Routledge and Keegan Paul, 1961.

Hendriksen, W. *I and II Thessalonians*. NTC. Grand Rapids: Baker Book House, 1955.

_____ *Philippians, Colossians and Philemon*. NTC. Reprinted 1981. Edinburgh: Banner of Truth, 1962.

Hengel, M. *The Pre-Christian Paul*. Translated by J. Bowden. London: SCM Press, 1991.

Henry, M. *Commentary on the Whole Bible: Genesis to Revelation*. L. F. Church ed. Grand Rapids, MI: Zondervan, 1961.

_____ *The Complete Works of Matthew Henry: Treatises, Sermons, and Tracts*. 2 volumes. Grand Rapids: Baker Books, 1979.

Hock, R. F. 'Paul's Tentmaking and the Problem of His Social Class.' *JBL* vol. 97, no. 4, 1978.

_____. *The Social Context of Paul's Ministry: Tentmaking and Apostleship*. Philadelphia: Fortress Press, 1980.

Hodge, C. *Romans*. Geneva Series of Commentaries. Reprinted 1975. Edinburgh: Banner of Truth, 1864.

Hooker, M. D. '"Beyond the Things Which Are Written": An Examination of 1 Cor. 4.6.' *NTS* vol. 44, no. 2, 1963-64.

Horrell, D. G. *The Social Ethos of the Corinthian Correspondence*. Edinburgh: T. and T. Clark, 1996.

House, H. W. *Chronological and Background Charts of the New Testament*. Grand Rapids: Zondervan, 2009.

Hughes, R. K. *Colossians and Philemon*. Westchester, IL: Crossway, 1989.

_____ *2 Corinthians*. Westchester, IL: Crossway, 2006.

_____ *Philippians*. Wheaton, IL: Crossway, 2007.

Hurd, J. C. Jr. *The Origin of 1 Corinthians*. New York: Seabury, 1965.

_____ 'Pauline Theology and Pauline Chronology' in *Christian History and Interpretation: Studies Presented to John Knox*. W. R. Farmer, C. F. D. Moule and R. R. Niebuhr eds. Cambridge: Cambridge University Press, 1967.

Huttar, D. 'Did Paul Call Andronicus an Apostle in Romans 16:7?' JETS 52.4 (2009).

Hylen, S. E. 'Women διάκονοι and Gendered Norms of Leadership.' *JBL* vol. 138, no. 3, 2019.

Jeremias, J. *Jerusalem in the Time of Jesus*. London: SCM Press, 1969.

Jewett, R. *Dating Paul's Life*. London: SCM Press, 1979.

_____ *Romans: A commentary*. Hermeneia. Minneapolis, MN: Fortress Press, 2007.

Jipp, J. W. *Reading Acts*. Eugene, OR: Cascade Books, 2018.

Josephus, F. *Jewish Antiquities, Books 18-19*. Translated by L. H. Feldman. Loeb Classical Library, 1965.

Judge, E. A. *The social pattern of the Christian groups in the first century: some prolegomena to the study of New Testament ideas of social obligation*. London: Tyndale Press, 1960.

Käsemann, E. *Essays on New Testament Themes*. London: SCM Press, 1964.

_____ *Commentary on Romans*. Translated by G. W. Bromiley. London: SCM Press, 1980.

Keener, C. S. *Paul, Women & Wives*. Massachusetts: Hendrickson, 1993.

_____. *Acts: An Exegetical Commentary.* 4 volumes. Grand Rapids: Baker Academic, 2012-15.

_____. *Galatians: A Commentary.* Grand Rapids: Baker Academic, 2019.

Kidd, R. M. *Paul's Prison Epistles: Paul and the Philippians.* Third Millennium Ministries, 2012. See Thirdmill, *www.thirdmill.org.*

Kirkland, A. 'The Beginnings of Christianity in the Lycus Valley: An Exercise in Historical Reconstruction.' *Neotestamentica* vol. 29, no. 1, 1995.

Kittel, G. ed. *Theological Dictionary of the New Testament.* Grand Rapids: Eerdmans, 1964.

Klauck H.-J. et al. eds. *Encyclopaedia of the Bible and its Reception*. Berlin: de Gruyter, 2009.

Knox, J. *Philemon among the Letters of Paul*. Nashville, TN: Abingdon Press, 1959.

_____ *Chapters in a Life of Paul*. Macon, GA: Mercer University Press, 2000.

Koester, H. *Introduction to the New Testament, vol. 2: History and Literature of Early Christianity.* second edition. New York: Walter de Gruyter, 2000.

Kohlenberger, J. R. III, E. W. Goodrick and J. A. Swanson eds. *The Greek English Concordance to the New Testament with the New International Version*. Grand Rapids: Zondervan, 1997.

Köstenberger, A. J. 'Gender Passages in the NT: Hermeneutical Fallacies Critiqued.' *WTJ* vol. 56, no. 2, 1994.

_____ 'Women in the Pauline Mission' in *The Gospel to the Nations*. P. Bolt and M. Thompson eds. Downers Grove, IL: InterVarsity Press, 2000.

_____ *Commentary on 1-2 Timothy and Titus*. Biblical Theology for Christian Proclamation. Nashville, TN: Holman, 2017.

Kruse, C. G. *2 Corinthians: An Introduction and Commentary.* TNCT. Downers Grove, IL: InterVarsity Press, 2015.

Lampe, P. 'The Roman Christians in Romans 16' in *The Romans Debate*, K. P. Donfried ed. Revised and expanded edition. Peabody, MA: Hendrickson, 1977.

Larkin, W. J. Jr. *Ephesians: A Handbook on the Greek Text*. BHGNT. Waco, TX: Baylor University Press, 2009.

Lightfoot, J. B. *Saint Paul's Epistle to the Philippians*. Reprinted 1908. London: MacMillan, 1898.

Lin, Y-J. 'Junia: An Apostle before Paul.' *JBL* vol. 139, no. 1, 2020.

Lock, W. *A Critical and Exegetical Commentary on the Pastoral Epistles*. ICC. Edinburgh: T&T Clark, reprint 2000.

Longenecker, R. N. *Galatians*. WBC. Dallas, TX: Word Books, 1990.

_____ *The Epistle to the Romans*. NIGTC. Grand Rapids: Eerdmans, 2016.

Lucas, R. C. *The Message of Colossians and Philemon*. TBST. Leicester: InterVarsity Press, 1980.

Lüdemann, G. *Paul, Apostle to the Gentiles: Studies in Chronology*. Minneapolis: Fortress Press, 1984.

Luther, M. *Commentary on the Epistle to the Romans*. Translated by J. T. Mueller. Grand Rapids: Kregel Publications, 1976.

MacArthur, J. *1 and 2 Thessalonians*. MacArthur New Testament Commentary. Chicago: Moody Publishers, 2002.

MacGillivray, E. D. 'Romans 16:2, προστάτις/προστάτης, and the Application of Reciprocal Relationships to New Testament Texts.' *NTest* vol. 53, no. 2, 2011.

Machen, J. G. 'Westminster Theological Seminary: Its Purpose and Plan' in *J. Gresham Machen: Selected Shorter Writings*. D. G. Hart ed. Phillipsburg, NJ: P & R Publishing, 2004.

Manuell, G. *Gender Wars in Christianity*. Brisbane: Connor Court, 2018.

_____ 'Prisca and Aquila: Exemplary Models of Gospel Obedience.' *RTR* vol. 80, no. 3, 2021.

_____ 'Apollos in 1 Corinthians: Praised by Paul but Defamed by Translators.' *Evangelical Action* 4, 2021.

_____ *The Letter of Jude: A Wake-Up Call to Christians in the Twenty-First Century*. Revised edition. Sydney: Tulip Publishing, 2022.

Marshall, I. H. *The Acts of the Apostles*. TNTC. Leicester: InterVarsity Press, 1980.

_____ *A Fresh Look at the Acts of the Apostles*. Sheffield, UK: JSOT Press, 1992.

_____ with P. N. Towner. *A Critical and Exegetical Commentary on the Pastoral Epistles*. ICC. Edinburgh: T. and T. Clark, 1999.

Marshall, P. 'Enmity in Corinth: Social Conventions in Paul's Relations with the Corinthians.' *WUNT* 2. Reihe 23, 1987.

Martin, D. B. *Slavery as Salvation: The Metaphor of Slavery in Pauline Christianity*. New Haven, NJ: Yale University Press, 1990.

_____ 'Review Essay: Justin J. Meggitt, Paul, Poverty and Survival.' *JSNT* vol. 24, no. 2, 2001.

Martin, R. P. *The Epistle of Paul to the Philippians: An Introduction and Commentary*. TNTC. Reprint 1983. Leicester: InterVarsity Press, 1959.

_____ *2 Corinthians*. WBC. Grand Rapids: Zondervan, 2014.

Mathew, S. *Women in the Greetings of Romans 16.1-16: A Study of Mutuality and Women's Ministry in the Letter to the Romans*. Library of New Testament Studies 471. London: T. and T. Clark, 2014.

McCarty, V. K. 'Recipe for Reconciliation: Paul's Charge to Syntyche & Euodia in Phil. 4:2-7.' *International Congregational Journal* vol. 14, no. 1, 2015.

McKnight, S. *The Letter to Philemon*. NICNT. Grand Rapids: Eerdmans, 2017.

_____ *The Letter to the Colossians*. NICNT. Grand Rapids: Eerdmans, 2018.

Meeks, W. A. *The First Urban Christians: The Social World of the Apostle Paul.* New Haven, CT: Yale University Press, 2003.

Meggitt, J. J. 'Response to Martin and Theissen.' *JSNT* vol. 24, no. 1, 2001.

Michael, J. H. *The Epistle of Paul to the Philippians.* MNTC. New York: Harper and Brothers Publishers, 1928.

Mitchell, M. M. *Paul and the Rhetoric of Reconciliation: An Exegetical Investigation of the Language and Composition of 1 Corinthians.* Louisville: Westminster John Knox Press, 1992.

Moffatt, J. *The First Epistle of Paul to the Corinthians.* MNTC. reprinted 1947. London: Hodder and Stoughton, 1938.

Moo, D. J. *The Letters to the Colossians and to Philemon.* PNTC. Grand Rapids: Eerdmans, 2008.

_____ *Galatians.* BECNT. Grand Rapids: Baker Academic, 2013.

_____ *The Epistle to the Romans.* NICNT. Grand Rapids: Eerdmans, 2018.

Morris, L. L. *The First Epistle of Paul to the Corinthians.* TNTC. Leicester: InterVarsity Press, 1983.

_____ *The Epistle to the Romans.* Grand Rapids: Eerdmans, 1988.

_____ *Expository Reflections on the Letter to the Ephesians.* Grand Rapids: Baker Books, 1994.

_____ *Galatians: Paul's Charter of Christian Freedom.* Leicester: InterVarsity Press, 1996.

Motyer, J. A. *The Message of Philippians.* TBST. Leicester: InterVarsity Press, 1984.

Moule, H. C. G. *Colossians and Philemon Studies.* London: Pickering and Inglis, 1902.

_____ *The Second Epistle to Timothy: Lessons in Faith and Holiness.* The Devotional Commentary Series. London: Religious Tract Society, 1905.

Mowczko, M. 'Wealthy Women in the First-Century Roman World and in the Church.' *Priscilla Papers* vol. 32, no. 3, 2018.

Murray, J. *The Epistle to the Romans*. NICNT. Reprinted 1973. Grand Rapids: Eerdmans, 1959.

Myllykoski, M. 'James the Just in History and Tradition: Perspectives of Past and Present Scholarship (Part 1).' *Currents in Biblical Research* vol. 5, no. 1, 2006.

_____ 'James the Just in History and Tradition: Perspectives of Past and Present Scholarship (Part 2).' *Currents in Biblical Research* vol. 6, no. 1, 2007.

Neudorfer, H.-W. *Der zweite Brief des Paulus an Timotheus*. Historisch-theologische Auslegung. Witten: Brockhaus, 2017.

Neuhaus, D. M. 'Paul: A Tentmaker.' in *Saint Paul: Educator to Faith and Love*. M. Ferrero and R. Spataro eds. Jerusalem: Studium Theologicum Salesianum, 2008.

Ng, E. Y. L. 'Phoebe as *Prostatis*.' *Trinity Journal* vol. 25, no. 1, 2004.

_____ 'Was Junia(s) in Rom. 16:7 a Female Apostle? And So What?' JETS 63.3 (2020).

Nobbs, A. '"Beloved Brothers" in the New Testament and Early Christian World' in *The New Testament in Its First Century Setting: Essays on Context and Background in Honour of B. W. Winter on his 65th Birthday*. P. J. Williams *et al.* eds. Grand Rapids: Eerdmans, 2004.

O'Brien, P. T. *The Epistle to the Philippians: A Commentary on the Greek Text*. Carlisle, UK: Paternoster Press, 1991.

Oden, T. C. *First and Second Timothy and Titus: Interpretation: A Bible Commentary for Teaching and Preaching*. Reprinted 2012. Louisville: Westminster John Knox Press, 1989.

Ogg, G. *The Chronology of the Life of Paul*. London: Epworth, 1968.

Olivers, T. 'The God of Abraham praise.' The Methodist Hymn Book with Tunes. No. 21. 34th ed. 1962. London: Methodist Conference Office, 1933.

Osiek, C. 'The Politics of Patronage and the Politics of Kinship: The Meeting of the Ways.' *BTB* vol. 39, no. 3, 2009.

Parsons, M. C. and M. M. Culy. Acts: A *Handbook on the Greek Text*. BHGNT. Waco, TX: Baylor University Press, 2003.

Perkins, L. J. *The Pastoral Letters: A Handbook on the Greek Text*. BHGNT. Waco, TX: Baylor University Press, 2017.

Peterson, D. G. *Commentary on Romans*. Biblical Theology for Christian Proclamation. Nashville, TN: B&H Publishing, 2017.

Pfitzner, V. C. 'Paul and the *Agon* Motif.' *NTest* Supplement 16. Leiden: E. J. Brill, 1967.

Piper, J. *The Chronology of the New Testament*. See Desiring God, *http://www.desiringgod.org/articles/the-chronology-of-the-new-testament*.

_____ and W. Grudem eds. *Recovering Biblical Manhood and Womanhood: A Response to Evangelical Feminism*. reprinted 2006. Wheaton IL: Crossway Books, 1991.

_____ 'Exposition or Imposition? How Gospel-Centred Preaching Can Go Wrong.' Sermon delivered on May 14 2020. https://www.desiringgod.org/messages/exposition-or-imposition

Pollock, J. *The Apostle*. Third edition. London: Hodder and Stoughton, 1987.

Porter, S. E. 'Pauline Authorship and the Pastoral Epistles: Implications for Canon.' *BBR* vol. 5, 1995.

_____ *The Paul of Acts: Essays in Literary Criticism, Rhetoric and Theology. WUNT* 115. Tübingen: Mohr-Siebeck, 1999.

_____ *The Apostle Paul: His Life, Thought, and Letters*. Grand Rapids: Eerdmans, 2016.

_____ and G. P. Fewster eds. *Paul and Pseudepigraphy*. Pauline Studies (PAST 8). Leiden: E. J. Brill, 2013.

Powers, B. W. *First Corinthians: An Exegetical and Explanatory Commentary*. Eugene, OR: Wipf and Stock, 2008.

Preato, D. J. 'Junia, a Female Apostle: An Examination of the Historical Record.' *Priscilla Papers* vol. 33, no. 2, 2019.

Prior, D. *The Message of 1 Corinthians*. TBST. Leicester: InterVarsity Press, 1985.

Prohl, R. C. *Woman in the Church*. Grand Rapids: Eerdmans, 1957.

Quarles, C. L. *Illustrated Life Of Paul*. Nashville, TN: B&H Publishing, 2014.

Ramelli, I. L. E. 'Origen, Greek Philosophy, and the Birth of the Trinitarian Meaning of Hypostasis.' *HTR* vol. 105, no. 3, 2021.

Ramsay, W. M. *St Paul the Traveller and Roman Citizen*. London, Hodder and Stoughton, 1942.

Rengstorf, K. H. '*doulos*.' *TDNT*. G. Kittel ed. vol 2. Grand Rapids: Eerdmans, 1964.

Richards, E. R. *The Secretary in the Letters of Paul*. Tübingen: Mohr-Siebeck, 1991.

_____ *Paul and First-century Letter Writing: Secretaries, Composition and Collection*. Downers Grove, IL: InterVarsity Press, 2004.

Riesner, R. *Paul's Early Period: Chronology, Mission Strategy, Theology*. Grand Rapids: Eerdmans, 1998.

Rist, J. M. *Human Value: A Study in Ancient Philosophical Ethics*. Leiden: E. J. Brill, 1982.

Robinson, B. W. 'An Ephesian Imprisonment of Paul.' *JBL* vol. 29, no. 2, 1910.

Russell, W. B. III. 'An Alternative Suggestion for the Purpose of Romans.' *BS* vol. 145, no. 578, 1988.

Schaff, P. and D. S. Schaff. *History of the Christian Church*. Vol. 1. New York: Charles Scribner's Sons, 1910.

Schreiner, T. R. *1, 2 Peter, Jude*. The New American Commentary. Nashville: Broadman and Holman, 2003.

_____ 'The Valuable Ministries of Women in the Context of Male Leadership: A Survey of Old and New Testament Examples and Teaching' in *Recovering*

Biblical Manhood and Womanhood: A Response to Evangelical Feminism. J. Piper and W. Grudem eds. Wheaton IL: Crossway, 2006.

_____ *Galatians*. ZETNC. Grand Rapids: Zondervan, 2010.

_____ *Romans*, BECNT. Second edition. Grand Rapids: Baker Academic, 2018.

_____ *Handbook on Acts and Paul's Letters*. Grand Rapids: Baker Academic, 2019.

Schüssler Fiorenza, E. 'Rhetorical Situation and Historical Reconstruction in 1 Corinthians.' *NTS* vol. 33, no. 3, 1987.

Scott, E. F. *The Epistles of Paul to the Colossians, to Philemon and to the Ephesians*. MNTC. Reprinted 1942. London: Hodder and Stoughton, 1930.

_____ *The Pastoral Epistles*. MNTC. London: Hodder and Stoughton, 1936.

Sharma, D. 'Cross-Gender Leadership: Priscilla, Aquila, and Apollos.' *Journal of Biblical Perspectives in Leadership* vol. 10, no. 1, 2020.

Slingerland, D. 'Acts 18:1-7 and Luedemann's Pauline Chronology.' *JBL* vol. 109, no. 4, 1990.

_____ 'Acts 18:1-18, The Gallio Inscription, and Absolute Pauline Chronology.' *JBL* vol. 110, no. 3, 1991.

Spencer, F. S. *Journeying through Acts: a literary-cultural reading*. Peabody, MA: Hendrickson, 2004.

Spicq, C. 'Loïs, ta grand'maman (2 Tim. 1:5).' *Revue Biblique* vol. 84, no. 3, 1977.

Sproul, R. C. *Romans*. St Andrew's Expositional Commentary. Wheaton, IL: Crossway, 2009.

Stark, R. *The Rise of Christianity*. New York: HarperOne, 1996.

Steinmann, A. E. *From Abraham to Paul: A Biblical Chronology*. St. Louis: Concordia, 2011.

Stewart, J. S. *A Man in Christ*. London: Hodder and Stoughton, 1935.

Still, T. D. 'Did Paul Loathe Manual Labour? Revisiting the Work of Ronald F. Hock on the Apostle's Tentmaking and Social Class.' *JBL* vol. 125, no. 4, 2006.

Stott, J. R. W. *The Message of Galatians*. TSBT. Leicester: InterVarsity Press, 1968.

_____ *The Message of 2 Timothy*. TSBT. Leicester: InterVarsity Press, 1973.

_____ *The Message of Ephesians*. TSBT. Leicester: InterVarsity Press, 1979.

_____ *The Message of Acts*. TSBT. Leicester: InterVarsity Press, 1990.

_____ *The Message of Thessalonians*. TSBT. Leicester: InterVarsity Press, 1991.

_____ *The Message of Romans*. TSBT. Leicester: InterVarsity Press, 1994.

Strong, J. 'Greek Dictionary of the New Testament' in *The Exhaustive Concordance of the Bible*. Reprinted 1970. London: Hodder and Stoughton, 1890.

Talbert, C. H. *Ephesians and Colossians*. Grand Rapids: Baker Academic, 2007.

_____ *Reading Acts: A Literary and Theological Commentary on the Acts of the Apostles*. Revised edition. Macon, GA: Smith and Helwys, 2018.

Tasker, R. V. G. *The Second Epistle of Paul to the Corinthians*. TNTC. Leicester: InterVarsity Press, 1963.

The Hodder and Stoughton Illustrated Bible Dictionary. Nashville, TN: Thomas Nelson, 1986.

The Strongest NASB Exhaustive Concordance. Grand Rapids: Zondervan, 2004.

Theissen, G. *The Social Setting of Pauline Christianity: Essays on Corinth*. Translated by J. H. Schutz. Philadelphia: Fortress Press, 1982.

_____ 'The Social Structure of Pauline Communities: Some Critical Remarks on J. J. Meggitt, *Paul, Poverty and Survival*.' *JSNT* vol. 24, no. 2, 2001.

Thielman, F. *Romans*. ZECNT. Grand Rapids: Zondervan, 2018.

Thompson, T. 'Erastus' in H.-J. Klauck *et al.* eds. *Encyclopaedia of the Bible and its Reception*. Berlin: de Gruyter, 2009.

_____ 'Eubulus' in H.-J. Klauck *et al.* eds. *Encyclopaedia of the Bible and its Reception*. Berlin: de Gruyter, 2009.

Towner, P. H. *1-2 Timothy and Titus*. IVP New Testament Commentary Series. Downers Grove, IL: InterVarsity Press Academic, 1994.

_____ *The Letters to Timothy and Titus*. NICNT. Grand Rapids: Eerdmans, 2006.

Trebilco, P. 'The Early Christians in Ephesus from Paul to Ignatius.' *WUNT* 166. Tübingen: Mohr-Siebeck, 2004.

_____ 'Why Did the Early Christians Call Themselves ή εκκλησία?' *NTS* vol. 57, no. 3, 2011.

van Kouten, G. H. 'Ἐκκλησία του θεοῦ: The "Church of God" and the Civic Assemblies (ἐκκλησίαι) of the Greek Cities in the Roman Empire: A Response to Paul Trebilco and Richard A. Horsley.' *NTS* vol. 58, no. 4, 2012.

Van Neste, R. 'Claudia' in H.-J. Klauck *et al.* eds. *Encyclopaedia of the Bible and its Reception* Berlin: de Gruyter, 2009.

van Unnik, W. C. 'Tarsus or Jerusalem: The City of Paul's Youth.' Sparsa Collecta 1. Leiden: E. J. Brill, 1973.

Vermes, G. *Who's Who in the Age of Jesus*. London: Penguin, 2005.

Wagner, J. R. '"Not Beyond the Things that are Written": A Call to Boast Only in the Lord (1 Cor. 4:6).' *NTS* vol. 44, no. 2, 1998.

Walker, W. O. Jr. 'The Portrayal of Aquila and Priscilla in Acts: The Question of Sources.' *NTS* vol. 54, no. 4, 2008.

Wansink, C. S. 'Chained in Christ: The Experience and Rhetoric of Paul's Imprisonments.' *JSNT* Supplement 130. Sheffield: Sheffield Academic, 1996.

Watson, F. *Paul, Judaism, and the Gentiles: Beyond the New Perspective*. Second edition. Grand Rapids: Eerdmans, 2007.

Welborn, L. L. 'A Conciliatory Principle in 1 Cor. 4:6.' *NTest* vol. 29, no. 4, 1987.

_____ *Politics and Rhetoric in the Corinthian Epistles*. Macon, GA: Mercer University Press, 1997.

_____ 'How "Democratic" Was the Pauline *Ekklēsia*? An Assessment with Special Reference to the Christ Groups of Roman Corinth.' *NTS* vol. 65, no. 3, 2019.

Westermann, W. L. 'The Slave Systems of Greek and Roman Antiquity.' *Memoirs of the American Philosophical Society* vol. 40. New York: Noble Offset Printers, 1955.

Wieland, G. M. 'Roman Crete and the Letter to Titus.' *NTS* vol. 55, no. 3, 2009.

Witherington, B. III. *Letters and Homilies for Hellenised Christians: A Socio-Rhetorical Commentary on Titus, 1–2 Timothy and 1–3 John*. Downers Grove, IL: InterVarsity Press, 2006.

_____ *The Letters to Philemon, the Colossians, and the Ephesians: A Social-Rhetorical Commentary on the Captivity Epistles*. Grand Rapids: Eerdmans, 2007.

_____ *Paul's Letter to the Philippians: A Social-Rhetorical Commentary*. Grand Rapids: Eerdmans, 2011.

_____ 'The Case of the Imprisonment that did not Happen: Paul at Ephesus.' *JETS* vol. 60, no. 3, 2017.

Woodhouse, J. *Colossians and Philemon: So Walk in Him*. Focus on the Bible Commentary Series. Fearn: Christian Focus, 2011.

Wright, N. T. *Paul: a biography*. San Francisco: HarperOne, 2018.

Yarbrough, R. W. *The Letters to Timothy and Titus*. Pillar New Testament Commentary. Grand Rapids: Eerdmans, 2018.

Zerwick, M. and M. Grosvenor. *A Grammatical Analysis of the Greek New Testament*. Vol. 1. Rome: Biblical Institute Press, 1974.

_____ *A Grammatical Analysis of the Greek New Testament*. Vol. 2. Rome: Biblical Institute Press, 1979.

Subject Index

T

V

W

Z

Scripture Index

Romans

2 Corinthians

Author Index

Also available from Christian Focus Publications ...

9781781919798

Cracking the Foundation of the New Perspective on Paul

Covenantal Nomism versus Reformed Covenantal Theology

Robert J. Cara

The New Perspective on Paul claims that the Reformed understanding of justification is wrong – that it misunderstands Paul and the Judaism with which he engages. The New Perspective's revised understanding of Second Temple Judaism provides the foundation to a new perspective. This important book seeks to show that this foundation is fundamentally faulty and cannot bear the weight it needs to carry, thus undermining the entirety of the New Perspective on Paul itself.

Robert Cara is a specialist and adds fresh arguments against the NPP interpretation. And yet, he writes in a way that makes the issues accessible to pastors who need informed responses to this influential trend.

MICHAEL HORTON
Professor of Systematic Theology
Westminster Seminary, Escondido, Califorina

Christian Focus Publications

Our mission statement

Staying Faithful

In dependence upon God we seek to impact the world through literature faithful to His infallible Word, the Bible. Our aim is to ensure that the Lord Jesus Christ is presented as the only hope to obtain forgiveness of sin, live a useful life and look forward to heaven with Him.

Our Books are published in four imprints:

CHRISTIAN FOCUS

Popular works including biographies, commentaries, basic doctrine and Christian living.

MENTOR

Books written at a level suitable for Bible College and seminary students, pastors, and other serious readers. The imprint includes commentaries, doctrinal studies, examination of current issues and church history.

CHRISTIAN HERITAGE

Books representing some of the best material from the rich heritage of the church.

CF4KIDS

Children's books for quality Bible teaching and for all age groups: Sunday school curriculum, puzzle and activity books; personal and family devotional titles, biographies and inspirational stories – because you are never too young to know Jesus!

Christian Focus Publications Ltd,
Geanies House, Fearn, Ross-shire,
IV20 1TW, Scotland, United Kingdom.
www.christianfocus.com